Voyager

Jeana Yeager trained to be
the first woman in space (the
project, privately funded,
was ultimately abandoned)
before meeting with Dick
Rutan and conceiving the
Voyager project

Dick Rutan learned to fly at
fifteen, and went on to fly
105 missions over North
Vietnam as a fighter pilot.

Also by Phil Patton

The Open Road
Razzle Dazzle

Voyager

JEANA YEAGER
and DICK RUTAN

with PHIL PATTON

Heinemann · Mandarin

A Mandarin Paperback

VOYAGER

First published in Great Britain 1988
by William Heinemann Ltd
This edition published 1989
by Heinemann · Mandarin
Michelin House, 81 Fulham Road, London sw3 6rb

Mandarin is an imprint of the Octopus Publishing Group

Copyright © 1987 by Jeana Yeager, Dick Rutan and Phil Patton

Photographs courtesy of the following: Carol Bernson,
Mark Greenberg, Dennis M. Luosey, Dick Rutan, Pat Storch,
Nayland Wilkins and Jeana Yeager, all for Visions Photo Group.

British Library Cataloguing in Publication Data

Yeager, Jeana
    Voyager
    1. World. Circumnavigation by aircraft,
    history
    I. Title   II. Rutan, Dick   III. Patton, Phil
    910.4'1

ISBN 0 7493 0061 2

Reproduced, printed and bound in Great Britain by
Hazell Watson & Viney Limited
Member of BPCC Limited
Aylesbury, Bucks, England

Contents

Oh Dark Thirty	3
Dick	11
Jeana	25
Beginnings	33
Design	40
A Paper Airplane and the Magic Door	50
Flying	69
Building	81
Hangar 77	94
Oscillations, Vacillations, and Paradoxes	106
The Trailer	130
Human Factors	140
The Inside of a Cow	160
The Last Rung on the Ladder	183
Rescue Mission	208
Bending the Bow	220
Shooting the Curl	237
Flying the Profile	247

CONTENTS

The Dark Continent   272

Red Light   292

Stormy Weather   296

Until the Fat Lady Sings   304

Compass Rose   317

Glossary   335

This book is dedicated to all those who, in the best pioneering spirit, provided the grass-roots support that made *Voyager* possible: to the *Voyager* volunteers, the *Voyager* Impressive People, our sponsors, contributors, families, and friends. Thank you for sharing a dream.

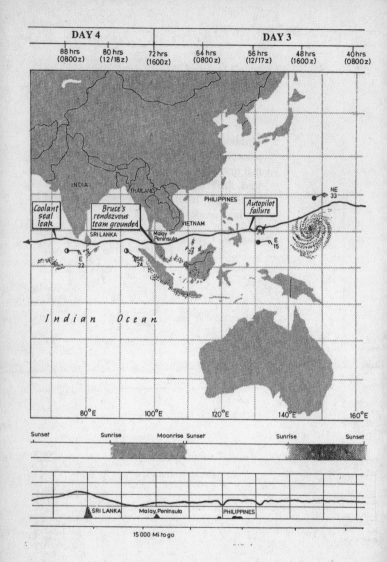

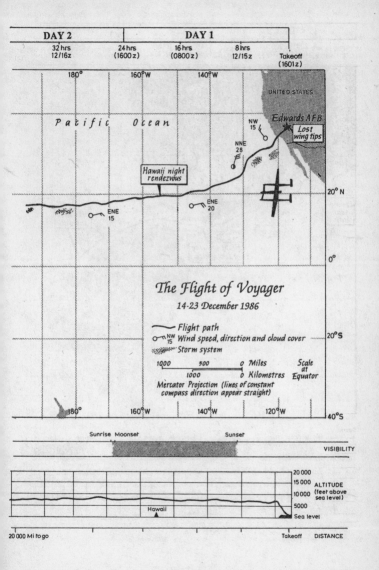

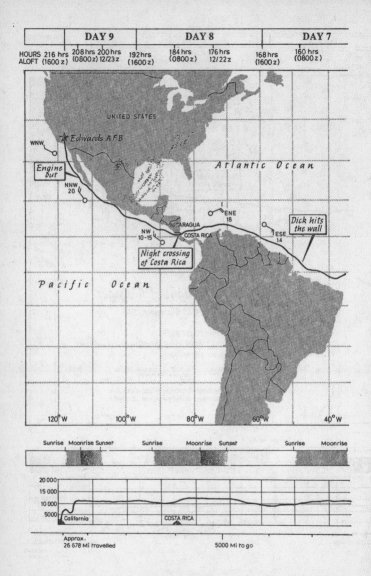

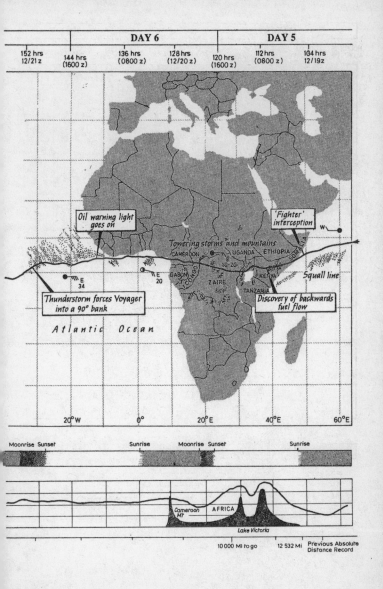

Voyager

Oh Dark Thirty

There is only one thing predictable about the wind at Mojave: it will be back. The wind drives down the San Joaquin Valley, roars through Tehachapi Pass, turns an orchard of windmills shaped like metal pinwheels or eggbeaters, and tumbles down the Horned Toad Hills like a waterfall onto the town of Mojave and its airport.

Sometimes the wind will lay off most of the day—and it is rare and wonderful when there is no wind in the desert—then slowly pick up in the afternoon and gust as the sun falls. Other times it will blow constantly for days, like an engine that runs all the time.

If there is one time that you can most often count on for quiet air, it's just after sunrise. It was then that *Voyager* would appear for its test flights—about half an hour before the sun comes up. "Oh dark thirty," we called it.

The wind is often still asleep then, and the neon light over the truck stop on the main drag is still flashing "Gas, Gas, Gas" against the darkness to the west. Big clouds to the east are touched with the sunrise so they look like flying wings or spaceships on the cover of some old science-fiction magazine.

That's when we would roll the airplane out—or, rather, crab it out, for *Voyager* would fit into the doors at Hangar 77 only diagonally, with Bruce Evans, our crew chief, orchestrating. Already Bruce would have been up in the air checking the weather, and he would brief the crew on conditions. The gear scissors would be disconnected, and the airplane carefully rolled down the ramped metal plates of its scales—for we are always checking its weight—and out of the hangar, with someone watching each delicate wingtip for clearance.

Then Jeana, who had been in the office taking care of paperwork until two or three the previous night, keeping us barely solvent, would come out carrying the chutes and flight test cards and checklists, sipping from one of the foil juice packets she always seemed to be carrying, and I in my black cowboy hat would quaff the last of my Shaklee shake.

Fergy Fay, with a technique practiced since his army air corps days forty years ago, would throw the back prop over and duck out of the way, throw and duck, throw and duck, until the engine caught. Lee Herron would pull the canopy out of its quilted bag, swap it for my black cowboy hat, and settle it in place. Then he would get into his white chase van, and we'd secure the canopy latches.

The fire engine—usually just a pickup truck with a couple of extinguishers—scoots out from the tower and stands by while we move out onto the runway, line up, and talk to the tower. Sometimes, even that early, we might have to wait until somebody ahead of us takes off in one of the Vari Eze's that my brother Burt had designed. A B-1B bomber, chased by an F-111, slices overhead on its way from Edwards Air Force Base. The sonic booms helped wake us up on those days.

Inside the cockpit, Jeana would work down the checklist: mags, prime, ramps, fuel. We always joked that it had to be the longest checklist anyone had ever seen for what was supposed to be such a simple airplane—five computer-printed pages—and already Bruce had had time to get the chase plane ready to take off behind us.

Finally we throttle it forward and start the takeoff run. Jeana would brace herself against a bulkhead and lean over my shoulder, reading airspeeds and calling them out. We had to be careful, because the ends of the long wings—sailplane wings, really—wanted to fly before the inboard portions had made up their mind to go along. So it was always tricky.

Eventually the wings would arc up and make like they wanted to hug a cloud, and we were off, heading toward the distant mountains. As we came overhead, the little ground owl dove back into his burrow at the end of the runway.

Depending on how heavy we were, those wings would start working up and down sooner or later, and you knew that was the time to not watch them anymore. It was just too chest clinching to see wings doing that. Because there was no way that Voyager was anything like a normal airplane, and no way that we would ever feel anything like normal or relaxed trying to fly it.

Mojave Airport is tucked into the shadow of the Tehachapi Mountains. Stubbled with vegetation like a face that's gone three days without shaving, the Tehachapis form the coccyx of the spine of the Sierra Nevadas, which rise in a great sweep to the northeast and north.

This is the high desert, native ground of the mean little Mojave green rattlesnake, of creosote bushes, some of which have been growing for a thousand years or more, and of tough jackrabbits. When it is a hard season and there is not enough to eat in the desert, the jackrabbits grow bold. They come right up to the edge of town and sit by the highway, staring impertinently at passing drivers as the wind ripples the fur over their thin ribs.

When the ground looks like that, you look up. The main thing in Mojave is the sky. With an average of 360 "severe clear" visibility days a year, that sky is almost never obscured. People talk about "the desert floor," a sign that they view the land simply as the bottom of the sky.

This is the last bastion of cowboy flying, and that is why we found ourselves there When the folks in the tower know everybody and don't get ticked off when you pull straight up as soon as you hit bug speed and then climb to the roof and come ripping back in over the desert at top speed and go rolling, corkscrewing, right by the open doors of hangars about fifty feet over the taxiways and then back up into the sky, looking for some poor sucker to engage in a friendly dogfight—when that happens, it's cowboy flying.

From that sky, the town recedes into almost nothing in the expanse of the desert. To the north, the neat grid of streets for a development that never developed offers reference points for aerobatic maneuvers. Far to the south, a small golf course looks like a green doormat dropped on the dust. The area is called the Antelope Valley, but no one has seen an antelope here for years. The animals never learned to cross the railroad tracks.

"How many people live in Mojave?" runs an ancient joke. "About half of them."

"It's not the edge of the world," goes another line, "but you can sure see it from there."

Mojave's main drag is Highway 58, which runs north, eventually to Bakersfield. On one side of it are the tracks of the Atchison, Topeka, and Santa Fe Railroad, with a wooden frame station the color of lime sherbet, covered with dust. On the other side are the leading establishments of the town: motels, truck stops with their parking lots full of silver eighteen-wheelers, service stations, convenience stores, and two or three national fast-food chains. "Fast food, fast gas," we liked to say.

Some of the stores and restaurants display old photographs that show how Main Street looked before it burned down in the 1890s: like a thousand clichéd false-front western towns, hotel, dry goods, general store.

The railroad built this town. The old twenty-mule borax teams converged here from Death Valley to transfer their cargo to the rails and all traffic, freight and passenger, to the north passed through Tehachapi Pass. The wind would take the derbies and Stetsons of unwary passengers and deposit them on the level land east of town that locals took to calling "the Hat Farm."

During World War II, the marine corps built an airport on the Hat Farm and established an aviation training center. It turned out pilots to fly Helldivers and Dauntlesses and later Corsairs and Phantoms.

Just to the south was the old Muroc Army Air Corps Base. After the war it flourished, and by 1950 it had become a great test center, renamed Edwards Air Force Base. The marine station at Mojave, by contrast, turned quiet when peace came.

In 1958 the federal government turned it over to Kern County. It languished until the early 1970s, rented out to sheep farmers for grazing. Raisin growers dried their grapes on the empty runways. Then civilian researchers, spinning off from Edwards, began to settle in at Mojave. Now the flightline is the home of a number of advanced aviation research companies.

It is a particularly convenient place to test out "home-builts." One of the attractions of the airport is that the surrounding area qualifies as an official "unpopulated area" as defined by the Federal Aviation Administration. It is therefore acceptable for flying the fifty hours of test time required to certify new experimental home-built aircraft.

Because of that, Burt Rutan came to Mojave to open Rutan Aircraft Factory—RAF—in a little barracks-style building on the edge of the airport, selling home-built plans and designing new planes. And because Burt was here I came to Mojave in 1978 to work with my brother.

It was at one of Mojave's finer eating establishments, the late lamented Mojave Inn, a couple of years later, that the idea of Voyager was hatched. It really did start on a napkin, one day, when Jeana and I sat down with Burt over a teriyaki steak.

Burt outlined his idea, and we could see he was serious.

"Why not?" Jeana said, and no one could think of a good reason why not.

I thought the notion still belonged to the same category of things as flying to Mars—some wacko engineering notion. And engineering ideas tended to make an uneasy transition into the practicalities of the cockpit.

As we thought more about it, we became excited by the idea. We all knew that nonrefueled, around-the-world flight was the last milestone in aviation and that whoever did it would be entering into history.

On the napkin, Burt sketched an airplane that looked like little more than a giant wing, an airplane that could fly 28,000 miles.

Flying around the world is not as simple an idea as it seems. As a formal category in aviation record keeping, around-the-world flight has always been poorly defined. The first such flight was accomplished by a virtual task force of airplanes and support facilities in 1924. Four army Douglas World Cruisers, open cockpit biplanes, started the flight, skipping in sixty-nine short hops, but only two completed the 27,000-mile loop. They took 175 days.

Later aviators flew around the world faster, but not as far: many of their flights were in fact rings around a portion of the earth, not around its widest circumference; Northern Hemisphere circles that were halos on the globe, not hula hoops.

In 1929 the *Graf Zeppelin* set a record of twenty days, four hours, although the records of airships and heavier-than-air craft are generally kept separate.

Wiley Post flew around the world twice in the Lockheed Vega he named the *Winnie Mae*. The second time he became the first man to do it solo, in seven days and eighteen hours, with stops. It was on an attempted around-the-world flight that Amelia Earhart disappeared in the Pacific near Howland Island in 1937.

Howard Hughes flew an around-the-world flight in 1938, using extensive staging facilities along the way. Each stop of his Lockheed 14 was accompanied by great hoopla: at Floyd Bennett Field in Brooklyn he was met by New York Mayor Fiorello La Guardia and squads of motorcycle police. He cut the world record to three days nineteen hours.

Due to the advancing technology in aviation new rules had to be established. A definition of world flight was not standardized until the FAI (Fédération Aéronautique Intérnationale) established that the minimum distance to qualify for a world flight had to be the distance of the Tropic of Cancer or Capricorn, equal to 22,858 statute miles. The true circumference of the Earth is 24,855 statute miles.

The first nonstop around-the-world flight was a U.S. Air Force demonstration aimed at impressing the Soviets with American air power. In

1949 the B-50 *Lucky Lady II* was refueled in flight and made the trip in ninety-three hours. The *Lucky Lady II* had originally set out, under orders from Strategic Air Command boss General Curtis LeMay, with two other planes on a multistop circumnavigational flight. But after one airplane crashed, he upped the ante. "Come back and start all over," LeMay supposedly said, "and this time do it nonstop." Someone worked out an air-to-air refueling system using dangling hoses and grappling hooks. It was extremely crude and the first of its type, but it worked.

B-52's made similar flights. The B-52H set the record for such a flight, with 12,532 statute miles. And the B-52 also held the absolute record for closed-course distance, the record that *Voyager* was to break on the California coast flight. Those four-hundred-ton airplanes flew 11,337 miles; *Voyager*, at a thousand-odd pounds, with 3,500 pounds of fuel, flew 11,600.

It was only the arrival of composite construction that made anyone even consider the possibility of flying this distance without refueling. Dr. Paul MacCready, the inventive creator of the first man-powered plane, the *Gossamer Albatross*, the *Gossamer Condor*, and a flying model of the ancient pterosaur, looked at the possibility. He decided that *Voyager* was so far ahead that he didn't want to compete. And he thought we had an excellent chance of success.

. . .

Voyager involved two kinds of challenge. One challenge was a public one: the challenge of innovation and leadership in design and technology.

Voyager would not have been possible without certain developments in the world of flying. One, of course, was the growth of the home-built industry, in which our work at Rutan Aircraft was so important. Even before that, however, was the existence of the Experimental Aircraft Association, based in Oshkosh, Wisconsin. The EAA was the brainchild of Paul Poberezny. He had founded it in 1953, and each year the membership grew until it numbered nearly a hundred thousand—a hundred thousand people all interested in new types of airplanes and new aviation achievements. And many of these people are the owners and pilots of aircraft they have built themselves, using new designs and new materials.

Behind the growth in the home-built market is the fact that private aviation in this country has been in a slump for years. The main factor is liability insurance. In 1978 there were about 1,400 single-engine airplanes produced annually; now it's down to just over a thousand.

By contrast, the home-built market has expanded tremendously. The

EAA estimates that around seven hundred home-builts are completed each year. You now pay around $30,000 for a small plane, or about three times what the same plane cost ten years ago. And, except for avionics, it's the same plane—and the same plane you would have bought thirty years ago. Developing and testing new planes is the last thing companies want to do in this litigious world. For the price of an average mid-sized car and a lot of time, you can put together a home-built in your garage, with much better performance than a store-bought plane.

Voyager is the largest all-composite airplane ever built. It points the way to the future—eventually, all airplanes will be built this way.

We stand now on the threshold of a change in aircraft construction as dramatic as the one that saw aluminum and monocoque, or shell-structured, forms replace spruce spars and doped linen. Already the new generation of fighter aircraft employs composites for as much as 40 percent of their airframes.

Ironically, though, it has been the do-it-yourself airplanes, more than those built in factories, that have pioneered composites of various types.

Voyager has long-term technological lessons. As we liked to say about the Vari Eze and Long EZ that Burt designed, "Don't laugh, the airliner you fly on in fifteen years may look just like this."

The technology Voyager embodies could lead to more efficient passenger and cargo airplanes, airplanes that take off and land in smaller areas, airplanes that are so inexpensive to build that people can buy them like pickup trucks.

For the more immediate future, the same lift factor that enables it to carry five times its weight in fuel makes it equally capable of flying very high—an ability useful for high-altitude "lingering" aircraft, used for reconnaissance, say, either manned or remote-controlled.

In another way, Voyager and its technology, like many of Burt's designs, and the organization that built it, point the way back—back to the day when you could build a plane in a garage or backyard, when the pilot was also the mechanic. Voyager is do-it-yourself high technology, and it recalls the days before it took huge government contracts and engineers measured literally by the acre of office space to turn out a new plane.

Voyager reasserts the importance of the pilot—it presents a test of flying skill, as well as physical endurance. The most advanced fighters, by contrast, long ago passed the point where the limits to their performance became not those of engines or airframes, but those of the people flying them. Engineers no longer worry about G-forces produced by loops and dives and acceleration pulling the plane apart. Instead they worry about the simple physical limits that, despite the best pressure suits and physical conditioning, have been causing pilots to lose control. The new phenomenon is not the traditional "blackout" but something more subtle and dangerous and far less well understood called "temporary loss of consciousness," or TLC, a moment's confusion in a turn or a dive. The pilot lucky enough to survive a TLC episode rarely even remembers it.

Speed is now a drawback to maneuverability, and experimental jets are designed to be inherently unstable—demanding that a computer, adjusting the control surfaces some forty times a second, assist the basic flying.

Pilots still have the right stuff. American test pilots and fighter pilots continue to be superb, and even computer-assisted there is no substitute for them. But the success of the engineers has taken much of the work load out of the pilot's hands.

The tests we would face as pilots would be very different, but equally stringent.

· · ·

The other challenge was a personal one—a dare you take personally, an opportunity that is also a danger. It is an age-old sort of challenge, and the tools it involves are only incidental. It may be compared to the challenge of climbing a mountain or sailing a wooden ship around the world, as Magellan and his sailors did.

People today tend to forget that Charles Lindbergh had many competitors in the race to be the first to fly from New York to Paris. Most of them were better financed and organized than he was. But none were as fully involved as he was in all aspects of the attempt: design, building, testing, and flying. And the interference of sponsors, the rivalry of participants in the more elaborate schemes, slowed them down. Lindbergh was careful and thorough, but daring. And he was also as lucky as his nickname suggests. We had all that involvement, but we needed all that luck.

We had our whole lives wrapped up in this personal challenge for more than six years. It was our personal dream, but as it became more public, we became something like hostages to it—captives of the expectations we had raised. It took all our days and many of our nights, and at times it threatened to turn into a nightmare. It brought us in contact with all sorts of people, and it lifted our spirits up and down as abruptly as the airplane itself, with its great flapping wings, tossed our bodies about. And yet in the end we came to suspect that it was what we were destined to do, what our lives had been leading up to.

Dick

In front of the main terminal at Mojave Airport stands a mothballed F-100 jet fighter, displayed like an artifact or museum piece. But when I saw my first F-100 it seemed like something straight out of the future.

I was a sophomore in high school, and the F-100 was brand-new, being shown to the public for the first time. It was the air force's hot new fighter, the "Super Sabre," and I knew right away that what I most wanted in life was to fly one of them.

It was at the Fresno Air Terminal, one of the many places the family would visit to see planes and pilots: a silver tube, almost all engine, with relatively small wings. Its long nose tapered to the hungry oval mouth of an air intake—a contrast to the snub nose, say, of the F-86's that fought MIGs over Korea. It had to be the slickest airplane ever built, and I made a vow to myself: "I'm going to fly F-100's in Germany."

Germany, because in 1954 it was still the front lines, distant and dangerous, still in the shadow of the last war and the Cold War. Germany stood for action, real combat.

I did keep that vow, but it was nearly fifteen years later, by which time the plane was already almost obsolete, supplanted by a whole new generation of fighters, and well on its way to being droned. But I clung to my loyalty to this airplane, long after others had become infatuated with the triangular-winged Delta Dart or the Starfighter or even the powerful F-4 Phantom.

Growing up, Burt and I were both obsessed with flying and with airplanes. The family would drive to any place where there were planes, especially to the air force bases in Fresno and Merced, to Castle Air Force

Base, March Air Force Base, near our home in the little town of Dinuba, on occasions such as Armed Forces Day when planes and pilots would be on display to the public. To me, fighter pilots were simply like gods; they were supermen.

The F-100 wasn't the fastest airplane in the world. Later, I would joke about "the slightly supersonic Super Sabre." But it was the last airplane in the U.S. arsenal that gave one guy the capacity to single-handedly deliver a nuclear weapon. The president would have to give the order, of course, and the security was incredibly tight, but once the word came down, that pilot would be on his own. All that firepower in one piece of machinery, under one man's control! It was a trip to think that you alone could be in control of enough power to wipe out the entire Los Angeles basin.

This was the fifties and the height of the Cold War, and I'll never forget one television episode of *Dragnet* that featured fighter pilots and the line about sonic booms. "When you don't hear that sound anymore," Jack Webb said, "it will mean we are no longer free. Because that is the sound of freedom." Now that's what people in the Antelope Valley say all the time to visitors who are jolted by the booms. "Oh, that? We don't mind that. It's the sound of freedom."

My parents, George and Irene Rutan, had met in Loma Linda, near Los Angeles. I was born down there, but it was the Depression and hard times, and they moved up to a farm Mom's father had in Oregon, near Estacada, southeast of Portland. They took all the money they possessed with them, changed into half-dollars and carried inside an old milk can. Burt and Nell were born in Estacada.

After serving in the navy during World War II, Pop went to dental school at the University of Southern California on the G.I. Bill. He went into practice in Dinuba, a small town in California's Central Valley near Fresno, and after Los Angeles most of my growing-up years were spent there.

Moving to Dinuba was like going home for Pop Rutan. His family had lived in the area for years, having settled there after the trip over the Oregon Trail. In the late forties and early fifties, Dinuba was booming, along with the rest of the Central Valley, as deep wells brought water up to nurture the fields and orchards and the oil fields began sprouting their own crop of drilling rigs and pumps.

Having lived in Los Angeles, we were city kids in the small town. Teenage life in Dinuba was a fifties classic: car cruising and car racing. There's a picture from the family album that shows the family looking like something on *Ozzie and Harriet*. We are all watching television. I have a kind of smirk on my face, and Burt looks thoughtful, as if his mind were somewhere else.

Burt and I lived in a room behind the garage, an old open woodshed our father had closed in and heated. It was so narrow that our beds had to be placed end to end, with our heads together. In later years, working on *Voyager*, whenever someone would say, "Well, Burt had this good idea . . ." I would reply, "Hell, I had that idea. I told him that when we were kids." It was a regular line that went back to the days of sleeping head to head.

Although we shared the room, to our parents it was always "Dick and the little kids." Burt was five years younger; Nell, who later became an airline stewardess, was four years younger.

I spent a lot of time with my motorcycle, fixing it up and racing, racing and fixing it up. In those days motorcycles evoked adult visions of Marlon Brando raising hell in *The Wild One*. Driving them was viewed as one small step removed from outright criminality. So I acquired a reputation as "wild."

I would get my friend Alden Berg to come by with his pickup and load the bike in and go off to race on one of the many dirt tracks in the area. We competed in "hound and hare" races, where one guy would set out ahead of the others, and the rest of us would ride like hell to catch up with him.

I hardly ever rode the bike on the highway, especially after one night, when I was coming home late and we came across a guy whose motorcycle had been hit by a truck. He was just lying there, bleeding. I had this leather jacket, all worn real soft. We called an ambulance, and while we waited for it to come I took that jacket off and put it under the guy's head. He died before the ambulance got there, and my mother claims I never wore the jacket again.

I had a lot of fun when my father gave me the family's old '49 Ford to fix up. I switched the wires so that when you pushed the turn signal the horn sounded, when you turned on the radio the windshield wipers started, and so on. Every control was somewhere else. Thanks to this little mechanical prank, of course, I was the only one who could drive it— which I guess was probably the point.

Burt was a little different. If I was the wild greaser, he was the pimply science kid, obsessed with airplanes.

Burt had begun building models when he was about eleven years old. He later took one to chemistry class and nearly flew it through the wall.

Soon the bedroom was also a workshop, full of tools and model airplanes and engine parts.

Our mother, Irene, would drive the family's Ford Skyline station wagon out over the foothills of the Sierra Nevadas with Burt in the backseat, keeping within radio-control distance of his planes before they flew over the horizon.

Pop was always urging Burt to get out and do things with the other kids, instead of staying in the workshop.

Both our parents, then, were overjoyed when Burt told them that he had decided to enter a school foot race called "the Turkey Trot."

So the track and other athletes wouldn't automatically win, and to make it more interesting, each runner in the race was given a handicap, like a golfer's—so many seconds. The handicaps were assigned fairly arbitrarily, on the basis of how athletic the student was thought to be, and Burt figured he could turn his reputation to advantage. He was sure he would get a large handicap.

He didn't even have a decent pair of athletic shoes or sneakers, so he ran in a pair of thick wool socks that gave out well before the finish line. He ended the race barefoot and bloody, but thanks to the handicap, he won. It was the competition that had lured him, and after the race he promptly disappeared back into the shop and continued building his model airplanes.

I was obsessed with airplanes, too, but mostly with real ones. I began taking flying lessons when I was fifteen and soloed after just five and a half hours of training, spread out over six months—it took me a month of working, cutting grapes or carrying raisin trays, to raise the money for each forty-minute lesson. Pop says that I was so taken with it that I persuaded him to take flying lessons, too, although I'm not sure he needed much convincing. Eventually he joined with several friends to buy a Beechcraft.

By my sixteenth birthday, I had about five hours of instruction, and Mom drove me to Reedley Airport so I could solo on the first day I was legally eligible; then she drove me downtown to get my driver's license. The instructor, Johnny Chakerian, did three takeoffs and landings with me and then got out and let me fly. On my sixteenth birthday, again the minimum age, I got my private license, and then it was on to commercial, instrument, multiengine, seaplane, and instructor certificates. I was never one to wait around.

Already I'd started to take a lot of pride in my flying skills. Even though most of what I got to do in the airplane consisted of throwing out toilet paper and chopping it up with the prop over the football stadium—an activity that later became a favorite of Burt's as well—I started calling myself the Velvet Arm and worked up all these arm-flexing poses out of the Charles Atlas bodybuilding ads in the comic books. (In fact, my body was so far from the Charles Atlas type that I was nicknamed "Pretzel.") Pop remembers that when I flew with him for the first time, in a rented Aeronca, I pulled a complete loop that left him pretty upset, shaking and fuming. He told me to never do that again.

After high school graduation, I decided for some reason to drive my motorcycle cross-country. I took off east in the June heat and on the road joined up with another guy, Ian McNealy. By the time we got up into the Rockies it was so cold that when we stopped I could barely move my hands. But Ian was worse off. I had to pry his fingers off the handlebars. I made it to the Mississippi River, then turned around and came home. That was far enough.

There was no question of what I was going to do after high school. I signed on with the air force air cadet program. I'd been so set on the service that I'd already gotten myself thrown out of one school. My parents sent me to a Seventh-Day Adventist high school, where they teach war is bad and expect their graduates to become conscientious objectors. After I stopped to think about that, it took me three days to get thrown out, much to my parents' dismay. I hitchhiked the thirty miles home and immediately registered at the public school for my last year.

After graduation I had to take the Air Force's written test. I did not do well enough on the test to qualify for a pilot slot, so I signed on as a navigator instead. The recruiter said it would be no problem, that once I got down to San Antonio, where the training began, I could easily switch. In fact, the guy told me, I could be a triple threat: navigator, bombardier, and pilot.

That was just recruiter talk. As it turned out, nearly seven years passed before I was able to get into pilot training. In between, the air force quite unintentionally was to provide me with as wide and deep an education in the skills I would one day require to fly around the world as I could have asked for.

Even for navigators, in 1958, there was a seven-month waiting list. While waiting for the telegram that would tell me to report, I decided to attend Reedley Junior College, a few miles from Dinuba. There I had a chance to work with aircraft engines, and I became fascinated. I had three weeks to go in the course when word came from the Air Force that I was to join up. The engines had come naturally to me, and my skill with them had impressed the instructor, who went out of his way to pack the last part of the curriculum into just a few days so I could finish. I took my test and came away with an official Federal Aviation Agency power plant license. I was an airplane engine mechanic as well as a pilot now.

Once at Lackland Air Force Base in San Antonio for preflight, I was scared to death.

It began as soon as I got off the bus and a senior cadet put me in a "brace"—or stiff attention. My sideburns at this time reached just below my ear.

"You, Elvis!" he called out to me. "Are you chewing gum, mister? Swallow it!"

"Now sing, Elvis."

And they made me do my best to sing and sound like Elvis.

At Lackland, away from home for the first time, I was homesick and terrified. I was too scared to eat in the stiff military stance the cadets were forced to assume at the table. I was too scared to go to the bathroom. I was too scared to study, even if I could have found time amid the barracks hazing by senior cadets. The new cadets weren't even allowed to wear uniforms for the first few weeks. In varied and unwashed civvies, we were disdained as "rainbows," scum, unworthy of the Air Force blue.

Because I couldn't study, I quickly found myself on academic restriction, forced to march the "tour ramp" in fatigues, around and around for an hour, then five minutes off, an hour for every demerit, while other cadets left for town leave on weekends. I would have quit, as many of the cadets did—of the seventy-two people in my class, only a dozen were left a year later—but I was too scared even to walk down to the office and say that I was quitting—I was terrified I would run into one of those fearsome upperclassmen.

I just barely made it through preflight, then went on to Harlingen, Texas, for navigator school. There, for half the course, it was the same old story. I worked hard but just barely made it by on the tests. Then, during the section on celestial and radar navigation, with the suddenness of a light going on, I found myself. Something about the subject appealed to the same instincts for the mechanical and systematic that had made me successful with engines. I finished at the top of the radar and celestial navigation class.

While most of the assignments were to cargo or SAC B-47's or B-52's

I still wanted to fly fighters and got assigned to Waco, Texas, for radar intercept officer training in the backseat of a fighter interceptor. I would be the scope dope—the guy in back with his head buried in the radar screen—but at least I was flying fighters.

I was assigned to Keflavík, Iceland, where in 1961 I had the dubious honor of flying the last active air defense scramble in an F-89 Scorpion. This ancient, bulb-nosed airplane, known for its proclivity to suck up rocks into its intakes, was so slow that it sometimes had a hard time catching up with the 707 jet airliners that had only a few years before begun transatlantic service. A 707 would go off course, the radar would pick it up, and if the Scorpions didn't get off to a good head start and pick the right angle of approach, in front and above, they would miss the intercept.

As a navigator on C-124 Globemaster transports, stationed at Travis Air Force Base, California, I first flew into Southeast Asia at the beginning of the big Vietnam buildup. We would drop into some isolated spot in Thailand, such as Khorat or Nakhon Phanom—"Naked Phantom," we called it—where there was little more than a steel plank runway and some tents dropped into a swamp. The heat and humidity were ungodly, but only the radar and electronics tent rated air conditioning. The air force people were flying F-105's, but there were other planes, C-123 freighters with commercial markings, unloading huge boxes under the direction of mysterious civilians—spooks. Once, I stopped one of these men to ask what was in the boxes. "Shoes," the guy answered without a smile. "Shoes."

One of these spooks came up to the base commander, who was equally in the dark as to the cargo contents, and asked him what he needed to improve the base. Buildings? Equipment? And he reached into his pocket and peeled bills off a huge roll of cash.

Navigating across the Pacific gave me a knowledge of the area and its weather that was to be critically useful later with *Voyager*. I developed a healthy respect for the storms there and knew how essential radar was to fly safely in that part of the world.

In 1966, after having applied for years, I finally got my chance at pilot training. I told the other guys I was going to fly F-100's when I finished. "Shoot," they told me, "there hasn't been an F-100 slot to come down for a year or more now." It became the joke of the class.

Naturally, I excelled: I had been getting ready for this for more than ten years. I worked harder than I ever had and finished at the top of the class. And sure enough, two F-100 slots came along, and as the guy at the top of the class I got first pick. I had my F-100.

I went on to F-100 gunnery school at Luke Air Force Base in Arizona, which was the only place for a fighter pilot to go, and I continued to do well.

It was 1967, and our entire gunnery class went to Vietnam—except for one graduate whose father was an air force general: he went to Europe.

From the beginning, I felt clearly the absurdities of the way the war was being conducted—on the ground, the emphasis on body count, of course, and in the air the method of bombing "sky spots." This was an adaptation of methods used for practice bomb runs in training. We would be directed over the radio to fly to a particular spot, on a radar vector. "Change course half a degree left," the instructions might go. "Now half a degree right . . . Pickle!"—which was the call to drop the bombs. Or they might go on like that and suddenly say, "And no drop!" Just testing you out. And your thumb would be poised on the button, and you'd have to reach over quickly and grab it to stifle the natural reflex to squeeze.

The target was never specifically identified, and you had no way to know whether you had hit it. You only knew that you had dropped your bombs and they hit the ground. Sometimes you doubted that there was anything except trees where the bombs fell. You had to get permission from the local Vietnamese officials to bomb, and with the South Vietnamese government's notorious lack of security, it was pretty much guaranteed that whatever had been there when permission was requested had moved on by the time it was obtained.

I spent about three months flying this sort of mission, from the base at Phu Cat, bombing trees, as we put it, and occasionally flying strafing missions—"shooting up water buffaloes," as it was called.

Occasionally we would be called on to support troops who were actually in contact with the enemy, and we enjoyed a rare feeling that we were accomplishing something. But still it seemed very distant, and the effects were unclear.

Once, I got a closer view of the ground war. I took a couple of days' leave and visited an army helicopter unit stationed at a forward base in the central highlands. The base was little more than the scraped-off top of a hill, with bunkers, inside a wire-and-trench perimeter.

I met a helicopter gunner and saw how he would take the M-60 machine gun out of its window station in the chopper and mount it on the edge of his bunker, overlooking the perimeter.

"What?" I asked. "You mean there's no one else out there guarding you? The Viet Cong could crawl right up here at night?"

The gunner said he guessed that could happen. He had scars all over his body from fire he had taken manning the window gun, and I could tell from the way he talked about things that he had lost hope of making it out of the country alive.

At the chopper base was a small prison area—a set of cages, really—at the base where VC suspects were interrogated. I was shocked to see a fresh young lieutenant who looked as if he had walked straight off an Ivy League campus begin talking in fluent Vietnamese to one of the prisoners, a young man, what was known as "a military age male," who was clearly scared out of his wits. All of a sudden the lieutenant just started beating the hell out of the guy, hitting him right and left, trying to get him to talk about some sort of weapons cache they thought he knew about. Then the lieutenant turned to me and explained what was going on. I was shocked to hear him speak English; after that long harangue in Vietnamese, it seemed Vietnamese was his natural tongue. I went away wondering how the military found people willing to fight this kind of war on the ground.

But I was still eager to find more action in the air. I still subscribed very heavily to the old gladiatorial mythology of the fighter pilot. It was an infatuation with life in the air and in combat, a disdain for those on the ground, summed up in the often repeated story of the guy who comes back after punching out of his disabled plane. "Didn't you worry about the plane hitting somebody's house?" he was asked.

And the answer that came back was, "Fuck 'em, that's what they get for living on the ground."

In this I was like most of the pilots, chomping at the bit for a dogfight, entranced with the idea of shooting at another airplane. Some of these guys were so eager to do this that sometimes, when one of their fellows was hit and flew to the ocean to bail out, they would cluster around, elbowing each other, for a chance to take a practice shot at the abandoned aircraft. The ejecting American pilot would be almost ignored as they blasted the plane he had punched out of.

I volunteered for an outfit called Commando Sabre—call sign Misty—whose pilots flew spotting missions over North Vietnam, along the lower end of the Ho Chi Minh Trail. Fast FACs, they were called in the air force acronymic. FACs were Forward Air Controllers, and they usually flew in slow Cessna Birddogs, finding "lucrative" targets for fighter bombers. But over the north those planes wouldn't have lasted five minutes in the ground fire, so they used F-100's—thus "fast FACs." They flew over the north and Laos looking for convoys and antiaircraft sites, supply depots, staging areas, and what were called "transhipment points." These were places where supplies were readied to be ferried on barges, in place of the bridges that had long ago been bombed away. When we spotted any of these targets, we marked them with smoke rockets and called in circling fighter bombers—F-4's and F-105's—for the kill.

It was a solo operation, two guys in an F-100F roaming almost at will, and in my first Misty mission, with Captain Mick Greene, sailing in through the murk, then dashing down into the weeds, I got more action and excitement than in my entire three months in the south. The unit had a loss-per-sortie rate five times higher than any other in the war. Some pilots were picked up, but I saw others stranded and captured. Others simply disappeared, unaccounted for to this day. The air force found this loss rate acceptable only because of the number of targets the Mistys identified and hit.

On my first mission, I was shocked by the amount of bombs dropped with so little apparent effect. The whole landscape had been re-created by the craters. The craters covered thousands of meters around old bridge-heads. The accuracy of the bombing was terrible. And still the shipments went on. The president and the generals kept telling the public how well the war was going, but the truth—the stupidity and ineffectiveness of the way the war was being waged—was obvious from the air.

Most pilots did one 120-day tour with the Mistys. I volunteered for a second and then a third. I went home with 105 Misty missions, 220 in the south, and I was able to claim what at that time was the highest total number of combat hours spent over North Vietnam of anyone in the war.

Sometimes I flew in front as pilot, other times in back, as the forward air controller, the observer who found the targets. Often the pilots would come back with holes in the airplane. I came to realize that I was addicted to the adrenaline of it all, hooked on the combat highs, and eventually combat-fatigued—short on patience, strung tight as a tripwire. I wasn't sure I'd ever be able to live on the ground again.

It was an exhausting routine, twelve-hour days, and little respite in between the missions. And there was intense rivalry among pilots to get the good missions.

The day would begin at three in the morning with a breakfast crammed down in the knowledge that it was certainly the last meal you would have that day and might, if things went wrong, be the last decent meal you would have for a very long time. There was a three-hour intelligence briefing on what to look for, and then into the aircraft. We would fly up the coast for twenty minutes, then snuggle in behind the KC-135 to top off on fuel. Dropping off behind the tanker, we'd tighten our harnesses, cut off radio emitters, and gird for battle.

I loved coming in from the sea over the North Vietnamese coast, quiet, lovely, and dead calm, with low mist clinging to the land. At this moment, sailing in at six hundred knots, you never said anything. You knew that as soon as you hit the coast, all hell was going to break loose from the guns down in the cover, and every day it did.

The fire would start like Fourth of July sparklers, and tracers would float up past them, sometimes so close we could feel the shimmer of the shock wave. We would start to jink and jag, depriving the gunners of the steady track they needed to lead the plane. Without doing that, we probably wouldn't last five minutes.

We would rack the plane out into the jinks at four or five G's, going in and out of afterburner for extra power. We became so used to the high G's that sometimes we wouldn't even notice them. Once I pulled around and froze our angle in one of the steady banks the backseat man needed to take reconnaissance photographs. I waited for the guy to let me know that he had the shot and we could break off. But the spotter couldn't even lift the camera. I looked at the panel and saw we were still holding nearly four G's.

It took practice to find the targets on the ground, to read the signs in the landscape of guns or truck parks. Five or six weeks of flying were required to learn to spot a bunch of leaves turned upside down, the square edge where the mottled canvas turned or fresh tire tracks. This process had been nicknamed "Camouflage College."

We had a strange sort of rapport with the gunners on the ground. We were supposed to mark the gunsites we identified with our phosphorus smoke rockets, and then the bombers or the navy attack fighters from carriers would come in after them. We would have what they called gun-killing contests. The Misty would roar in and fire the smoke rocket at the site, then pull steeply up and away, and the bombers would follow. Once spotted, the gunners knew it was them or the planes, and they fought viciously.

Even if they survived the bombs, the gunners would have to move—an exhausting process of disassembly and assembly that would take them all night. But sometimes we'd see the guns and leave them alone, re-membering the locations for the next day and not venturing too close, but not trying to kill them. The rule was, if you harassed them too much, the guns would move and you couldn't find them the next day: they might be able to surprise you. So you did just enough to keep them off balance. And sometimes the gunners would not fire at the planes that passed over-head, knowing the rings of smoke they left would give them away.

There were good shots among the gunners and bad ones, and the fliers would leave the bad ones alone and try to kill the good ones. One very bad shot had his station high on a formation of limestone in Laos and became famous as the "Kid on the Karst." His tracers would go sailing off hundreds of yards from the planes. So the word went out to everyone in the unit, "Nobody touches the Kid on the Karst." But at last there was some new guy in the unit, a rookie who hadn't gotten the word, and after he came back one day the news spread: "Somebody killed the Kid on the Karst." And the rest of the group were so angry they said they could have killed the rookie, too.

A few guys did a second tour, but I volunteered for a third and began to become notorious. I was the "high time" guy in the unit, and friends were telling me it was time to knock off, that I'd flown too many missions, that I was hanging it out too much. The commanding officer kept urging me to hang it up now and go back to flying with a normal squadron over South Vietnam.

Now I was training other pilots in the Camouflage College, and I was so strung out that I would lose patience and yell at them, "Can't you see that? You damn fool, you almost got us shot." And finally, one day, we did get shot.

It was the final mission of the tour for my seatmate—the champagne flight, they called it—so he got to fly, and I was in the back. The pilot, who was named Chuck Shaheen and came from the same part of California I did, was called the Crazy Arab for some of his exploits, and he wanted to go out with a big mission. He took us strafing too low, and we took ground fire. It hit us with a sound like somebody pounding the bottom of the airplane with a baseball bat. The plane was burning, bleeding fuel at a tremendous rate, and as we set out for the water and safety, forty miles away, I felt certain that the fuel would go before we could make it. But he lit the afterburner, which burned the fuel faster and kicked us along at maximum speed, and we aimed the plane up to get maximum altitude. The lighter we got, the faster we went, and we made the coast just as the engine quit. We were just supersonic when it flamed out, and we glided down and out over the water. You might say it was a never-to-be-forgotten lesson in fuel maintenance.

We ejected—I'd always been curious about that, how it would feel, but now I closed my eyes and barely felt anything until the tug of the canopy. The water was warm and calm, and we spent three and a half hours in the raft before being picked up. I fell asleep on the Jolly Green, the helicopter back home, because I knew the war was over for me and that I would be going home.

The next day I went to the commanding officer, the guy who had been begging me to lay off, and said, "Sir, is it okay if I don't go up there anymore?"

.   .   .

I went on to less stressful assignments and spent pleasant years in northern Italy and Turkey, in England, and in headquarters at Wright-Patterson in Ohio.

In 1975 I moved to Davis-Monthan Air Force Base, near Tucson, where I was assigned as flight test maintenance officer of the 355th Tactical Air Command squadron, commanding the 450-person maintenance squadron and administering a two-and-a-half-million-dollar budget. The unit was so riddled with drugs at that time it was known as "the Drug Store," and I had to clean it up. It took all sorts of tactics, including three-o'clock-in-the-morning raids of the barracks, drug-sniffing dogs, and twelve general court-martials, but I did it.

The next logical step for me was to command a fighter squadron, and I was the next logical guy. That job was the pinnacle of a fighter pilot's career—to have your own squadron! One day I was called in to see the wing commander. He told me the new squadron head had been picked: it was not to be me, but a protégé of one of the generals, a golden boy who had just been transferred in from another base, after only a few months in his previous job—too few, in fact, to be strictly legal. I knew that his transfer had been against regulations, and now I knew why it had been done.

I was silent.

"Don't you have anything to say?" he asked me.

"No, sir," I said. I took three steps, saluted, turned on my heel, and walked out. Then I went directly to put in my papers for retirement.

This is no place for Dick Rutan, I thought. This is not where I should be. The politics were more than simple turf protection—some of the top officers struck me as pathological. I had always had a problem with the idea of "superior" officer. The guy with the higher rank was a senior officer, but he was not superior to me, nor I to my subordinates. I always corrected juniors who referred to me as a superior, and perhaps that should have been a sign to me that I would never adapt well enough to the military view of things.

This was not a game I could play. I was too straightforward. I would end up in a desk job someplace, and that was not what I wanted.

Still, it was a big blow. The Air Force was all I had known, and now I was starting over at age thirty-nine.

My wife, Geri, didn't like my getting out of the Air Force at all. She had put up with all the years of transfers and overseas moves, waiting for the day when life would stabilize in a command and a more regular home—and now this had put an end to it. It was a major disagreement, but I had no other choice than the one I made. And eventually it led to our separating.

Burt and I talked about my going to work with him. I had already become interested in what he was doing in Mojave. He needed a test pilot, couldn't afford one, and I'd done the test flying on the Vari Eze prototype when I was still in the air force and flew it to the EAA Fly-In at Oshkosh in 1975, setting a closed-course distance record right there in front of the crowd.

Mom and Pop had a house at Big Bear, where we would all get together for Christmas and other holidays each year. Most people would have wanted to look out on the lake or mountains, of course, but our house looked out on the airport, where the most moving part of the scenery was the windsock.

It was at our house that Pop agreed to grubstake Burt's incorporation of Rutan Aircraft Factory; it was on one holiday there that our sister, Nell, came up with the name Vari Eze for Burt's new airplane. And it was there one Christmas that I decided to go to work for Burt.

Jeana

Growing up, I learned that I could do anything I set my mind to if I was willing to work hard enough. My parents never tried to force me into any pattern nor did they tell me that because I was a girl I had to do things a certain way. Sometimes I would dress up and be ladylike but other times they let me be a tomboy and climb trees, hunt tadpoles, and go stream fishing.

I've always been curious about things and wanted to see new places. When I was very little we moved a lot. My father was employed by LTV— Ling Temco Vought—and they kept transferring him to different facilities in the Dallas–Fort Worth area, with a three-year stint in Oxnard, California.

Travel was always a delight for me. When we went on vacation, I loved to sit in the front of the car and just watch the landscape change as we drove to California or one of the national parks. They tell me that when we stopped at the parks I would tend to go exploring on my own, and they always knew where to look for me: at the top of the nearest pile of boulders.

My first spoken sentence was "I want a horse." I was put up to it by Judy, my older sister, but it pretty well reflected what I would be talking about for a good part of my life.

It was not until I was three or four that we got our first horse, a large pony named Buffalo, and that was the beginning of my love for horses. I could easily walk under her without even bending my head.

Buffalo was Judy's horse except when Judy was at school. Then I would go out into the pasture to get her, slip a rope around her neck, and lead her back to the house.

I was too little to get the bridle and saddle on by myself. But where there's a will there's a way. Being small you learn to be resourceful. I tried fences and tree stumps. Then I thought of the picnic table.

I guess all horses must know the trick of taking one step away just as you get ready to jump on—Buffalo surely did. I climbed off the table and pushed her back close to it, then got back on the table. *She did it again.*

This time I climbed down from the table, moved it so that there was just enough room between the table and a tree for Buffalo, moved her into position, climbed back up, and jumped on her back.

With no bridle, "Getty up" and a flapping of my little legs were the signal for "go." Turns were in any direction Buffalo desired. "Whoa" did not exist and the clothesline was low enough to brush the pony back.

It was time for some new strategy. I slid off and went looking around— and found a bamboo fishing pole.

I jumped over onto her back again, looking like a knight with jousting lance but no armor. Turns were simple now: I just tapped the pole on the side opposite the one I wanted to go. Now I could ride.

. . . . .

When I was four we moved from Fort Worth to Garland, just north of Dallas. Behind our garage there was a wisteria vine, with branches strong enough for me to climb. I would take my toy horses and scramble up into it and be lost in play there for hours, just enjoying the warmth of the sunlight coming through the canopy of flowers and the scent of the blossoms and the hum of the bees.

It seems I always established a corner to claim as my own hideaway, some place I could address the problems of my life. When we moved to a lovely white house facing Route 101 in Oxnard, California—with a lemon orchard on one side and a strawberry field on the other—the wisteria vine was replaced as my hideaway by a little attic room. I was always organized, and in this room I laid out all my toys in order. My palomino horses were all together; the grays, blacks, whites, and sorrels were all together, and each group was arranged according to sizes and names. Even if I was blindfolded I could retrieve any one of them.

In 1963 Dad was transferred back to Texas and we moved to Garland again. I was starting the fourth grade now, and the school was just a couple of blocks away so I got to walk almost every day.

Later I got involved with the local track team. In track, I learned discipline and stamina. I was a naturally relaxed runner and growing up I had learned to imitate the gliding stride of the horses I loved. Running gave me a free and strong feeling, a feeling of sharing the beauty and strength of horses and the ease with which they flew across the land.

From track, too, I learned sportsmanship, all about trying and succeeding and winning and losing. My best event was the 440-yard run and my toughest competition came from the black girls on another team we often faced. Against them, I always seemed to hold my own until the homestretch, when they always had just a bit more to give than my body could come up with. At best, I usually finished third.

To make the finals at one meet I had to get at least that third place. In the homestretch, I had it, just one step ahead of the girl moving up behind me. I was determined that place was mine and I stretched out my stride and tried to pull ahead. But at the moment I did, I lost my footing and all of a sudden I found myself on the ground, my left leg underneath and behind me and my right leg, the thigh raw with gravel burn, stretched out in front of me. My right toe was just three feet from the finish line.

It was my first major defeat. I was disappointed but not angry with anyone—not even with myself. I had tried. And because I had tried I knew I could never really fail.

I knew my friends would still love me, my coach would still work with me, and I would still be able to run other races.

Once we went to a state meet. There was no 440 in my age division, but my coach came up to me and told me he had entered me in the 440— in the senior division.

The girls in that group were four or five years older, including some from a team we had never competed with, two of whom were reported to be very good. I still had a good chance at third.

The coach also mentioned that he'd had to lie about my age and if the committee questioned me I could be disqualified. And if I won, I might have to forfeit any medals, if complaints were filed. He asked me if I wanted to take the chance.

I beamed with pride, knowing the coach must have thought I was pretty good if he was willing to enter me against these older girls.

He told the team that if my age was questioned and I was disqualified, the whole team would probably be disqualified too.

The 440 was not until late in the afternoon and I had all day to worry about it. The coach had entered the five of us on the team in almost all the events, even those in which we didn't specialize, and as a result the team was third in overall points.

We had done well, and built up a lot of points. We had won ribbons and medals. I quietly prepared for the race.

My heart pounded. I tried to remember I had a job to do. I carefully set up my starting blocks, then did some trial starts, readjusting the blocks several times. I breathed slowly and deeply, pacing and waiting for the call to position.

The gun went off. I had a good clean start and got off to the lead. I maintained a good strong pace for over three-quarters of the race. Then, with their more mature and trained muscles, very steadily and very easily the other girls pulled past me—one, two girls—their best. They were very coordinated, disciplined, and experienced, and it felt as if they had just started to run the race. There was nothing I could do except maintain the pace I'd already established. I pushed myself harder and yet it was all I could do to keep from slowing down. I hung on and as the coach predicted I took third place.

The coach explained afterward that they had used me as a rabbit to pace themselves, reserving their energy for a final sprint. Sprint was a new word for me, but as I gained experience I learned how to pace myself.

For third place, I got my first medal, and I was prouder of it than of any of the medals that were to come later. I had matched myself against girls five years older than I and held my own—and more important, I had learned from the experience.

. . . .

Track lasted only a couple of years for me. When I was in the tenth grade, we moved to Commerce, Texas. There we found a house with a barn and twenty-three acres—at last a proper place for my horses. In Garland, we had to drive thirteen miles to a pasture we had rented outside of town to feed the horses. In Commerce, they would be right there with us.

It had all started at a registered quarter horse auction at the Circle E Ranch in Garland. We got our first breeding horse when, the family story goes, Judy nudged Dad and he yelped—a sign the auctioneer took as the winning bid on a mare with a pretty young filly.

It was a few months before we got to take possession of her. Dad had grand expectations of raising registered quarter horses and becoming wealthy. Miss Star Lone was now waiting to be bred to get this business going.

The first baby born was Hickory Snip (Snip), then King Peppy Top (Pep). Next was Joker Jude (Jude) and finally Liberty Bob (Liberty). Four years later Dad woke up to the fact that the horse business was not such a gold mine. Perhaps it was because I had made pets out of all the horses. They were all my children.

Horses were always the center of my life; school was just someplace I had to go to. Occasionally when I was bored in class I would doodle, usually drawing pictures of horses, and although I never showed them to anyone and would throw them away, I liked to draw. I decided to take a course in drafting and the skills I learned turned out to be important to me years after I graduated.

On April 8, 1972, just before I turned twenty, I married Jon Anthony Farrar. Jon was a lieutenant deputy in the Fort Bend County, Texas, sheriff's department, involved with criminal investigation. He was a kind and gentle person, the sort of guy everyone liked, and a wonderful husband.

After five years of marriage I had become restless and felt there were more things I had to do. I couldn't just live and die in Rosenberg, Texas—not without seeing what the world held for me. My instincts told me there was something I had to do in my lifetime that couldn't be done there. I decided I would pull up roots and head for the unknown. It was time for a change in my life. I packed up and drove to Santa Rosa, California—north of San Francisco—where Judy lived.

I made the drive in two days, from Rosenberg to El Paso, then straight through to Santa Rosa. On the way, I was lost in thought—about California, about the past, and about how sad I was that I was hurting someone I cared very much for.

I moved in with Judy and found a job drafting and surveying for a geothermal energy company. We had not seen much of each other over the years and it was much like meeting my sister all over again—probably the happiest time in both our lives.

Four months after Jon's and my divorce had become final, Jon was killed in an automobile accident. In spite of my leaving, I still loved him. There had never been any bitterness between us, and his death left an emptiness that remains in my heart.

. . .

What first attracted me to flying was a fascination with helicopters. They reminded me of dragonflies, hovering and maneuvering so lightly in the air. I remember seeing dragonflies when I was little, swimming at a lake or fishing in a stream. Sometimes I would just stand and watch them for a while or chase them.

Before I could learn to fly helicopters it was recommended that I get my fixed wing license. I learned to fly in Santa Rosa, at the Piper Flying School at the Sonoma County Airport, and got my license in 1978.

I was ready to move on to helicopters. The lessons were expensive; I had to put down a large deposit with a company that gave lessons—and then the company ran into financial difficulties. I never got the lessons; I felt fortunate even to get most of my money back. That money and everything else I had later went into *Voyager*. I still intend to get my helicopter rating someday.

A friend told me about a man who was building a rocket in his backyard. I was curious and went over to see what the place was like. It was a five-car garage turned into a workshop, and a couple of rockets out front, with his children and pets. It was an unlikely setting for a space program.

The man in charge, Bob Truax—Captain Robert Truax, U.S. Navy, ret.—is one of the true pioneers of rocketry. He's been at it since 1937 and is one of the few people who worked with both Robert Goddard and Werner von Braun. He worked on the rockets that went into the X-1— the experimental airplane in which Chuck Yeager broke the sound barrier. He helped create JATO—jet-assisted takeoff—rockets and he developed an innovative concept called Sea Dragon, for launching rockets at sea, in which the ocean itself provides cooling and launch pad cushioning.

Now he had started his own company to launch rockets. While working for the navy on rockets, and later for Aerojet General, he had become convinced that we were going about getting things into space all wrong. Most rocket designs had begun with payload and "engineering parameters" and worked back from there. Cost was incidental.

Bob's idea, which he worked on for a while before he retired from Aerojet, was to begin with cost—to look at what was already available and design the rest of the system from there.

Some of the resulting ideas were to use already developed components for his rockets—and to separate the cargo carrier, which constituted most of the weight, from the people carrier, for which very high reliability was demanded.

Bob's ideas were sound and well thought out but he was having trouble raising funds; he'd spent a quarter of a million dollars on the project, but he needed more. People believed that only a huge company or the government could do what he was trying to do.

As soon as we had achieved the necessary reliability of the rockets, Bob was going to launch one carrying an astronaut, more for the sake of getting public and investor attention than anything else. When people asked him about life-support systems, he noted that the first flight would only be a suborbital dash into space and "you could practically hold your breath that long."

Bob and I hit it off right away. He sort of adopted me from the start. He treated me like another one of his children and became as good and trusted a friend as I have ever had.

He would always introduce me by putting his arm around me and saying, "This is Jeana, she's my astronaut." In fact, while I was the astronaut for all the mock-ups, he never quite asked me to be the astronaut for the real flight and I never committed myself to it. I suspect he was too fond of me to ever ask—he was probably afraid I'd say yes.

I went to work for Bob, drafting at first, and then, as I went along, I learned about all sorts of other things such as rocketry and systems engineering.

Bob would give me an assignment and then just let me go off on my own, watching me out of the corner of his eye when he didn't think I noticed. I learned how to do the work the way I had learned how to train horses—by experience and trial and error.

One day Bob told me to build the launch pad for static testing. I drew up the plan and showed it to him. He calculated that it was just adequate to handle the thrust, suggested I increase the dimensions slightly, and sent me on. We agreed on a suitable site, at Fremont Airport, and I hired the contractor and helped build the launch pad. I think I often surprised him.

Bob had a friend named Martin Hollman who had designed and built a two-place gyroplane. Martin would go around to airshows publicizing his aircraft. He was a gentle giant of a man, nearly seven feet tall, and he kept inviting me to go along to the airshows and help hand out flyers and talk about his gyroplanes. I was a little concerned about his intentions and kept finding polite reasons not to go, but by the time he invited me to the 1980 Chino, California, airshow, I had run out of excuses. Martin had cleared it with his wife and with Bob and I soon found myself making the long drive to Chino, which is near L.A., in an underpowered Volkswagen pulling a trailer.

When I got to Chino I noticed the Rutan Aircraft display, with Vari Eze's and Long EZ's sitting behind ropes. I knew Bob was interested in buying a Vari Eze so I thought I would drop by, pick up some of their brochures, and ask if anyone knew of a Vari Eze for sale.

The whole Rutan clan was there: Burt, Mom and Pop Rutan, Mike and Sally Melvill, and Dick. I talked to Mike first. He was called away and sent Dick over to talk to me.

Dick gave me a lot of attention right away and for most of the rest of the day he kept entertaining me. When the time came for the long drive back to the Bay Area, Dick offered to fly me back instead. "Well," I told him, "I came with Martin—you'll have to ask him."

Towering over me, Martin seemed very protective, as if he had been my chaperon. Dick finally mustered up his courage and asked Martin if he could fly me home—and Martin turned him down flat. "Bob told me to bring Jeana down here, take care of her, and bring her back, and that's what I'm going to do," he said.

The whole scene struck me as hilarious. Dick was not afraid to strap on his Long EZ and throw it across the sky doing aerobatics, but he was intimidated by Martin.

"Why am I doing this?" Dick asked. "I feel like some kid asking a father for permission to take out his daughter."

We looked at each other and both burst into laughter. When it was time to go our separate ways I knew it wasn't the last time I would see Dick.

Beginnings

I came to work for Burt and Rutan Aircraft Factory (RAF—pronounced as an acronym and not like the Royal Air Force) as chief test pilot and production manager. I tested the new planes, put them through their first flights, tracked their performance, and helped improve them. There was the Vari Eze, which I flew to Oshkosh and then, with thousands of Experimental Aircraft Association members watching, piloted through a record-breaking closed-circuit flight. Others were the Microlite and the Next Generation Trainer and the Long EZ and the Defiant and the Vantage, an 85% scale version of the Starship I executive plane for Beech.

I also flew aerobatic exhibitions, great loops and rolls in the tiny planes that were as exciting as anything I had done since Vietnam—they were like combat with an audience. There was a lot of flying skill to it and necessarily a good deal of danger. I had been reading Abraham Maslow's theories of personal development, and aerobatic flying seemed to represent, to me, what Maslow called one's "level of self-actualization."

The aerobatics bothered Burt, however. He was afraid that people who didn't know what they were doing would take up aerobatics, crash, and give a bad name to the world of home-built airplanes he had done so much to create. The FAA had been very lenient with the home-builts, but a run of crashes could bring pressure to stiffen regulations.

Burt had not really wanted me to go for the records. Generally cautious, he had told me that I could prepare for those flights only after I had put my regular hours in at Rutan Aircraft.

It was the first of a number of disputes we would have, in which two natures, that of the daring pilot and that of the innovative but painstaking designer, were at war.

We disagreed about the company, and we had loud and painful arguments. I wanted, for instance, to take the Long EZ to airshows, to fly fancy aerobatics with it, to jazz it up with better avionics, to turn it into a sports car of flying. I thought the company should be selling dreams.

Burt didn't want to do any of that. He approached things more cautiously. He was afraid it could all get out of hand, that people would push the planes too far, accident rates would rise, the FAA might drop in on the little space of freedom of the home-built world like a lead sled.

But it was Burt's company. I was an employee and felt more like one with every fight we had. I felt my talents were being wasted, that I had become nothing more than a technician putting together airplanes. And Burt could have hired any number of those. I felt that I was not doing what I wanted to do, that I wanted more control of my life.

Even the aerobatic flying I did at fly-ins, which once had held so much excitement for me, began to pale.

The fundamental problem was that I was Burt's employee. We disagreed over the course the company should take. As brothers we argued long and hard, but as the boss Burt always won. The direction of the company was out of my hands, and sometimes I felt almost like a hostage.

Burt had dozens of innovative, brilliant designs for airplanes in his head and on his drawing board. But to me it always seemed that the company built the wrong ones. RAF could build only one plane at a time, and Burt did not want to expand.

The planes Burt built were usually those that challenged him as a designer, not the ones with the best chances for commercial success. With the Solitaire, Burt won a contest for glider design, but there seemed to be little market for it. And the planes for which he sold plans—the Vari Eze and the Long EZ—put money in the pockets of other companies, those that sold materials and parts, and very little into RAF. To me it seemed that Burt made a lot of money for other people without getting what he and RAF deserved.

Burt has a freedom of thought that makes him successful; that is part of his genius. He doesn't constrain his thought processes with old ideas, but takes a fresh look at every problem, and it is amazing to see him work.

He is an intuitive designer, but he also follows each possibility to its rational consequences. He bought an early Apple II personal computer and ran the equations for wing loadings and airfoil shapings on it. For the

Solitaire sailplane, he went through seventy-six designs before settling on the seventy-seventh. And he did not freeze that shape until after an extensive series of load tests that involved piling dozens of lead-shot-filled sandbags atop the wing and canard.

He has always avoided complex systems in his aircraft. For all the innovations of his designs, his fundamental instinct is for what he likes to call the KISS principle—keep it simple, stupid. First out of necessity, then out of choice, he has demonstrated an affinity for the easily available, the off-the-shelf, the do-it-yourself. It is typical of Burt that he designed and built a solar water heater system to provide the hot water for RAF's hangar.

He chose to work with "high-tech materials" not because they were new, but because they would carry more with less weight. His innovations have been in methods—many of them extemporized—for working the material. He has always chosen the simplest and cheapest item that will do the job. The first Vari Eze was powered by a Volkswagen engine. The generator on the Long EZ prototype was taken from a Kubota tractor. And when I flew the closed-circuit record in the Long EZ, I kept track of my fuel flow using a Sears fuel meter.

But Burt's very genius and confidence in his designs have sometimes limited his sense of what is really possible, of what will fly—and what will sell.

When the first Long EZ was being tested, for instance, I told Burt for months that the Long's wing was not right; whatever the drawings and tests said, it did not handle well. The stall speed was too fast and the roll rate inadequate.

Burt thought that the design could be "tweaked"—modified slightly with the benefit of experience. So I flew the original wing on fifty-one test flights, which resulted in more than thirty modifications. About six months later, Burt eventually recognized that the wing had to be entirely redesigned.

Other planes Burt designed simply had no market. The Grizzly was Burt's design for a bush plane. The market was severely limited to begin with—most of its potential users were kicking around in ancient rebuilt aircraft because they fit the budget. And for all its innovations—its ability to take off and land in a short distance, its ease of control—it had a severe limitation: access to the cabin was difficult. It would have been almost impossible for the backwoodsman to load his caribou quarters, snowmobile, camp gear, or whatever.

The Defiant, with its twin, push-me-pull-you engines, one on the rear and one on the front, was one of the designs Burt was proudest of. He had hoped for a while to build it commercially, but as he got involved in other projects, that fell by the wayside.

. . .

I was separated from my wife then and lived in a small apartment in Mojave, working at RAF all day and into the night. My air force benefits went to her and our two daughters, and I lived a Spartan life, focused on my work. If that work wasn't satisfying, then what did I have?

As Burt became more and more concerned that home-builders would see us doing aerobatics at shows and be inspired to do something they couldn't handle, he tried to talk me out of taking the Long EZ prototype to any more shows. But this was what I loved doing. I had come to RAF to fly, not to be a shop technician. So I resisted. Finally, one day, Burt literally took the key to the airplane away, like a parent grounding a teenager: "Can't use the car anymore." It was, after all, his airplane.

One weekend that summer I went to an airshow in Chino to fly and show off Rutan airplanes. Jeana came by the booth. She was thin, with long brown hair and fine features. She looked about fourteen years old, and I thought she was the neatest girl I'd ever seen.

I didn't fly Jeana home that day, but I started phoning her and went up to see her the next weekend and the next, and she began to come down to Mojave.

She was, I felt, all I could have dreamed of in a woman, beautiful, smart—and a pilot to boot.

One of our first dates was a trip to Lake Tahoe. I will never forget how we walked down the street, arm in arm. Jeana fixed her eyes only on mine, not looking ahead of her or at where she was putting her feet, just relying on me to guide the way, total faith and trust and love in her expression.

. . .

Soon we had decided to build our own Long EZ. Mike and Sally Melvill, who had joined RAF shortly before, wanted a Long EZ, too, and in June of 1981 we all started building what were to be the second and third Long EZ's in the world.

Mike was to turn out to be one of the best test pilots I'd ever known, and all of us were to become close friends. We worked for Burt during the day, and as soon as the day ended we ran across the airport to a little room we had rented and went to work on our airplanes. Mike and I both had some ideas of how to improve the plane, based on what we had learned during the testing of the prototype.

For the basic parts, we worked on a form of semi-mass production to speed things along. I would build all the bulkheads, for instance, and Mike the sides, and we'd flip a coin on which airplane each part went into. When we got the basic pieces done we went on to customize the airplanes the different ways we each wanted.

Since the new wing worked so well, I thought I could do more to improve the Long EZ design. I persuaded Burt to design an aerobatic airfoil for the canard so I could fly inverted, enlarge the ailerons, and install a bigger engine—and all the changes eventually caused bugs that had to be shaken out later.

Jeana would come down on weekends and work with me on the Long EZ, learning the techniques as she went, enjoying the work, and learning about composite construction and seeing the plane take shape.

During those weekends, we found we had a lot in common. We were both hard workers, but we couldn't stand nine-to-five jobs, whether in an office or in a factory, "bolting on fenders," doing the same thing day after day.

We wanted to be challenged by something new all the time, and neither one of us minded taking chances to do it.

Jeana enjoyed life on the flightline. You really had a chance to get your hands on things and make them work.

Bob Truax's project was about to run out of money, and Jeana thought she was about to be out of a job. By the end of the year I persuaded her to move to Mojave. It seemed the right thing to do, the right change to make—a gamble maybe, but one she would take.

She brought along some furniture that filled up my tiny apartment. It was cramped and simple, but I have never been happier in my life. I would be working in the cramped kitchen, and she would scamper up onto the counter like a little cat, cross her legs, and sit there just watching everything I did and looking into my eyes. We were very much in love. Life felt like one long honeymoon, and the skies were big and blue when we would go flying together.

Once or twice, though, a warning cloud would appear. One day we went into Reno's, the restaurant on Mojave's main drag, and I sat down across from her at the table instead of beside her. She took offense; she thought it was a terrible thing I'd done to her.

He didn't want to sit beside me. Dick had seen someone he knew and was afraid there would be gossip. I told him that if he was going to date me, he had better not be ashamed of me. And I moved to another table.

I explained to Jeana that I could see her face better sitting across from her, but she was very deeply hurt by it. She rarely ever sat beside me again. It was the first of many things—a Christmas tree I forgot to pick up, a promised bathing suit I never got around to buying. They were little things, those broken promises, but they remained like scars.

. . .

I would go off to work each day, but Jeana didn't have a job. I could see she was looking for something to dig her teeth into. She was not the kind of person to sit home and wait for me to return at the end of the day. Once I bought her a VHF radio kit to solder together, but by noon she had it all assembled.

Before long, as we discussed my unhappiness working at RAF, we came up with plans to start our own company. We would take one of Burt's many designs, produce it, and pay him a royalty. That way, we thought, Burt and I could work with each other instead of for each other.

I wasn't sure I could do it better, but I felt I could do no worse. And both Burt and I would feel better without the constant arguments. So it was agreed: Jeana and I would produce an aerobatic plane designed by Burt. We would start a company, to be called Monarch Aviation—until we found out that company name had already been taken.

Then we had our famous lunch with Burt at the Mojave Inn.

It was Burt's impulse to begin with. We sat in a horseshoe-shaped booth inside the restaurant and ate steak teriyaki and salad and chatted about forming our own company—until Burt brought up the idea of flying around the world. He was as casual, in his way, as if he were suggesting a nice vacation trip. "Sure," he said, "you can do Monarch, but why don't you just do this round-the-world flight first? It won't take very long—six months or a year."

I had heard Burt talk about various record flight attempts before, and a lot of them were joking—like man-powered aircraft ascending to orbit. He would always wear a little smile, the corners of his mouth just turned up a bit. But this time I looked at his face, and the corners of his mouth were completely level. I looked into his eyes, and I could see he was dead-nuts serious.

I looked at Jeana, who was as intent as Burt. She sat in the middle and finally said, "Why not? Let's do it." We all thought for a moment. No one could think why not. All interest in food vanished, and the plates were pushed away.

Burt explained that he thought the state of composite construction now made an airplane with the necessary fuel capacity possible, how we wouldn't have to use any exotic engines. He laid it all out.

Like Jeana and I, Burt had been doing some hard thinking about his future, and specifically about what he had achieved, what he would be remembered for. Burt had always been very serious about what he intended to do, and now, despite enjoying his reputation as the most innovative airplane designer of his time, he thought about posterity.

And by the time we walked out into the hot Mojave sun and got back in the car, all of us were hooked on the idea.

Design

We weren't sure we could do it—weren't sure anyone could fly around the world on a single tank of gas. But we were sure that if anyone could design a plane to do it, it was Burt.

Burt had already helped create a revolution in aircraft design. From age ten Burt had been obsessed with airplanes—models first, of course. Once, seeing his interest, our mother offered to go to the store and buy Burt a model airplane kit. A kit! He just laughed. Burt never built a model from a kit in his life—he built his own airplanes. And when I would fly a model and it crashed, he would take the wreckage and rebuild it into an airplane he liked.

He enjoyed a considerable measure of fame in the world of model aviation. He had built a model of a navy-carrier-based fighter that succeeded in almost hovering above the ground. He carried off so many prizes that model associations began changing their rules. He got a taste of publicity: his picture began appearing with regularity in the modelers' magazines, and he liked it.

Almost incidentally, he learned to fly "full scale" airplanes. When he was sixteen, he soloed in an Aeronca 7AC Champ and became an excellent pilot.

Later, while I was in Vietnam sending taped recollections home, Burt would also send our parents his thoughts on cassette, from Edwards Air Force Base where he was working. On one of them he pondered his goals and confessed his ambitions: "I want to really make something of myself in aviation," he says, and talks about how lucky he was to have had the experience of flying models. This was in the unsettled late sixties, and he ponders how model airplanes would make kids happier and better. It makes him sound like a high school counselor's dream come true. Statements like that, George Rutan recalls, made people think of Burt as "an apple polisher," but, his father is convinced, the sentiments were entirely genuine.

He was having similar thoughts that day in 1981 when he first conceived of *Voyager*, of what goals he wanted to set for himself, how he wanted to be known.

All of Burt's airplane designs have been in a sense an extension of his fascination with building model airplanes. The Vari-Viggen, his first airplane, was like a giant model, built mostly of plywood instead of balsa. Its handling was intended to provide in a tiny airplane an accurate scale rendition of the feel and handling of much larger and faster jet fighters.

The legacy of modeling is physically visible in many of his planes. He used model builder's materials on early planes. The Solitaire sailplane actually uses model airplane wheels on its wingtip landing gear. In *Voyager* the trailing edge of the wing was originally of balsa wood and fabric; the trim tab on the canard, jokingly called a "sparrow strainer," is a radio-controlled model part. But most fundamentally, the methods of modeling live on in *Voyager* in the stage of design after the plans are drawn, the period of "tweaking," the "cut and fit" method that only composites make possible.

Burt always wanted to retain the same control over the design as model airplane building afforded; he did not want to be pushed into manufacturing. Sometimes he was in love with the design of an airplane to the exclusion of market considerations.

And in a sense he's still in the model business, with Scaled, which he sold to Beech Aircraft, part of the giant Raytheon Corporation, in August of 1985. He builds half or 80 percent mock-ups and knows how to apply the results of performance tests with aircraft of that size to predict the performance of the full-scale aircraft.

. . .

Burt never wanted to leave the models in the workshop bedroom he had inherited after I went off to join the air force. But our parents persuaded him to go to college, at California Polytechnic in San Luis Obispo. There he began working on another plane, a larger one, the Vari-Viggen—a stubby, canard-equipped plywood thing.

He made up for his lack of a wind tunnel by attaching an airplane model outfitted with measuring instruments to the top of a 1966 Dodge Dart station wagon and driving at night. He would run straight for ten or twenty miles at eighty miles an hour. He was never stopped for speeding.

After college he began working at Edwards Air Force Base as a civilian test engineer. He was assigned to a program involving the F-4 Phantom, a workhorse fighter bomber of the Vietnam era. Many pilots disliked the F-4, which was solidly built but heavy. Worse, it had a disturbing tendency to enter into unprovoked spins, especially in its later models or when loaded with fuel tanks or bombs.

In 1969 and 1970, when Burt was working on the program, it was of critical importance to the air force to solve the problem. There is no way to test ways of escaping from a spin except to throw the plane into one. As a safety measure, the F-4 test plane was equipped with a special parachute, deployed by a mortar, that would bring it out of the spin.

Burt flew in the backseat on these tests behind a pilot named Jerry Gentry. On one flight, the airplane spun seventeen and a half times. Then the mortar chute was fired, the plane jerked stable, and landed. The day after that test the plane went back up. This time, after the spin, the mortar parachute came loose. The pilot and observer ejected, but the plane ended up a junk heap on the desert floor.

On the basis of these tests, Burt put together a manual for pilots to get out of a spin and found the air force grateful. He became known as "the man who saved the F-4 program," and it was clear he could have pretty much written his own ticket in research at Edwards.

But with our parents' encouragement and a $10,000 loan from our father, he left to pursue his own designs. It was the Vari Eze that made Burt famous, when Dick flew it to the annual Experimental Aircraft Association Fly-In at Oshkosh in 1975.

It was a fiberglass composite, and in just a few years some eight hundred of the airplanes were flying, an astonishing total for a home-built design.

Originally, plans sold for $50. Suppliers such as Task Research, Aircraft Spruce, Ken Brock Manufacturing, and Wicks Aircraft provided parts and did very well, while Burt scraped by.

Before long Burt had become legendary in aviation circles. He turned out more innovative designs of more varieties of aircraft than probably anyone since the days of John Northrop or Kelly Johnson of Lockheed.

For NASA, unsolicited, he turned out the shape for a curious-looking "skew wing" airplane—the wings, which looked like an oversized pair of scissors, were supposed to test ways of reducing transonic drag—and had it built for a mere $250,000, barely a jot on the agency's budget. Some NASA scientists looked at it admiringly but, when they found out the price, decided it couldn't be worth anything. "Didn't cost enough to be any good," they said.

Burt's design trademark is the canard, the "front wing," which, although it has cropped up on various innovative airplane designs through the years, has pretty much been out of favor since before World War I.

The canard was a feature of all the Wright Brothers planes and was critical to their success—indeed, it repeatedly saved their lives. The Wrights found that the most dangerous feature of flight, gliding or powered, was the stall. The Wrights added the canard to their airplane after hearing about such stall-caused crashes as the one that killed German glider pioneer Otto Lielienthal.

When a canard-equipped airplane stalls, if it is configured right the canard loses lift before the main wing. The canard—and nose of the plane—then dips, increasing speed and restoring lift. The canard is in effect an automatic pitch regulator.

Canards were abandoned when puller engines began to be installed on the front of the plane—the Wrights, of course, had pushers on the back, and the tail assumed its familiar shape and position. And Burt's aircraft, from the early Vari-Viggen and Vari Eze, had the props on the back, to simplify the flow of air over the airfoils.

But airplanes like the Swedish Saab Viggen fighter brought the canard back for the sake of maneuverability and short runway takeoffs—a variable-pitch canard has more surface to bootstrap a plane into the air from the ground than a simple elevator. The Viggen was designed to be stored in bombproof shelters, then rolled out to take off on highways or other short-paved surfaces in case of war—the plane can take off in 1,500 feet. These planes came out beginning in 1962; by 1964 Burt had already put a canard on one of his model airplanes.

The canard appealed to him not only for its stall resistance and safety, but for the handling it offered. When he set out to build his first home-built design, which he was to call the Vari-Viggen in homage to the Swedish fighter, he wanted to create a plane that handled like a jet fighter, that climbed and rolled dramatically. He gave his interests away later when he painted his own Vari-Viggen in the colors of the Air Force Thunderbirds' aerobatic team—the plane was consequently nicknamed "Thunderchicken."

The idea that a stubby little aircraft could handle like a jet fighter was as striking as the possibility of building it in your garage.

Burt's, of course, was not the first home-built aircraft design. Among others, there was a man named Jim Bede, of Newton, Kansas, who hired Burt away from Edwards. Burt put the disassembled Vari-Viggen on the moving van that carried his household to Kansas.

Home-builts had a particular attraction in an aviation industry whose innovations had been crippled by liability problems. By the sixties, new small airplanes were simply not being introduced. The Pipers and Cessnas and Beeches that made up the heart of the private aviation market were mostly designs dating from the forties or fifties.

Since the manufacturer of a home-built airplane was also its owner and pilot, the burden of liability was removed. There was, strictly speaking, no such thing as, say, a Rutan Vari Eze. It was a Smith Vari Eze or a Jones Vari Eze; each plane was certified by the FAA as a separate aircraft type. They might share a common set of plans, but the actual construction might differ markedly—from the topnotch expert builder to the builder who neglected to put in the bolts holding the wings to the fuselage.

.   .   .

Burt has been compared to the innovators of the personal computer: he was interested in making flying available to the many, just as Steve Jobs and Steve Wozniak of Apple were interested in bringing computing to the many. But unlike the founders of Apple or other computer pioneers, he had no interest in manufacturing. The last thing he wanted was to become another Cessna or Piper. And he has consistently made business decisions, many of them against his own financial interests, to keep his role from expanding beyond designing and testing airplanes. With the Vari Eze and Long EZ, for instance, it was the suppliers of parts and materials who really profited.

Certainly the builders of Rutan aircraft are as fervid as any Apple or Commodore computer buffs. They swap tips with each other, talk tech, and share flying stories.

Like the early computer hobbyists, the builders of Burt's airplanes felt a personal kinship to each other and to him. They would meet him at Oshkosh or at other fly-ins. Many of his employees came to Mojave after casual meetings. Mike Melvill, who was to become Burt's right hand, was working in an Indiana tool and die shop when he met Burt and began building his Vari-Viggen. Mike's wife, Sally, was the bookkeeper at RAF.

Burt needed a bookkeeper and a technical man, so in 1978 he persuaded them both to move to Mojave.

Lee and Diane Herron were running an aviation nostalgia shop in New Jersey when they met Burt. They became more and more friendly, spent more and more time in Mojave, and finally decided to move out when Dan Sabovitch, the airport manager, suggested they move their shop to the tower building in Mojave.

There was a familylike feel to RAF—I was there, after all, and our parents were always around, forming the nucleus—and the owners of Rutan planes felt like part of the family. For Burt's fortieth birthday, we threw a fly-in party: forty-five Rutan airplane owners brought their craft to Mojave. I flew an aerobatic show, and Mike, Burt, and I did some formation flying. It was a general aerial festival.

Despite this, Burt acquired a reputation for being elusive and private. Often he seemed preoccupied and busy, with more time to listen to his talking African gray parrot, Winglet, than to listen to visitors. Although he worked consciously on becoming better at dealing with people, even in the middle of a conversation he was sometimes unable to tear his eyes away from the drawing on his desk.

In the summer of 1985, however, Burt got out of the home-built business. He sold Scaled Composites to Beech Aircraft, although he continues to run it. He is, above all, a designer. He is not interested in manufacturing or simply supporting a customer base.

I had heard Burt broach the idea of flying around the world before but I had never taken it seriously. To him it still inhabited the category of things that included flying to the moon. Some flakey engineering concept.

On the napkin at that lunch at the Mojave Inn, Burt had sketched an airplane that was essentially a single huge wing, fronted with another tiny wing or canard in front. He took the napkin, stained with teriyaki sauce, home and worked out more detailed drawings in his notebook. The cabin— a stubby cigar shape with an engine pulling at the front and one pushing at the back—would be pressurized, with a bed for the off-duty crew member. The vertical stabilizers were on the tips of the long, slightly swept wing. Burt labeled the design "number 76." He had drawings for seventy-five previous airplanes in his notebook.

Seeing a real airplane in plans, I began to take the idea seriously for the first time, and Burt began to work out the range and performance requirements for the finished airplane.

Every aeronautical engineer knows the Breguet theorem, as every phys-

ics student has learned $E = mc^2$. Louis Breguet, one of the founders of
Air France and of the French aircraft manufacturing industry, developed
the standard formula for determining the range of an airplane:

$$\text{Range} = 375 \times \frac{\text{thrust efficiency}}{\text{specific fuel consumption}} \times \frac{\text{lift}}{\text{drag}} \times \log\left(1 + \frac{\text{fuel weight}}{\text{gross weight at end of flight}}\right)$$

Not quite as simple as $E = mc^2$, perhaps, but something definite to use
for running numbers through your computer.

What the formula boils down to is that to develop an airplane of great
range, you need a lot of lift, high gas mileage, and a high proportion of
fuel weight to total weight.

For a round-the-world flight, Burt planned an aircraft with a range of
some 28,000 statute miles. Breguet's formula showed that unless the aircraft
was to be larger than any ever built, it had to have a very high lift-to-drag
coefficient—a lot of wing per pound, in other words, and very efficient
engines.

The first sketch, the flying wing, with a tiny canard to obtain the most
lifting surface possible, seemed to answer the requirements. The ideal
flying wing offers perfect "span loading"—weight and lift are even at any
given point on its axis.

The "flying wing" was a concept that had a long and troubled history.
It tended to be unstable and hard to control. The largest flying wing ever
built was the YB-49, an airplane of highly dubious handling qualities. It
had been flown only a few times before it crashed, right near Mojave,
killing the test pilot, Glen Edwards. And the name of Muroc Air Force
Base had been changed to Edwards. It was from the runway there that
Voyager would eventually take off.

But when Burt ran the design through his computer, he found that
he didn't need the flying wing. It didn't provide enough fuel capacity. And
toward the end of the flight, when it was nearly empty of fuel, it would
have been easily tossed about by the slightest headwind. So he turned to
a notion he had been tossing around in his head for a long time: twin
booms or outriggers, which produced a design for Voyager that looked like
a catamaran sailboat crossed with a glider.

From that idea, the airplane almost seemed to design itself, and there
was a logic about the new sketches, which Burt finished up in March
1981, that made an immediate visual sense. The canard became a natural
brace for the twin booms. It canted back in a slight sweep to attach behind
the front engine. The vertical stabilizers moved from the wings to the rear

of the boom tanks, and tiny winglets appeared at the end of the long, now very thin wing.

The twin boom shape was a clever way of distributing the weight— the great bulk of which was to be fuel—evenly along the wings.

Burt had wanted to build an airplane using this concept for some time. But Voyager's wing was very long—longer than a 727 jet airliner's—but very thin, so that it resembled an oversized sailplane wing.

It also looked like some oversized version of Kelly Johnson's classic World War II fighter, the P-38, although the concept was very different. The P-38 was also a twin-engine plane, and Johnson had used the booms for mounting the engines. The fuselage proper was simply a teardrop-shaped capsule hung on the wing between them.

But because Voyager was to use the engines in stages, Burt put them on the fuselage, front and rear. Two engines are needed for takeoff and climb; the front one was to be turned off for more efficient cruising. The booms also allowed the vertical stabilizers to be placed far away from the prop wash of the rear engine. The winglets at the tips of the wing, used on some craft to "fool" the wing into behaving as if it were longer by smoothing resistance at its ends, turned out to function mainly in keeping the fuel vent outlet elevated from the main wing.

All this Burt finally worked out in just eleven drawings. Jeana quickly drew more formal plans, using pages of coordinate numbers generated by Burt's computer, and did a perspective view of the airplane, in India ink. It began to take on a sense of reality. She gave it the name. It popped into her mind as inevitable; there were no other serious contenders, and she quickly designed a paint scheme: a series of blue, V-like wingshapes radiating from the canopy. She painted the stripes on the airplane, and the name, and the word "Experimental" beside the cockpit.

. . .

The wings, booms, and fuselage were to be in effect a series of fuel tanks. The graphite structure itself, partitioned with bulkheads and pierced by the light plastic tubing that, joined with safety wire, was to serve as fuel lines, would hold the fuel. There were to be none of the interior tanks used in traditional aircraft design. Voyager was the tank. And its main cargo was fuel, a planned 8,934 pounds, 1,489 gallons of one hundred octane aviation fuel. Keeping weight down became imperative: for every pound added to the 939 pounds of basic fuselage and wing, 6 more pounds of gasoline would be required.

The fuel system is the epitome of the thinking involved in Voyager's design. It provides redundant systems, but without redundant equipment.

There were sixteen fuel tanks in the wings and fuselage feeding into a common fuselage feed tank. Electrical pumps move fuel to the feed tank; mechanical pumps move fuel from the feed tank to the engines. But if either set of pumps fails, the other, with a bit of valve shifting, can do both jobs. If there is an electrical failure, the mechanical pumps with valves open can suck fuel from the wing and other tanks, using the feed as a conduit. And if a mechanical pump on one of the engines broke down, the electric pump could feed the engines as well.

We worried about overflowing the feed tank, if we were distracted or busy, and the possibility of losing fuel or putting it somewhere that would make the plane unstable. Dick himself did it on Voyager's second test flight. The backup system for that eventuality on Voyager was to run the overflow into the left forward fuselage tank, one of the first that would be emptied and one close to the plane's center of gravity.

Another example is the crude but clever fuel-gauging system. There is only one fuel gauge proper, and it is of the old-fashioned transparent tube sort that Lindbergh used. It would take fifteen hours to fuel the Voyager completely, through tiny, ⅝-inch fuel caps. It indicates the amount of fuel in the feed tank; the amount in the other tanks is figured mathematically by keeping a record of the transfers in a log book. Fuel can also be transferred overboard, in the case of a forced landing, and drained at the rate of seventy gallons an hour total.

A specially fabricated eight-to-one valve handles the necessary switching. This fuel tank select valve had been custom made by Jim Billups of Meer Instruments. It was a sort of glorified version of the valves that mix the hot and cold water going into a shower head, only these valves switched the feed tank to draw from one of the sixteen tanks to another.

A transducer that measured the amount of fuel coming out of each tank is rolled back to zero, the desired amount of the transfer is set, and a countdown timer accompanied by a flashing white light and headset tone tracks the transfer and tells the pilot when to shut the pump off as a reminder not to overfill the feed tank.

To determine the distribution of the fuel's weight among the wing tanks—a critical factor, since too much of it near the end could induce excessive strain at the root of the wing—the pilots are required to sight through marks on their side window. These they line up with another mark on the wingtip to gauge the amount of wing bending.

The forward/aft balance of fuel is also critical because, if the plane becomes too nose heavy—if the center of gravity moves too far forward, enough to require more than one or two degrees of canard elevator—the autopilot may be driven out of whack and quit. We could lose control and fall in a deadly dive. It could also cause structural damage, and we knew that monitoring fuel balance would be a constant worry requiring constant attention. To help with the job, we added a deck angle gauge that showed our angle of attack. *Voyager* was the only plane we ever heard of that would take off, fly, and land at the same angle of attack.

. . .

Almost everyone who saw *Voyager* in flight for the first time associated it more readily with the ocean than with the air. The catamaran shape and pairing of the booms, and the canoelike configuration of the fuselage with its tiny, almost unnoticed canopy, lent this impression. So did the seemingly unpowered, sailing character of its flight, with the glider-inspired wings, affording a high thirty-four-to-one aspect ratio, and the occasional bobbing on the sea of air. When the white wings would lift and fall, the immediate association was with a great flapping gull, while, seen from the side, with the fuselage seemingly slung between the foreshortened wings, viewers might think of a humpback whale, leaping out of the water with forefins extended.

Like the sea, the air plays tricks with the sense of size and scale. Sometimes it made *Voyager* seem little more than a pencil line in the sky; at others it could make *Voyager* look like one of the great old B-36 bombers, or one of those thirties "futuristic" designs for airliners as big as ocean liners. At other times it seemed like a toy, a model. And there were some who saw in *Voyager's* assemblage of parts something like the *Star Trek* spacecraft *Enterprise*. Aesthetically, it was an inspiring shape. Its sheer beauty took people's breath away. But whether it could do the job was another question.

A Paper Airplane
and the Magic Door

We set out to build this plane. The idea seemed straightforward at the time: to find a corporate sponsor for the project. We set up our corporation, Voyager Aircraft, and immediately set about putting together proposals to send to potential sponsors.

The first months of the project were ones that we were to remember as the happiest in our lives. We lived in an old military tract house Dick's parents had lent us, nothing fancy, a fairly ragged sort of place, in fact, but free. Later, Dick's parents bought a different house, and we worked hard—Sheetrocking, carpeting, everything—to fix the house up. It was also our office.

Dick drove an ancient Toyota station wagon with fake wood paneling that the wind had sandblasted smooth. I had an ugly brown Buick Riviera. Both were paid for. We were unencumbered by mortgage or car payments or jobs. We wore jeans and running shoes and Dick wore his old Air Force jacket. Mom Rutan would come by every now and then to put a load of groceries in the refrigerator. We didn't have anything, but we didn't want anything, either.

We were quite infatuated, like a couple of kids in love. But we knew the project would be getting more complicated, that the quiet time couldn't last. We told each other even then that someday we would look back on this time and realize how fortunate we were.

From our "office"—Dick's desk was the kitchen table, mine a drafting table—we began work. It was a great idea, a dramatic project, a wonderful publicity vehicle. Surely we would be able to find backers. We spent eighteen months putting together our proposal and circulating it among potential backers; every day, and then the next day and the day after that, we expected a letter informing us that someone was willing to build the airplane and back us. The idea from the beginning had been to find one big company that would sponsor us for the sake of publicity. They would pick up the tab for building and supporting the airplane. Burt thought we could hire Ames Industries, a contractor that had built airplanes for him before, to do the actual construction.

In this effort, we were working in an established tradition. From the very earliest days, aviation milestones in America have been supported by private individuals and companies. There was the famous cross-country flight of a Wright airplane called the Vin Fiz, after the grape-flavored soft drink whose makers put up the cash. Today, Vin Fiz would be almost completely forgotten if its name hadn't been attached to that airplane.

But we weren't going to turn the airplane into a flying billboard for soda pop or fast food. We didn't want government to do the job, either, and this spirit was shared by those who worked with us. When one of our volunteers came to work on Voyager after a career in the military and aerospace industry, he said he'd be happy to volunteer, just as long as the government didn't have anything to do with it.

We were so naive. We sent out packages of material containing all the proprietary technical information on how we intended to proceed, with a meek request to return them if the recipient was not interested. Experienced business types must have laughed themselves silly at that simplistic sort of trust. Anyone could have ripped off our whole design and plan if he had wanted.

We went to the Reno Air Races in the summer of 1981 with a man who had made a tidy little fortune publishing a "counterculture" magazine.

He was different, but he was very enthusiastic about Voyager. He drove around in this motor home and put ads in the magazine to meet women to travel with him—he said he had hundreds of responses. We drove the motor home to the Reno Air Races while the publisher and one of his friends made themselves comfortable in the back. And at Reno, after the races, he said he wanted to fund Voyager.

"Let's do it," were his words.

"Call my lawyers," he said. "They may give you trouble, but just tell them to talk to me. We're going to do it."

We had planned a raft trip down the Grand Canyon—a guided trip we had put a big deposit down on—and we canceled it waiting to hear from him. We had been saving up for this trip and put down nonrefundable deposits of more than $2,000, and we were really looking forward to the time together. But we just couldn't run off now. It would be a bad omen to take a vacation at this point. You take a vacation after you've been working hard, not before, and we were that sure we were about to begin building Voyager. Dick even noted in the project log, "Voyager funded!"

Then the difficulty started. As the publisher had warned us they would, his lawyers tried to put us off. But when we followed the rest of his instructions and told them to talk to the publisher, there was a problem: no one could get in contact with him. "He's on the road," they said. "We don't know where he is or how to reach him."

We tried everything, left messages all over the country, even called his parents, trying to locate the man. Time went on and on. Finally, one of the lawyers called. "He's decided not to participate." We were hurt and disappointed. The publisher didn't even have the consideration or guts to tell us himself. The raft trip was lost, and so was the Voyager funding.

.   .   .

Maybe what we needed was competition—a race, like the race to cross the Atlantic and win the Orteig Prize when Lindbergh and his rivals were flying.

Well, we had some, but we didn't take it too seriously.

Two of our neighbors down the flightline, Tom Jewett and Gene Sheehan, had produced a home-built called the Quickie, for which Burt did the original design, and they were hard at work on a strange plane to be used to set some records.

What we didn't know for a while was that they—or Jewett, who was a former flight test engineer for the B-1 program—planned to fly that airplane around the world nonstop, nonrefueled.

It was a kind of overgrown sailplane, equipped with a Polish Franklin Pretzel engine. They called it Big Bird.

Both Jewett and Sheehan seemed somewhat suspicious of us, and after word leaked out in the spring of 1981 of what we planned to do with Voyager, they accused us of stealing their idea of flying around the world.

We found out that they claimed Big Bird had 24,000 miles of range; we couldn't see from the data they released how it could be any more than 16,000 miles, even if flown perfectly. Jewett was planning to sleep using oxygen at high altitudes, for ten out of the ninety hours the trip would take—an extremely dangerous proposition. I had flown with oxygen a lot, and I knew that if your face relaxes, or your head falls back, it is just too easy for the seal of your oxygen mask to be broken. The results can be brain damage or death. And I could never feel easy about the idea of the only pilot of an airplane being asleep.

We didn't regard them as serious competition, but they resented us. Reporters would come out to talk to them, and they'd hear rumors we were working on something similar and stop by to talk to us. "Aren't they way ahead of you? Why are you bothering?" We tried to bite our lips and not to say anything—after all, we didn't have an airplane, we didn't have a sponsor—but sometimes I couldn't resist. I used a line I had heard from Dr. Paul MacCready, creator of the man-powered *Gossamer Albatross*— "It is nice to be in competition with those who have absolutely no chance of success."

They didn't like the sound of that. Things weren't helped by the fact that I went out one day for some "cowboy flying" in the Long EZ and "jumped" Sheehan, in his Quickie, above Mojave. Even though I knew Gene wanted no part of dogfighting, I couldn't resist. It was the sort of playful dogfighting everyone did around Mojave, but Sheehan got very angry. Back on the ground, he yelled at me.

Aside from such episodes, we had coexisted along the flightline—it was like the main street of a small town and you had to do that. Jeana had even been doing some drafting for Quickie Aircraft, Jewett and Sheehan's home-built company.

We were always having a falling-out. And the last words I said to Tom Jewett before we stopped speaking to each other were, "I just want to tell you, as one pilot to another, that sleeping while on oxygen at high altitudes is extremely dangerous."

The morning of July 2, 1982, was clear and bright. The day before had been Dick's birthday, and I had given him a birthday cake—right in the face. We were feeling good, got up early, and had gone out together jogging in the desert near the house. We heard the noise of an engine, looked up, and saw *Big Bird* coming around on approach to runway three zero at Mojave, about 1½ miles away. At about ninety degrees to the runway the airplane rolled steeply, the nose went down, the airplane turned almost vertical—and then it disappeared from our view behind some trees. We heard the impact, and I raced back to the house, Dick trailing after.

We jumped into the car, drove to the airport, down the runway, and out to the crash site.

We walked over to within a hundred feet of the wreckage. Gene Shee-han stood there, looking at the body of his friend and partner.

"Jeana," I said, "we have no business being here."

We walked back to the car and drove home.

I was relieved that I had not considered *Big Bird* competition enough to bring on any feelings resembling gloating, now, but also a little sad that I had not been friendlier to Tom.

Jeana felt that if Tom had to die, at least he died doing something he believed in. I felt similarly about *Voyager*. I hope when I die, I go in my sleep or doing something I believe in, something I've committed my life to.

.   .   .

Through an EZ builder we knew, who shared a hangar with his corporate jet, we got an introduction to Barron Hilton, of the hotel chain. Hilton had been active for a long time in soaring and other areas of aviation, and we thought he might be the one who could understand what we were doing. We went up to his office, and Jeana could tell from halfway down the hall that he smoked cigars. He was enthusiastic, and prospects for Hilton's support at first seemed very good. If Hilton would fund us, I had decided I could even learn to live with cigars.

As in so many other cases, things with Hilton just dragged on. Then the funding was off, and just as suddenly it was a possibility again. We gave him a budget of $800,000, of which he agreed to provide half a million—provided we could come up with the other $300,000 and would basically sign over all our publicity rights to him and insure the project through his company. And where the hell were we going to come up with the rest of the money?

For eighteen months we rode a roller coaster of hopes and disappointments. And then, gradually, it began to dawn on us that maybe everybody else wasn't as excited about flying around the world as we were. Why it took us so long to accept, we don't know. Chalk it up to nearsightedness, or naiveté, or romanticism.

"This is just a paper airplane now," Jeana said, "a dream. No one sees it as something real. This is not an airplane that will ever be mass-produced. There is no chance of a potential profit in it, only publicity. And if something goes wrong, that publicity might turn out to be bad."

Every potential sponsor seemed to have a vision of the airplane turning into a giant fireball, making a spectacular piece of TV footage—and clearly showing his logo through the flickering flames.

It was extremely frustrating. "Doesn't anybody see what this thing is all about!!!???" I scrawled in the log one evening.

Wealthy people we contacted all seemed to have the same story: they thought it was a great idea, but they couldn't help. However, they did have a friend who might be interested, and in a position to help . . . and so on.

We finally realized this was an elaborate way of saying no. Eventually it became a joke between us, and we had to suppress laughter each time the tale would begin again. One such person was a wealthy oilman named Howard Keck, who had just sold his company and could have funded *Voyager* out of the change in his pocket. He had helped Burt with seed money to start Scaled Composites, and Burt kept saying, "Gee, I think I've got Howard Keck sold on funding *Voyager*."

"It will be the same story," Jeana warned, and when we met him it was. At first he seemed quite interested. But as soon as he heard we had talked to Barron Hilton and Hilton had declined to participate, he became obsessed with that fact alone. "Why didn't Hilton do it?" he asked, and he kept coming back to that.

We just sat back and smiled to ourselves, watching the scene unfold. And sure enough, pretty soon he mentioned that he knew about a college in the Bay Area that had a foundation that did just this sort of thing, and he was friends with people there, and he was sure they would fund us. And we looked at each other and winked.

Burt couldn't understand what had gone wrong. "I thought I had him talked into it," he said after Keck left, shaking his head.

We met some fascinating people, and we learned about the rich. Along the way, someone told us the story of the rules of wealth.

Every rich person, it goes, has to appear before the god of wealth. And the god of wealth says, "I will make you rich, but you must agree to two rules, which you must never violate, or I will immediately make you poor.

"First, you must never do anything with your own money. And second, you must never give anything away."

It always seemed that the generosity of the people we dealt with varied inversely with their socioeconomic status. Once we were lured to a fancy banquet held in Long Beach by the public relations man for a leading airliner manufacturer. The guests of honor were customers for its planes from all around the world, and we were star attractions. "You'll meet all kinds of wealthy people who will be eager to finance your project," he told us. We gave our talk and showed our slides, had a fancy hotel suite, and ate the huge shrimp put out with the cocktails and the chateaubriand dinner that must have cost $100. But there was no honorarium, no support for building Voyager, and no interest from the fat cats. Plus the company even reneged on its promise to pay our expenses, and we went home feeling foolish and angry.

A couple of days later, we went to another gathering, at El Monte Airport, of working aviation people. The response was just the opposite— we sold a lot of the shirts and posters we had made up, and guys chipped in with contributions. They really understood the project, and they were excited to be part of it. We began to get a clearer idea of who was going to support this thing.

We appeared at all sorts of fly-ins and airshows, doing low-level aerobatics in the trusty blue Long EZ, ten or fifteen minutes of loops and rolls—pure cowboy flying. For one, in Kingman, Arizona, we figured that the $300 fee was barely worth our while. Still, we flew out there and did our aerobatics—only to find later that the airshow had lost money. We were never paid.

With people who had money, the story was always, "There's a guy I knew who knows a guy who knows a guy—" At a banquet at Edwards Air Force Base we met a fellow who knew the man who owned Caesars Palace. He told us he was sure he could get us support—if we could take off and land from Las Vegas. We said we would have to check on the length of the runway at McCarran Field, the airport there, or maybe we could use Nellis Air Force Base, and then there's the question of density altitude, and . . .

"Oh, no, no, no," he replied. "You would have to take off and land from the parking lot." He was referring to the parking lot at Caesars Palace, well-known site of heavyweight boxing title bouts, Formula One auto races, and Evel Knievel motorcycle leaps.

There were sponsors we rejected. We both abhor smoking and abhor tobacco; we think it is as dangerous as heroin. We had interest from an agent with contacts with a British tobacco company that is active in motor racing. He told us he could get us a couple of million dollars if we accepted support from tobacco companies. But we were not going to fly around the world with a cigarette logo on the tail. "You don't have enough money," we replied, "for us to put a cigarette on this airplane."

Dealing with the press was vital to spreading word of the project and getting people interested, but we really didn't know much about how to do it.

We got several calls from a tabloid newspaper. The flight was hardly the stuff of searing supermarket headlines about aliens, Bigfoot, and voices from beyond the grave—but still they wanted the story. In fact, they wanted exclusive rights to it. Dick didn't want to get them angry, so they simply made up a story, but we had no intention of selling them any kind of rights, so Dick just laughed at the figure they offered.

We were not interested in any sort of exclusive deal. This enraged their representative. "I demand," he said, "I demand that you tell me how much you want."

We learned something about the press, too. A reporter from *The Washington Post* named Pete Early came out. He was easy to talk to and spent several days with us. Although Jeana told me it was not a good idea, I began to talk with him about politics and religion and a lot of things you can count on offending somebody or other by talking about. As he left I asked him not to put that material in his story. The reporter promised he wouldn't, but he did anyway—and even included the fact that we'd asked him not to include it!

. . .

We did get offers of help—from strange quarters. We followed almost all of them up, because we were keeping an open mind about any new system that might be usable on the aircraft.

A man from Texas, Howard Tourney, who was just getting involved in the composite aircraft construction business, offered us $25,000 to let him bring some of his engineers around for a look. Dick and Bruce Evans worked out a whole show for him. We demonstrated how to make and cure all kinds of composite materials, and we even had finished samples ready for him—the way Julia Child has the finished dishes she pulls out at the end of her cooking shows. We gave him the samples and books and videotapes on how to handle the stuff.

When the group arrived, the Texan took Dick aside and said, "Don't mention anything about the money to these fellows." Dick knew it was a bad sign, and sure enough, the Texan shook hands warmly at the end of the day, took all our materials, flew home, and never mailed the check. We must have spent six or seven hundred dollars just on materials, and we asked him just to pay for those and for our time, but he wouldn't even do that.

Strange technical suggestions, too, would come in, unsolicited, from inventors and basement technicians. One fellow claimed to have a power pack that ran on iridium—used in hospital X-ray machines. It was about the size of an automobile battery and would generate 35 kilowatts at fifty cycles for the half-life of the iridium—for decades. He had one running, he said, but he was afraid to produce it because someone would steal the concept.

Dick called him and said, "Congratulations. You know, don't you, that your system has solved all energy problems and put the Arabs out of business." We were promised a demonstration, but somehow it never came about.

Another one claimed to have a system for burning fuel in a "nuclear plasma" without exhaust or waste heat or light. We wouldn't even need a new airplane, he said; just put it in the Long EZ and fly two or three times around the world. "I can make it any size," he said. "Do you want a two hundred horsepower? Three hundred horsepower?" To finish it up, he needed just $3,500.

A man from Switzerland wrote, suggesting himself as a substitute for Jeana. He didn't think a woman could bear up under an eleven-day flight, he said, and offered his own heart and respiration rates as evidence that he could.

Another correspondent, whose return address was a California penitentiary, described a fuel system that operated on air and water and again, of course, would operate for months. He found himself at his current location, he added, because of a misunderstanding occasioned by what he referred to as "an accidental act of euthanasia" involving his father.

One man sent a letter with a drawing of a shark holding a pennant in its mouth that read "Amelia Earhart Fan Club." "I will join your VIP club," he wrote, "and send $100 if you use the money to send Jeana back to Texas and replace her with an autopilot. Your airplane is a lightning rod, and it will surely blow up and you will both join the Amelia Earhart Fan Club."

. . . .

Don Lopez, assistant director of the National Air and Space Museum in Washington, D.C., was a big help. He offered us space in the museum for the command center and expressed eagerness to acquire the plane after the flight. After Walter Boyne became director of the museum, he also became an enthusiastic supporter.

We thought we were home free when Walter Boyne called the project a golden opportunity to revive the romantic spirit of aviation. "The *Voyager* project," he wrote in an aviation magazine, "has the potential to have the same effect on the aviation industry today that Lindbergh had in 1927." He could not understand, he added, why the aircraft industry, which would benefit so much from the success of the flight, did not form a pool to provide funds to finance it. Each company's contribution would be barely an eyeblink in its budget.

The National Air and Space Museum is the world's most popular: fifty thousand people a day enter its doors—a potential audience any number of marketers could use. Walter Boyne wrote a letter to a major oil company, calling the chance to support the project "the opportunity of a lifetime." Dick figured a letter like that—the endorsement of the director of the leading aviation museum in the world—was practically worth its weight in gold. But the company curtly declined—only later did they come on as a sponsor, supplying the synthetic oil and fuel for the testing and flight— and other corporations found the appeal equally easy to resist.

We also approached major American corporations in areas not directly connected with the airplane, seeking support equipment and sponsorship money. Chrysler Corporation built an automobile called the Voyager, so we talked to people there. A fellow named Paul Sheridan, who worked on advanced engines for Chrysler, had come out to talk to us about composite power plants. He understood the technical innovations involved in *Voyager* and became our supporter within the company. He recommended us to all sorts of his higher-ups within Chrysler. We requested the use of a couple of the Voyager vans for badly needed ground support, and Chrysler's logo would be visible on them, but we kept getting polite rejections from all of them, right up to vice-president.

Our request finally reached Lee Iacocca himself, a man (we figured) who, by his reputation, at least, would have been eager to support a project like *Voyager*, which boosted American technology, daring, and enterprise. But Iacocca declined: he did not, he said, want to overrule the decision his vice-presidents had made—that's what they were paid for. Paul later sent us a whole file of the letters and memos involved in our request, each of them stamped with all sorts of cover-your-ass "date received" and "cc" stamps.

While we had numerous contacts from overseas auto firms, we wanted as much as possible to link up with American industry. But after searching for a year and a half, we still couldn't find any interest among the American auto companies, and we accepted the sponsorship of Audi. We instantly fell in love with the cars they provided. They were a far cry from the old

Toyota and ailing Buick we'd been putting up with, and Dick provided his ultimate compliment: "This is almost like flying."

We talked to Ross Perot, the Texas computer magnate famous for his rescue of employees imprisoned in Iran. Dick had also been appreciative of his efforts to find some comrades still in Vietnam.

Our two and a half hours with him were the most educational meetings we had with any of the "rich" people we talked to. He was totally honest and sincere and perceptive and did not lead us on. But the first thing he said was, "My biggest problem is that you two are not married."

He felt that would open him up to criticism by his liberal enemies, who would use any excuse to get at him. It made me feel as if I were left out—Perot couldn't seem to talk to me. He only wanted to talk to Dick.

He warned us that we were going to have a hard time finding sponsors until we had something people could see or touch, and that they were still going to be afraid of something with their name on it falling into the sea.

. . .

Grasping at anything now, we explored the possibility of establishing a nonprofit organization to handle the financing. We had been warned against this method by the first lawyer we talked to, and we later wished we had remembered the warning.

Another lawyer came by and said he could set up a nonprofit corporation in six weeks. "A collateral nonprofit corporation," however, needed 501-C federal tax-exempt status, and after nine months we found it took a long time to obtain this. Only 50 percent of what we would take in could be spent on the program; the rest would go to running the corporation. We even hired a professional fund-raising firm.

The complexity was in how the profit corporation, Voyager Aircraft Inc., would relate to the nonprofit Voyager Foundation. It was so complex the accountants couldn't figure it out. But when they finally started arguing over whether we could go to jail over some of the shifts of funds, we knew it was time to abandon the idea. "That's it, stop it," we said, and went away heartsick that again it had all come to nothing, that all that time and money had been wasted.

. . .

But if we found no Americans interested in sponsoring us, we did have support from other quarters. We came very close to a deal with JVC

(Japanese Victor Corporation), the Japanese electronics company, and their ad agency, Dentsu, which is one of the largest in the world.

Larry Newman, the balloonist, introduced us to JVC/Dentsu and started negotiations. Somehow Ben Katz came into the picture and took over negotiations. For publicity reasons, JVC/Dentsu wanted us to fly over Europe and over Japan—neither of which was on our planned route and presented major weather problems. And after we bought all the extensive insurance they were requiring and gave a share to RAF, the money would have been tight at best.

Nor did we feel comfortable with Ben Katz. Katz was an economics professor who came along and tried to get us to create a limited partnership deal—offering what were essentially tax shelters for the wealthy. This might have worked, but it was not an idea we felt comfortable with.

Jeana noticed that he always seemed to be full of jokes and yarns that he insisted on telling before he got to the business at hand—if he ever did. He kept assuring us that the deal was just about clinched, everything was right around the corner. "Go ahead and begin picking out new cars," he told us.

Things were complicated by the fact that Burt was in the process of setting up Scaled, his company that would build composite partial-scale prototypes of aircraft for manufacturers. Burt was using Ben Katz to help him find financing for Scaled. And Ben was often presenting *Voyager* and Scaled together, as part of a package, to potential investors.

At least, though, JVC and Dentsu understood what we were trying to do. They were ready to sign us up, providing the financial support needed in return for the rights to market all aspects of the project. But they wanted partial control and a firm schedule, for $500,000, with $100,000 of it as bonus after the world flight.

Then, just before the contract was to be signed with Dentsu, in the fall of 1982 Burt was invited to give the prestigious Lindbergh lecture at the National Air and Space Museum. We went along, and before the speech, I walked through the Milestones of Flight hall, past the *Spirit of St. Louis*, past the original 1903 Wright Flyer, with its canard. A Japanese-supported airplane could never hang there, among the other famous milestone American aircraft where it belonged.

We decided to reject Dentsu's offer and try to fund the project another way.

We would build the airplane ourselves, using materials we could scrounge from our friends in the home-built supply business: Aircraft Spruce and

Specialty, Wicks, and Task Research. We counted on being able to get materials from Hexcel and Hercules. The building of the airplane would be done in the RAF shop, by us. It would then be turned over to Voyager Aircraft for testing and flying. RAF and Voyager Inc.—Jeana and I— would each own half the plane and be entitled to half of any income it produced.

We would be working at RAF without pay. We were both determined not to be working for Burt again. Still, it required a lot of deep swallowing to go back to RAF in any form. We knew it would not be easy. We would have to learn all the fabrication methods: we had built foam and fiberglass aircraft but never worked with graphite and the oven and vacuum-bagging methods required. But we could learn.

And we would keep looking for sponsors.

Thinking about it then, we realized how important it was to us to finance things in a particular way—an American way. It was as important to us to do that part right as it was to fly. Aviation records had been set and the firsts accomplished mostly by Americans. We wanted this one to be done by Americans, and we also wanted it to reflect the best values of the American system.

It would have been impossible for Voyager to happen as it did in any other country. In most countries, there are all sorts of restrictions to keep you from hurting yourself. This is especially striking in the area of aviation. In Japan, for instance, owners of home-builts are restricted to takeoffs and landings at a single airport. Here, the FAA certifies your home-built airplane but can withhold that certification only if you endanger somebody else. The FAA can require that the airplane be tested over an "unpopulated area," but it has no authority to approve or reject anything concerning its design or construction.

When we finally did prepare Voyager for flight, our dealings with the government consisted of filling out just two forms: one for the tail number and one certifying it as an experimental aircraft. The risk, as it should, remained ours.

We don't believe that protecting you from yourself is anyone else's job. We're all concerned about danger, but the greatest danger—far more threatening than any kind of physical danger—is the danger of losing your freedom.

. . .

I felt partially relieved with the decision. I had long been pushing to keep this project as close to the grass roots as possible. That, coupled with our lack of success in attracting corporate support, is why I came up with the Voyager Impressive People Club—the VIPs. Dick and Burt at first had little confidence in this idea, but I kept pushing it, and it paid off later. Each member would contribute $100 and help create a wider, grass-roots involvement and interest. The VIPs were to become the primary sponsor we never found in the corporate world.

They became not only financial boosters, but personal ones, calling in to find out how things were going, making repeated visits to the hangar, bringing their friends by. We couldn't have made it without them and all the contributors of smaller amounts, too. That's why we framed and put on the wall—so you see it just as soon as you enter the hangar—the letter from the guy who sent a couple of bucks. "Don't laugh," he wrote, "I don't get lunch today."

Even with those sponsors who came along with us, it was sometimes frustrating. We were low priority; we didn't hold out the promise of profits. That made perfect business sense, but when deadlines slipped for the arrival of equipment, when people failed to show up for scheduled meetings, as happened again and again, it was still extremely frustrating, bang-your-head-on-the-wall frustrating. Beggars can't be choosers. We often felt helpless and without control over our company or our destinies.

We kept a very careful log of the people and companies we approached and those that approached us. Often it was hard to keep a tone of discouragement and frustration out of this record. When things looked good, Dick would draw a happy face in the margin and when things looked bad a sad face with downturned mouth.

One day I would write, "An interesting possibility . . . very helpful . . . looks good, we'll see." But the next Dick would write, "A real low . . . rejection . . . found that the prop spinners don't fit . . . the Toyota broke down. . . . I'm tired of begging, getting down on our hands and knees. . . . Can't anyone see what this thing is all about??!!!"

Hard as the job of fund-raising was, there also seemed to be some kind of force working in our favor. Just when we needed something desperately, it would walk in the door. When were down to our last few dollars, some sort of job—flying for a movie or television production, a test-piloting job for Dick, things like that—would come in.

A man who had developed an exotic and, he believed, highly efficient new aviation fuel paid us to test it out. He was an Indian doctor and very secretive: we met him in the dark back room of a bar in San Jose, where, after making us sign a nondisclosure agreement and swearing us to secrecy on pain of death, he wrote the composition of the fuel—code-named "bug juice"—down on a napkin, all the time looking furtively around him. He flashed the napkin briefly in front of us and then dramatically burned it in a candle on the table.

He wanted us to put the fuel in the Voyager. Instead we agreed to help him buy a small airplane and test it for him in that. We did the test and told him the truth: the fuel was not very good. He paid us—even though he may not have been happy with the results. OPEC is in no danger.

Later Dick was hired to do some flying for the pilot program of a television series called Midas Valley—a Dallas- or Dynasty-style evening soap. We took the Long EZ up, and while Dick flew, I delighted in watching the actors doing scenes on the ground. They reminded me of circus animals, trotted out of their trailers like lions from their cages to do tricks and then sent back until their next scene.

Two big breaks were Dick's jobs testing the Starship I for Beech (Burt was producing an 85 percent test version of it at Scaled) and a job for Northrop on a classified project called Vantage or "Sneaky Pete."

With these breaks, and the contributions of materials and money that somehow managed to come in, we made it through.

I started calling the door to the hangar "the Magic Door" because of all the miracles that kept coming in. We began to have the feeling that there was some favorable force out there, helping us, some kind of serendipity working in our favor.

Every time we needed something, it would appear. We would be just about to go borrow money to buy something when a job came in to pay the bills.

Dick was sitting around one morning thinking about the avionics for Voyager. He was looking at a stack of magazines and brochures on avionics that towered from the floor to above his desk top. He had already spent weeks making comparisons and decided that King Radio had the best and lightest stuff we needed in just about every category—radios, radar, navigation systems, autopilot. We were trying to figure out the best way to pitch the project to Ed King, the owner of the company, when the phone rang. It was Ed King, calling to say he wanted to put his avionics on Voyager.

The value of the equipment alone that King provided was maybe $250,000, and the modification, installation, and consultation would surely be valued at least that much.

We tried to interest the directors of SAMPE, the Society for the Advancement of Material and Process Engineering, the trade association for the composite industry. We figured that the project would be a boon to this organization and its members.

When they put us off, we went to the SAMPE convention in Anaheim and dashed from booth to booth all over the floor, picking up cards and brochures to get all the addresses and make up a mailing list. We wrote to the presidents of all the member companies, asking them each to give us a thousand dollars, saying that whether or not their specific product was used in the airplane, its success would be a shot in the arm to the whole industry. And of the dozens of letters we sent we got just two responses. One was from Union Carbide saying that they thought it was an excellent idea and they were happy to be part of it and here was their thousand dollars.

The other was from a smaller company owned by a large petroleum corporation. And they said, If our material is not in your airplane, we will have no part of it.

The $1,000 from Union Carbide barely covered mailing costs. As a group of manufacturers supposedly on the cutting edge of technology, their lack of vision was shocking.

We made a formal request for support from Dupont, which had backed Paul MacCready's human-powered airplanes. They said they were interested only if it was a totally Kevlar airplane. Kevlar was not appropriate for the whole *Voyager*, however. We used aramid (the generic name for Kevlar) with its good tensile strength, in leading edge and floors, for instance, but not for making up the whole airframe. Hexcel was to provide us with Nomex honeycomb.

A marketing study had showed that Dupont received some $52 million worth of publicity for the few thousand dollars they spent in support of MacCready's Gossamer airplanes. Their refusal to help us typified much of the shortsightedness we found in big corporations.

We did use their materials, obtained via Hexcel, but we took our small revenge in banishing from our vocabulary Dupont's trade names for them— Kevlar and Nomex—and resolved forever after to say "aramid" and "honeycomb" instead.

Then there were people like Walt Jones, who, working within their own companies and standing up to their bosses, wouldn't take no for an answer.

Walt Jones was a salesman for Hercules, which manufactures the carbon used throughout the aircraft. He had worked with Burt on some projects, and he was a believer from the start. He kept trying to get Hercules to help out. He would be on the phone every few days telling us, "Well, they said no, but I'm going to try again." Dick would talk to them: "Hell, you throw away more material in one day than is in our entire airplane." Finally he just wore them down, and Hercules provided us use of their forty-foot autoclave, the high-pressure oven that was crucial for fabricating the spars and other parts, and materials and technicians. We went through this procedure with all sorts of suppliers, and after a while we came up with the standard phrase for it: "We'll just have to beat somebody up for that," we'd say.

People at Hercules had estimated that it would cost something like $35,000 just to build the tools—the molds—for the airplane's spars. Burt had a conniption when he heard that, and he and Bruce worked out some do-it-yourself fabrication schemes using steel forms that cut the cost to a few hundred dollars, and then Dick and Bruce went up to their plant and worked with their people to do the job on the cheap.

And Walt had already accumulated the materials, bit by bit. Some was material rejected by a tennis racket manufacturer; some came out of his budgets for materials for sales demonstration purposes—a little bit here, a little bit there. He even managed, somehow, to get hold of some super-advanced high-performance graphite we needed for the fork of the landing gear. It was legitimate, although maybe not by the letter of things. Walt had a lot on the line, but as we got further into building the airplane Hercules became one of our most avid supporters.

Not that the companies involved in this way didn't get a lot out of it—not just publicity, but technical knowledge. We in effect did an extended R & D program on the Teledyne Continental engine, the IOL 200. We gave King a leg up on their competitors in information about adapting avionics to composite aircraft. We probably ended up helping Hercules sell more materials because a lot of the people Walt was selling to—military and civilian alike—were impressed by Hercules's involvement in a project they realized was at the cutting edge. People he would call on—the military people, especially—would always ask him right off about Voyager.

All this was in the best traditions of American aviation—Ryan aircraft and Curtiss Wright engines proved out their equipment on the Spirit of St. Louis. Lindbergh helped establish the metal frame and the high-wing monoplane and the radial engine.

. . .

Jeana came up with the name for the airplane and the company, designed a paint scheme and a kind of logo, an angular series of V's that fanned out something like a wing. She painted the stripes on the airplane, and the name, and the word "Experimental" beside the cockpit.

But she also organized and ran the office.

We felt a little bit like a pioneer family. I spent most of my time on technical things, working on the airplane in the hangar and trying to round up equipment. Jeana, besides working on the airplane, ran the homestead—created the corporation, maintained the business side, the letters and the accounts and the paperwork, the selection and ordering of souvenir items for the shop. It was about half a dozen jobs in one, all layered on top of her basic job of training and flying.

And our work was constantly interrupted by the need to dash off for some appearance. About 80 percent of our time was spent trying to raise enough money to keep going from week to week.

We appeared at all sorts of groups, showing films and slides, selling signed posters, hats, and buttons.

It's hard to estimate just how many groups we spoke to, everyone from aviation gas retailers to Rotary clubs, experimental test pilots to airliner salesmen.

These appearances were all different, but one close to home might stand for all of them. A Kiwanis club in Bakersfield invited us up to speak, the Bakersfield East Oildale Kiwanis Club.

The program director had his nine-year-old daughter act as the chief salesperson for the *Voyager* posters and shirts we spread out on a folding table.

These were heartland people, who have a "freedom shrine"—reproducing a series of great American documents—on the walls of their meeting place and begin their meetings by reciting the Pledge of Allegiance. They work in the oil fields or the cotton fields or the orchards. Merle Haggard, the country and western singer, is from Bakersfield, and in one of his songs he talks about the people there as the seeds of the Dust Bowl.

We flew the Beech Sierra up, and the program chairman and his daughter met us at the airport. They fed us on hearty barbecue and good country biscuits called "fly speck"—after the bits of pepper mixed into the dough— and peach cobbler. Everybody got up and introduced the friends they had brought along. Dick made most of the speeches. I was good at answering questions and talking with people in ones and twos and threes informally, but it has never been easy for me to stand up and talk to a whole room full of people.

The speeches brought out the natural ham in Dick. The basic speech had been restructured and refined over the months of giving it again and again. It had its laugh lines—Dick would often lead off with the story of how the waste disposal system would work; he would hold up a fecal containment bag and talk about how we had tested it by dropping ripe bananas. And it would always end with Dick talking about freedom in America, how only in America would the government allow people to build airplanes in their garage and fly them. And how the dangers to that freedom lay in the growth of bureaucracies and regulations, from the creeping limits laid down by people who wanted to protect you from yourself. And how Voyager stood for something done privately, the old-fashioned way, an American do-it-yourself way.

The Kiwanians stood up and clapped at that. We flew back with a small cardboard box stuffed with the cash proceeds from the sales of the shirts and posters.

The one thing we always said at the end was, Please invite us back after we've really done this thing. Thanks for supporting us when we haven't done it yet. We began to feel a little embarrassed by being hailed and cheered just for saying what we were going to do. We both have always believed in the rule, Don't talk about it, Do It. But in this case we had no choice: we had to talk about it to get the means to do it.

Flying

Mike and Sally got their Long EZ finished in six months but it took us longer. Our Long EZ was not completed until April of 1981—not long after we had begun planning for the *Voyager* project in February. After a lot of working out of the bugs, we ended up with a fine, fast airplane, a lovely light blue baby in which we were both to set some records. Boy, we were proud of it; it was like our kid.

The registration number was N169SH, and we called it "Shit Hot," after those two last letters and Dick's fighter pilot boasted of its performance. In polite company, we changed that to "Sierra Hotel," and later, when the hangar was full of visitors, we had it painted up with the name "D&J's Key." For Dick, the name of the airplane was a response to Burt's having taken away the keys to his Long EZ. The name was also a joking reference to the fact that it was our key to getting out of the imprisoning isolation of remote Mojave. It has been the airplane we could fly anytime, anywhere we wanted to. And as it turned out the flying we did in it was also the key to the experience and confidence we needed for *Voyager*.

We intended to set some records with the airplane. That would help establish our credibility, maybe help get attention that would help bring in funding for *Voyager*. And besides, that was what we did—that was what gave us fun and excitement, planning for the records, doing the flying, getting our names in the record books and on the plaques. We loved it. It also turned out that overcoming the problems we faced setting those records taught us a lot. We had our share of adventures during those days, and we got to travel some.

In May of 1981 we took Shit Hot to Alaska. Dick was aiming to set a distance record in the international C1b category—the category for airplanes weighing less than 1,000 kg—and if he could, to exceed 5,000 miles in doing it. We were confident that Shit Hot was the best airplane of its weight in the world.

It had a 160-horsepower Lycoming engine in it, and we fixed up extra fuel tanks for the distance run. Dick went down to the local waterbed store and bought a waterbed mattress that would serve as a collapsible fuel bladder, fitting sixty-five gallons right into the cockpit behind Dick, filling every nook and cranny. The plastic got stiff after exposure to fuel, but it would work at least once. We managed to get twenty-four more gallons into a fiberglass tank that fit up in the canopy.

We sent the fiberglass tank up to Alaska via an Air National Guard C-130 and flew up together in the Long EZ. Our last stop was at Sandpoint, Idaho, and we flew nine and a half hours all the way over Canada and landed at Northway, Alaska. The customs inspector there looked at us funny; he had a hard time believing we hadn't landed somewhere in Canada.

In Anchorage we stayed with Fred Keller, who was to later build the second example of Burt's Defiant, and had to wait twelve days for decent weather before we could take off.

We didn't mind the delay too much. We spent the time hiking through the glacial wilderness. One day on an outing to Mount McKinley National Park with Dave Daily, we stumbled right on a mother moose with two calves—a mean and dangerous creature, especially during the Alaskan spring, which is calving season.

The moose charged—half a ton of angry animal, seething with protective maternal instinct—and Dave and I headed for the cover of a small tree, the only cover around, about six inches wide. But Jeana stopped and confronted the creature head on, in the middle of the trail, until it came right up to her nose—and stopped. She stood it down like it was nothing more than a cantankerous quarter horse in a Texas corral.

Later we learned that more people are killed and injured by moose than by any other creature in the Alaska wilderness.

The episode showed me a new side of Jeana, and I was convinced that Jeana possessed her own special brand of courage. In the future I clung to it like an amulet.

· · ·

Finally the weather cleared. At three in the morning on June 5 Dick took off from Anchorage International with plastic bags around his feet to keep out the cold and a set of *Green Hornet* radio tapes to keep him awake, aiming to fly nonstop all the way to St. Thomas in the Virgin Islands.

I started off with excellent tail winds, but the vacuum pump failed as I crossed into the states, and soon the weather, too, began to go to hell. There was a huge front from Kentucky all the way to Georgia, and in Tennessee I ran into a wall of rain. The water started to come in through the edges of the canopy, and I lost my transponder. I was down to one electric turn-and-bank instrument and an airspeed indicator, flying with minimal visibility in the rain. I picked up radar vectors from air controllers along the way and tried to keep going through the storm. It was nearly the end of me. I had no parachute, and there was hail and lightning and more rain from midnight until dawn broke, somewhere near Atlanta.

Meanwhile Jeana took a commercial flight to Orlando and we rendezvoused about dawn in a Long EZ belonging to Johnny Murphy, the mayor of Cape Canaveral and the NAA (National Aeronautical Association) official. We flew on together. The five thousand miles we had hoped for were now out of our reach: the weather had seen to that. There were still six gallons in the tank, but not enough fuel for the next island, so, around noon, I put the Long EZ down on Grand Turk Island, after thirty hours and eight minutes and 4,563 statute miles. I had broken the previous record long before, in the rain somewhere near Chicago. And we resolved never again to depend on a vacuum pump; we did not use one on the *Voyager*.

Later that year we got a contract for a television film to fly up Angel Falls in Venezuela, the tallest in the world. We flew down via Texas en route and stopped at an EAA airshow in Georgetown, just north of Austin. We did our aerobatic show there and got up early the next morning ready to take off at dawn, heading for Brownsville, Texas, and over the Gulf to Venezuela. The weather was terrible—drizzly rainy with tops at a thousand feet. We climbed above the clouds to a clear bright morning.

We leveled out at about twelve thousand feet, and it wasn't long before we noticed a slight vibration. It would stop if you pulled back on the power, but it gradually kept getting worse and worse. We told the air controller in Houston we had a problem and asked if there was anywhere close by we could land. He said that everyplace was socked in.

Then the vibration just quit. Boom—it was perfectly smooth. At the same time we both looked over our right shoulders and saw our beautiful new prop and the spinner over its hub departing the airplane end over end.

The first reaction was denial. *This can't happen.* The vibration had stopped, problem solved! I actually pushed the throttle forward—and was brought back to reality by the scream of the engine without a prop. And then we had to recognize we were in deep trouble.

It took us twenty-three minutes to glide down. The undercast was thin vertically, and as we passed over it we could look down through a sort of notch in it and see bits of the ground underneath. But once we got down inside that stuff, we knew, we would not be able to see anything horizontally. Looking down, we could just barely make out a black strip— maybe a little airstrip! We declared an emergency and raised Houston center control, who had us on radar and told us that it was, indeed, a deserted airstrip. And we locked in on that in a tight left orbit.

As we orbited down, knowing we wouldn't be able to see anything once we got in the fog, we memorized the landscape, talking back and forth. "There's a barn." "Here's a road . . . a powerline." "Remember that pumphouse." Jeana undid her safety harness so she could bend forward close to me, and we discussed our plan. "I hate these emergencies where you have all kinds of time," I said.

We descended into the fog and were in it all the way. We could barely see over the nose. But the landmarks we had memorized showed up all right. "There's the barn . . . the road . . . the powerline." And as we turned on final approach right next to the pumphouse, the runway appeared right on centerline. We landed, dodging the cowpies on the runway, and came to a stop, took a deep breath, relayed back to Houston through an airliner overhead that everything was okay and thanks and please close our flight plan.

It was deadly silent—a Sunday morning with no one around, no house, nothing but a couple of curious cows, who wandered over, chewing their cuds. The adrenaline was still pumping in our veins while we pulled the airplane back to a parking spot and tied it down.

We tried to hitch a ride, but nobody would pick up two strangers out on a Sunday morning—a couple of folks looked at us as if we were crazy— so we ended up walking the three miles to town.

We got Burt to ship us one of the props off his Defiant and when we went back to the airplane we found it full of ants. We had planned to fly across the Gulf of Mexico, but now we thought better of it. After the plane was fixed up we stuck pretty close to the coastline, even though it was the longer way to Venezuela, and we still didn't feel any too comfortable during the three or four hours we had to spend over the Gulf.

The producer's idea was that we would fly straight up Angel Falls for his cameras. After he first called us back in Mojave, Dick took the Long EZ out and ran it up to top speed, then pulled straight up.

We found out that, as we had anticipated, there was no way any airplane could fly all the way up the 3,212-foot waterfall in one go. So we would make no claim to a record of any sort. What we did do was fly up the falls in pieces, and the producers spliced the film together. The result was some terrific footage of dramatic flying in front of dramatic scenery.

The resort that was our base (Canaima) was located far back in the jungle, and everything had to be flown in—food, fuel, even material for the runway we had landed on. It was a breathtaking place, and after we had assured ourselves there were no piranha in the water, we went swimming in the swiftly flowing river nearby.

On the way back from Venezuela we worked our way up the Lesser Antilles, again not looking forward to the time over open water. We landed in St. Martin, one of the nicest of the Caribbean islands, where it seemed that everyone had a job and was happy and friendly. Usually when we land somewhere we don't know, we ask people at the airport for a recommendation of a place to stay; but here we just decided to take pot luck. We took a taxi to the center of town, and once we were there we found a little hotel run by Americans, who took us in very warmly.

We spent several days driving around the island, from the Dutch to the French side, where there was a little village, and going out on the beaches with that dreamy bright blue Caribbean water teeming with colorful fish. It was idyllic, and later, when things got tough back in Mojave, we dreamed of those days and of going back there.

. . .

In February 1982, we took Shit Hot up into the Central Valley of California to set some long-range speed records. We knew this was a great airplane, we had worked out the bugs, and we were very excited about taking the whole handful of records we felt it was capable of taking.

The course was laid out between two little-used airports, at Shafter and Gustine. The five-hundred-kilometer lap ran over the rich agricultural land of the valley, across neat squares of whole sections of land devoted to cotton and alfalfa and fruit. A soft, humid haze rose from the plants and cushioned the ground. Birds and jackrabbits were everywhere. We could set five-hundred-, one-thousand-, and two-thousand-kilometer records, taking our best laps for the shorter distances.

The course ran against the grain of the section lines, and it was hard to navigate. We flew low to get maximum speed, right in the weeds. In the morning the air was crisp and favored speed, so we started out bright and early and didn't finish for six and a half or seven hours.

It was tough to navigate because of the haze and because the course was laid out angling across the grain of the section lines. The only landmarks were roads and canals. And they all looked alike. Dick flew the first day, going for the two-thousand-kilometer record. After a good start, all of a sudden he realized that he was using a lot more fuel than he should have been. We could hear that the engine was making a funny sound, so he kept leaning it out and leaning it out. But by the second lap the fuel consumption was really going to hell. By the third we all realized he could barely make it back to the airport and land.

As I taxied in I heard people yelling and screaming: "There's fuel coming out of the airplane!"

A fitting had broken off the fuel line right at the carburetor. Just enough fuel was going into the engine to keep it running, but the rest of it—about five gallons an hour—was being pumped right into the engine bay and overboard.

I got the switch turned off—holding my breath—and while the airplane was still rolling I gingerly slipped out of the plane.

The whole engine bay was bathed in fuel, and great blue-green fuel stains were running down into the root of the wing and out the top. And when I saw that, I nearly threw up.

It was a miracle that the airplane hadn't exploded or caught on fire. The only reason that it didn't was that the slipstream of the airplane had pulled the fuel fumes out the exhaust and away from the engine. If I had stopped before I tried to turn off the engine, it would almost certainly have blown sky-high.

Even if it had only caught fire—only!—running that close to the ground, the fire would have burned through the main spar, the wings would have come off, and there wouldn't have been a prayer of getting out. "I don't know why I didn't die," I said, and I went around shaking my head in wonder for quite a while.

Still, I got back in the airplane early the next morning and tried to put all that out of my mind. I did just one lap, to get the five-hundred-kilometer record, a perfect lap flat out and on the deck, busting over the pylon and setting the record. The same day Jeana took her turn.

We put extra ballast in the nose to maintain the center of gravity for my light weight and placed a couple of cushions on the seat. Still, I could just barely see out of the canopy.

Dick had taken me up for a quick survey of the course the day before, but by the time I could look for each landmark, it had already passed out of view under the wing. The course was almost impossible to remember. I was supposed to follow one of a pair of roads that split off at a fork, and in the haze on the second lap I simply took the wrong one. I ended up almost in Stockton before I found myself on the map. When I did, I just climbed up, throttled back to save fuel, and headed home.

Dick and the others who had come along waited at the pylon for me to complete my second lap. They waited and waited. Hours went by with no sound, no sighting, no word on the radio. Dick was getting worried. Finally, he talked someone into lending him a Cessna and was about to take off to look for me when I came in. "Where the hell have you been?" he asked me, but he could tell how down I was about it, and laid off. A front was coming through, and the next day was rainy. It was Dick's turn again.

It was hard to see, and I was constantly having to wipe off the inside of the windshield. The rain, at the speed I was flying, actually wore away part of the prop.

When I got near the pylon, we navigated by a combination of radio and sound. The ground crew would guide us over the pylon from the ground by the noise of the approaching engine. "Do you hear me yet?"

"Yeah, yeah, turn left, turn left!"

And I'd turn, and then they'd see me come right overhead.

I got the two-thousand-kilometer record, but the rain and bugs battered the airplane and prop too badly for us to try any other records for a while. We gave it up for a couple of months, fixed Shit Hot up, and came back in April. Jeana went after the two-thousand-kilometer, and at this time of year the area was teeming with bugs.

I dashed across the fields and didn't get lost this time, and when I finished up—it was more than six hours, but it seemed like only one, I was concentrating so hard—I had not only broken the women's record but bettered the record Dick had set in February. The airplane was green with the bugs, so completely covered you couldn't see the paint. I was exultant; I didn't even mind hearing Dick say, "Well, hell, I should have gone up there and taken that record back." We had now set four records, and we had taken all of them away from Eastern-bloc countries and brought them back to the United States.

In August of 1984 I got another record, this time for distance: the C1a open-distance record, 2,427.1 statute miles in a Vari Eze that belonged to a friend named Gary Herzler, flown between Meadows Field at Bakersfield and Merced.

I made the mistake of letting someone talk me into taking a sleeping pill the night before the flight. He knew I would be in the air eighteen hours or so and wanted to make sure I got a good night's sleep. Well, I sure did. In fact, I was still not quite awake early the next morning when Joan Richey came by the motel in Bakersfield to get me showered and dressed. At least she told me she did; I don't remember it. I was in a fog, just staring at one spot, when they weighed me in. I jogged around beside the airplane to get the blood moving and got into the airplane, but I was still just barely awake—more like a robot—when I took off and not awake enough to even remember the first lap.

Dick flew beside me in the Long EZ for the first two laps. He left on the third lap. It was not daybreak yet and I almost flew right by the turnpoint. That gave me a jolt, and I began to wake up. I drank one of the Cokes I had along and was all right from then on. It would take eight laps for the record, and I had it set on what Dick calls the "gobblety rich" cruise—burning too much fuel. I was in sight of the turnpoint in Merced when we realized I wouldn't have enough fuel to make it there and back. You have to complete a lap, or the whole record is invalid. I was about two gallons short when I had to turn back, frustrated.

Of course I tried again—and only took a quarter of a sleeping pill the night before and didn't feel any effects the next morning. This time I made the eight laps to break the record and started on a ninth. I didn't really have the fuel for that extra lap, so we chickened out and came back in. I didn't want to risk losing the record.

. . .

Not all my flying days were that happy. One year I entered the CAFE 400 with Shit Hot, the blue Long EZ. CAFE stands for Competition for Aircraft Fuel Efficiency, and the winners are chosen according to a complicated formula, determining who achieves the highest miles per gallon at the fastest speed and highest payload. There are different race categories for different sizes of airplanes.

The race is run every year from Santa Rosa, about fifty miles north of San Francisco over northern California. The course involved a number of checkpoints and many changes in altitude. Much of the terrain covered was rough—the foothills and peaks of the Sierras.

Dick flew another airplane in the race, a Dragonfly, and I flew with a passenger, a fellow named Dave Ronnenberg. This year the Long EZ was not able to place—but I wanted to fly so we decided to establish the fastest speed around the course, just for fun. I knew I had to run it pretty much full out at a target speed of over two hundred miles per hour and navigate and fly with extreme precision.

I had crossed the first checkpoint 2 knots slow and at the second checkpoint I had the engine really cranking when I lost about 60 percent of one prop blade. The vibration was terrific—it shattered instruments and punched holes in the engine cowling. On any metal plane, it probably would have torn the engine completely off. This experience made me a true believer in composite construction.

There was only one place to land: the middle of busy Interstate 5, carrying traffic north toward Oregon. I had to get down between a couple of big trucks and an overpass bridge. The big trucks were moving along the road, and there wasn't much room: I had to hold up a little, then dive, to slip the airplane into the gap between the trucks and the overpass. The airplane hit hard, the front landing gear folded up, and Shit Hot skidded along on its nose—right through the overpass—and right up to a small car moving in the same direction. I didn't even feel it, but the canard nicked the back of the car and broke, ending up skewed around at about a forty-five-degree angle to the fuselage.

Almost as soon as we had dragged the airplane to the median strip, five or six highway patrol cars showed up with lights flashing.

Dick, flying in the Dragonfly, got a radio message from one of the airplanes ahead of him. "Isn't that your blue Long EZ down on the highway?" He looked over his left shoulder and saw us in the middle of the freeway, surrounded by CHP cars. He began to think about breaking off the race and coming down to help out, then realized there was nothing he could do. He spent the next three and a half hours agonizing over what had happened, but he still went on to win his category of the race. If he had landed, I probably would have shot him.

The lucky thing was that if it had happened three to five minutes farther around the course, we would have been in the High Sierras, along the Feather River Canyon, where there is nothing but pine trees and cliffs and absolutely nowhere to land an airplane without getting killed.

. . .

I enjoyed setting the records, and I was proud of it, but there were other times when I felt frustrated with flying. I always wanted to fly, and so did Dick, and neither of us was comfortable in the backseat. Usually Dick won out; I got to ride shotgun.

I always respected Dick's natural ability with aircraft. He's been in an airplane practically since he was born. He shared a oneness with his airplane the way I did with my horses, something special, when instinct and reflexes respond together. It isn't something you can learn.

Once while I was riding my favorite horse along a road, a motorcycle went by. We both jumped, at the same time and in the same direction. There was no jolt. We both floated the same way; we had the same instincts and reactions.

That is the way Dick is with the airplane: he makes the airplane an extension of himself, totally in his command.

Flying brought us together, but because we both loved to fly so much, it also pushed us apart. We each wanted the controls and that was a problem.

Dick had very little patience when I flew; he was the worst sort of backseat pilot. I learned early that putting up with Dick in the backseat was a burden.

At one fly-in, a home-builder with a new model asked me if I thought Dick would like to try it out. "I don't know," I said, "but I would."

The man was taken aback, but he gave me the chance, and I loved it. Wow, I thought, I got to fly something before Dick.

Once I was flying formation with an experienced pilot who said, "You know, you are a really good pilot. You just need more confidence." And I realized he was right. Dick had bullied away much of my confidence.

In 1982 Mike Melvill wanted to take his Viggen, Burt's first built design, to Oshkosh, and with Dick flying our Long EZ, I was asked to fly it. Because I was so light, we put a twenty-five-pound bag of lead shot in the nose to maintain the center of gravity. Mike checked me out in it and I set off.

Dick flew aerobatics in the blue Long EZ at Oshkosh that year, carrying a movie camera for a film company, and picked up some funds for the kitty that way. For those few days the Viggen was mine, and I polished it top and bottom and took care of it. On the way back we stopped off to visit some friends who had a cabin in the Wisconsin woods, beside a lake with an island where ospreys nested. There we fished and canoed, picked raspberries into cones of rolled paper, and made tea of the leaves.

The Viggen didn't have much range, and we had to stop often to refuel. One of the stops was Yellowstone Park, and as we walked around there, Jeana was looking at everything but me.

It reminded me of how different things had been when we went to Lake Tahoe. I wished things were still the same, wished I knew some way to recapture her heart.

Zigging and zagging the Long to stay back with the slower Viggen, barely staying in the sky, Dick moaned and groaned and complained about having to make all these stops, but I loved it. When we stopped, people would gather around and look at the two planes. I got a kick out of the fact that they thought the larger Long EZ was the reason we had to refuel. "Me fly!" I exclaimed in the log book when I got back. I felt like Cinderella when the clock struck midnight. "I had to give back the keys," I wrote in the log. "My Cinderella trip in the Viggen was over. I'll just keep my fingers crossed that I lost my glass slipper out there, and I'll get to fly the Viggen again."

But I never did.

.   .   .

For his 1979 record flights, Dick was awarded the FAI's 1982 Louis Blériot medal, and in September we went to Brussels for the presentation and then on to Paris for a week. Money was always a problem, of course, but Dick's sister Nell, who is a stewardess with American Airlines, was able to get Dick a pass and I managed to get a discount rate and once we got there we were treated to most everything by the European home-builders.

Jean Blériot, the son of the aviator who had been the first to cross the English Channel, presented the medal to Dick. There were some of our astronauts and some Soviet FAI representatives in attendance.

We took some time to visit Belgium and France. The trip blurred into a kind of rapid succession of train rides, very good meals, tours of castles, and introductions to people with whom we shared only enough language for the simplest airplane conversation.

I had planned to visit a lot of places in Europe, but Dick wanted to spend most of our time with EZ builders and pilots. Often it seemed that we were two people who just happened to be there at the same time. But the trip gave me a taste of things in Europe; I hoped to come back someday, and I brought home some good memories.

At one little restaurant in France, the waiter took a shine to me. He grandly asked Dick for permission to make me a small gift. "In Paris," he said, "there is a statue called the Angel of Smiles. The way you smile reminds me so much of her." And he solemnly pinned a stickpin bearing the image of the Angel of Smiles to my vest and kissed my cheek.

Dick spent about half his time reading maps—finding our way through the streets of Paris, through the galleries of the Louvre. "Once a navigator, always a navigator," I teased him one day as he stood in the middle of the Champs-Elysées studying the map. Each day we would get back very late from a wonderful French dinner to a darkened hallway, stumbling toward our room, running into things while trying to find the light switch, giggling and making so much noise we thought we would wake up the whole place.

It was moments like these we would always remember, more than our visits to Versailles and the castles of the Loire—via Long EZ.

Seeing the castles made me wish I could take a time machine to visit the past and see the people who lived then and how they lived. I've always wanted to live in a castle. And while I was at it, I wished I could travel ahead to the future and explore it as well.

Building

In the hands of Superman, a lump of coal becomes a diamond. Graphite, like coal and diamond, is mostly carbon. Drawn into fibers, heated and pressed in the mechanical equivalent of Superman's fist, it takes on physical properties somewhere between the two. It provides strength, flexibility, and lightness. It is one-half of the weight of steel and five times as strong. It is used in fishing rods and tennis rackets, and without it *Voyager* would have been impossible.

Graphite is an expensive material, and it is expensive to work with. It requires highly trained technicians and a special high-pressure, high temperature oven, or autoclave, to cure the parts. Unless, that is, you do it yourself. And do it ourselves is just what we did: we and Bruce Evans did the majority of the work in building the *Voyager*.

When we finally started building the airplane in the spring of 1982, we knew very little about how to do this work. The Vari Eze's and Long EZ's from which we had learned most of what we knew about building airplanes had been of solid, not negative construction: the process there simply involved shaping foam cores and covering them with fiberglass sheeting.

But for *Voyager* the parts would be hollow, and the process was the opposite. *Voyager*'s construction in effect required building three or four airplanes, negative and positive, female and male molds, bent from metal or carved from plastic foam, of which only one set would fly.

Making some of these parts required a sculptor's skill. Gary Morris makes his living cutting foam the way Rodin cut stone. He created the forms that gave lovely contours to the fuselage.

The basic structure of the airplane is a sandwich of Hexcel honeycomb, a resin-impregnated paper that really does resemble the bee's product, surrounded by two layers of carbon fiber cloth imbued with epoxies. Binding the fabric to the honeycomb was a polyurethane adhesive. The layers of cloth had to be carefully aligned, with the direction of the weave correctly oriented. And each part had to be cured under heat and pressure.

Not until it undergoes this process does the material take on its strength. And even after that it retains a certain delicacy. The honeycomb can be easily dented by a blow. It returns to shape, seemingly unharmed, but once compressed the cell structure loses the majority of its strength. For this reason, the plane always had to be protected from careless visitors.

.   .   .

Voyager looks sleek and smooth, but in fact, when compared with professional composite construction, there are many imperfections and signs of do-it-yourself shortcuts. The wings bear ripples, two or three thousandths of an inch high, that have little effect on performance but saved untold man-hours of labor. They are the result of the rippling of steel molds under heat.

We worked chiefly on the TLAR method—"that looks about right"—and our main form of theorizing was the SWAG—or "scientific wild-assed guess." The original design called for the wing and canard both to taper out from the fuselage. That meant that each of the supporting pieces for the molds, which occurred about every eight to ten inches, would have to be different in shape.

Bruce, Jeana, and I got tired of making new shapes for each piece, so we went to Burt and asked him if there was anything to do. He redesigned the portions of the wing and canard inboard of the booms so all the pieces could be made identical. This provided a cruder approximation of the ideal airfoil but allowed for much simpler fabrication. We mass-produced the templates for the tools in which these were to be shaped, routing them on a table. Bruce cranked them out at top speed.

The aircraft's apparent symmetry is misleading. The right boom tank extends beyond the canard; its tip encloses the radar antenna. There is only one rudder, on the right vertical stabilizer, which means turns to the left are slower and more cumbersome—the effect is to make the plane's handling asymmetrical as well. And the canopy is set to the right side of the fuselage top, over the pilot's seat, which can cause a lot of misleading visual effects (vertigo).

Most subtly, the wing spars are overlapped. Because of the overlap the left wing is two and a half inches farther forward than the right—a fact that has no effect on its aerodynamics but means, we liked to joke, that if we ran into a parallel formation of birds, they would hit the left wing first.

Spanloading—spreading the load as evenly as possible along the wing—was a critical aim. The point was to avoid concentrations of load that require reinforcement. If an airplane's weight could be perfectly span-loaded, its airframe could be built of tissue paper; the lift provided by its form would counteract weight at every point. That is the theory behind flying wings.

Many airplanes require a heavy boxlike structure at the juncture of fuselage and wing. On *Voyager*, the wing spars do not even attach directly to the fuselage but pass through it.

The spars are the aeronautical equivalent of a skyscraper's girders—the structural skeleton—and the most critical parts of the airplane. We would have to construct them in an autoclave.

The other parts we could build at Mojave. The skins and ribs of graphite fiber sandwiching the resinated honeycomb paper cured at relatively low temperature (250°) and atmospheric vacuum pressure. For them, we used a homemade oven we built from a gas-fired home heating furnace, a blower we had found at a flea market, and scrap aluminum siding, all joined by ordinary pop rivets.

By December of 1982, Dick and Pop Rutan were working long days trying to get the oven working, defeating the numerous safety shut-down bugs, and finally got it to maintain a steady temperature of 300 degrees Fahrenheit.

The oven was about four by five by seventeen feet, but there was so little room in the shop at Rutan Aircraft Factory, where it was to be used, that a Rube Goldberg scheme was devised to raise it to the ceiling on pulleys, build parts underneath, and then lower the oven on top of them.

Molds or female tools had to be made for each part. At first we tried to make the molds of aluminum, but it expanded so much with the heat that it totally distorted the shapes. We switched to steel, so it was back to the foundry to find the metal. Still, the metal would expand an inch or more in the 250 to 350 degrees of the oven and could throw out of whack a part that had been laid out with a micrometer to the thousandth of an inch.

On December 9 we ran a test sample, and it looked terrific. "A little more work," Dick noted, "and we should be ready to do an aircraft part for real at last. . . ."

.   .   .

Before the oven was completed, Bruce Evans came by and was formally hired as a contract consultant to help build *Voyager*.

We knew Bruce by reputation in the home-builder world, where he was respected as a skilled craftsman and good pilot.

Bruce Evans was to become not only the crew chief, but the heart and soul of our project. Bruce was a born builder, a house contractor from San Diego who picked up the various skills needed to work on *Voyager* with the felicity of a natural athlete taking up a new sport. He had built his own Vari Eze and gotten from it a satisfaction he never quite had from the houses he built. He had built it very carefully and finished it perfectly, but it was a little heavy. That also made it slow, he thought, so he painted the name "Sky Slug" on the airplane. (He found out later that his airspeed indicator was slow; the airplane was as fast as any EZ, but he left the name on anyway.)

Bruce flew up to Mojave one day in 1982, when *Voyager* was still a rumor mostly confined to the home-built crowd. He was curious, and besides, interest rates were high, and it was tough to get financing to build houses. He planned to stay a few days and look around; almost instantly, he agreed to work on *Voyager*. He ended up staying four plus years and became our ground crew chief—and our best friend.

Every so often Bruce would go down to Baja, Mexico for recreation. He had always done this, and he made it clear when he decided to stay and work on the project that he reserved the right to continue doing it. We had agreed, but it was still frustrating. We didn't really blame him, but Bruce had become so important to the project that it was hard to do without him.

Bruce liked his beer. He had one of those T-shirts that read "Everyone has to believe in something, and I believe I'll have another beer." But he was careful when it came to flying, never drinking before getting into the airplane—or working on *Voyager*.

He had favorite bars, some in Mexico, some nearer to home, for what he called "recreational elbow bending," seedy survivals of the Wild West, where, the joke went, they checked for knives at the door—and if you didn't have one, they gave you one.

Once, the morning after an evening in one such bar, he had been wandering along a dry riverbed in Mexico when he came upon a cache of machine guns. He looked at them and then thought about taking one and then got away from there as quickly as he could.

Occasionally he would talk about Baja and the fishing and snorkeling and daily life there.

"We know it won't last forever, but now it's still like a private lake. There are a bunch of us, but we can go for days and not see anybody else.

"Oh, it's tough," he would joke, "and the days repeat themselves. You get into arguments over where to have the midday dive. That's the big decision of the day.

"Then you go fishing on your own, because everybody knows the best place to go, and nobody agrees with anybody else.

"The absolute nicest part of the day is when the sun goes down. You pull your chair right up to the edge of the surf and have the seafood cocktails right out of the water and then real cocktails—the tequila is something like three dollars a bottle—and pretty soon the last little light fades and the stars come out and it's time to think about cooking dinner.

"The fish you've caught are just there waiting for you, and you either get up and make a big five-course knockout seafood dinner, or else the cocktail hour runs a little too long, and you forget about dinner altogether."

Bruce remained a sort of a loner, although he had a wonderful ability to get along with people. We offered him, and no one else except Mike Melvill, a chance to fly in *Voyager*. He declined the invitation: in a sense, the day the plane first flew, he had fulfilled his commitment. He went off to Baja a few days later. He had planned to leave for good after that but was persuaded to stay on. He had become indispensable.

Bruce didn't much like the press, although he was polite and informative when he talked to any single reporter. He stayed away from the hangar for two entire days to dodge the television crew from 20/20. "There are only two heroes in this story," he would say, "Dick and Jeana." But if there were any heroes at all in this project, he would be right at the top of the list.

Bruce was focused on the building and refinement of *Voyager*. At one point he even confessed that he was "ambivalent about the world flight." The process was more important to him than the end result. Tacked on the wall above his desk was a postcard someone had sent him, bearing the words of an ancient Zen saying: "To travel rather than to arrive."

Because we were each often away from the hangar for one reason or another, Bruce was the one who did most of the building. He never wanted to work at a quiet pace: he would either go full out or not at all.

Jeana felt that even though they didn't speak a lot of words together, he was the closest thing to a brother she'd ever had.

Dick would be off flying the Starship or working inside the cockpit, and Bruce and I would work side by side, not saying much, but communicating almost by telepathy. He never really asked anything of me, and he was always there to help me.

When we first started working together he seemed to dread it. He wore an expression that seemed to say, "You're a girl—you're going to be nothing but in the way." But as time went by we found we worked well together.

We rarely spoke except to explain what needed to be done. We were both perfectionists. "Try for perfection," he would tell me, "and be satisfied with the best you can do." We found ourselves to be a very efficient team. Dick tended to be less patient; he wanted to just slap things together and go. That worked on the Long EZ, but not on Voyager, where weight was so critical.

Bruce also played another role, calming and mediating in the debriefings and planning meetings between Burt and me, when some disagreement would arise. Just as often he would pick up on something Jeana said in her quiet voice and help her get her point across. Bruce has an ability to see different sides and balance different opinions. But the key factor was that he was totally honest, and everyone knew it.

These qualities enabled him to help Burt communicate with me, through all the static of our arguments. He knew both of us better than almost anyone else. Often, instead of going through one of the major scenes that would inevitably come about if Burt and I sat down together to discuss some question, Bruce would go down to RAF on our behalf and work things out with Burt. He was like a brother; the relationship was that close, and he felt that special.

Bruce was the most conscientious sort of craftsman. He wouldn't be satisfied with anything unless he thought it was just right. He took pride in doing everything himself, and if he didn't know how to do something, he would find someone who did and watch that person and train himself.

He learned to fly formation in "the Dick Rutan formation chase pilot school," which I operated just like fighter pilot training. He was extremely conscious of the protocols of the air, which in flying chase can save your life. One time he accidentally flew through a controlled airspace where he wasn't supposed to be and came back to the hangar devastated. He was going to turn himself in to the FAA until I talked him out of it. As we were to learn many times, he was completely unflappable; he never panicked.

. . .

Finally, on December 18, all was ready for the curing of the first part, the bottom fuselage shell. The sheets of carbon fabric were laid over one another with the weaves at thirty-two degrees for the proper "torsional rigidity"—resistance to twisting force—and the mold had been carefully waxed.

A vacuum pump, also home-built, drew the air out of the temperature-resistant plastic bags that surrounded the mold and material, drawing the material toward the tool that was to give it shape. Keeping the pieces together was like holding down a bunch of springs.

We put the part in the oven, holding the temperature steady at 250 degrees for twenty minutes, watching over it like a nervous chef, then raising it to 300 degrees for two hours. Finally, we lifted up the oven, let it cool, and began to unwrap it. But when we tried to pull the shell from the mold, it was impossible: the heat had bound the two firmly together. The wax release compound had failed to do its job. The part and the three hundred dollars' worth of materials it represented were ruined, and we were heartsick. Even worse, the mold appeared to be ruined. But Jeana took some thin strips of fiberglass and began working them between the mold and the part. Soon, although her fingers were cut and bloody from working with the sharp edges of the carbon, parts of the piece began to release with a popping sound. There was no way to save the part itself, but we did save the mold. We turned the damaged part into a display sample to show visitors the lightness of Voyager's construction.

It was back to the beginning. We made a series of test squares of the material and tried a number of new release waxes. We called up experts, plane builders, aerospace contractors. Finally we found the one thing that worked: polyvinyl alcohol, PVA, a strange substance that dissolves only in water. Sprayed on over the original wax in a very thin film, it worked, and the pieces popped out smooth and whole.

On Christmas Eve we tried again, this time on a bulkhead part. "Did not release," Dick noted sadly.

Then, with two days left in the year, we did a lay-up of a second bottom fuselage part. The process took fifteen hours, but it cured and cooled and released from the tool. In the log Dick exalted, "At long last we have a part of Voyager."

"We drank the May wine at last," I noted. This was literally true: we had a bottle Dick had given me a long time ago that I had been saving for a special occasion. "We are ready to make *Voyager*." And in the margin Dick drew a big smiling face.

.   .   .

The homemade oven was not adequate to build the spars. They had to be made in an autoclave.

The critical idea was to use pieces of steel as the molds or tools for the spars. In April Dick and Bruce took RAF's beat-up old Chevy van, borrowed a trailer used for transporting a glider, and drove up to Salt Lake City, where the Hercules plant was located. They stopped at an iron foundry and hand-selected pieces of channel iron and T squares, looking for the least bit of warping. The foundry workers couldn't understand it: Dick and Bruce would reject the very best building steel, with maybe a rough spot here and there, and handled the pieces carefully as if they were china, not metal, so that they wouldn't be nicked or bent. The foundry workers thought they were nuts.

These they brought back to a shop in Salt Lake City that Ed Smith, one of the Hercules engineers, had lent them and welded them into female forms for the spars. It took three solid days of welding, grinding, and smoothing. Then they loaded the finished parts back onto a flat bed trailer that a homebuilder friend in Salt Lake City let us use, climbed into the beat-up van, and drove them, under cover of darkness, out to the Hercules plant.

Because of union rules, we weren't supposed to do any physical labor. Walt Jones had finally managed to persuade Hercules, whose middle management had been somewhat reluctant, to provide a couple of technicians to help. These excellent workers, Larry Doxford and Don Ajer, worked two and a half shifts each day, and so did we, all night, through the swing shift and the graveyard.

We would come in around three-thirty in the afternoon to talk to the engineer in charge and were ready to go when the day shift ended. We worked all night long, laying up the carbon a layer at a time, materials a few thousandths of an inch thick that had to be built up to something over four inches thick. When they were finished, the parts would be vacuum-sealed and run into the autoclave—if the autoclave wasn't already full of some top-secret, high-tech military project that naturally had priority and that we didn't even have clearance to look at.

We came in cowboy hats and rough garb and played Willie Nelson music while we worked. The technicians there said they'd never seen anything like it. They had never seen techniques like this or seen anyone work so hard at the job or get so much done so fast. We were worried that the managers were going to find out how we'd showed up their methods and throw us out—as bad for morale. The truth was, we were running on sheer adrenaline and excitement. Hell, we were going to fly around the world!

The steel tools expanded in the autoclave, and the spars came out two inches off in length! And then, as they cooled, tiny longitudinal cracks between the layers began to appear—one of the Hercules guys sawed a little slice off the end for a test, sprayed water on it, and the whole thing crackled and quivered. But it held together, and the cracks weren't bad enough for us to reject the part; there was no significant loss in strength (we hoped). But if they'd been intended for any serious aerospace client, they would have been discarded immediately.

Each part had to be sanded and put through the autoclave in stages—each layered part of the six big spars. I wore out four pairs of gloves sanding.

We would work until we couldn't work any more, then get back to the motel where we were staying around eight each morning. Bruce and I would have some breakfast, then collapse in the Jacuzzi and drink beer, fall into bed around ten, and get four or five hours of sleep. We were there for a month. Jeana came up and worked with us during the last weeks.

I hadn't seen her in weeks, and I wanted to go over some instrument training while we were up there.

At the end of my stay Dick and I loaded the spars up in the glider trailer for the trip home, and on the way Dick got it in his head that we had to worry about the spars bending or having their ends crushed on the turns. He wanted me to get out and run alongside and make sure they were fine, which I knew they were. I refused because it was on a busy freeway and I wasn't going to run alongside to look at the spars when I could see them from the back window. He got very angry and yelled at me. The whole trip back was that way, tense and unhappy.

Worst of all, it was my birthday. I didn't even call my sister, Judy, because I didn't want her to know I'd been crying. I was so mad and so hurt. If I hadn't been committed to the project, I'd have gotten out of that van and he would never have seen me again.

. . .

As the airplane took form, the old conflicts between Burt and Dick would also surface again, now ostensibly as conflicts between two organizations called Voyager Inc. and Rutan Aircraft Factory Inc. They were the old conflicts between the weight-saving engineer and the pilot. But they were also the even older conflicts between two proud and stubborn brothers, each of whom brought his own special skills and viewpoint to the problem and each of whom was sure he knew the right way.

Many of the conflicts were about features of *Voyager*'s design. Burt, as the designer, was rightly trying to keep weight to a minimum. But we, as pilots, were also trying to make sure the plane could be flown safely and successfully. He was trying to imbue within us an abhorrence of weight so that this airplane did not take the usual course aircraft take while they turn from plans to planes: grow heavier, lose range, become more compromised. We used the line "If you can throw it up and it comes down again, it's too heavy." And in pushing us toward this attitude, Burt was right. But while the overall philosophy was correct, in many cases the decision against weight would have been the wrong one: it could have killed us.

Burt, for instance, didn't see any need for radar. He said that he'd flown for years without it. It would add too much weight, and it would ruin the parallel shapes of the twin booms, one of which would have to be extended to hold its antenna.

Dick felt differently. He was flabbergasted that Burt objected to radar. There was no piece of equipment we considered more important.

He had flown with radar for years, as the "scope dope" in interceptors, as the navigator on cargo runs across the Pacific. And if there was one thing he was sure of, it was that he was not fool enough to fly across the Pacific Ocean without radar in an airplane as light and vulnerable as the *Voyager*.

Dick insisted on radar. "It's my ass out there over the Pacific," he said. "Run into just one of those storms out there, and we'll be finished. I'll be damned if I'm going to drive blind across the whole ocean." There were arguments, loud voices—"very large discussion," as it became referred to. It went on for over a month and a half. Burt originally wanted us to carry no radar, no radios, no navigation aids. We would have other airplanes with that equipment fly ahead of us and lead us. The whole notion was incredibly naive. What if there was a storm? We were supposed to attempt a rendezvous in the weather and be led through the thunderstorms? It would have been certain death, we thought.

We began to think that Burt was looking for an excuse if the mission failed—it was because Dick put all that extra stuff on the plane. He didn't seem to have a direct feeling about the life-and-death issues involved; that came later. Now, he was already referring to "the second attempt," when, he imagined, we would strip out the avionics and try it his way.

This was an example of the flip side of what has made Burt a successful designer. He clings to his ideas, and he usually makes them work. But he hates to be wrong. Sometimes this tenacity served Burt wrong and turned into simple stubbornness; he simply wouldn't listen.

I told Burt that we would put the radar on when Jeana and I took control of the project, after construction was complete, but that it would be easier to install it now. Finally he relented.

Such "large discussions" became a regular feature of life with us. At RAF I was seen as an unbending, dogmatic figure. They called me "the Colonel." And Burt was equally set in his ways and his opinions. Jeana spoke less often, but when she did, it surprised everyone and usually made an impression. Conflict between Burt and me tended to exasperate people.

Once when Burt and Dick were arguing, I sat listening and doodled two rams, butting horns. That was the way our discussions seemed, with all the huffing and puffing that went on for what seemed like hours before we finally got down to whatever technical question was felt to be at stake.

. . .

Now, with the spars back in the shop at RAF, the big work began in earnest. All of 1983 would be devoted to construction. We would spend a whole ten-hour day or longer to get just one piece. The work went on late into the night, and pretty soon we had some parts that looked like they might really add up into an airplane.

All those hours, all those late nights of work seemed to blend into one interrupted only by Dick and Bruce's occasional dart game and beer.

It was kind of a ritual that when we would finally get a part in the oven at ten or eleven o'clock or midnight, we would just sit together, Dick and Bruce with their beers, I with my Coke, for an hour or more, happy at the progress we were making and just happy together. Bruce knew how to work hard, and he also knew how to relax.

It was a good thing that I had kept notes in the log, so we could see we were making progress and be aware not just of how far we had to go, but how far we had already come.

Building *Voyager* was not all we were doing, however. I was working on Shit Hot, patching it up after my landing on Interstate 5. Dick made some other modifications he had wanted to do for a long time. I was fixing up another house now and, later, the hangar—Hangar 77, the home-to-be of Voyager Aircraft. There were offices to be outfitted, carpets to be installed.

By fall we began to put parts together, and the shape of the airplane gradually began to emerge. "Sept. 19," I noted. "Forward boom tank installed today.

"Sept. 20. Bruce started on nose section of the left side. Jeana prepped aft boom tank.

"Oct. 13. Start on the control system. Finish up rt. vertical. Attach fin.

"Oct. 30. Work on gear installation."

In November we began to plan for the larger space we would need when the airplane was finished. We were rapidly outgrowing the back room at RAF—it was already so crowded that Bruce built a footbridge so we could walk over and among the scattered parts.

In December we got Hangar 77 for real—made the first payment.

Dick told Burt we had gotten a hangar of our own, and Burt was hurt and angry. "How long do you expect to keep us poor?" Dick asked him.

The work continued in the new year—1984. "Jan 7. Lay up outer wing section.

"Started the left wing tooling and got it into a cure cycle.

"Jan. 24. Spar glued in.

"Jan. 26. Prep upper skin to close the wing.

"Jan. 27. Got the ribs into cure.

"Feb. 23. Whoopee! moved the parts to 77 for fit-up.

"March 9. Prep work to attach upper fuselage, canopy, gear.

"March 14. Templates for leading edge and trailing edge. Sand prep to attach the top fuselage.

"March 15. Top goes on—everybody helping. I now have the most cockpit time in the *Voyager*," I noted. " 'Little Kid' gets the hard-to-get-to jobs.

"March 26. 110-mile-per-hour wind blew the hangar doors open and tried to carry off parts.

"March 28. Bruce started the aft cowl.

"April 4. Dick worked on lay-up for cowl, fuselage stiffener.

"April 5. Dick picked up the landing gear from Ken Brock."

By May the pieces were mostly assembled, the fuselage and wings and cowlings all together on the gear, ready for its paint, wearing a soft gray primer. After two years of work, we finally had something that looked like a whole airplane standing proudly under the lights of Hangar 77.

Hangar 77

Hangar 77 was a sea-green prefab steel building, like the other off-the-rack buildings up and down the flightline at Mojave, some of them bright blue, some of them a soft yellow, all pressed-aluminum slabs along with a couple of the old wooden hangars, like sets from a World War II movie, fighting the relentless Mojave sun and wind.

If the hangar doors were closed, the wind would rattle them like some giant creature, about to rip them off. If they were open the slightest bit, the wind would lick into the hangar through any open door, grab cardboard boxes full of airplane parts and turn them over onto the floor, take hold of the demounted cowlings and send them tumbling, even threaten air-planes inadequately tied down.

Early in 1984 Hangar 77 became Voyager's home, and within a few days we had 110-mile-an-hour winds blowing outside. Jeana, George and Irene Rutan, and Joan Richey fought the doors shut just before the wind got in and started throwing parts around. There was no one else around to help. Later on we would be joined more and more by volunteer workers.

It was mostly from among the ranks of owners of Rutan home-builts that volunteers who composed the crew came to the Voyager project, people who had already proved their dedication to flying by spending hours build-ing their own planes. They made up the loose team of people who worked with us on and on into the night with desert winds scouring the steel doors with sand.

Most came in casually, as spectators, and a few stayed for months or years. There was a rule around Hangar 77 called the seven-minute rule: we would stop work and be sociable to anyone who came in for seven minutes. But after seven minutes, the rule went, one of two things had to happen: the visitor had to leave, or he had to begin to do something useful—fetch a rat-nosed file, hold a bolt box, sand a patch—just be useful.

It was an aviation tradition that goes back to the very beginning, to the Wright brothers, who pressed into service everyone who would come out to their field near Dayton or their demonstrations in Europe. When Wilbur Wright first took his airplane to France, it seemed that every count and marquis in the realm turned out to watch. He enlisted the spectating aristocrats into tugging the cables that set the weight on his launching catapult.

Lee Herron was a former race car driver and avid pilot who runs a shop at Mojave called Aviator's World, a room inside the main building at the airport where he and his wife, Diane Dempsey, sell aviation memorabilia—patches, oxygen masks, throttles, pressure suits. He had helped costume the characters for the film *The Right Stuff* when it was being shot at Mojave.

For each test flight, Lee and Diane would close up shop and drive their van down to Hangar 77 to serve as a chase vehicle. Lee would usually turn the propeller on the rear engine to fire it up and then hop in the van, talking to me through his hand-held radio as Diane drove chase down the runway.

Most of the time Fergus Fay would do the propeller turning. Fergy was our living link to the early days of aviation. His career stretched from the barnstorming days to the space shuttle. With his flat-top haircut and little mustache, Ferg looked a little bit like Smilin' Jack, the flier in the funny papers.

He had even seen Lindbergh, when Lindy came to Montana on the tour after his flight across the Atlantic. Fergy was just a kid. It was not long after that, he says, that "airplanes bit him in the ass" and infected him with a fascination he was never to get over.

He was fifteen years old when he learned to fly in Montana, at a time when there were no more than forty airplanes in the whole state. His first job was as mechanic for Red Morrison's flying service, an outfit that specialized in giving country folks their first airplane ride at county fairs and rodeos—fill the seven seats of the Fokker Superuniversal, climb, then cut the engine to save fuel and glide back down. The fare was a dollar and a half, and they could keep the planes flying until ten at night. It took that long, during the northern summers, for it to get dark.

They went around to the rodeos and the county fairs. In Livingston, for instance, the rodeo was a three-day bash when everything in town shut down but the bars and the hotels. A county fair was a county fair, and you damn well better be there, or people would ask, "What's wrong with you, were you feeling puny?"

All the cowboys and mountain men and every conceivable character came out of the hills for an event like that. And in those three days they would spend a significant portion of their entire annual income.

Big farm families would come up and look curiously at the planes, hesitating about whether to take the ride. Ferg remembered how the old farmers would always make the same joke—"Yeah, I'll fly, if I can keep one foot on the ground, heh, heh." They thought that was the funniest line ever.

They would go back to the hotel after the fair and count the piles of money on the floor. Old Red would pay Fergy and the other guys and say, "Take whatever you need and go get a steak."

Then when winter came, they would fly medical missions or dump bales of hay to stranded cattle and wait for the summer season when they could really make money.

Ferg's father was in the mining business and thought flying was something for the idle rich. His father wanted him to go to the Montana School of Mines and then into the business. Ferg didn't want to. He had seen enough of Montana to know that it looked better from the air than from the ground, and it looked even better the farther away you were. So Fergy went into the army air corps. Before long he was helling about in a P-51. He didn't believe in weather until one day in a storm over West Virginia he learned about ice buildup. He had to park the Mustang on an Appalachian slope and go over the side. On the way down, he tried to think up a good excuse for boring a hole with one of Uncle's airplanes.

They must have forgiven him. He went on to fly up and down the western Pacific from Java to the Philippines and ended up a light colonel commanding jets.

Several times when he was in the air force Ferg had flown in the northern latitudes, where he could see the aurora borealis, that great shimmering, electrified rainbow. It looked so close that he always thought, If I fly just a little bit higher I'll be inside it, just a little higher, just a little higher. And of course he never could reach it.

He spent two decades working for North American Rockwell, on such projects as the B-70, the B-1, and the space shuttle. There he learned about bureaucracies, corporate and governmental. And he learned about the limits of aircraft design. Time and time again he saw some neatly laid out design have to be radically tweaked to make it work. The day they shipped the last parts for the *Atlantis* space shuttle, Ferg left. He came away with a firm belief that aeronautical engineering, even today, remains about 40 percent science and 60 percent a black art.

So nothing that went wrong around *Voyager* fazed him. "I've seen how badly the big boys can mess things up," he would say, "and we aren't doing half-bad.

"This whole project would have taken government or industry fifty times as many people, and they would end up doing it worse."

At Rockwell he had been a design coordinator, meaning that he helped work out compromises among, say, the electrical people and the hydraulic people and the people who watched weight when a new conduit or pipe would be added to the system. The meetings would sometimes leave him frustrated and angry.

It is not surprising that when he happened on the Vari Eze, a building project that would be free of such conflicts, of which one man, the builder and pilot, would be in charge, the idea held tremendous appeal for him. He already owned and flew a conventional airplane, but after attending a seminar of Burt's he knew he had to build one of those planes. It was, he said, the best pure flying airplane he had ever seen, a "strap it on" kind of plane that gave him even more satisfaction in the air than the P-51 Mustang or the F-80.

Ferg had been part of Jeana's ground team for the Long EZ records up in the Valley. He came to Mojave again when he heard about *Voyager* and became a key member of the crew, working on the engines, talking the plane down on landings, driving chase with his black Ford Ranchero, strapping on thick rubber knee pads to kneel on the tarmac under the *Voyager* to hand prop the aft engines.

He had a particular talent for summing up things around Hangar 77 in a diction that mixed the old West and aerospace tech with three years of Latin at a Jesuit school and the ministrations of his mother, a former New England schoolteacher, who, he said, "torqued us kids into proper speech."

. . .

Glenn Maben came by one day after his job working as a Grumman test engineer on one of the hottest programs in the aerospace business, the X-29 project, down the road at Edwards. The X-29 was a plane no pilot could fly alone—inherently unstable, it required the constant operation of an onboard computer, adjusting its wing surfaces forty times each second—and one no engineer could contribute to except as a part of the whole human machine. He enjoyed the work for Grumman, but the hands-on work at *Voyager* was a welcome change from his days, analyzing reams of computerized data and looking for patterns, and he felt more at home in Hangar 77 than he did among the engineers who looked down on the technicians who did physical work. He was a degreed engineer, but he had begun as an unlettered mechanic and sympathized with the blue collars as well as the white. Dick also ran him through the "Dick Rutan formation flying school." His own airplane was a Pitts Special, a classic aerobatic biplane. His was painted in red, white, and blue stripes.

Working with Burt at Scaled Composites was a brilliant young man named Doug Shane, who was also a superb pilot. He had a feel for every aspect of airplanes—he worked out a lot of the graphs integrating the data from our test flying, providing the basic model for the airplane's performance—but he was also a very witty guy who lightened the atmosphere whenever he came around. He was an excellent photographer and took a lot of stills and videotapes for the program and often flew chase for us—Dick had trained him too. He often helped me get out of the office and go flying, no matter how many excuses I came up with. Dick thought his combination of skills made him a perfect astronaut. "You really should apply to the astronaut program," everyone told him, but he was happy with the work at Scaled and after hours at *Voyager*.

Neal Brown called himself a "recycling engineer." He had worked on the Alaska pipeline and now lived in Bigfork, Montana, where he did things like buy old wood stoves and remake them. In Mojave he also called himself "a hangar rat" because he lived in a small tent he set up on top of the offices.

He had grown up in Nebraska, on a farm set between the two forks of the Platte River. Railroads ran along both the North Platte and the South Platte, and on the farm in the winter Neal and the family could tell which way the wind was blowing by which train whistle you could hear.

He was a rough-hewn sort of guy, who would have been at home in the old West of trappers and mountain men, but he also knew how to work with composites—he'd helped build a couple of airplanes—and he had a sense of history. He liked to read such books as *The Journals of Lewis and Clark*.

Gary Fox was a Volkswagen mechanic who had gotten a job in fabrication at Scaled Composites. He came down before and after work; he took his few vacation days to work on the airplane. In addition, he fixed all the ailing Volkswagens around the place, including the blue one Mom and Pop Rutan lent the company. He talked his parents, who were retired, into coming up in their motor home and pitching in at Voyager. Soon they were two of the most devoted and valuable volunteers around the hangar.

Dan Card became general manager of the office operations in early 1986. He was a park ranger at Yosemite, who had been flying his own airplane down to Mojave from time to time. He had invited us to ski and backpack up there, and we became friends. Dan had a background in administrative work and in dealing with the public, and these were the sorts of skills we needed right then. Plus, he joked, he was already used to carrying a walkie-talkie around in his belt.

He found us a bunch of bargain IBM-PC clones and got the office computerized, straightened out the phones, and helped take care of enough of the office work so I didn't have to do everything.

. . .

One day when working on the plane, I found two short lengths of safety wire in the cowl underneath the rear engine. Safety wire is the stainless-steel wire used to secure engine bolts against vibration, to choke off tubes, and to do a thousand other things on an airplane.

Those bits of wire constituted foreign objects of the most ominous sort: they could be blown up and pierce an oil pipe, they could puncture a radiator hose, or they could be turned into flying needles that would splinter and destroy a fast-turning propeller.

So when I mentioned the pieces of wire to Jeana and the group re-mounting bushings on the engine, there was a tense silence. I did not accuse anyone of leaving the pieces of wire, or get angry, but the fact was that Jeana and I were flying the plane, not they. The usual banter that punctuates the work in the hangar vanished, and for a while all that was heard was the hissing of the mercury lights. The moment passed, and everything went back to normal.

There was a line everyone used from time to time that dissipated such tensions: "You just can't get good volunteer help these days."

Sometimes, though, the dependence on volunteers really did get to us. They would leave at all hours, as they had a perfect right to do, but often before a job was finished or a modification made.

And there was real concern, too. Even professionals made mistakes. Everyone around Hangar 77 had heard my "foreign object damage" story. I had been flying an F-100 out of Lakenheath in England when my oil pressure suddenly went to zero. The engine continued to run for twelve and a half minutes, time enough for me to turn around and head back down, when the engine blew up. It took me a second and a half to level off, aim the plane away from a nearby village, and eject. Thirty seconds later, I would have been too late to punch out, and as it was I swung twice under the parachute and watched the F-100 go in and explode.

I was going into some trees and almost hit a big dead branch. I jerked myself away at the last minute. Once on the ground, my heart beating like crazy, the old Vietnam instincts took over. I thought about hiding my chute and going into the evasion and escape procedures, trying to make my way to where I could be picked up.

A forester chopping wood nearby in the Queen's Forest saw the explosion. He watched something that looked like a chair on fire, a smoking, flaming throne, fall out of the sky. Then someone crashed down through the branches near him.

He saw a man in a tight suit and a helmet with a gold visor down over his face. A spaceman. A German? A Russian! He saw the man run up to him and heard him start babbling about how there were indigenous around and he had to E and E. He said, "I'm Major Rutan and I'm alive." Then he pulled a rope, something exploded, and a huge yellow thing started flapping and hissing. The forester dropped his axe and started to run.

The man in front of me looked at me with round eyes and began to edge away. And then I remembered that I was in England, and it was 1970. I pulled the ring on my survival pack and raft. The raft inflated, and I pulled out my radio to let the tower know I was okay.

A technician, it seems, had left an oil sample bottle loose in the F-100's oil tank, and when I pulled a zero-G maneuver it lodged so no oil could get into the engine. Cause of crash: foreign object damage, FOD.

. . . .

So there were some things that I trusted no one to do. Just as, during my air force years, I had always insisted on watching my parachute being packed, I now determined to install the entire fuel system myself. It was one of those elements of the plane that were highly unconventional. The fuel lines were all plastic tubing, secured with safety wire. If the wire was twisted too tight, it could cut the soft plastic tube; too loose, and it could come loose and leak fuel. So I did the ties with my own "Velvet Arm."

Always there was the consciousness of weight, of literally cutting corners to reduce weight, and what amounted to an absolute disgust for metal. Securing the battery, for instance, was done not with the bolt-and-bracket system of conventional aircraft or automobiles, but with a basket of fiberglass strips, laid up and cured in a sort of baker's oven as a "spare time" project by one of the volunteers, sewed together and mounted with Kevlar thread.

Part of the fuel system required valves that were, inescapably, of metal. Burt's design had stipulated aluminum valves, but none of the proper size could be found. We had to use brass valves. I knew that if Burt saw them, he would absolutely refuse to accept them—"obscene" was the way we all began to think about heavy items. So I weighed the valves, then took each one of them to a lathe and ground off every corner, every bit of excess metal I could reach. I put them on the scale again: the weight had been cut in half. Finally, I painted them to look like aluminum. It made me feel a lot better, and when Burt came by and peered into the still open fuselage, standing there like a canoe, he felt comfortable with them, too. Burt may have known they were brass underneath, but weight conscious-ness had become so much a part of our mental training, so ingrained, that at least psychologically he could accept them more easily.

For every part, every bit of maintenance, every "mod" or "tweak," one question was always asked: "Will that go around the world?" It was a jocular way to emphasize the seriousness of the goal. Working over possible designs for new scoops one day, to control the flow of cooling air over the engines, someone might say, for instance, "Those are big ugly totally unacceptable scoops that will never go around the world."

· · ·

Inside, a special sort of concentration and focus takes over, and the world outside the hangar recedes from consciousness.

It lent a special camaraderie to the group, the teasing and quibbling. Dan Card, the Yosemite Park ranger, was naturally known around the hangar as Ranger Dan, and after a segment about Voyager appeared on a television program and became part of the material screened for visitors, he teased Dick relentlessly about the narrator's portentous line, "Lone Eagle no longer flies alone. He flies with Woman at his side."

Sometimes it seemed that the airplane would never be finished. It was flying all right, but at night, and between flights, something was always being worked on. These fixes and mods were a constant demonstration of the flexibility of composites. Tweaking the intakes and flaps that carried cooling air over the engines and radiators, say, or installing antennas, would have been a nightmare with a metal plane. But with the composites it was as easy as patching up a model plane that had come to some grief.

When, for instance, it turned out that the antenna for the Omega navigation system suffered horrendous interference in the cockpit—the generator was the apparent culprit—it had to be reinstalled on the right boom.

An ugly-looking trench was gouged out of the fiberglass foam of the trailing edge to hold the connecting cable, and Dick, Lee Herron, and Glenn Maben spent hours filing a hole through the rear of the cockpit to connect with it. Dick didn't trust anyone else to do the critical cutting there, and late at night, with all the lights except a single fluorescent bulb turned off to save on the power bill, he filed and sawed, rearing up occasionally in the open cockpit with a hand bent to his spine and a grimace of pain from the old backache, induced by the two ejections from disabled F-100's and reactivated by scrunching down for long hours into the corner.

. . .

I thought the people who came to work at Voyager all seemed to have a remarkable versatility. There was a philosophy that held if something needed to be done, you got it done. And if you didn't know how to do it, you learned. The volunteers had in common a dexterity learned in one area—Bruce's carpentry, Glenn's or Fergy's engineering backgrounds, Lee Herron's experience as an automobile racer as well as a house builder. With classic American handiness, they adapted these skills to graphite and fiberglass and electricity and engines.

The work involved a combination of roughness and care, "hacking" and delicacy. Hangar 77 was no clean room, no white chamber, but after every bit of cutting or sanding, the big industrial vacuum cleaners were called into service to make sure dust and fragments didn't end up sneaking into and disabling some piece of equipment. Many of the volunteers would come in after their regular jobs, so work would begin in the early evening and often go on into the night. People would eat when they could, making a sandwich from food in the refrigerator in one corner of the hangar or grabbing a Shaklee energy bar.

There was even a sort of hangar mascot, a hang-around cat Bruce had picked up. The cat was black as graphite, so he was called Magnamite, or Maggie for short. Actually, there were two Maggies.

The first Magnamite was a real cool cat, would hop into a car and go riding—highly uncatlike behavior. They had even thought about taking that cat up in a plane.

When the first Magnamite disappeared during our annual migration to Oshkosh, I later brought the new one from the stable where my horse was kept.

The cat was a talker, meowing constantly. Maggie II, whom some people just called Replacement, finally shut up. But then he started to grow. Everyone fed the cat, and it grew huge. Seeing a fat cat drove Dick crazy. The struggle against weight was so ingrained in him that he couldn't stand the fat cat. He ordered that no one should feed it, that he alone would do it. Every now and then he would give the cat a single handful of chow. More often, though, he forgot, and the animal was quickly starved down to trimmer dimensions.

But some of the people around at the time thought the second Magnamite inferior to the first. He had no class, they said, he was just strange. The new Magnamite had a tendency to throw himself on his back, stick his legs in the air, and go to sleep. He would lie like that for hours, like a stuffed animal turned upside down. Lee Herron said he was "the deadest cat that had ever lived."

The old cat was like the old days, the days when we were just two or three people in the desert building an airplane. The new cat was the new time, of the press and fund-raising and testing. The tone and the atmosphere were changing. More and more people were showing up.

Everything at Voyager—mods, maintenance, flights, and so on—happened amid a constant stream of visitors. They would look at the plane and view the videotapes about the program upstairs and, we hoped, buy a couple of T-shirts and posters on the way out and maybe even join the VIP Club. The guest book, which we had everyone sign, was filled with addresses from all over the world—Australia and Austria, Norway and New Hampshire, Germany and Georgia.

We had to be careful about damage to the airplane. The visitor area was roped, but still the hangar was very public. Sometimes people would come looking for industrial secrets, which always gave us a laugh since there wasn't much of anything that was secret. Some people from a large aerospace contractor came one day and got Dick to show them all around in the hopes that they could learn things applicable to one of their programs. During the coast flight, a former CIA agent turned industrial spy showed up on the premises, with wife and son for cover. He spent hours around the place, looking and tape-recording everything, however inane, that anyone said. Somebody got a kick out of taking a video camera out and casually panning around the office. The guy automatically raised his hand to shield his face.

. . .

I designed a paint scheme for the airplane and a company logo, an angular series of V's that fanned out something like a wing.

One whole afternoon Michael Dilly and Larry Lombard were putting tape on to get the stripes even. It was hard; the tape kept getting wavy, and Dick kept snapping at me about it. Finally I apologized to Mike and Larry and just ripped off all their work and started all over. An hour later I had it all laid out.

I organized and ran the office. When we started, neither of us knew anything about the technicalities of establishing and operating a corporation, but I learned all that as I went.

The money situation was getting more and more difficult; we weren't finding corporate financing, and we weren't even getting the promised help from Burt and his employees at RAF. But when some source of funding did loom up—like a mirage, as it always did—RAF was always quick to claim the share our agreement had entitled it to.

I kept pushing for the VIP Club. We had many meetings, and not all of them were pleasant. On March 7, 1984, I noted in the log, "Another big meeting with RAF. This time I did some talking. Upset everyone, but we need to get some RAF hands-on participation. It's like the fairy tale story of the Little Red Hen. We plant, till, harvest, everyone takes credit. . . . I lost some friends."

In April, seventeen months after we began to build Voyager, completion of the airplane was in sight, and we had more meetings on the subject. I said that we had to go with a primary sponsor or the VIP plan. The two didn't go together. And I insisted on having full control of the VIPs. "It is a lot of responsibility and work," I said, "and I'm willing to do it, but I have to have complete cooperation and control." And finally I convinced Burt and Dick to give it a try. We had to work out what you would get as a VIP member. The most appealing part of it was that your name would be carried around the world on the airplane and would go with it in the log books to the Smithsonian if we were successful. We started a newsletter, to give VIPs periodic updates.

The VIP Club snowballed after we had an airplane to show and particularly after we flew the plane to Oshkosh. In the shop for T-shirts and other items we had going, we gave everyone a VIP flier. Mom and Pop Rutan, who minded the shop on weekends for us, helped sell the memberships. We sent our flyers to all the EAA chapters, and many would join together, as a group. It surprised everyone how quickly the club grew.

One worry remained, however: What if we did find a primary sponsor, one who was really willing and able to pick up the budget for all or most of the program? Would we have to return all VIP money?

When Wanda Wolf came in to see *Voyager* on her way to apply for work at General Electric, I latched on to her as receptionist and secretary and just about everything else, and in January of 1985 Voyager Aircraft had its first full-time paid employee. Wanda became the voice of *Voyager* to the outside world, and before long the manners and soft tones of her native Georgia began to be mentioned repeatedly in articles and television features about *Voyager*.

I also got more volunteers in the office. There was a lot of work—the shop accounts, correspondence, mailing lists, the newsletter—and a hundred miscellaneous things that cropped up daily. All over the place were my notes and reminders, written on yellow tabs of stick-on paper in a thin, exact hand.

I often looked at the people who came into the shop in the hangar and thought; There is an aura about all this. You could see the skepticism and curiosity in people's eyes when they came in, and when they left you could see faith—they knew the project was going to work.

Oscillations, Vacillations, and Paradoxes

Sitting at the end of the runway, in a brand-new airplane, a machine that has never flown, there is always the same feeling: one of total uncertainty. I had flown maybe a dozen airplanes on their maiden flights, and I had always felt that way. You know the engineering studies and the design parameters say that it will fly, but it never has flown, and now it's all up to you, the test pilot. It's where engineering stops and piloting starts. You make a quick survey of what the next five minutes of your life are likely to be like, and you take a deep breath, because until you get up and out of ground effect, you know you are going to be holding that breath.

We had been taxiing the *Voyager*, getting a little bit of a feel for the airplane, but until that moment we didn't know for sure if it would really fly, much less if it would be possible to handle it, or if it had the range. Flying it around the airport was what we wanted then; flying it around the world was still way off.

There was no way to know except to do it. So we installed a couple of used engines we got from Burt, giving them nothing but "a rag overhaul"—one quick inspection and a hopeful swipe of the cloth.

Jeana put the canopy on and then ran to the Grizzly that was to fly chase and threw herself across the backseat, behind Burt and Mike Melvill, straining to look out the plane's little window.

Alone inside now, I thought of different scenarios, reviewed what I would do in different situations—and what could happen. What if this thing pitched up or rolled over or there was total loss of control? What would it feel like just before it hit the ground?

Sure there's fear. Subconsciously you'd like to find an excuse to get out. If someone told you a tire was flat, you'd be happy. Only ego and self-respect and peer respect keep you there.

But you know you are going to do it, and you ask yourself why you are having this argument with yourself. So stop agonizing, relax, press on.

And the funny thing is, once you release the brakes, it's all gone. There is no fear whatsoever. You slow down and get more methodical, not more hyperactive.

I released the brake, pushed the throttles forward, and started the takeoff roll. As the airplane picked up speed it changed gradually from being a machine on the ground to being one ready for the air, and when I eased the stick back it slipped right up. "A gorgeous gal," I said.

Voyager did fly on that beautiful day, June 22, 1984, old engines and all.

I was about a hundred feet up before I dared to look out the window—and saw that shadow, that crazy long network of shapes, spread out across the runway. "Holy bananas! Look at that shadow! What have we done?" I said, and when Jeana in the chase plane heard that, knowing I was still in ground effect, she reminded me to pay attention. The airplane could still turn around and bite me.

Mike Melvill, flying the chase airplane, slid underneath the *Voyager*. His eyes swept across the back engine looking for smoke or oil and then worked their way up the bottom of the fuselage. And when he got to the nose he saw oil bubbling and oozing out into the nose landing gear well and running back in a black streak.

"You have a major—I say, major—oil leak in the front engine," he told me calmly, professionally, doing it the right way: describe the emergency plainly, then let the pilot decide what to do.

"Roger, shutting off front engine," I said, and I reached down and pulled the mixture control back to idle cut-off. The front prop windmilled for a while, then gradually stopped.

"That's why we put two engines on airplanes," Burt said. And we went on with the test flight.

We looked at the stability of the control system and worked on airspeed calibration with the chase plane locked on the wing as a pacer. We checked the controls for flutter by pulling back to slow speed and pulsing the stick, hoping everything damped itself out but alert for the funny little feedback that, if you're lucky, you get right before the flutter starts. And then again, at higher speed, and higher speed.

I was in the air about forty minutes. Before I landed Mike reminded me to come in on runway 30, which was uphill, and to be sure not to come in long because there was likely to be oil on the front gear strut, the only brake on the aircraft. It was a strange flying bird, but I managed to make a halfway decent landing.

Jeana was the first one up to the plane. I always want the canopy off right away, and the rear engine was still running when she climbed up over the right wing and onto the fuselage and perched herself sidesaddle. She pulled the canopy up as soon as I had unlatched it. I reached up and rubbed her head, savoring the moment, proud of both of us, and then she swung her legs down into the cockpit, and I hugged them.

Afterward, as always after first flights, we had a party—a "glad to be alive party," and there was champagne and beer and the feeling that at last we had a real, flying airplane, more than three years after we started a program we thought might take us a year.

We had learned that the handling was pretty marginal. The plane was sensitive in pitch, the aileron forces were heavy, and roll was very slow. The rudder was just barely enough to do the job. The elevator forces were too light, and we added an elevator antiservo tab or "sparrow strainer" made from radio-controlled model parts to improve the pitch force. The rest of the handling was just adequate—nothing fun to zip around in, but slow and lumbering and wallowing. We figured we could live with it.

It was on the second flight, shuttling back and forth above windy Mojave, that I ran into some thermals and first saw the wings really flailing. The motion felt strange: wings and fuselage were not in sync. All my flying experience had taught me to expect that when the wings went up, the fuselage would go down; but with *Voyager* I noticed that when the wings were on their upward cycle the nose would be pitching up, too. At the slow speeds and light weight of that test, the motion dampened out, but it was uncomfortable. It bothered me, and it planted the first seeds of doubt about the airplane in my mind. I resolved never to look at those wingtips when they began to move up and down

I came along with Dick on the second flight, and the way the airplane felt instantly reminded me of one thing: a sailboat. It rocked and rolled as if on the ocean, like the boats I had sailed off the Texas coast when I was married. Even my view was more like being below decks in a sailboat, looking through the small portholelike windows and seeing the lines of clouds like the ocean horizon and the booms like gunwale rails.

The way the airplane tossed us around was not like the big stomach raising of a commercial airline on a bumpy final approach or a small aerobatic airplane.

No, *Voyager's* wallowing flight was a direct reflection of the way its sensitive, long wings magnified the waves of the air so that they felt as powerful as the waves of the sea. You didn't feel jolts, but you were riding waves all the time and got caught up in the cycle. You couldn't sit still. Your body was constantly, instinctively working to brace itself to follow the cycle and prepare and brace for the next wave. For the first time in my life, I felt something like seasickness. It was like riding on the back of a pterodactyl. Sometimes there would be completely different types of waves in each wing and you could watch them coming toward you. But while *Voyager* looked very fragile, in many ways she was a tough and durable bird.

The discomfort I would have to put up with was clear from the first moments of the flight. I wore a backpack parachute, with straps that cut into my legs. It was so stiff I couldn't curl up into the fetal position but had to lie stretched out on elbows and knees. Because of the chute, too, the only way to raise my head to look forward to see the instrument panel and watch Dick was to turn on my side. There was a three-inch drop-off from the back compartment to the console area, so most of my weight came directly down on my elbows, and my shoulders quickly began to ache. I felt like a dog sticking out of a doghouse.

We had strategically placed the windows at the most awkward points, too high to look out of when I was lying down, too low when I was in the pilot's seat. To look out, I had to push my face right up against them. They were so difficult to look out of they might just as well not have been there at all.

Even though it was a short flight, I came back with badly bruised elbows. The composite floor was almost as soft as concrete. My position meant that I never had more than one hand to work with; the other was always braced beneath me.

I realized I had to have some way to get my weight off my elbows— a kind of a little bucket seat, or two panels, really, forward near the fuel-switching area. Dick said it was too heavy and we didn't need it, but Lee Herron finally got it built for me—but not until nearly two years later, just after the coast flight.

. . .

We planned two parts to our testing program. Phase one would test the range and handling. Phase two would test the world-flight engines and the feasibility of living inside the airplane.

We had a press rollout, and it seemed that everyone got the impression we were about to fly around the world the next day. Originally, Burt had figured we would have about ten test flights and be ready to go. But it didn't turn out that way. With every day, the program was getting more and more complicated. Problems cropped up and had to be fixed.

Being public now helped in many ways. A photographer named Mark Greenberg who showed up at the rollout stayed around the hangar for several days afterward and as we talked to him he suggested his agency handle images of the *Voyager* for publications all over the world. Mark had a friend named Peter Riva. "You need Peter," he told us, and we talked to him about serving as our representative in dealing with corporations. Right then, however, he had other commitments. He gave us a lot of good advice. About a year later Mark suggested Peter to us again. This time we came to work together.

We had a lot of testing to do on the airplane. First of all, Burt was afraid that he might have miscalculated the wing loads by not taking into consideration the pressure the fuel would produce when the wings flexed. So we tested a sample wing cross section under water pressure. We filled a tank full of water, ran a hose from it twelve feet up the side of the building, and pressurized it.

The water pressure on one square inch of Hoover Dam at a given depth is the same as on the whole dam no matter how big the lake behind the dam, and so with the wing: we could duplicate the load generated on the whole wing by testing just one area with the stack of water in the standing pipe.

Burt said that if the section could stand just three feet of water pressure, it would be okay. We reached that level and kept building the pressure up and up—four feet, five feet, six feet—and it held. Burt kept saying, "Stand back, it may explode," and edging away—seven feet, eight feet, nine feet. Burt couldn't believe it. And finally, after everyone had retreated back to the walls, we put the whole twelve feet on it. Nothing. Then, just to see what would happen, we hooked the hose to a faucet and threw the valve open all the way. The wing section wrinkled and pillowed—the failure took the form of an inner shear of the honeycomb—but even in its failure mode it was flyable. After that we felt very confident.

Our biggest concern about the structure of the airplane was whether those long wings might, in effect, flap themselves right off. Taking advantage of the qualities of composite construction, we had designed them to move as much as thirty feet up or down—a sixty-foot arc. That can look pretty scary, but it's not dangerous unless the flapping gets out of control and amplifies itself, or the wings go in opposite directions. This is what the engineers call a "low-frequency high-amplitude divergent flutter mode."

Normally, if you vibrate something, the waves will tend to diminish in amplitude, like a diving board that bounces but gradually returns to being stable after you dive off. But if you have the wrong combination of material and frequency of vibration, then the waves can build up—the diving board just keeps working farther and farther up and down—and the waves build up and destroy the vibrating object.

On our first, lightly loaded flights, we were happy to find out that Voyager's wings tended to dampen out the flutter. Sometimes, though, in turbulence, we would have one side of the airplane doing something almost completely different from the other. And because the wingtips moved up and down so far, Dick was quick to make it a rule not to watch them. It was a disturbing, sometimes sickening sight. And later at higher weights we were to find that the story was even worse.

Originally, there were just two fuel cells in each wing outboard from the boom tanks. But we found that when the wings went up, the fuel in the outboard tanks all ran inward toward the roots of the outer wing—a kind of sloshing. This interfered with proper span loading, and we were also afraid that it might put too much pressure on the bulkhead dividing the two tanks. To solve the problem, we divided the outboard tank into a mid and tip tank by cutting the wing open and installing a dividing bulkhead. The problem, however, was that there was no way to run another fuel line out to the new tip tank. For a while, we were baffled as to what to do until one day Dick got the idea of an electrically controlled valve to simply open the new tip tank and let it flow into the mid when needed.

We knew that Burt, with his fanaticism about saving, would be appalled at any addition, even of wire for this valve. He had even opposed having wingtip lights because of the weight of the wires.

But there was a handy alternative. Planning to use an electrical auto-pilot servo, we had run a couple of extra wires from the cockpit inside the wing out to the tip. That plan had been scrapped, but now the wires came in handy. At the local Mojave automotive parts store, I got hold of some solenoid valves designed for switching fuel tanks on a recreation vehicle. These he soaked in fuel, then activated numerous times. He disassembled one to make sure there were no open breaker points that might spark. Assured that the valve was totally sealed, he finally attached the solenoids to the wires and put them in place. We would use the fuel in the tip tank last, when the wings were bent up. When we opened the solenoid valve, fuel would flow by gravity into the mid wing tank and through its existing fuel line to the feed tank.

.   .   .

We decided to take *Voyager* to the annual Experimental Aircraft Association Fly-In at Oshkosh in August of 1984. Oshkosh was critical for touching what Jeana was calling our ground support: the enthusiasm of the hundreds of EAA members and others there.

Burt figured we could just hop in, fly out there, do two or three laps between Mojave and Oshkosh, and set a distance record. That was plan A, and Jeana quickly vetoed it as impractical. Plan B was to fly straight to Oshkosh, all day and all night, and land on opening day. This was the alternative we chose.

In a week and a half we got the airplane ready to go. We had just signed King Radio on for avionics support, and right away King sent out John Grogan, Carl Wolf, and Craig Kristie; Doug Henkell for the Omega; and Jim Leyfeld for autopilot. Part of the agreement was that we were to use only King equipment, but I told Jim we had already put in a competitor's autopilot, and he said we could leave it in for Oshkosh and replace it afterward with the King autopilot. That saved us some time. King shipped out temporary radios, which we put in hurriedly, and a full avionics package, which we didn't even have time to install formally—we just hung it from the ceiling.

We rigged up a primitive electrical system from two motorcycle batteries and a Toyota auto alternator modified for twenty-eight volts. We lashed in some crude cockpit lighting, and off we went, with Bruce flying chase in the Sky Slug, his Vari Eze.

We didn't even get to the other side of the Antelope Valley before things started going wrong. First, the rudder autopilot servo broke loose from its bracket on the floor and slowly began snaking its way up my pants leg. Then two bottles of Hot Stuff glue and its accelerator came open in the storage area, ran together, and produced acrid fumes that burned our eyes and nauseated us.

It was a comedy of errors; Jeana had already filled two pages of the flight card problem notes, or "gig list."

We decided this was not our day and began to head back to Mojave. I'm not an abort kind of guy, and it was tough coming back. But sometimes it's the proper thing to do.

The remnants of a Mexican monsoon were sweeping through the area, bringing a lot of convective activity and rainshowers. Near the restricted area at Edwards, about fifteen miles south of Mojave, we encountered a verga, or mare's tail, a shower that starts from a high cloud and evaporates before it hits the ground. It was like a waterfall, maybe half a mile wide but a quarter-mile thick.

Some canard aircraft have trouble with rain cutting lift on the canard by disturbing what the engineers call laminar flow. We had to know whether this one would behave that way—and better sooner than later. The verga seemed to be an experiment ready-made for the purpose, so we headed right for the middle of it.

Just as we started picking up the first few drops of rain, the airplane started to pitch down. I corrected with the back stick—more elevator—but it kept coming down. The stick forces became very heavy, and as I kept coming back with the stick, I had a horrible feeling in the pit of my stomach that the airplane was coming down and I couldn't stop it.

I pushed the power up. No matter what I did with the stick, we were going down pretty steeply, and I looked around for some way to get out of the rain. But the only thing to do was press on through, looking at the ground and at the edge of the shower and hoping we got through the shower before we got to the ground.

Jeana got the parachutes ready, stowed the loose items, and went through the other emergency procedures, but there was no way I was going to bail out. I kept fighting it, fighting with such concentration and belief that I could save the airplane that I'm sure, if we hadn't come out of the shower, I would have stayed with the airplane all the way to the ground.

But we just did make it through, the canard started to dry off, and we turned and flew around the shower and landed at Mojave.

We immediately called Burt and John Roncz, his airfoil designer. Obviously we weren't going to make it to Oshkosh on opening day. But we still felt tremendous pressure to go. We wanted to share this home-built with our aviation family and were counting on getting the VIP Club started here.

We fixed the servo and cleaned up the glue. Burt and John didn't seem too concerned about the canard; just sand it, they said, to roughen it up. That night Jeana went all over it with six-hundred-grid sandpaper, sanding it at a forty-five-degree angle across the canard. We just took the sheen off to give it a kind of velvet finish.

We set out again the next day. It was far too ambitious a flight and premature to think we could do it, and the trip turned into a nightmare. The autopilot was temporary, makeshift, and not yet tailored to *Voyager*;

it couldn't handle the turbulence, and we couldn't control pitch adequately. I spent most of the time hand-flying the airplane.

We got the same type of weather we had the day before: convection and showers. I will never forget trying to pick our way through mountain passes and thunderstorms over the Rockies. We knew that if we could climb three thousand feet, we could get above much of the turbulence, but without oxygen we were trapped. Once we got over the plains it was the same thing. It was afternoon, and the heating of the plains set up tremendous thermals that rattled us all around. Jeana took the brunt of the punishment.

I was bounced all around the cockpit, spent half the time on the ceiling, and came out battered and bruised. Dick was totally exhausted from hand-flying the airplane, picking our way through the mountain passes. Even our cockpit lighting was inadequate. It showed us how far we had to go.

For the first and only time I felt something close to claustrophobia inside the airplane. It was also my first encounter with seasickness—my stomach was churning the whole time, and I got out of the plane with a terrible headache. I desperately wanted to sit up. Somehow, over those hours, I taught myself to forget everything else and just focus in on what I had to do inside the airplane, to reconcile myself to the discomfort of the situation.

We sweated it out for eleven hours and then finally had to land in Salina, Kansas, just before sunset. Dick was fed up with the whole project. Dick swore he never wanted to see Voyager again and threatened to burn the airplane and take a train home. My head was aching and my stomach was churning. I dreaded the confinement, the hours spent prone, but I never thought of quitting. I recognized my discomforts but I just had to push them aside.

Any thought of a three-day record flight was out of the question. We realized that we had to stay out of turbulence, and for the next two and a half years we could never stop wondering whether the airplane was really going to be able to fly in the bad weather we were sure to encounter somewhere around the world.

That was the moment when we realized, all of a sudden, that this great big adventure of flying around the world was going to be really tough, when we began to sense that the dream had a nightmare side to it. We knew that the airplane would not be fun to fly, with those wingtips flailing up and down, but we never anticipated how bad it could get. Dick admitted from the beginning that it was the only airplane he had ever feared. We were both scared of it—and any pilot would have been a fool not to be.

Many of the things about the airplane that looked good on paper didn't work out so well in reality. The cabin, whose twenty-inch height we had so cavalierly accepted in the plans, was a torture chamber. There were things we couldn't change, but more that we would have to change, and things we would have to add. It was clearly not going to be the quick effort Burt had originally envisioned—something to get our company started, just a few test flights and then go.

We learned an awful lot from the trip, the hard way. We confirmed that we needed radar to avoid the storms. And so often we saw that if we could only have gone another three thousand feet higher, we could have avoided most of the turbulence. Going to that altitude—fifteen thousand feet or higher—meant taking along oxygen. Suddenly oxygen became a very important part of the mission.

Burt wasn't at all happy about our having landed in Salina. He thought we should have flown the airplane on through. He was disappointed and maybe a bit embarrassed that he didn't have Voyager there to show off that day and that we wouldn't set a record right off.

We finally did arrive, a day late, and when we landed it almost wiped away whatever lingering distress we felt. There were a quarter of a million people, waving and cheering and flicking their handkerchiefs in the air. Oshkosh has seen a lot of strange airplanes in its day—Dick well remembered the astonished response he got when he flew the first Vari Eze there in 1975—but probably none received a warmer welcome than Voyager. And this wasn't simply an emotional lift; it had a practical side. These were the people we were counting on to help us fly this thing around the world. And, from that point on, they were counting on us to do it.

The first thing we had to do when we got back home was figure out the problem with rain on the canard. First Burt told us to put some narrow strips of duct tape on the leading edges to "trip the boundary layer" and simulate the way the rain disturbed the airflow.

It was a big job to put on this duct tape, in quarter-of-an-inch strips, and we worked into the night on it. The next morning we taxied out and started down the runway. On takeoff the wings came up, but the canard didn't fly. We drove on through the normal takeoff speed and then eight knots faster, and I started playing with the elevator to try to get the nose up. When it finally did come up, it shot up, immediately stalled, and fell violently back. The airplane hit and rebounded, then began a porpoise motion. I started to try to fly it, but the elevator now had no effect whatsoever. So I shut down both engines and waited for the oscillations to die down. The tail booms hit the runway and kept the nose from coming up and we were able to roll to a stop.

It scared me badly. I hadn't even been aware Jeana was there, and she was getting banged around, holding on for dear life. For some reason she began giggling, watching my frantic efforts to get the airplane under control, and asked me, "Are we having fun yet?" If the porpoising had gone to higher amplitudes, we could easily have collapsed the gear or stalled the airplane into a crash.

It was a really stupid experiment. We had almost lost the airplane in the rain, and now we were going to simulate the condition on takeoff, without even a chance to bail out?

We came back and told Burt about it. He's a fixer, and he thought he had another fix. On his advice we took all the tape off the main wing and canard bottom and then went out and tried the takeoff again. This time Burt was there watching. And the same thing happened, only this time it was worse. He had suggested we push the airplane to a higher airspeed, holding it down, and then take off. But this led to even more violent oscillations; we bounced the nose gear to the bottom of the strut, and the booms had left long scrapes on the runway when we were finished.

It even scared Burt, and when I got out I told him, "We are not going to fly this airplane again until it is fixed. We are not going to do airfoil development in flight testing; we'll do that in the wind tunnel."

He agreed. He talked about building a new canard, which meant another year. But then he began to think we could solve the problem by flying the airplane differently. Well, he said, you only have a problem when you fly slow, so just land faster. And just fly fast in the rain, and just don't land in the rain.

What if I'm in a driving rainstorm and have to find New Delhi some night? I thought. Burt had never really understood what was involved.

We went to John Roncz, the versatile genius who is Burt's favorite airfoil guru. John was a rotund Hungarian who had worked out the shapes of the airfoils for the *Voyager*, but before that he had applied himself to the study of Egyptian hieroglyphics, classical music, and computers. He turned to airfoil design because it was a problem that challenged him. He actually thought it was fun. And soon he was the best around at it.

For the canard, in particular, he had worked out a shape that had a huge amount of lift—a 132-to-1 lift-to-drag ratio as compared with the 20-to-1 ratio of a standard wing. It may have been the "most lifting" airfoil in the history of aviation, and in Breguet's formula it translated straight into range.

John also designed the shapes of the propeller blades we had Gerd Muhlbauer build. To do the job right, he and his colleague, David Lednicer, had to prepare an entire aerodynamic model of the *Voyager* using a $70,000 program called VS Aero that runs on a Digital Equipment VAX computer. The result was a series of beautiful color drawings of the airplane, tinted according to the amount of drag at each point. The airplane's drag creates turbulent air going through the rear pusher prop, and John had to model that airflow exactly in order to give the prop its correct shape.

John took his job seriously. We were worried about what sort of a mess ten days of bug strikes would make of the wings, so John did a crash course in entomology. This was not just an aesthetic problem—that many bugs could cut down lift even more dramatically than rain. John figured out what types of bugs we would find all around the world, how many at each altitude, how many per square meter, how big they were. He really did it up, and he worked out the shape of the airfoil so they would hit just where he wanted—not splat and stick, but glance off. He even figured out how to distinguish different types of insects according to their wing loading.

One day John was running a test sample of the airfoil in the wind tunnel using the smoke generated to observe drag, when a real bug somehow got into the system. It hit just where John's calculations said it would hit and made only the smallest ripple in the smoke. And John was ecstatic.

He made a full size mock-up of the canard that we took to the wind tunnel at Ohio State University. We got permission from the directors of the wind tunnel, Drs. Michael Bragg and Jerry Gregorek, to go in late at night and run our tests. We were the first outsiders ever allowed in there without supervision. I ran the tunnel, and John ran the computers that were hooked up to Pitot tubes in the tunnel, working away on the test sample until two or three in the morning.

What we found was that the rain disturbed the smooth passage, or "laminar flow," of air over the top of the canard. Each drop, at the moment it beaded on the canard, had the same effect as if it had been a solid bump on the smooth surface. "Nature," John Roncz said, "sees each drop as a rock." Sure enough, we lost 65 percent of the lift on the canard when it was wet. No wonder we were falling out of the sky in that shower.

To fix the problem, Dr. Gregorek suggested we try vortex generators, 210 tiny angled tabs, which look like little teeth or shark's fins, glued to the canard with Hot Stuff glue. These kept the air swirling over the airfoil and stopped the drops from appearing. As an added precaution, John later had us sand the leading edge down so the water didn't bead up. The vortex generators added about 2 percent drag, but as John put it, that was a very inexpensive premium for the life insurance they provided.

We left about a foot and a half of the canard untreated with these tabs and put tufts of material on its trailing edge to see if they really worked. And sure enough, the tufts behind the untabbed area stood almost straight up, indicating the absence of smooth airflow and therefore of lift, while the tufts behind the vortex generators lay down smooth with the flow of air. That wind tunnel demonstration of the fix was so convincing that later on I never felt any need to test the airplane itself in rain.

. . .

The flight to Oshkosh marked the informal end to phase one of testing, which, under Burt's management at RAF, was to provide an airframe with mission-adequate flying qualities and the aerodynamic range capability to fly around the world. Phase two was our responsibility: to outfit the airplane with world-flight engines, avionics, and other systems, to test the airplane, and to make the world flight.

The most critical part of the task involved the engines. Using two engines for *Voyager* was fundamental to the whole project. The requirements for getting the fully loaded plane off the ground were much greater than those for efficient long-distance cruising. Nor could the fate of the plane and pilot be trusted to a single engine, running constantly for ten or twelve days. We would need a second engine as a lifeboat engine, if nothing else, and we would need it if we had to climb.

So Burt employed "engine staging," using two engines, one of which would be turned off after takeoff and restarted as necessary to climb or if something went wrong with the other engine.

We tried to keep as open a mind as possible about which engines to use. For its first test flights, *Voyager* was equipped with two old "rag overhauled" Long EZ engines—Lycomings. These were always carefully concealed so no one would know their manufacturer. Whenever the airplane was on public display, we had all the air intakes closed up. We wanted to preserve the sponsorship value for the manufacturer of the engines we would ultimately choose. We didn't want his participation tainted with the information that we'd started out with a different kind of engine.

We would use the temporary engines for the first phase of our tests to determine that the plane could be flown and that we actually had the range to go around the world. We had found we did—we had so much range, approaching 37,000 miles, we figured, that the joke was we should fly around the world and then on to Paris and land at Le Bourget.

In retrospect, though, putting on temporary engines turned out to be a mistake. If the final engines had been installed from the beginning, we would probably have saved a year—a year that turned out to be filled with problems and stress. As it was, the new engines had to be fitted and tested and the engine mounts and cowlings completely rebuilt.

Our original idea was, Never fly a new experimental airplane and a new experimental engine at the same time. If you've got a new airplane, fly it with a proven engine. If you've got a new engine, test it out first on an airplane you know and trust. Otherwise, you're asking for double trouble. So we planned to use off-the-shelf engines. What would make Voyager unique would not be its engines, but its airframe—the design of the airfoils, its immense fuel capacity, and its very light composite structure.

We looked at engines of every kind: diesel, rotary, high compression, Mazda radial, exotic engines like stratified charge, and even a Porsche engine used on the one in their 911 sports car. The big problem was finding an engine that burned very little fuel and was very efficient at the low power settings we would be using during the long stretches of the world flight and when we would be relatively light and going quite slowly.

Then Don Bigler of Teledyne Continental called to tell us about a new liquid-cooled engine. It had been developed for a hush-hush military reconnaissance project, we found out.

The very first airplane engines were liquid-cooled. It is a more efficient process and allows detonation and other combustion factors to be more carefully controlled.

But, from the twenties on, no one really worried that much about fuel economy, and most aircraft designers decided to do away with the extra apparatus of the liquid-cooling plumbing and cool their engines directly from the air.

Teledyne Continental claimed their engine had a .355 fuel specific— meaning it burned that many pounds per hour per horsepower—which was phenomenally good. It was 20 percent better than what anyone else had.

We had a meeting at NASA's Lewis Center in Ohio, where they work on advanced engines, to see some of the new developments in the field. Phil Ming of NASA introduced us to Don Bigler, who went over the hard data with us, backing up the figure, based on thousands of hours running in a test cell at Teledyne Continental's facility in Mobile, Alabama.

It was so good that we bent but did not break our rules—we compromised and decided to fly with one of each, an air-cooled engine and a new liquid-cooled engine. On the back, as our main cruise engine, we would put the new liquid-cooled IOL 200, which turns out 117 horsepower. It had an astonishingly high compression ratio of 11.4 to 1, with fuel-injected, high-turbulence cylinders for better homogenization and flame pattern—all of which meant in plain terms that it crammed the air and fuel mixture down into the cylinders, beat it all together, and got just about as much explosive power of that mixture as could be gotten. Later, TCM would name not only this engine but its whole line of liquid-cooled engines after *Voyager*.

Most of the new engine, in fact, was actually an old engine. Only the cooling system, the water jacket, and the cylinders were new.

On the front we would put a dependable plain vanilla O-240—a standard air-cooled engine, with 130 horsepower, carefully built but all of stock parts. We took the starter off the back engine and put the coolant pump where it had been. We only planned to start the rear engine once— the old-fashioned way, by hand. In one of the favorite lines from his standard talk—one that generally got groans from his audiences—Dick called that way "the Hemingway starter": one slip, and it's *"Farewell to Arms."*

The engines provided less horsepower but better fuel economy than we originally planned for, and with that improved engine performance, we would not have to take off with full tanks. We could take off at nine or ten thousand pounds instead of eleven or twelve thousand—a big difference, especially when you're heading down that runway figuring how much of it you have left and wondering seriously what the next minute and a half of your life are going to be like.

. . .

As promising as the new engine was, it was no use to us unless we had it installed on the airplane, and we waited month after month for Teledyne Continental to deliver that liquid-cooled engine.

By the spring of 1985 TCM was seven months behind on delivery, and we were picking up ominous rumors from the aviation world that they had lost interest in the program. We were extremely frustrated. Dick called Peter Riva, with whom we had originally talked in the summer of 1984, and asked him to join us in Mojave. We needed someone to deal with corporations, someone who understood how they thought. When we had first talked to him, he was committed to other projects and couldn't join us. But he neatly outlined what he thought we needed—someone to deal with corporations for us and someone to deal with the press—and he warned us about the problems we were likely to encounter in those areas.

Talking to him, Dick said, "You were right. We don't have any engines." Peter was able to join Voyager. He moved quickly. In London on business, he called Don Bigler at TCM, told him that his company had either to deliver on its commitment for engines or get out of the way and let someone else do it. And he got things moving with other corporate sponsors. He understood that public exposure was the key thing we had to offer sponsors. One of the first fruits of that effort was a rollout we had in November 1985 to show off the new TCM engines, which had arrived just a few weeks before, packed in two big blue wooden crates.

Peter would come out to Mojave and set up in the office with a telephone headset—a key item of his equipment, since he rarely put the phone down—and he was a veritable whirlwind of activity.

When he arrived, Peter promised he would never give up, and he never did. On many occasions he saved the program. Before and during the flight he became as essential to the *Voyager* program as the mission control center or even the airplane itself.

. . .

With the installation of the world-flight engines, we were finally able to begin the second phase of testing in earnest. All Teledyne's testing on the new engine, however, didn't prevent us from having to do our own extensive research and development program to break the new engine in, find out its peculiarities, and get solid data to predict its performance. It was all part of the process we called kicking around the alligators.

Ferg Fay, who was keeping track of the problem, wrote a title on the front of his oil log book: "Oscillations, Vacillations, and Paradoxes." Right there was the story of our whole testing process.

We were really running research and development on a lot of equipment at a time when every problem loomed large under the pressure of a slipping schedule and shoestring finances and hopes stretched taut from years of effort. Every day it would seem we had something licked, only to have it come unraveled the next day or have a new problem crop up.

There were a lot of things we weren't expert in—all we wanted to do was make them work, and if we had to learn something about them to do it, that was incidental. None of us was very patient with traditional engineers—even Glenn Maben, who was a degreed engineer. They were always coming up with complicated explanations and terminology rather than fixing the thing.

An example of engineeringspeak that drove us crazy was just down the flightline, where a company was developing a new kind of engine they called an "unducted fan."

"Unducted fan!" Dick exploded one day. "Don't tell me what it isn't, tell me what it is. 'Horseless carriage.' 'Wireless telegraph.' 'Unducted fan.' Hell, I had an unducted hat once. I wear unducted shoes."

That was the thing that got us about a lot of engineers: they'd often rather tell you what things aren't, not what they are, what won't work, not what will.

. . .

We found that every problem that came up took about three times longer to solve than we expected. And about this time we developed the "one-hour rule": Nothing takes less than an hour to do. You would start out to take care of some tiny detail, a wire or a tube—"Oh, it'll just take me a minute"—and then you couldn't find the right tool, or you had to take something else out for access, and it had taken you an hour.

But a lot of the problems took weeks and months. For some reason a problem developed that had never manifested itself in the test cell, and it had us stumped. This was the infamous "oil burp." At high RPMs the engine would literally dump all its oil out the breather pipe. The odd thing was that it happened on both engines, the front and the back, the old and the new. Bruce put plastic plates, like windows, into both engines to observe what was happening. It took us two or three weeks to wrestle the problem out and fix it. We relocated the breather pipe on the front, and on the back we modified the oil standpipe. But we never really did figure out why it had happened.

We had no experience with liquid-cooled engines, and when we started installation we barely knew where to start. It seemed a crude system to just dump the heat from the radiator through the engine compartment and out the back, but then we realized that was what cars do. Cars! Right— so we tested out how things worked on the poor old Toyota station wagon.

We put instruments in the Toyota to measure pressure and tempera-tures at different airflow rates. And we got the different airflow rates by blocking off more and more of the radiator. We finally overheated the poor car so much that it was never quite the same again, and we ruined the air conditioning completely.

We found out that while the oil radiator was getting rid of more of the heat than it was supposed to, the coolant radiator was getting rid of less.

And we got these terribly high oil temperatures—on the standard front engine as well as on the back liquid-cooled one. The problem lay in the air pressure across the radiators—the delta-P, as the engineers call it. The radiators that cooled the oil had been designed to work at a delta-P of 3.3 inches of pressure. In fact, we were only getting 1 or 1.5 inches. What we found out was that the engineering predictions—basic formulas—were just flat wrong. And it took us a long time to figure it out, because we were naive enough to trust the engineering knowledge.

The formula for delta-P versus airspeed said that delta-P was supposed to increase with the square of the velocity; in other words, the pressure went up exponentially with your speed. But when we slowed down, we found we lost delta-P faster than we should have. This was important because we were going to be spending a long time at relatively low speed, and we needed that air coming through to keep the oil cool. We found that when we slowed down twenty-five knots, we lost half of delta-P. We instrumented *Voyager*, to measure just how much air was coming through, and then for comparison we instrumented a lot of other airplanes. What we concluded was that the engineers were basically wrong about low speeds. The numbers for the actual system were only half of what was theoretically possible.

The only thing to do was increase the size of the radiators. We talked to the experts at Stewart-Warner, and they built us 40 percent larger oil radiators. And even they were only marginally acceptable.

Then, to get more air flowing through, we put a kind of kicker ramp in the air exit scoop—something like a spoiler on an automobile. We fixed it so we could open it up for climbs and then close it down for low speed cruise. This was one of the great things about the composites—we could do little fixes like this without major machining.

Burt wasn't happy with this kicker at all. He looked at it as a gross addition of drag. In fact, the cooling drag—the openings and channels and so on—represented 20 percent of the drag on the airplane—the overall shape was that slippery. This kicker added maybe 2 or 3 percent, and we made it as small as we could; but it wasn't pretty, and it was going to offend anyone who was an aerodynamic purist. But the engineers could say what they liked; we had to live in the world of practicalities. We were the ones flying the airplane.

Sometimes we had to accept a little more weight for safety. For the fuel system, for instance, we at first tried out the manual system Dick had wanted, in which we would just change tubes by hand to switch tanks. The first time we tried it we got fuel all over the place, just as everyone had predicted. It was clearly unworkable. Then we had a rotating valve, like a shower mixer, specially fabricated by Meer Instruments to handle the tank switching.

The use of the plastic tubing seemed awfully clever at the time, but we had barely stopped patting ourselves on the back for thinking it up when we discovered some sort of strange rot in the tubes—"fuel line arteriosclerosis," we started calling it. Chemical fumes of some sort were rotting away at the plastic tubing. We exposed samples of the tubing to every kind of fume we could imagine, and none of them emerged as the clear culprit. So we had to replace all the tubing with a resistant type. All the tubing, that is, that we could reach, since a good deal was inaccessible now, and we had to cross our fingers about that. Six months later we found out that the rot was caused by fumes from the acid in the motorcycle batteries we had installed to make the flight to Oshkosh.

. . .

The props naturally had to be light and durable. They had to be of variable pitch—providing the equivalent of an automobile transmission—for maximum efficiency. They also had to be featherable—capable of being immobilized with the least amount of drag—for long periods so we could shut the engines off in flight, and the rear prop had to be reversible.

We looked around, and with the advice of our local expert, Victor Haluska at Santa Monica Propellers, we decided on props made by an outfit called MT Props, owned by Gerd Muhlbauer and based near Munich, West Germany.

Europeans are wild about gliding—none more than the Germans—and many of their sailplanes are equipped with engines that carry them to height and are then shut down for gliding. This requires extremely light propellers that can be feathered—just about the same specs we had—and the Germans use wood for them. The leader in manufacturing such props was a firm called Hoffman, and for fifteen years Gerd Muhlbauer was Hoffman's chief design engineer. Then he left to start his own company, and many people who knew more about these things than we did thought he made props that were even better than Hoffman's.

I flew over to Germany in January 1985 to watch the props—made of laminated spruce—being finished up and to bring them home with me. I was worried, coming through customs. These were very expensive props.

Even though they had been donated, I worried we might have to pay customs on their market value. That would put a deep hole in the bank account; Jeana would be very upset. And they were too big to hide.

As I stood in the customs line, I noticed that the inspector in front of me seemed like a really tough case. He went through the luggage of one woman so thoroughly, he could have been hunting for smuggled microfilm. He didn't look as if he would be very understanding about the situation.

Just then another inspector came up. "Would you step over here, sir?" he said to me. I was carrying a flying magazine. We were getting some attention by now in the press, and there was an article about Voyager in it, mentioning our financial struggles. I told the inspector about the props and showed him the picture in the magazine—and he recognized it. He was a big aviation buff, it turned out. "This plane?" he said. "For this plane? I have read about it."

Then he looked around to see if anyone was watching and said, "Go right on—and good luck."

And as things turned out, we needed all the luck everybody could wish us and more.

. . .

We planned that Dick would handle all the landings and takeoffs. The only way I would ever be landing the Voyager was if Dick were incapacitated. The airplane was very hard to land, even in calm conditions. Moving the airplane from one runway to another at Oshkosh, for instance, Dick had to make several passes. He found the airplane didn't want to leave the air. It just kept floating. Finally he resorted to the tremendously delicate and dangerous technique of coming in, planting the nosewheel, and letting it bleed off speed until he could get the mains down.

As we flew at heavier weights, we found out even worse things about the airplane: we discovered that, at a point just above eighty-two knots, we had a major pitch oscillation problem—pitch porpoising, we called it. What happened was that in an updraft the wings bow, the tips go up, and the wing roots go down, carrying the fuselage with them. This in turn pitches up the nose and canard. The motion becomes a wave, repeating itself and growing in magnitude—a heaving, or "porpoising."

We had known we were facing the danger of an airplane that was a flying bomb, a huge tank of fuel that could be detonated by a single spark, with no lightning strike protection and a nonstandard electrical system that often behaved strangely. Now we also had to accept the fact that we were facing the danger of an airplane that had a basic aerodynamic flaw, an airplane that could come apart around our ears if we made one single, momentary mistake.

For a long time the movement of the wings had seemed nothing more than a testimony to the resilience of Voyager's composite construction. People would ask how far the wings could bend, and we would answer jokingly, "Until they touch." The composite construction did give the wings a remarkable amount of resilience, and the fifteen or so feet of wingtip movement we often saw was not in itself a concern. But when that movement got out of control, there was danger—extreme danger.

When we flew at the heavier weights, the flapping became serious. The flights were showing that at exactly eighty-two and a half knots of speed, the flapping of the wings went out of control—the oscillations, in technical terms, "became divergent." The flapping began to increase in height, doubling with each cycle. Unless the pilot or autopilot stopped it, the wings would literally flap themselves off in about ten or twelve seconds. If you let go of the stick, this airplane would come apart.

The question became, Was there any way to fly the mission with this defect? Voyager would have to fly for at least three days above the critical speed, just to generate enough lift to sustain its weight.

Jeana had never handled the plane under those conditions, and with something that happened so fast, it seemed there was no way for her to learn. One learning mistake, and that was it.

Could I catnap in the seat during that time, trusting the autopilot, trusting that I could wake up and take control quickly enough if major turbulence set off the oscillation or the autopilot failed? And could I sleep, knowing that being able to wake up was critical to saving our lives?

Dick never allowed me to handle the Voyager above the dangerous weight. I was able to get little flying experience with Dick in the off-duty position and when I did he was near panic not being able to get his hands on the controls. Burt and Doug and the others pushed him to let me train but I knew that Dick would not be able to cope with the mission if he had to be in the back.

It was something whose seriousness we couldn't really acknowledge, not to the public and not even to the people in the trailer or the volunteers in the hangar.

If you attack the porpoising wrong, it gets worse. It can easily turn into "pilot-induced oscillation." The only way to control it is to lead the wave by ninety degrees. When the nose is at the bottom of the curve, you give it forward stick, even the stick as it passes the horizon, then, as it reaches to the top of the cycle, pull back.

It only works if you anticipate the cycle and hit it right on the head, nail it. And if you let go, it won't go back to normal, it won't stabilize, it will just get worse until within just a few seconds it will destroy the airplane.

You sit there almost pumping the stick, but with great delicacy, against that porpoising. It took 90 percent of Dick's considerable skill to handle it, and several times he had felt he was within a millisecond of losing it. He had come so close to not catching it in time. In any other situation, any other reasonable pilot would have walked away from the airplane and abandoned it for what it was: a fundamentally unsafe craft, a flying death-trap.

Probably the sensible thing to do was to call a halt and ground the airplane. But we were too deeply involved to quit now: we had nothing else. For years now all our energies, all our hopes, all our time, had gone into *Voyager*. Our lives were worth a lot less every time we climbed into that airplane, but on the ground we had no lives outside of it. It was our life now.

Unlike Jeana I hated the airplane and feared it. It was the only airplane I had ever been afraid of. I had never gotten used to the flailing wings. I would tell myself that the structures could take that motion, but I wasn't ever really convinced. It was a gnawing, grinding fear, and it never went away.

On mornings when we were scheduled for a test flight, I would sometimes look out the window and see that the wind was blowing too hard to fly and feel relief. And when we did fly, it would take all the willpower I could muster to descend back down into the thermals at Mojave and land the airplane.

The fear of the airplane infected me even in other aircraft. For the first time, I was afraid of flying. It followed me even into the cockpit of the Long EZ, where I was used to reeling off loops and rolls and chandelles—cowboy flying. I no longer even liked to turn or bank an airplane. That motion reminded me instantly of what such a movement would have done in the *Voyager*.

I would even look down out of the Long and feel fear of the height— something I never felt, not even on my first airplane flights. I had always felt fear looking down from tall buildings, but never in an airplane. Now I could not stand to look at the ground. Flying the Long EZ, I would tell

Jeana about it, and I knew it couldn't give her much confidence in her co-pilot.

I've got a no-shit fear of flying, I realized. And for the first time in my life I actually felt empathy for those afraid to board airliners.

I had to retrain myself. I had to go up in that airplane and tell myself, I love flying, I'm good at it. I even thought of talking to professionals about the problem, but lack of time, an aversion to their methods, and, I knew, ultimately my pride led me to decide to try to treat myself.

So, during the months when we were grounded for the installation of the new engines, I pursued a thorough course of therapy to conquer this fear.

I took up the Long EZ as often as I could, telling myself again and again, I love flying, I'm good at it, I can do this, putting myself through my old cowboy aerobatics, with more and more daring, gradually working myself back into the old groove.

When it was time to get back into Voyager to test out the new engines, I felt that I was 90 percent back to normal. As time went on it got better. The fear was still there, lurking, and it would never entirely leave, but I felt it was controlled.

I had talked one day to a psychiatrist who had come around the hangar. He told me how fear can make someone do things to avoid a situation— to do things that are almost suicidal.

Sometimes people whose business is failing end up having a bad accident. They do not do it purposely—they don't drive their car off a cliff— but if a dangerous situation arises not of their own making, subconsciously they might not use every bit of skill to save themselves. They relax a little and let disaster happen when they could have avoided it.

I had to be constantly aware of any manifestation of this.

I felt a special respect for the airplane, too, different from Dick's fear. My warning mechanism was different. I had never felt on the edge of panic, wildly wondering, What do I do next? Sometimes I felt that I was lacking some part of the fear mechanism that most people had. What I did have was a kind of inner voice, one that sometimes assured me, sometimes warned me.

I thought, I've always talked to things as if they were alive, and they've talked to me. I had a strong sense of just how far Voyager could be pushed.

Sometimes my senses instilled a fundamental confidence that somehow things would work out, that Voyager was something that was supposed to happen.

Many times the voices took on warning notes, like the subliminal sense of a mother whose child is in danger.

These were stressful times for me, too. I took solace in horses. It had been a long time since I had spent much time riding or around horses, but now I needed an escape. I made time to get down to the stables south of the Mojave airport.

There I met Terri Smith, who later came to work for us in the trailer. Terri loved to ride and had two horses, a tamer one and a "greenbroke" sixteen hand dune named Dusty who was pretty spunky. One day when Terri was brushing Dusty she asked me if I wanted to ride him.

Sometimes I would shock people who were used to seeing my quieter side. And on this day Terri was a little taken aback at the aggressive way I handled Dusty. But soon she was cheering me on.

I got on Dusty and the first time he bucked with me we discussed it with a whip. Before long Dusty caught on and we began riding around having a good time.

I got to ride Dusty several other times, and every time it was an improvement. At first I was a little concerned about being with a green horse like that. It had been so long I thought I'd forgotten. But it all came back, like they say about riding a bike.

Judy knew how much I missed horses, and she had been threatening for years to get me one. I always resisted, trying to be practical, until one day she called and told me that, whether I liked it or not, she was giving me a horse for my birthday. Well, when I heard that I just turned to jelly; all my resistance vanished.

Dr. George Jutila, our flight surgeon, and his wife Sylvia were driving down from their home in Fortuna. They swung by Santa Rosa, where the horse was, and soon arrived in Mojave towing a trailer in which they brought Gem, the name of my new lady. I quickly took her to the stables and immediately began pampering her. I kept the stall scrupulously neat, with every bridle and brush in its place, so even in the dark of the night, which was often the only time I had to go there, I could find anything instantly. From now on, if I wasn't at the hangar I was at the barn with Gem. It became my refuge from the pressures and frustrations at Hangar 77.

It was not just the riding that I loved, but simply being with my horse, feeding her, brushing her, talking to her, sometimes using her big old shoulder to cry on. Gem was my private and special little world.

Thanks to Judy, I stopped denying myself, and I resolved I would never again be without the horses I love so much.

The Trailer

We flew around the world dozens of times—and all the flights but one were made in the trailer beside the hangar that was our mission control, simulating every scenario we could imagine.

We were determined to keep our course as flexible as possible. If you can change course to avoid bad weather or find tail winds, you increase the chances of success immeasurably.

This was one reason for flying over the ocean: there is more room to maneuver, to go searching for the good winds and avoiding the bad. Over land, you are limited by political overflight restrictions—not the least of which is the possibility of some nutty dictator or crazy insurgent group taking a shot at you.

To pursue our method successfully, we had to have a good ground control operation. *Voyager*'s mission control was set up in a mobile-home-sized trailer beside Hangar 77, with two or three antennas guywired up beside it like oil derricks. On the roof were a dozen tires to keep the Mojave wind from blowing it off—something that, from the sound inside, it often seemed about to do anyway. Inside the trailer were tables covered with computers and other equipment and, at one end, a closed compartment full of the radios. On the wall was a Geochron global clock, tracing the real-time movement of sunlight and darkness around the world. The clock was virtually a mission-critical item. It showed the people in mission control whether we were in light or darkness and how long until sunset or sunrise. That was important because we wanted them to be inside our heads, to understand what we were up against, to have a tangible sense of such principles as not flying us through weather at night—in short, to make the same decisions at each point that we would have made.

During the exercises and the flights, the command post became a kind of world in itself, little touched by changes in daylight and operating on time scales different from the rest of Mojave—on Zulu, Greenwich mean time, or the local time where the airplane was flying.

It was hardly the Johnson Manned Space Flight Center. But, with the same sort of combination of high-tech equipment—almost all of it begged and borrowed—and makeshift handiwork that characterized the whole *Voyager* program, it did the job.

In charge of outfitting and staffing the trailer was our mission control director, Larry Caskey. Larry came to the program relatively late—early in 1986—and he had to do a lot of work very fast to get things in place.

Larry was uniquely prepared for the job. Born on a farm in Oklahoma, he was lured by his early love of flying to the aircraft industry in southern California just when we were about to be drawn into World War II. He learned navigation flying transports over the Himalayan "hump," supplying our bases in China. After the war he was stationed in Germany and helped coordinate and direct the Berlin airlift that successfully defied the Soviet blockade.

Larry went on to become a test and chase pilot at the "Skunkworks," Lockheed's famous development shop where the great designer Kelly Johnson turned out the P-80—the first U.S. jet—the F-104, the U-2, and Mach 3 SR-71 Blackbird. He was involved in the test program for Lockheed's L-1011 airliner.

He knew flying, he knew navigation, he knew communications, and he knew weather. He had spent a lot of time in the Pacific, a critical area of concern for the weather along our course. He was no stranger to the dreaded Intertropical Convergence Zone, the ITCZ or "Itch," where tropical storms spawn and massive thunderstorms might threaten *Voyager*.

Originally we had planned to accept the invitation of Don Lopez and Walter Boyne of the National Air and Space Museum in Washington to set up our mission control center there. The idea was that the public could share directly in the flight, walk by and look in, get constant updates, and feel a part of the project. This appealed to us as part of our grass-roots approach.

W. A. "Rodie" Rodewald had volunteered to serve as a mission controller. Rodie was a good friend who has had a long flying career and constructed several home-builts, one of them a Long EZ in which he'd flown from Hawaii to Oshkosh.

But the more we looked into this scheme, the more problems emerged. We began to realize that we needed the control center near at hand for planning and practice. Rodie could not be in Mojave for the months of preparation we needed, so he suggested we use other professionals. Washington was just too far away. We also figured out that at the National Air and Space Museum we would have to have professional security people twenty-four hours a day. The price tag for that was something like $175,000, which was money Voyager Aircraft simply didn't have and could hardly expect the museum to come up with.

So we settled the trailer down right beside old Hangar 77, and Larry Caskey settled into a spare bedroom in the house, flying back on weekends to his home up the coast in Paso Robles—when he could get away.

Larry put together the communications and navigation team. He brought on Don Rietzke, another alumnus of the Skunkworks, as chief radioman. His team included Dick Blosser from Rockwell, who served as chief of the radio room during the world flight, and hams from all over. Stu Hagedorn came up from NASA's own mission control in Houston. Dave Bearden's regular job was on the shortwave at the Seventh Street police garage in Los Angeles. Walt Massengale, from Yorba Linda, practically lived in back of the house where Richard Nixon was born. Gil and Isabel Fortune left their home in Florida to be on duty constantly in Mojave.

Jack Norris, who knew everything from landing gear to fuel pump and whose first job involved working on the F-100, came in to figure course, fuel, and speed. Helping him was Brent Silver, who had known us since the airplane was just a collection of pieces in the back room at RAF.

Others of the crew brought experience that stretched back a way. Don Taylor had flown a number of record flights himself—without satellites or electronics and with "seat of the pants" navigation—including one to the North Pole and back. He was the first home-builder to fly around the world.

Conway Roberts was a NASA pilot, another one of those guys with a twang—and also a heck of a lot of professional experience with the best.

In the airplane itself, our navigation was done by the King KNS 660 VLS Omega navigation system, a whole little computer that in effect locked on to radio waves miles and miles long from stations all over the world to obtain fixes. It displayed information on a four-inch screen, and in its silicon-chip memory was information about hundreds of airports around the world, just in case we had to make use of any of them. Supplementing it was a satellite-linked global positioning system, which would allow us to take a position fix from satellites passing overhead. The only problem was that not all the satellites had yet been put in place, and there were only four hours a day when we would be in contact with them and could use the system.

The Omega antenna was originally mounted inside the cockpit. Although the cabin area had been constructed of Aramid fiber, which, unlike graphite, is transparent to radio waves, a problem developed: there was major interference from the alternator. So we moved the antenna out to the right boom tank. We had to hack up the wing, dig a big trench to run a cable through, then fill it up and fair off a bubble on top of the boom.

In addition to the King KHF 990 HF and KX 165 VHF radios, we were eventually able to add a critical radio capability: UHF satellite communications. Working through the State Department, Peter Riva obtained special clearance to use frequencies on government and military satellites—the tiptop communications systems in the world. These communicated directly with satellites in geosynchronous orbit, which relayed the signal back to earth stations. This meant that every word traveled some 46,000 miles, up and back down, but it was to provide a clarity that shorter distances on the ground could not offer. For the UHF link, we looked at a number of systems and finally chose the Motorola LST-5, which weighed only seven and a half pounds.

The primary radio was the King KHF-990 long-range shortwave radio. Its antenna trailed from the left boom, a sixty-inch stinger that we had to be very careful about. When the airplane was in the hangar, we had a sawhorse that sat just underneath it to keep somebody from stumbling into it and breaking it off.

The information we got from Len Snellman back in the trailer would give us our general weather guide—the strategic picture—but for immediate local conditions—tactical information—we were counting on the radar whose inclusion on board had been such a subject of dispute with Burt. Len compared it to golf: he would handle the long strokes and get us down the fairway, but when we got close we would have to do our own putting.

The radar was a King KWX 58, with a screen that shows weather patterns in four colors. It looks like the screen of a very sophisticated personal computer, because that is really what it is—a device that digitally processes the radar return levels picked up by a twelve-inch phase array antenna, clustered inside the radome (the housing of the radar unit) on the front of the right boom, and sorts them according to intensity. Each intensity is displayed in a color: the weakest returns show up in green, stronger ones in yellow, and storms in red and magenta. Magenta indicates thick weather, saturated clouds, danger—the stuff that can kill you.

Equally crucial was the autopilot, a modified King KAP 150, which had to be specially fitted and adjusted to the airplane's dimensions and handling qualities and have the numbers burnt into its computer chips. This was a difficult job, because the aircraft handled so eccentrically. The autopilot had to be adjusted for the fact that there was only one rudder, and the rudder was used to control roll instead of Voyager's ailerons, because of the large air loads.

Because of those good old flapping wings, and the longitudinal oscillations we had been suffering through almost from the first day we flew the airplane, the autopilot was assisted by something called a pitch stability augmentation system, a special rate gyroscope for the pitch control that had been such a problem on this big, wallowing airplane.

On this combination of computer chips, gyroscopes, and servomotors, we were betting our lives. If we lost the autopilot, unless we were within a few hours from a suitable landing field, we would lose the aircraft. And the autopilot was critical to helping us maximize fuel efficiency—it was our cruise control.

Without satellites, it is fair to say that Voyager's flight would have been impossible—at least the way we planned it. The use of UHF satellites assured us of being in touch with the navigation, performance, and weather people at home. Weather satellites provided the raw information that let them help us make decisions about the course to fly. And a set of satellites in the SARSAT (Search and Rescue Satellite) system made sure that we would always be in touch with the rescue people, even if we lost all our power or went into the water, through a quick burst of computerized data transmitted by a battery-powered "bug."

The SARSAT transponder bug was small enough to put in your pocket— and that was exactly what we planned to do with it if we had to go over the side. If we went down, rescue people would know where we were almost instantly; even if worse came to worst, there would be no Amelia Earhart–style search.

We also had help from the Lockheed Dataplan, a computerized system that airlines and other fliers use to obtain information on weather, figures, and the best courses and to arrange political clearances.

Of course none of this would have been any use if we didn't have what Ferg Fay liked to call "expert rainmakers, who know when to shoot off the right cannons and do the right dances."

We began to research meteorology with a trip in 1982 to the National Weather Service headquarters in Maryland. There we met Rich Wagoner, one of the service's top men, who was enthusiastic about the program and said he would help us out—on his own time, unofficially, of course. At first we knew so little about the weather that we planned to fly from west to east. Rich explained to us that the equatorial trade winds would be a big help, and they are westerlies—they were the reason Columbus discovered America.

It was then, too, that we learned we would have to face the Intertropical Convergence Zone, the storm-generating belt that runs around the earth's oceans and throws up typhoons and hurricanes. "You'll have to find a hole in the ITCZ someplace," Rich told us. "The guy you want," he said, "is Len Snellman."

The course we planned would carry us southwest across the Pacific, finding some break in the ITCZ, over Australia, through the Indian Ocean, and across southern Africa. Then we would head home through the Caribbean and across Texas, New Mexico, and Arizona.

We didn't know too much more about weather than cloud names like "altocumulus standing lenticular"—and other bad guys pilots have to stay away from. So we were incredibly lucky to have lined up Len Snellman as our chief meteorologist.

When we told people Len was working with us, they couldn't believe it. "Snellman? But he has all these five-figure consulting contracts. Everybody wants him." They were right—Len is one of the top weather gurus in the country.

Len is a classical meteorologist who also knows how to use the new technology of satellites and computers. He teaches at the University of Utah and, in his spare time, coaches a girls' softball team called the Aeolians. Len, who worked in meteorology for the air force before becoming the National Weather Service chief for eight western states, wears the characteristic garb of his trade while he works, a sort of modified butcher's apron, with one pocket for grease pencils and another for lead pencils. The apron's muslin color is streaked and darkened with experience—it bears the marks of thousands of storms and fronts.

"Some of the grease pencil on this apron," Len will tell you proudly, "is thirty years old."

"Don't you ever wash it?" people ask.

"No," he'll say, "I never thought it needed it."

At Voyager, we were able to get Len the best satellite images available and the equipment to store and display them. In the trailer were huge video screens, where big pictures of the planet kept sweeping on and off the screens in loops—in a sequence of the pictures strung together, animated, showing some delicate tendril of clouds growing into the threatening claw of a storm that grasped at the West Coast or a blossom of cloud activity in the south Pacific, erupting and expanding in just a few hours. The video clips compressed the action of hours to seconds, from a tiny dot of a cloud into a tropical storm.

You could call up three days' worth of pictures, taken at six-hour intervals, and turn them into a dramatic little show, a weather saga, that kept replaying, looping back and forth.

The machine that creates these pictures is called a D-WIPS, an acronym that stands for digital weather information processing systems, put together by a brilliant man named Clarence Boice.

It would handle all the satellite weather pictures we needed. The D-WIPS's precious memory was housed in a large, upright blue box in the corner of the trailer. Above it Larry Caskey posted a sign banning the presence of all beverages, on pain of death.

You could use the mouse drawing device attached to the system's terminal to draw lines and shapes on the screen, marking a course or delimiting an area of interest. Occasionally people in the trailer would doodle with the mouse and draw a smiling face over Africa or a crude "Hi!" over the Atlantic.

.   .   .

Unlike some modern meteorologists, Snellman has never regarded satellites as having made the weatherman's job easy, and he never thought of the weather as a mechanical, analyzable system. He tends to talk about "Mother Nature" and "the weather gods" with a facetious tone but the clear implication that not all can be understood, that there are plenty of jokers left in the atmospheric deck of cards.

Snellman is highly respected by the fellow members of his profession. He has succeeded in putting the new technology of the trade in perspective. In 1977 he achieved a measure of international notoriety by warning at a world conference that weathermen were relying too much on technology. Overdependence on satellites and computers, he said, had produced a "meteorological cancer" that threatened the entire profession. Now, he complained, weathermen fascinated by these new tools no longer made basic observations.

Snellman's speech drew all the more notice because he had been one of the pioneer "synopticians"—weathermen who use satellite photography and computer analysis. He had been given some of the profession's most cherished awards for this work.

Len believed in using all the information that satellites and computers could produce; it was just that he didn't believe in stopping there.

As he once explained it, "A lot of people say something like, 'Well, there's moist air from the Gulf, so it's going to rain up here.' But it's not so simple. Most of the times there is a serious drought in the Midwest, say, there is probably more moisture in the air moving over the area than usual. What really matters is the atmospheric dynamics—and to understand that, you need the local winds and pressures at different altitudes."

To get this information and supplement his satellite images, Snellman arranged for detailed maps to be sent to the trailer via modem from the NOAA (National Oceanic and Atmospheric Administration) in Washington. He had them flowing in over phone lines, automatically and almost constantly, charting winds and pressures at five, ten, and thirty thousand feet.

These maps exist because weather forecasting is one of the few areas of human endeavor in which almost all the countries of the world cooperate. Twice each day, meteorologists all over the planet launch radiosondes—balloons carrying a variety of weather instruments—and the results together produce a set of world data for varying altitudes. This data goes into the computers, but it also goes on maps.

Aviators more than most people are in a position to understand Len's point. They have noticed that even as more and more technology has become available to weathermen, local forecasts have become less and less reliable. One reason for this is that the National Weather Service has become more centralized—more weathermen in Washington, fewer in Bakersfield or Butte or Birmingham. And the reason there are more weathermen in Washington—and in other big urban centers—is that they are tending computers and writing and refining programs.

The computer programs, Snellman believes, are the problem: however sophisticated the hardware or the software, it cannot crunch or "brute force" all the data into a pattern. There is simply too much information. And to prevent the machine from choking on all that information—much of which, when encountered by its circuits, seems contradictory—the programs are made to generate limited models.

Some of the models are descriptive. Others are predictive, generated from historical data. Snellman has a particular problem with these. When they replace the local guy who knows the history, has a feel for the area, and can read the detailed local maps, something is lost.

To produce the neat weather maps you see in newspapers and on television, the computer models are equipped with "smoothers," mathematical features that round off the numbers. This produces an impressive rendition of the large picture, but a relatively poor one of local conditions, the local zigs and zags smoothed off the curves.

It is, he says, a little bit like the guy with one foot in a bucket of 120-degree water and the other in thirty-degree water. Don't tell him about the general average—he is feeling the local conditions.

When Snellman talks about these smoothers, he makes them sound like some sort of food additive—a stabilizer or preservative. He would prefer the natural product. "Only Mother Nature," he says, "always seems to integrate the equations correctly so that the results come out in the clouds."

One day Len was reviewing a weather service map. "This is wrong," he said. "This low-pressure area is not going to move down here. Mother Nature would never do that."

He got on the phone to the weather service and told them they'd made a mistake. No, no, they said, no mistake. Len made them send him all the data that had gone into the map—ten feet of printouts—and he went over every number until, all of a sudden, he stopped and said, "They missed Roseland."

He called the weather service back, and sure enough, there was an error. That local reading was wrong. The low did not move where the map said it would move. After that we had a faith approaching awe in Len.

From then on, too, we understood why Len wanted the satellite pictures supplemented by the raw data, the maps with the information on them representing the local peaks and valleys the computer would smooth out.

He worked with Peter Riva and SISCorp to get the trailer hooked up with DIFAX—the international meteorological facsimile system that put him on a sort of computerized subscription list and saw to it that he was automatically sent the maps he needed. Supplementing this during the world flight was the service of Ocean Routes, which provided information from the European Centre for Medium Range Weather Forecasts. Len even went back and looked at Charles Lindbergh's weather maps—and was shocked at how crude they were and how lucky he was to have been successful. "Lindbergh's weatherman was God," Len would say, shaking his head.

Every six hours the weather people and the performance people would get together to send us an updated course projection. The tricky thing would be to balance fuel economy with a route through the weather that avoided dangerous storms and maximized tail winds. Complicated trade-offs were involved. Was it worth diverting this way to pick up a tail wind? Should we climb to avoid a head wind and use precious oxygen? There were all sorts of choices.

We would be counting on the people in the trailer to get us through. But we didn't even begin to anticipate just how important their role would be.

We had to have the trailer all set up for extended flight. Before, for test flights, it had just been Fergy and a tape recorder beside the radio. For our next flight—the Pacific coast closed-course flight—we would need the whole command post up and running. And the flight would test out how it would work over a period of days, just as much as it would test how we and the airplane would work.

Human Factors

The cowboy and the Indian ride up to the tent, high on a mountainside. They get off their horses and tie them up. I can see the weathered lines of the cowboy's face and the engraving on his saddle. I recognize the rifle the cowboy carries as a .30/30, and I can hear the mumble of their conversation.

I fly toward them for five minutes or so, until I am close enough to see that the figures are actually great rock outcroppings, there on the edge of the Sierras, formations hundreds of feet high. A few more seconds, and I would have flown the Long EZ right into them.

For more than a day now, I had been flying in a great circle, on the way to setting a new closed-course distance record in the little plane with its stubby, Donald Duck–legged landing gear. It was dark, and the lamps of the instruments, glowing weakly, shed just enough light to cast a wide funhouse-mirror reflection of my face across the canopy.

I was exhausted, on the edge of collapse, just barely remembering what I was doing. Time had stopped. I had seen Orion coming up in the sky and at first waited for it, then willed it, to move higher. It refused.

The cowboy and the Indian had been preceded in the waking dreams of fatigue and sensory deprivation by spaceships, flying formation with me, making high side passes around the Long EZ, apparently so close and so sharply defined I could see faces looking out of their portholes. They had been accompanied by "encounters." They dragged huge nets along the ground, sweeping up sagebrush and boulders and swinging them toward me, so real I almost veered to avoid them.

At another point I saw Life and Death in debate, half-embodied apparitions, two personalities battling each other, and I could float away from the plane, it seemed, right through the fuselage, and watch them.

The cockpit lights spread out my image across the canopy, wide and distorted.

The organ music again welled up in my ears and great philosophical questions of reality and illusion, meaning and purpose, began to debate themselves of their own accord. I was drawn into the debate, and suddenly I found myself talking to a small black elfin creature that had appeared on the canard in front of me.

I saw these things clearly, full and solid, and I would have sworn they were there even though I knew they couldn't be. I fought the apparitions, curiosity and fascination arguing with fading reason, as in a dream when the dreamer clings to a tiny spark of the understanding that he is dreaming.

This is what dying is like, I thought. I thought it must be like one of the "out of body" experiences I had read about, where critically ill people float to the top of a room and look down on their bodies. It scared the hell out of me. I could never forget it, and I never wanted to experience it again.

I had been flying, around and around in a great loop, and I didn't know whether it was all wasted, whether I could hold out long enough to break the record. I had circled over the Owens Valley between Bishop and Mojave, aiming for the closed-course record, until each pass had begun to seem as dizzying.

I had gotten off to a bad start, tensed up and nervous. I had been working late on the plane for the three previous nights; I couldn't sleep, and finally at three in the morning I had gotten up and gone running in the desert, trying to wear myself out enough to sleep.

I was tired when I took off at seven-fifteen on December 15, 1979, in Burt's prototype Long EZ, and a day and a half later I was entering the phase of exhaustion and sensory deprivation, where the mind, like an overtaxed and underprogrammed computer, begins to rebel against its instructions, crashes, throws up its hands, and begins to dump—to reach back at random into its memory banks, extracting odd images and sensations and tossing them out.

The apparitions, I later learned, were the creation of a tortured mind trying to make sense of the shapes of broken blood vessels appearing at the periphery of my vision, a mind ransacking its memory for concepts to attach to these strange shapes.

I held myself together, pulled back from the visions. I mumbled bits of poetry and thought about technical specifications for engine and aircraft parts I knew. I slapped myself in the face again and again, until my face was numb and it no longer did any good. Finally the daylight began to break and with it a real world around me. I flew on for twelve more hours, and I had enough spirit left at the end to do a flashy little cowboy loop before I set the Long EZ down, just before dark.

In 33.7 hours, I had flown 4,800 miles. The record for class C1b aircraft (1,102–2,204 pounds) was certified by the Fédération Aéronautique Intérnationale, the official world record-keeping body.

That night I went to bed at nine o'clock, slept until noon, was up for three hours, and went back to sleep for six more.

.   .   .

Two years later, flying for another record, from Alaska to Grand Turk Island in the Bahamas, this time on a straight-line course, I took precautions against a recurrence of the waking nightmares.

I read about the effects of extreme fatigue and sensory deprivation. After Jack Cox published the story of the flight in *Experimental Aircraft Association* magazine, I received all sorts of letters about how to fight the debilitating effects of long flights.

This time I took along tapes of old radio serials, *Green Hornet* and *The Shadow*, which Jeana had given me. They made my mind work just hard enough to keep it occupied.

And I got plenty of rest before the flight, running and hiking in the Alaskan wilderness, eating and sleeping well, waiting for the weather to clear. I took off well rested, having learned that what was critical in such situations was the ninety hours before a flight. After the Alaska/Grand Turk flight, which had covered 4,563 miles in thirty hours, I had dined with the governor of the island, gone to sleep at my normal bedtime, and felt fine the next day.

The experiences of the record flights conditioned planning for *Voyager*. The nightmare visions over the Owens Valley, in particular, were an experience I never wanted to go through again. And they taught me something about myself. I knew that I tended to push myself too far. In the military I had stayed awake for long hours, first while flying as navigator for cargo planes, later to pack in as much action as possible in the F-100.

I had run on almost sheer adrenaline in Vietnam, getting up at three in the morning for a briefing, coming in over the North Vietnamese coast just at sunup, flying for six or seven hours, then coming back in. You couldn't do that day in and day out without wearing yourself thin.

Many times I had taken off in airplanes when I should not have, planes with something mechanically wrong with them, or gone on with a mission because I hated to turn back or abort. I was not a "turnaround" guy, and that could be dangerous. This was information I had to file away in my flight plan, just as much as engine specs or navigation patterns.

Strange things can happen in flying, and a lot of them are the sum of physical discomforts, abuses, and stresses that individually don't seem so great.

We had been concentrating so much on making sure we had the range to fly around the world that we didn't notice the physical burden we were preparing for ourselves. Go more slowly and save, spend another two or three days? Why not? Dodge thunderstorms? No problem. We didn't know—literally—what we were getting ourselves into.

In retrospect, what is surprising is how hard we made it on ourselves, how easily we accepted physical deprivations in planning our own airplane. It was an index of our determination to do this thing—without considering the cost to ourselves.

Somewhere in the rules for setting world aviation records, Burt had found an obscure provision that required the pilots "to survive any record flight by forty-eight hours." Any life expectancy in excess of forty-eight hours, he liked to joke, represented wasted range capability. But before the *Voyager* program was over, there were times when we wondered how much of a joke it really was.

After all the planning given to the airplane itself, we felt that we were something of an afterthought. Originally, remember, we were going to have a roomier, pressurized cabin, and fewer days in the air. But then we had agreed, quite casually, after Burt had come in from a weekend of doing design calculations, that we could live with a smaller cabin and no pressurization. We would spend three more days in flight. In return, we would get an airplane with more range. It was a decision that would come back to nag us many times.

We thought we had designed the cockpit carefully. Long before the airplane was finished, we built a mock-up and practiced moving around in it, to be sure we could really change places and function. Jeana traced the plans out onto plywood, we cut and glued the pieces into a floor and bulkheads, put stringers of one-by-two around it for the cockpit, and worked out the specific placement of the canopy and stick the same way.

We put the seat on the right instead of the left, as in a conventional aircraft. The airplane was a side-stick controller, like jet fighters or the Long EZ, and to leave space for the off-duty pilot, the seat and stick were set close to the right side wall. The throttles were low, and the pilot sat virtually on the floor, in a contoured, articulated seat that tilted up or back. To accommodate my frame the seat was set so low that Jeana had to place both hands on the armrests 10–12 inches higher and lift herself up to see out the canopy.

Between the floor and armrest on the left side of the seat were the throttle and mixture controls for the front engine. The mixture and prop pitch control for the rear engine were behind the pilot's right elbow, and to get to them you had to reach across with your left arm. The control lever for the rear mixture was made extra long for better fidelity—the mixture on that engine would be critical for getting the most out of every pound of fuel. The prop pitch control for the front was forward underneath the pilot's left leg.

We practiced the acrobatics of the change. First, the pilot slipped the seat all the way back, then slid to the left, head to the back. The other crew member climbed over the pilot's legs and into the seat. It was a tough maneuver. After we tried it, Burt took two inches off the sides, added two on top, and moved the center bulkhead four inches back.

Now that it was finished, the cockpit somehow didn't seem as big. We called the space in the back "the hole" or "the cave" or sometimes just plain "hell."

We realized that we had somehow left ourselves nothing to live in but a seven-and-a-half by two-by-two space—a horizontal telephone booth. And with the engines going, that telephone booth felt as if it were being dragged down a cobbled road by a Mack truck with no muffler.

It was a serious problem—to have come all that way and not be sure we could spend the required time in the airplane. There were other factors as well: I was concerned about being able to let go enough to trust Jeana at the controls while I slept, to trust the autopilot, to be able to be ready to wake up in case of emergency, yet also be able to relax enough to sleep.

Inside that cockpit, the biggest problem was noise. We learned on the flight to Oshkosh that we just could not take more than a certain amount of turbulence because it threw us around so much, so we avoided it all we could. But there was no getting away from the noise. After just a few flights, I noticed a soft ringing in my ears that was to remain with me throughout the program—and is there to this day.

The noise added to fatigue. It was debilitating; it's the aural equivalent of those intense lights they shine in prisoners' eyes in the movies when they give them the third degree. In the end, the prisoners always break.

The noise ranged up to 110 decibels, and we had a hell of a time finding anything that could stop it. We tried earplugs and thickly padded headsets, and still it penetrated. When Dick slept, his head was right up against the aft firewall, and the sound came roaring right through the earplugs. I slept with my head the other way, on a sheepskin, but after the coast flight we both experienced temporary hearing loss. For the world flight, we had to be prepared for some permanent loss. There would be parts of the opera we would never appreciate.

We had all sorts of plans in the works for hearing protection, and like so many things in the program, they kept falling through. One person had some sort of conformable foam that fit over the earlobe completely, inside a headset, but that didn't work. Tony Bongiovi of the Power Station, the top recording studio in New York, came out and spent a lot of time carefully mapping the intensity and frequency of the noise; he came up with specifications for helmets to protect us from it. He contacted a number of leading helmet manufacturers, but none of them were willing to fabricate the helmets he'd designed.

But using Tony's model of the noise, we were able to work with the Bose Corporation adapting experimental noise-defeating electronics they'd been developing. This machine was a sine wave generator that registered the shape of sound waves and created waves that canceled them out directly.

Don Rietzke brought the Bose folks in one day, and we tried their machine out in the office beside a big electric fan. You could put your head down beside a running airplane engine, wearing the earphones from this thing, and it seemed as if someone had turned that engine off. We were stunned. "This crazy black box really works!" Dick said. "Sign 'em up, sport!"

The earpieces themselves were lined with a double ring of the same sort of silicone used in breast implants, and they sealed better and felt more comfortable than anything we had tried.

The body adapts to all sorts of things. It's the period of adaptation that is the hardest. The first couple of days on the California coast flight, for instance, were difficult, especially for Dick. He took catnaps in the seat—something we had once vowed was too dangerous—and found that waking up suddenly was like trying to get out of bed and start running right away. And it took Dick nearly three full days to learn to sleep decently in the airplane. After that, we settled into a rhythm that, although it wouldn't have been fun, was at least something we felt we could have kept up indefinitely. It gave us confidence that we could endure the world flight.

* * *

The sense of taste is different at high altitudes. Spicy things, for instance, become too intense, downright repulsive, so the food tended to be fairly bland by ground standards. We selected some of the soup and shake mixes and energy bars prepared by the Shaklee Corporation and also more complete meals from the Yurika Company. These were foil-packed and could sit on the shelf for months or years.

The normal sense of thirst is also thrown off, and it would take us a long time to learn that we had to force ourselves to drink water on long flights. Later, we were to have a stern lesson that brought home what Dr. Jutila had been saying on this subject.

Dr. George Jutila had been an air force flight surgeon, and now he had a practice in Fortuna, California, and spent his few free hours free-diving for the abalone that is the local delicacy. Sometimes he would dive as deep as forty or fifty feet searching for abalone. The hobby had given him prodigious lungs: he had been known to swim underwater around the entire perimeter of a large pool. When he came to Mojave he would cook up abalone chowder for the gang and minister to everyone's miscellaneous ailments. He spent long hours traveling down, pulling his motor home behind the car, and he sacrificed a lot of time and money to be part of the project.

We went to Fortuna in September 1983 to meet him and his family, and he won us over at once: the fact that he had horses on his place did it for Jeana. We got into his car, and right away he said, "If you're a smoker, you can get out right now." We knew we were going to get along just fine.

He had arranged for us to be given a whole series of tests at the UCLA Medical Center to see how we handled altitude and to measure our oxygen consumption. Doc drove us down to UCLA, and the doctors explained the tests. We were to ride stationary bicycles with our noses pinched off and oxygen tubes in our mouths. It was not until we lay down on the exam table that they explained they would be inserting a catheter in an artery near one elbow. Every twenty seconds a valve in the catheter tube would be opened, and blood would squirt directly from the artery into a vial. The doctors tested the blood to see how much of the oxygen we absorbed and simulated higher altitudes by lowering the percentage of oxygen in the air we breathed through the tubes.

The whole scene looked like some exotic torture chamber. We pedaled away, attached to the tubes and the EKG sensors on heart and head, while a bank of multipen sensors wiggled back and forth on two-foot widths of paper, recording the amount of energy we expended, our respiratory rates, pulse, and blood pressure, and the amounts of oxygen we breathed in and carbon dioxide we breathed out. The technicians had blood all over their white coats.

We learned that as you fatigue your blood gets to a point where it can no longer carry the amount of oxygen your body requires from the lungs to the tissues, no matter how deeply you breathe. You go into oxygen debt, and the body begins scrounging energy from other tissues.

They pushed us to exhaustion, and they did it again and again, every two hours, four or five times a day for two days. In front of you on the bicycle was an ergometer gauge, and you had to keep pedaling so that you kept the needle of that gauge at a fixed point. When you got so exhausted you couldn't do that, you were supposed to warn them about thirty seconds in advance. But when you did they'd say, "Keep going! Keep going! A little bit more!" to make sure they had worn you absolutely out. And then you slumped down over the bike. Then they would take the last blood sample.

The first day went all right, but on the second day the head physician himself was on the scene to put the needles and catheters in. The old pro! Well, he's the last guy you want doing something like that. The person you want is a nurse who does it all the time.

The doctor deadened the arm with Novocain first and then began to probe with the catheter needle—and probe and probe. He couldn't find the artery, and he kept complaining about the quality of the needle, and he kept probing.

And the needle hit a major nerve in my arm—the Velvet Arm! It felt as if it had been plunged into a fiery furnace, or run over and crushed by a truck, and the middle two fingers were numb and paralyzed. Every time I moved my elbow the nerves would scrape and I would grab my hand in pain.

That scared me, and I walked around for a couple of months with my arm elevated. If I straightened it out, the burning pain came back in my hand. Finally it began to feel almost normal again, but the fingers have never been quite as mobile since.

We had already learned something about what can happen without enough oxygen. In September of 1981, when we were first starting out with the program, we went to the altitude chamber at Edwards. Inside, the atmosphere was lowered to the equivalent of 25,000 feet in a mild rapid decompression. The idea was to familiarize us with the symptoms of hypoxia.

It hit me first, after about five minutes. Jeana was still fine, but I began to feel warm and stuffy, there was a strange feeling about my skin, and my mind grew lazy; I found the number test difficult. My vision dimmed, and I felt sleepy. Jeana fared better.

It took me awhile longer—the tests showed that I needed only about half as much oxygen as Dick.

That, and the flight to Oshkosh, combined to impress on us the need for a good oxygen system. But finding one that would be light enough for our purposes proved incredibly difficult. We must have followed up about ten different leads before Dr. Sidney White, an expert on high-altitude medicine, showed us a "demand oxygen controller," or DOC system, that was light and dependable enough. It used canulas—nose feeder tubes—that released oxygen with each breath instead of in a steady stream. The mechanism adjusted itself to the individual rate of breathing. There was a light that showed when each pulse of oxygen was released; watching it, you felt almost like Pavlov's dog, automatically breathing when it flashed. This conserved the supply, so we were able to carry three and a half to four days' worth of oxygen, compressed in a small tank to an extreme pressure of about three thousand pounds per square inch. This required a special tank, provided by Ron Richelieu of Structural Composites. These were the best around—they are used by NASA and in the manned maneuvering units astronauts strap on to take space walks—and we went to the plant to see them produced and were impressed by their testing and quality control procedures.

The tanks were rated for 1,850 psi, but we saw as we walked through the plant that they were periodically tested to 3,000 psi and did not burst until the pressure hit 5,000 psi. It was illegal to fill them so high, but we filled ours as much as we legally could, then rented smaller high-pressure bottles and illegally repressurized them to 3,000 psi. The whole system only weighed about twenty pounds.

We tested the DOC system by taking a turbo-powered airplane Dr. White had rented up to 25,000 feet. He figured out the amount of oxygen each of us would need at a given altitude. We had a device called a Biox IV that measured the amount of oxygen in our blood by detecting the color of blood passing through the fingers. At each altitude we decreased the amount of oxygen until the blood saturation level dropped to 78 percent of normal—the level Dr. Jutila had defined as acceptable. I was in pretty good shape when the level reached 78 but I could tell hypoxia was coming on. Jeana never dropped below 88 percent. The tests showed that her body used oxygen extremely efficiently and Dr. White took to referring to her as "a little dynamo." From these experiments the doctors drew up a chart of the oxygen flows we should use at each altitude for us to carry along in the checklist book on the world flight. The only problem was that we did the tests at a time when we were well rested, well fed, and healthy— something that was to have serious consequences later over Africa.

. . .

The first question we always got asked was, "How do you plan to go to the bathroom up there, yuck, yuck?" After a while we began every one of our talks by holding up one of the fecal containment bags that Dr. Jutila had gotten for us.

The bags were of the same sort used in hospitals and in the Gemini space program, with a peel-off tape covering adhesive to attach them to your buttocks with a seal. You stick it on, go, then remove it.

We planned to drop these out a little door in the bottom of the cockpit. We tested this system using very ripe bananas, to be sure the bags would drop clear of the rear prop. We would throttle the front engine back as much as possible to reduce the slipstream that might push the bags back into the rear prop. We wondered what people out walking in the desert might think if they came upon these plastic bags with bananas in them.

The system worked fine with bananas, but when we tried it with the real thing, the results were not so good. We hadn't figured on the toilet paper. The bags would barely fit through the drop door. And they were so light that they might blow back into the prop. The stuff came awfully close to hitting the fan.

So, unpleasant as it was, we finally decided that we would have to stow the waste on board. We reserved one of the compartments in the right main wing root for the purpose.

. . .

To be prepared for a parachute landing in the ocean or a ditching, I took an air force survival course similar to one Dick had years ago when he was in the service. Dick has always been something of a survival nut—in the air force he took every possible course they had on the subject—and we had to go all the way to the secretary of the air force to get an okay for me to join this program. The air force told us, yes, civilians could take the course, but only on payment of a fee that was way beyond our budget. And no one in uniform had the power to waive the fee; it took the direct intervention of Secretary Vernon Orr to do it, and he agreed.

I loved the course, three days at Homestead Air Force Base in Florida and a series of exercises that were like a grand amusement park.

We had to traverse an obstacle course, swim under a parachute canopy spread on water, and make simulated parachute landings from a tower into a pond. I learned how to turn a life raft upright and get in, and how to use all sorts of rescue equipment—smoke flares, pen light, signaling dye. Then we went out to sea. I hung from a beam extended from the boat, learning proper body position for releasing myself from the parachute harness. And I learned all sorts of interesting facts I hoped I would never have to remember.

The highlight was riding the parasail—half kite, half parachute—to simulate a parachute landing. They put an old football-type helmet on my head. As the boat towing me started off I shot straight up into the sky. It was grand sailing along up there and I wanted them never to let me down. When they did, I made a good landing.

The group all clapped after each of us made his or her drop. The course was run very much on a "buddy" ethic—"help your buddy"—and it gave me an insight into something I was unfamiliar with, the sort of military group bonding Dick had spent his life with. And I also ended up understanding Dick better, and how feelings of camaraderie could lie under a lot of bluster and seeming toughness.

The course gave me some assurance I could handle any of the flight's what-ifs: What if we had to bail out? What if Dick and I were separated? What if Dick were injured or killed?

. . .

In Manley Butler, of China Lake, California, we were lucky to find a man who was just as fanatic about weight reduction as we had become. Manley put together our parachutes and survival gear—all of which came out weighing less than thirty-two pounds—about a third the weight of conventional gear.

The harnesses were custom-fitted to each of our bodies, and the parachutes were especially designed, with extra-small canopies sized to our body weights. Dick's weighed just over nine pounds, mine only seven! We would not have to wear the chutes all the time. We kept our harnesses on, and the chutes and accompanying survival pack, containing such items as flares, signaling mirror, flashlight, knife, life vest, and raft—and money, passports, and MasterCards—stood ready to be clipped onto the harness in a matter of seconds.

The chutes didn't even have a ripcord or a pilot chute. Instead there was a red tag, held down by Velcro, that you pulled to tug the chute out, and then you had to unfurl the canopy by hand to catch the airstream.

The life raft was a navy model, which turned out to weigh a third as much as the air force one. I would carry an ELT rescue beacon, while Dick carried a SARSAT beacon, an experimental 406-megacycle beeper whose coded signal would be picked up by any of two Russian or three U.S. satellites. The code would identify the specific beeper immediately as belonging to *Voyager*, and if they heard it, rescuers would contact our mission control and launch a rescue. We tested this many times on the ground, and it worked perfectly.

Still, it would be a hairy deal if we ever did have to get out of the aircraft quickly, and Dick worried about it. It was going to be particularly hard for the off-duty pilot. The plan called for Dick to go first, which he didn't like at all. When he envisioned escape scenarios, he imagined that in fact he would have to try to reach back and physically hurl me up and out.

And if we did end up in the water, we couldn't last long there. We didn't rate our chances of surviving a ditching as even fifty-fifty. The gear we had was rescue gear, not survival gear. The only way we would make it would be if someone found us—fast. We did not carry any water. We figured we could survive for forty-eight hours without it, and we told them back in mission control if you don't find us within forty-eight hours, forget it, we're gone.

. . .

Everyone was telling us we should practice living in the cockpit. But there wasn't much you could do for practice. It would never be comfortable, and it would never be anywhere we wanted to spend more than the minimum amount of time. Living in the cockpit, Dick would say, was like going to the dentist—and how do you practice going to the dentist?

A group of NASA scientists at Ames Research Center volunteered their advice on adjusting our circadian rhythms. We would have to reset our body clocks, they explained. We should probably aim for a six-hour day, offset from each other. That fit in well with our normal working modes— I had always been a night person, while Dick worked best during the day. We made careful plans to reset our circadian rhythms to what John Lauber, one of the NASA scientists, said was called "the local social environment," and we hoped to take several days before the flight to adjust to the schedule.

That was a joke. There was no way we could do it. The problem was that we were not only pilots, we were administrators and everything else in the program. We didn't have the luxury of taking time to adjust our body clocks.

. . .

We knew we had to give ourselves a break every now and then if we were to keep going. But even when we took a holiday, crises seemed to come up.

Flying the Long EZ one day, we had noticed a couple of remote lakes behind Mount Whitney, a lovely place near Horseshoe Meadows, eight or nine thousand feet up in the Sierras, where we felt sure few hikers ever visited.

We both loved backpacking—all of it, Dick said, except for carrying the packs on our backs—so we thought it would be great to take some horses up to those lakes. I borrowed two horses to carry our equipment, and we set out with them in a trailer.

We had taken some photographs from the air and used them instead of a map to find our way up there. The only problem was that the pictures didn't show the trails or how rough they were, and on our second day we found ourselves around noon in a very rocky area leading the horses along a trail that was really too rugged for them. It ran along the side of a steep ravine with water at the bottom.

Dick was trying to pull his horse up the trail when it got confused and Dick let go. She rolled over twice on jagged rocks and ended up in front of me. Dick didn't know what else to do. He just looked at me and then let go of the horse.

Dick could see right away there was a major gash on her right flank, two or three inches deep and eight inches long. We knew right away our vacation was over.

I knew that the only way to save the horse's life was to get her down the mountain before she became lame, so we packed all our equipment on the other horse and headed down. We stopped at a little meadow with running water to look at the injured horse. The meadow was teeming with mosquitoes, and the horse turned almost black with them. I tried to sew the horse up with a needle and thread, but the skin was too thick; I was able to get one stitch in, but the horse naturally wouldn't hold still for any more. So all we could do was dissolve a bottle of iodine tablets in water for disinfectant and flush the wound.

To get back by nightfall we were practically running downhill. It was so exhausting that about a mile from the car Dick started throwing up beside the trail. "Boy, horse," he said, "I sure hope you appreciate this."

We loaded the horses in the trailer just as it got dark and made it back to Mojave about midnight. We couldn't find a vet until the next morning, and it was too late to sew up the gash. The vet just gave her antibiotics. The horse would end up with a bad scar, but she was alive. And we went back to work more exhausted than before our vacation.

. . .

We had always joked that after we got out of the airplane after eleven or twelve days together in the tiny cockpit, we might not ever want to see each other again. But the joke wasn't sounding very funny anymore: tensions were developing between us long before we got off the ground to fly around the world.

We had both always believed and continued to believe to the end that no other team could do this flight. As many conflicts as we had with Burt, we had looked at our relationship with him the same way: fight as much as we did, what came out of it was something we couldn't imagine other people being able to accomplish.

We knew each other's strengths and weaknesses. We had flown many hours together, and we had come through many crises. But that didn't mean it was easy.

The project left us no time for anything else. It was not just Dick and Jeana, it was "Rutan and Yeager, Voyager pilots." The trips we had taken together in the early days of the program, the adventures we'd had, were all in the past. There was little time for any of that now.

Our roles as Voyager pilots—and manager and engineer and fundraiser and shop boss—all took over from everything else.

We didn't have time for ourselves. We rarely sat down to a meal together anyplace, and when we did it was never at home. There were many days when we barely saw each other. Dick would be in the hangar working on the airplane all day and then again, on a sort of second shift, when the volunteers came in after their regular jobs ended. But still he would get home before me. I was at my desk until two or three in the morning almost every day—and back by eight the next morning. I had always been a night person. I had never needed much sleep, and now with people coming in and the telephone ringing constantly during the day, I needed the quiet night hours to deal with the masses of paperwork that grew larger as the program went along. We were running a corporation and a retail operation and a fund-raising drive as well as an aviation research and development program. These were my special provinces, and Dick never got involved with them.

. . .

The hardest thing was that I realized, despite all the difficulties, I still adored her. I was jealous of the time she spent in the office—or with her horse, Gem, her few hours of relaxation. I realized I had lost her completely.

I also saw that the demands of running the office were taking Jeana away from flying.

One night Doc Jutila was arriving by commercial plane at Ontario Airport. Somebody had to fly down and pick him up.

"Take the Sierra and go get the doc," I said to Jeana. "You need the time to work on your skills."

"No," she told me. "I've got too many things to do around here."

"Go get him," I said, and walked away.

When I came back an hour later, Jeana had not gone. Bruce and Glenn went instead, and she was working in the office.

"Why didn't you go get the doctor?" I asked.

"I had other things to do," she replied, and went on with her work. It was a standoff.

. . .

I began to perceive Dick as a burden that I had to bear through the program. I felt there was a softer, more sensitive side to Dick. In the first days after we met, he was more gentle and solicitous. Now I hardly see that side of him at all.

More and more I was aware of his limitations—the cowboy pilot side of him, bold and daring but also short on patience, often as impulsive as an adolescent.

Many times, I felt, his frustrations with delays and problems, the slow pace of things, his frustration with and fear of the airplane, were shifted to me: he would blame me for things, nag me to train harder or learn some system. In the cockpit he would yell at me if he thought I had made a mistake running the UHF radio or the oil system.

But I did not know what else to do except put up with him. We were the agents of this thing, the tools. It was for everyone, for the people. We didn't have any choice about it anymore.

I felt more and more that I was the mother to this project, the main force keeping it going. I had never stopped short of finishing anything before, and I wasn't about to now.

I would have left if I could, but I had made a commitment. People were depending on me. People had faith in *Voyager*.

. . .

The strain showed to others as well. We had always teased each other, but it was affectionate and playful. The teasing served to discharge any competitive tension we felt then, but now the teasing stopped working that way. It took on a hard edge.

One night after supper in the hangar Dick grabbed me around the waist. I tried to shake his hands loose. We got into a wrestling match. Once, it would have been playful, like a couple of kids, but now we started in earnest, and Dick was surprised at the bitter force he felt from me. And while he was amazed thinking about this, too amazed to bring his own strength into play, I got astride his chest and pinned him on the concrete floor.

"Next!" Dick said once he'd gotten up, as if he had won and was ready for the next challenger. The others of the team, finishing their suppers after a long day of work in the hangar, felt embarrassed at what they had witnessed.

That episode hurt us badly. But there was no time to deal with it. The project was going on at such a pace that personal things were not allowed. They were there and they hurt, but there was nothing we could do about them.

Jeana and I were now two methodical individual air crew members. There was harmony and coordination, but it was a matter of her doing her job and me doing mine. There was no personal feeling to it, with the exception of a few occasions of crisis or extreme stress when I would get so down about the airplane and my fear of it that she would jump in with her intensity and determination and the force that kept driving the project. She never considerd quitting or failure even as words in her vocabulary. She simply would not accept the possibility, which I thought was very real, that for all our best efforts, it just might not be possible to complete this project. Her makeup did not allow any doubt. And I knew that was the same quality that kept her from forgetting and forgiving old hurts.

. . . .

We were still "partners, in the air and on the ground." We hadn't hidden the fact that we lived together, either. Now the partnership was easier in the air than it was on the ground. But it was far from smooth even in the air.

The problem that grew from this strain endangered our ability to make the world flight successful. Neither of us knew how to resolve it satisfactorily. The technical factors could be worked out, fixed, tweaked. The human factors were much harder.

Neither of us ever forgot that the airplane was fundamentally unsafe. We always talked proudly about how its construction made it essentially a flying fuel tank, but it was also a flying bomb. The electrical system was full of gremlins and mysteries. Strange arcs of static electricity would show up every now and then, and plumes of smoke, and fuel smells.

This is an airplane that human beings should really not try to fly, Dick thought. This is an airplane that should only be flown by black boxes, by electronics, or not at all.

Dick pressed me to spend more time training. "You've got to get out of the office and do some flying. You're losing your proficiency and sharpness."

He felt I was being stubborn—and I was the first to admit I was by nature stubborn—in refusing to learn.

But he was not the teacher I needed.

I felt he was trying to force me out of the program so he would be off the hook and able to satisfy his pride. He was venting his anger and frustration and fear on me. He was looking for a way out.

Dick had no patience. Maybe it was a legacy of the military, but in training he left no room for human feelings. He was always bullying, not explaining. He jumped from one thing to another, and he thought he had told me things when he hadn't. I had to read his mind. It was like trying to teach somebody to read by taking a pile of alphabet blocks, pulling one out and then another, and expecting it all to make sense.

For one thing, the instrument panel kept changing practically every day with new modifications—Dick's modifications. And I became gun-shy: it was hard to concentrate if you knew you were going to be yelled at.

He got more and more frightened and more and more angry. But his anger rarely showed up in flight. And I made sure that we went through our preflight briefings and postflight debriefings so that he could work out his feelings with an audience he could command.

After a while he gave up on the training, too, and we would just go through the motions. We would go out to the plane for him to describe some system to me, but then he would get distracted by something else in the hangar and go off and not come back.

. . .

I was frustrated she would not train. I begged and pleaded, but she wouldn't even discuss it.

So I wrote her a formal letter, partner to partner, pilot to pilot, urging her to work on her flying. Your lack of training, I wrote, puts too much of a load on me, and I don't deserve it. You are endangering both of us and the program. I even threatened to find another pilot to fly around the world. In fact, I realized she was irreplaceable, and the mission could not be done without her, but what I wanted was to shock her into the realization that she needed to do more training.

Peter Lert of *Air Progress* magazine mentioned that there were air ferry services whose pilots delivered airplanes to owners or dealers in Australia. I thought that riding along on a trip like that would be good training for Jeana.

Jeana had always had a problem talking on the radio, and I thought this would be a good way for her to get experience in doing that as well as sharpen up her instrument skills. A pilot who flew across the Pacific frequently could also teach her about winds and weather and how to read the clouds. More important, she could learn the names and frequencies of the air traffic control facilities along the way.

We contacted two ferry companies, and soon one of them called up saying that he had a twin engine going to Australia, a seat was open, and she was welcome.

She made the trip and on the way felt that she learned a good deal about the clouds and winds; among other things, they ran through a major typhoon going into Australia.

She stayed a few days, until we finally talked Qantas into providing her a seat home.

But when she got back I found that she had made no attempt to talk on the radio and had learned little about the radar or air traffic control system. As far as I was concerned, the trip had been totally useless.

When it became obvious that I was not going to be able to train her, for her own credibility as a pilot we sent her for instrument and multiengine training with Beech in Wichita, Kansas, where she spent several weeks and got those ratings. I took Mike Melvill along on one test flight of the *Voyager* while she was gone.

The whole team was in on the need to help lighten Jeana's work load and get her more flying time. Peter Riva's wife, Sandy, for instance, would phone when Jeana was the only one around and say she needed Peter home in Tehachapi right away, and Jeana would fly him up in the Beech Sierra.

.   .   .   .

The pitch porpoise problem was the focus of the crisis, the point where all the other strains seemed to come together.

I felt I could learn to handle the oscillations. Dick would never lie there quietly and let me learn, but I knew I could do it. I was sure I could train to do it, but I was also sure that Dick could not be the one to train me. But who else was there?

As much as I urged Jeana to take time to train and learn the aircraft systems, I didn't feel I had the time or the guts to train her to handle the big problem. I was not sure I could sit and watch her oscillate the airplane through the pitch porpoise.

We did try a few times to train on the pitch porpoise problem. In the early summer of 1985 we set up a clip-on second or helper stick, set up behind the seat. I had to reach around behind the seat to grasp the second stick. It was awkward, and I was concerned about how hard it would be if she could not control a pitch oscillation and I had to try to stop it. If it went one more oscillation, I might be floating in the cockpit and unable to do it.

One of those times, she was trying to fly the airplane with the oscillations when she got scared and wanted to get out of the seat. I looked into her eyes and saw a distinct fear. It was the first time I had ever seen her scared of the airplane, and I knew she didn't think she could handle it. I knew then I would be spending a long time in the seat on the world flight.

.   .   .

Because Dick was frightened lying on his stomach, unable to reach the controls, he was irritable and impatient with my every move. So the end was a stalemate. We reconciled ourselves to the reality—the reality of our personalities, our strengths and weaknesses, the reality of the human factors.

I knew that unless the pitch porpoising could be controlled, Dick could not be comfortable out of the seat until the weight and speed of the airplane dropped below the danger zone. And that would not be for at least three days. Remember, we would slow down as the flight went on and more fuel was burned. It would take at least that long to get below eighty-two knots, the point above which the airplane was vulnerable to the worst oscillations.

Bruce, Glenn, Doug, and the others on the ground could not accept this, and Dick felt that none of them, not even Bruce Evans, really understood the magnitude of the problem.

They provided me with consolation—a shoulder, a hug, when I got frustrated. And they kept urging Dick to let me get some training at the heavier weights on the pitch porpoise.

"How can you practice what you have to do right the first time?" he would reply. "It's like trying to verbally teach somebody on the ground who's never done it before to land an airplane. It just can't be done."

Doug Shane kept after Dick right up to the end. On one of the last test flights he repeated his suggestion, and Dick got very angry. "Comment noted, Doug. End of discussion. I don't ever want you to bring up the subject again."

. . .

I knew that Dick was a rare and superb pilot, that he had skills even he was not conscious of, skills that came to the fore automatically when some critical situation called for them. And I knew that every one of them would likely be called for. This airplane was like an only partly tamed animal, and its wild side could emerge at any moment. It never allowed you to relax.

So we both reconciled ourselves to the fact that Dick would spend the first three days of the flight in the seat, ready to take over if the autopilot failed, and all that was required of me was to help Dick keep going, to maintain his spirits and his confidence as well as the aircraft.

It meant I would have to watch him like a hawk, watch for fatigue, watch the systems, watch for mistakes, and do it all from that awkward twisted position in the cockpit. Dick would be flying the airplane, and I would be flying him.

It wasn't the best way, and it was a dangerous way, but it had become the only way.

The Inside of a Cow

By the late spring of 1986 we felt we had just about wrestled out all the alligators in the engines and avionics. Larry Caskey had almost finished setting up the mission control center. We had our food and survival equipment in place. Now all we had to do was learn to live inside the airplane. It was time to fly overnight.

It turned out to be a hell of a lot harder than we expected.

Before our first overnight flight, Jeana had her long hair cut. She didn't like to have to do it, but inside *Voyager* long hair could be a hazard. It might get caught in one of the open control cable tracks. With the static energy of the cockpit, it tended to float around. And for flights of several days, cleaning it would be difficult.

As the nearly waist-length locks fell to the floor, I watched.

I had always joked with Jeana that cutting her hair would save us fuel, and she replied by suggesting we trim down my long nose. But now, although I hammed around, putting a great swatch under my nose like a Pancho Villa mustache, seeing the hair cut bothered me. It touched the deep feeling I had for her. It felt as if, by losing that beautiful long hair I loved so much, a part of the old girl was lost and gone forever, that another part of our relationship had been taken away, and I couldn't help feeling that it was very sad.

It took Jeana awhile to get used to it. For days afterward she would feel the imagined weight of her hair and reach up to push it off her shoulder.

There is no way to fly at night without some sort of horizon, and the question was whether we could do the job just using the instrument horizon. Bruce suddenly wondered if we could even fly the airplane in the dark.

I hadn't thought of it that way, and the idea disturbed me.

Maybe, I thought, the only way I've been able to correct that pitching at all has been by some sort of subconscious clues—the kinesthetic cues of the bucking up and down you feel in the seat of your pants, the visual cues of the wings going up and down. These might be essential to handling *Voyager* and especially the pitch porpoising. In the dark, with my vision reduced from a 180-degree panorama to a little deck-angle gauge, and the attitude indicator in a little three-and-a-half-inch hole in the instrument panel, I might not be able to control the plane.

To find the answer, we arranged crude blackout curtains—big sheets of black paper taped to the canopy and windows. It was like Jimmy Doolittle's first instrument flying experiments—if we couldn't fly on instruments, we'd quickly reach up and tear the paper off.

We pasted up the curtains, turned up the cockpit lights, and simulated nighttime. I disconnected the autopilot and started to hand-fly the airplane on instruments for about five or ten minutes. That was no problem.

Now it was time to try the pitch porpoise. This was like Russian roulette—if we could not control the oscillations in the dark, then we had to come up with a live chamber. We were ready to bail out.

"Okay, this is it," I told Jeana. She put her hands on the two left window screens, ready to tear them away, and I peeled off just a quarter of the paper on my right window.

We looked at each other again.

I gave it a little pitch input, elevator down, then up, and I knew it would go into its oscillations. I let go of the stick, and we could feel the pressure of the motion in our seats. And now I grabbed the stick and attempted to stop it—and I found I could, easily!

We looked at each other with a big sigh of relief. I did it again, two or three times, with no problem. "Piece of pie, babe," I radioed Bruce. "I can really do it."

There had been a lot of rough steps on this ladder, and this may have been the big one. But we got through it pretty easily.

We felt good that we had achieved this plateau. We peeled the window curtains off, and as the sun went down we felt a little more confident.

Our first three tries at sleeping overnight were failures. We kept coming up with various little technical problems, and Dick realized that they were more excuses for not flying at night than anything else. Once, we realized, with some embarrassment, that we weren't sure we had enough oil on board. If we ran out in the middle of the night, we might have to make a landing in the dark—something we had never done and never wanted to do. We finally pressed on, deciding we could make an emergency landing on the illuminated airport at Bakersfield if we needed to.

It was getting ridiculous. We were talking about spending eleven or twelve days in this thing, and after three tries Dick still hadn't been able to sleep.

I had learned to sleep in the back, but only lightly and never comfortably or deeply. And never without occasionally opening my eyes to check the instruments and see whether the movements of Dick's arm were getting jerky. That was a sign of trouble. I had learned to let go and accept where I was—it was something I had begun to teach myself on the torturous flight to Oshkosh.

I lay with my head at the bulkhead, so I could see Dick, or sometimes curled up completely in back. I would lie on my side with the headset uncomfortably pressed to the floor and shift sides every now and then.

Even when the autopilot was working fine and the air was smooth, even right in the seat, with Jeana hovering by the panel, taking care of everything, I could not sleep.

All my experience with flying at night had required me to stay awake, and now I had to undo that training to sleep in the seat. Flying the Long EZ down from Alaska, flying it on the closed-circuit course near Mojave, all those hours had been conditioning in staying awake.

What is involved is letting go, trusting, feeling that you are safe. And the process involves working the mind down through several levels of resistance to sleep.

At first there is a psychomotor level. Your inner ear tries to persuade you that the airplane is rolling. You feel motion—"There is ten degrees of bank, twenty, thirty"—and your eyes pop open, and you grab the stick. After several episodes like this, I would get mad and tell myself, I'm absolutely not going to open my eyes, and shake my head to disturb my inner ear, to remove the signals it was giving my brain. Then I would feel the motion and resist it and resist it, and finally I couldn't hold out any longer. It was like a game of chicken; I told myself that whatever happened I wasn't going to open my eyes—but then I always did.

Finally after fifteen or twenty minutes you assure yourself that the airplane is stable, and you get down to the aural level—you start to hear things with the engines. Gee, that sounds like a main bearing. Is that a mag? Wow, isn't the prop surging? And then I would jump back up again and say, "Jeana, is everything working okay?" And of course it was.

The lowest level is one of simple belief in your safety. If you are hanging over a cliff on the end of a fraying rope, there is no way you are going to sleep, however tired you are.

And when I had finally convinced myself that I was safe, the airplane was stable, the engines were working fine, then I would lie back and doze—until my tongue fell back and blocked my windpipe and I woke up, breathless.

And I never did really sleep.

The ground crew was getting exasperated with us. Bruce threatened to advertise the airplane for sale: "one owner, low mileage, always hangared."

But under pressure of time, we decided to go ahead with our big closed-course flight without having conquered the sleep problem. Things were dragging on, and we all needed to see some progress. Dick's birthday was coming up, and everyone in the hangar got together and signed a card for him that showed a bedraggled bird in flying gear. "*Voyager*, not just an adventure but a career," Bruce Evans wrote above his signature. Dick thought of the program then as being as droopy as that cartoon bird.

We were up late into the night working on the plane, stowing food and equipment, before the scheduled test flight number 46, the California coast flight. We spent a restless night. It was still dark on the morning of July 8 when we got to the hangar.

We planned to fly four and a half days on a circuit from a point twenty miles off the coast near San Luis Obispo to Stewart's Point, a point at sea northwest of San Francisco. We explained to everyone that this was first of all a test flight, and we would remain within reach of good airports and close enough to Mojave to get back for repairs if needed. But if all went well, we could also break the closed-course distance record that the B-52H had set in 1962. Twenty laps around the points would do it.

There was a lot of satisfaction to be had in breaking that record. To show that a home-built composite plane could do something that one of the largest and most powerful metal planes couldn't.

Finally, we were doing something with this crazy airplane that had cost us so much time and toil. And we were facing the big test: to learn if we could live inside it for day after day. If we couldn't, then the program was at an end, and, as I quietly told everyone in the hangar, "This may be the only record attempt we ever make."

The airport beacon on Mojave tower swept its beam of light through the night. It was windier and gustier even than usual for Mojave. Flags were beating against their poles. Somewhere back toward town, a rooster crowed.

I felt very up and kept flexing my biceps in the best Velvet Arm mode—a bit of macho completely defused by an ungainly costume composed of sweat pants and a Voyager T-shirt, sunglasses, and a King Radio cap.

The thing I noticed was all the new video equipment in the hangar, cameras and these tremendous monitors that showed the weather pictures from the D-WIPS processors. And the press: we had dozens of TV, radio, and print reporters. We were finally getting some attention from the outside world. We were being taken seriously. It felt good and a little strange.

Bruce and the crew had looked the plane over very carefully and fueled it up the night before, to just under half the planned world flight fuel load, and none of us had gotten much sleep. Now, Pop Rutan began wiping the plane down affectionately with a cloth, and Burt came by. He walked around Voyager, surveying everything, checking out the airplane he had designed with a proprietary air.

Before the plane was rolled out, we all got together in a huddle, football style—the ground crew, the mission control people, the pilots. Everyone had his or her official Wear-Guard uniform now, navy blue with patches and names sewn on so we had at least the veneer of a pretty crack outfit.

Rich Hanson, the official from the National Aeronautical Association, arrived wearing a red tropical tourist shirt covered with bright feather shapes, a big shirt because he was a big guy, a casual outfit for an official. He would be supervising the seals on the fuel caps and the barograph to certify the record. Radar from Los Angeles and Oakland air control centers would be verifying our turnpoints, using prearranged squawk codes.

We were both excited and a little nervous, and the adrenaline was going already. There was a lot of hugging and handshaking, soaking in the support from all our friends to carry us through the four days ahead. Still, it felt like another test flight.

As we got the airplane ready for takeoff, we could see a whole troop of reporters and photographers move down the runway, some in cars, some on foot, in an assemblage that looked like a demonstration of some kind and led by Peter like the Pied Piper.

The wind was stiff, coming across runway 30, and we took off toward the north, aiming right at the Tehachapis. Burt was quite concerned about the crosswind, but I knew that, thanks to its slim profile and small rudder, Voyager is less vulnerable to crosswinds than a standard airplane. Still, I

1. Some of Burt Rutan's airplane designs

2. Burt Rutan's house, 1982. *Left to right*: Burt, Sally Melvill, Mike Melvill, Jeana and Dick

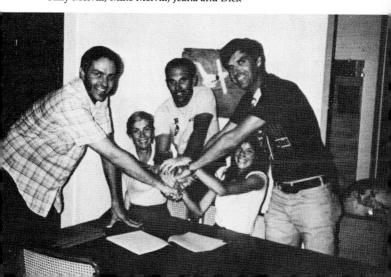

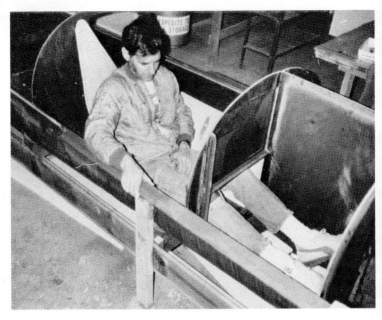

3. Dick in the mock-up of the *Voyager* cockpit

4. *Voyager*, after more than two years work

5. *Voyager* made sixty-seven test flights
before flying around the world

6. Jeana and Dick
testing the demand oxygen controller system

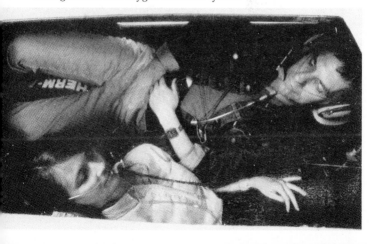

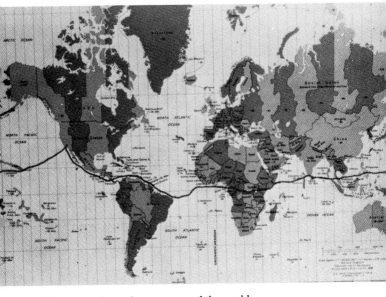

7. *Voyager*'s planned course around the world

8. Jeana packing for the world flight

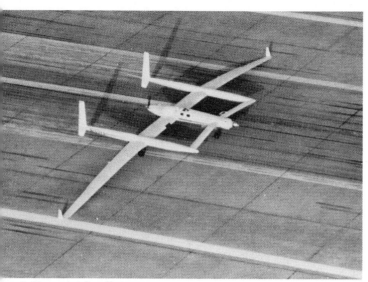

9. *Voyager*'s take off run
   with the wing tips scraping the ground

10. The wing tips were ground away so far
    that the winglets were just barely hanging on

11. The fifth day of the flight.
    Dick's beard made him look like an outlaw

12. In the radio room. *Left to right*: Stu Hagedorn,
    Conway Roberts, Mike Melvill, Burt Rutan and Len Snellman

13. Burt and Mike and Sally Melvill meet us in the red-and-white Duchess

14. We couldn't believe how many people were lined up on the dry lake

15. Burt, Jeana and Dick are presented
    with the Presidential Citizens Medal

16. Burt, Jeana and Dick

started off way over to one side of the runway and angled across with the wind.

To those on the ground who had never seen *Voyager* take off, the sensation that the airplane was flapping those wings was inescapable. And even those who had seen a number of takeoffs thought the flapping much more than usual.

The airplane seemed to be heading straight for the mountains. In fact, of course, the mountains were far away, but the perspective of the desert and that big sky made them seem much closer.

We couldn't see the people lining the runway, only the wings working up and down. As we turned, there was a distinct rippling of the right wing. The thermals were so localized that the right wing was in one and the left was not.

We turned, swung around over Mojave, and headed west to the course. Most of the press people cleared out, and the hangar was quiet again. And as far as everyone knew, all was going well.

In fact, it began as a very tough flight. The autopilot computer was overheating; when it ran too long and got too warm, it would hunt up and down for the proper orientation. We would have to shut it off for a few minutes until it cooled. Stan Magnuson of King was already figuring out a fix, so we weren't worried, but flying without the autopilot increased the work load by about ten times.

Then, at about three o'clock, when were just completing the first lap by the south end of the course, in long-distance cruise configuration with the front engine off, I was about to turn the plane over to Jeana when I noticed a slight increase in RPM. The rear prop was slowly speeding up.

I reached over to the electric RPM switch and turned it down. Nothing happened. I turned it again and again. But not only were the RPMs not going down, they were creeping up. The pitch of the propeller was gradually going flat and no longer biting into the air.

"Something's wrong in the electronics," I told Jeana. But this wasn't supposed to be able to happen. The electric motor changed the prop blade angle with a screw-jack sort of mechanism. If the motor wasn't driving that mechanism, it was supposed to lock. How the hell could it go backward?

To try to stop it, I flipped the emergency override, a special switch that puts full energy directly to the prop pitch motor; its circuit breaker blew immediately. I waited about ten seconds, reset the circuit breaker, and flipped it again. Once again it blew.

The pitch of the propeller was completely flat now, and the prop was out of control, running wild. The back engine was at hard idle but running at the red line, overrevving. "How can this happen?" I asked Jeana, who was up by my shoulder now, and I pointed to the RPMs. It was like shifting into low at sixty miles an hour—no engine likes that kind of treatment.

Now, with no thrust, I had to disconnect the autopilot and push the nose over to keep from stalling. We were going downhill, with the back prop producing no thrust, just a spinning disk dragging behind us.

The front engine had to start.

That was no simple job. Jeana pulled out the checklist, and we began to go down the procedures. We powered down the avionics and lights. I unfeathered the front engine, which took a minute and a half, with my left hand on the unfeather button and my right hand flying the plane. We had to do about eight things to start that engine, and we ran down them— carburetor boost pump on, mags on, cowl doors open, mixture to full rich. Then I primed the engine, pumping the throttle four long strokes with my left hand, let go of the stick with my right, and pushed the starter button. The engine turned over once, turned again, and then—caught.

We gave it a couple of minutes to warm up and then pushed it gradually up to full throttle. We powered back up, and Jeana watched to be sure the oil temperatures came up normally in the engine compartment. But even at full power we could not maintain level flight with the front engine by itself. We were coming out of the sky.

And then I thought of something Burt told me. He had found in testing the Defiant, an earlier two-engine push-me-pull-you design, that you just can't maintain level flight with the rear engine windmilling. Trying to fly with that spinning prop was like dragging a huge solid disc behind you. The slipstream of the front engine runs right into that rear prop and creates all kinds of drag. You have to be able to feather or stop the rear prop to fly on the front engine.

So we had to stop that back engine from windmilling. I reached back to the aft engine mixture control and pulled it into idle cutoff to shut off all the fuel, with almost no effect. It was the slipstream of the front making the back prop windmill, and the first thing we had to do was reduce that slipstream. I pulled the throttle on the front engine back to idle, right on the ragged edge of a stall, and slowly pulled the nose of the airplane up. We'd never tried to fly the airplane this slowly before, and we didn't know how it would handle—we could get some odd pitch problem—and I just hoped I could keep control.

It seemed to take forever, but finally, with agonizing slowness, that prop slowed down and stopped windmilling. Now we pushed the nose over again. "Don't start again," I begged it. If the back started windmilling again on its own, we'd either have to try a dead-stick landing or bail out.

But we both knew instinctively that we wouldn't bail out. If we had any chance at all to save the airplane, we knew we'd stick with it. And with full power on the front we leveled out, holding our breath, and the rear prop stayed still. No windmilling. Now we could fly and just barely climb.

We thought first of heading back to Mojave, but the airplane was too full of fuel for a go-around if we had trouble landing. We no longer had the rear prop we could reverse as a brake. And the trip home would take an hour and half—what happened to the back prop could happen to the front. Then Edwards came to mind, but it was a long way off, over rough terrain.

At just about the same time, I looked out the window and saw Vandenberg Air Force Base, with its unused runway for the space shuttle. Vandenberg was a restricted area—it's the Pacific missile test range, but we could use it in an emergency.

Jeana had the frequency for the Vandenberg tower right at hand, and we called them. "We'll help you all we can," the tower said, "but first you have to say the magic word."

"Okay," I replied. "Mayday, Mayday." I had never been one of the school of pilots who hate to use that word, who regard it as some sort of admission of failure. "It's too much paperwork," they complain. Not to take advantage of all the help you can get is bad judgment. To needlessly subject yourself and your passengers to risk is stupid.

"Roger your emergency," came the reply from the tower. "You are cleared into restricted area. What is your location and altitude?"

Vandenberg is right on the coast, and the coastal fog creeps up every morning to cover most of the base. That day was no exception. Although it was afternoon, only part of that fog had dissipated. It burned off from the land toward the sea, and at the edge of the burn-off was a layer of convection and turbulence. We would have to fly over the fog, come around, land on the clear runway, and roll out into the fog.

We turned south and started down, coming over the base at about 1,500 feet over the runway in a teardrop-pattern approach. This airplane glides flat and lands fast—with only one nose brake it had to be done just right. Once we got the gear down we were committed. We couldn't maintain level flight with the drag of the gear.

The runway was only half-visible through the fog. We had no way to go around, we couldn't overshoot, but we were still a little high, and I had to make an S-turn to kill off some altitude. As we came up on the edge where the fog was burning off, all of a sudden we hit the turbulence. The wings started their flailing, and it was all I could do to keep control and put the airplane down, bump, bump, about a third of the way down the runway.

We touched down at three-fourteen in the afternoon, wiped the sweat from our brows, and set about figuring out what went wrong.

The chase aircraft was down for refueling, and we were out of contact with our radio people when the problem surfaced. Their antennas weren't in place yet. So on our way down we had given the phone number in the trailer in Mojave to the tower at Vandenberg and asked them to call our mission control.

We pulled the airplane up to a hangar belonging to the Air Sea Rescue people. They lent us tools and an ohmmeter to troubleshoot the prop problem. We hooked up the ohmmeter and found we had a dead electrical short and traced it to the prop motor. We took the spinner off, removed the motor, opened the housing, and the two halves of the armature magnet of the motor that adjusted the blade's pitch fell out in my hand. The magnet had fractured; the armature wire was in charred bits. The polarity had somehow reversed, and instead of reducing pitch, the motor had been increasing it. At high RPMs, the centrifugal force had turned the whole setup backward. In theory it was impossible, but it had happened, and we duplicated it later.

And we were counting on those motors to take us all the way around the world.

Bruce was exhausted after flying chase all day, but Mike Melvill flew him up to Vandenberg just before nightfall, and we considered what to do.

At Vandenberg we were received like heroes. "I used to be in this man's Air Force," I said as soon as I got out of the plane. "You did?" said one of the young airmen on duty. "For twenty years," I told him, and the airman became very solicitous.

A cordon of camouflaged MPs with automatic rifles was thrown around the aircraft. The base commander came out and peered curiously at the engine as we worked on it.

Since just about all NASA operations were shut down in the wake of the *Challenger* disaster, there wasn't much happening at Vandenberg, so our arrival was a big deal. The public relations types snapped a lot of photos, hurried to the darkroom, and made prints for us to autograph. We posed for more pictures with the *Voyager* and a lot of the Vandenberg personnel.

The local television camera crews were notified, and they immediately came down. "This is a test flight, and we are happy to be allowed to use the facilities at Vandenberg. We will evaluate the problem, fix it, and continue the test flight as soon as possible," I told them.

Pretty soon, the whole world seemed to know we'd had a problem.

What they didn't know was that something far more frightening had happened earlier, something that the public had not been told: *flutter*.

There are three extremely dangerous things that can happen to an airplane in flight: structural failure, fire, and flutter—the uncontrollable flapping of a control surface that, very quickly, can tear an aileron or elevator loose from the airplane.

Flutter is something few people are lucky enough to live to tell about. Heading north on the first lap, we had begun a series of performance tests at five, ten, and fifteen thousand feet. Flying at fifteen thousand feet, I pushed both engines to full throttle, heading for maximum speed to take our first performance point. We had reached 108 knots when all of a sudden there was a whirr and heavy pressure in the stick. At first I thought the autopilot had run away. I reached over to disconnect it, but the stick continued shaking, so badly I could barely hold on to it.

Then Jeana looked out the window and saw that the elevator was vibrating. She calmly told me and at the same time began to pull the chutes forward, but I didn't notice; she had to tell me again. I immediately pulled both throttles back to idle and pulled the nose up. The flutter stopped as quickly as it had started.

We were lucky we didn't lose a control surface completely. The elevators were never designed to withstand that kind of flutter. It was a close thing.

The reason behind it turned out to be ridiculously simple. Because the pitch control of the airplane was at first too sensitive, we had added an elevator trim tab, or antiservo tab, a small winglike structure behind the canard stuck on a couple of pretty flexible little shafts. That had artificially given us more elevator. It still wasn't enough, so we added another one on the opposite side. These were made up from radio-controlled model airplane parts—real hometown technology—and they were informally known as "sparrow strainers."

Now if all the control surfaces are balanced, there should be no flutter. And we'd balanced them. What we hadn't figured on was that just before the coast flight Bruce had put some paint on the airplane. With all the little modifications we had been making, it had begun to look a little ragged; a lot of press and public were going to see it, and we were hoping to set this record. It was only a tiny bit of paint, but more of it ended up on the trailing than on the leading edge and unbalanced the tab. The tab had begun to flutter on the north leg of the lap, as we were turning, and it was at the bottom of the lap that the prop started running away.

There may have been a certain symbolism in the fact that it was the paint we put on for the public that had caused the problem. We felt really pushed by the attention we were getting—and the attention we needed. But at the same time we could not reveal such a critical problem as flutter.

Those sponsors who had backed us despite the potential of a fiery crash would hardly have been reassured by that news. So we were caught between our desire to keep the program open and public and our need to keep confidence in the airplane and in what we were trying to do.

We felt sure the flutter had to do with the high speed and altitude at which it had occurred and were not especially concerned. There was no reason to get the airplane characterized as dangerous by the media.

. . .

When Burt, who was out of town, called in the evening after the emergency landing, Bruce explained what had happened. He told him how the sparrow strainer had fluttered and the prop motor had failed; how the magnet had broken neatly in two and the halves had popped out in Dick's hand when he opened the housing; and how the armature wire was shredded. Together they tried to figure out what made an electric motor do something like that. The best guess was that the vibration had been at fault, that the prop must have been running at a specific frequency to which the magnet was sensitive, and that it had cracked like a wineglass when the soprano hits the high note.

Burt was more concerned about the flutter, and the problem with the elevator. We hadn't determined the cause for sure yet, and he thought it could be solved with a modification to the sparrow strainer. Working with his accustomed inventiveness and quickness, he described a fix for it. Bruce sketched it while they talked. They hoped to make the modification before we took off again. To make sure there were no slip-ups, Burt agreed to draw the adjustment to the sparrow strainer on graph paper. He then read out the key coordinates on the phone to Bruce, who transferred it to his own paper. Pretty slick work.

Bruce thought the modification could be made on the ground at Vandenberg. But Burt wasn't very happy with the idea of us taking off again the next day; he wanted us to come back to Mojave and start all over again. He told Bruce to tell Dick that if the elevator was pounding, put the airplane down right away. "Remind him of what happened to Tom Jewett," he said.

. . .

The Air Sea Rescue people took us in. They rearranged their helicopters so we could put the *Voyager* in their big hangar, and we spent a restless night in a motel in the nearby town of Lompoc. But at least we got a night's sleep—that was more than we had gotten the night before, when we'd worked on the airplane into the wee hours.

The next morning we got up and had a terrible breakfast at some local grease palace. "A hell of a way to start a world record," Dick said with his stomach already feeling the effects.

We went out to Vandenberg, and Dick finished up installing the new prop pitch control motor. The motor that failed had a hundred hours on it; I figured it would at least carry us through this flight. I was much more uneasy about the main prop blade retention bearings, which had been wearing even before the flight. Our general confidence in this whole MT propeller system had dropped pretty low.

That morning the base was shrouded in fog, and we wouldn't be able to take off for a while. We thought we might have to return to Mojave to reweigh the airplane, but since the fuel tanks and barograph were all still sealed, Rich Hanson, the NAA representative, okayed our restarting the record flight from Vandenberg—a little good news.

That morning Gerd Muhlbauer, the prop maker, called from Germany. The motor that had failed had been obtained from an outside supplier, but he was embarrassed nonetheless. He didn't have an explanation for what might have caused the problem.

We could replace the prop control motor and take off. It wasn't what Burt would have called for; he was more concerned about the flutter and felt that a more conservative plan would have been to fly back to Mojave, check everything out, and then start again.

There was another factor. We were learning that "press" was only the first half of "pressure." Peter had worked very hard to persuade Jay Lamonica, producer of ABC's 20/20 program, to do a story on *Voyager*, and the twenty-minute segment, concluding with a live interview with us in the plane, was scheduled for the next night, Thursday. Twenty minutes of prime-time television!

If we weren't in the air, they might very well jerk the segment. It shouldn't have been the basis for making a decision to fly, a decision that might mean the difference between life and death, but in fact it was important. Dick felt the continued existence of the program could be at stake.

. . .

The motor was fixed and tested out. Again there was fog at Vandenberg, and it wouldn't burn off enough for a takeoff until nearly three o'clock. Around eleven, I retreated to an empty, dark training room at the back of the Air Sea Rescue hangar.

In it was a single table, and the only light came streaming in through a high window. It felt like a prison cell, and after a few minutes I put my head down in my hands on the table.

For half an hour in that room I thought and worried and searched my soul, feeling all my frustration about the program and the airplane. There was a lot of pressure from Burt and Bruce to go home and start over later. I thought back over all the things those prop pitch control motors had done to us: the way one had shed the two little screws that held it on and torn loose in the test cell at Teledyne Continental, the way the retention bearings had been wearing—that bothered me the most. But the motor that failed was a hundred hours old; the new one should make it through the hundred-odd hours planned for this flight. The flutter, I was sure, would not recur if we kept our speed and altitude down.

I tried to make a list of pros and cons but ended up deciding not according to any rational calculus but according to a basic feeling that we had to go on and an instinct that said we could make it. It was time to shit or get off the pot. If we went back to Mojave, the program might end. We might not get another chance. This might be the only important thing we ever did with this airplane, and we should do it while people were watching.

I came out and gathered everyone around and said, "We're going to finish this thing." And everyone agreed.

. . .

There was fog at Vandenberg, and it wasn't until nearly three o'clock that enough of it had burned away for a takeoff. Even then, visibility was poor, with tops at only eight hundred feet and the turbulent layer where the fog ended waiting for us as we would come up off the runway.

We went down the checklist and lined up. Rich Hanson stood by to record the takeoff time. Knowing the turbulence would be there at the edge of the fog, Dick asked Bruce to fly chase in tight formation, and as we took off Bruce tucked the Sierra practically up in behind Voyager's wing. Bruce was amazed to see close up the way the airplane oscillated as we got into the layer of turbulence. But as soon as we climbed through the weather, it was perfectly smooth and bright.

That day—Wednesday—we made one lap, and on Thursday, about an hour before 20/20, I got in the seat.

Dick went in the back but didn't sleep. I was looking out the window and saw a star go slowly by the window. I pulled my knees up and slid forward on my back so I could see the attitude indicator: it was steady. But then I saw the standby indicator, and its horizon was slowly tilting. Stars don't move: we were slowly rolling!

The roll was too slow for either of us to feel. We had inadvertently opened a circuit breaker and cut power to the main attitude indicator, and, deprived of power, the gyro that it used as a reference was slowly spinning down. The autopilot was orienting us to a false horizon.

Dick calmly told me what was wrong. I turned off the autopilot, slowly brought the airplane back level, reestablished the attitude indicator, and turned the autopilot back on.

If we hadn't caught it, we would have rolled on our back and surely died.

That night while Jeana flew, I watched 20/20 on a tiny television set perched on my stomach. Jeana had given me that set for my birthday when we were first going together. It was the only one we had then, and I remembered how in those poor but happy times we had eaten dinner together in the cramped apartment, watching it on the table in front of us.

We were just off San Francisco, and, picking up a local station, I lay with my head to the rear firewall and watched with pride—and some frustration: I had left the earphone home. I could either put the set to one ear with a hand over the other one to block out the engine noise, or I could watch, but not both. I finally decided just to watch. At the end of the tape segment, we went to radiotelephone patch for the live interview with correspondents Tom Jarriel and Hugh Downs.

Back in the hangar they watched, too. Everyone was in high spirits and laughed and clapped when a sponsor's name or logo made its way into the broadcast: the King logo on Dick's hat, the uniform patches, the signs on the plane. They even laughed at Dick's jokes.

The 20/20 people had produced a fancy computer graphic, a schematic drawing of the airplane showing the fuel tanks. The tanks lit up one by one in turn. Somebody said, "Well, now Bruce knows where they are."

We had agreed to drop a sample of the synthetic oil the next day so the company could evaluate its performance by measuring its metal content. Again, however, the real factor at work was publicity.

We never should have agreed to do it, but the oil sponsor was insistent.

"People shouldn't be asked to do this sort of thing without any sleep," I said, but I felt committed to do the drop, although Jeana was against it and so were Doug Shane and Larry Caskey on the ground.

"This is crazy," Doug said. "This is the tail wagging the dog. We shouldn't be thinking about what's convenient for the press or the sponsors, we should be thinking about what's best for the test flight." And he was right. The whole maneuver was one big screw-up.

The sample had been placed in a carefully padded container with an attached streamer. We descended from our cruising altitude out of the stratus clouds and came low over San Luis Obispo airport, dropping the bottle out the bottom waste door and hoping that Dan Card, on the ground, would be able to track it as it fell. But Dan lost sight of it as it neared the ground—the whole exercise was for nothing.

The climb back up was painfully slow. Dick finally decided to restart the front engine, and he was so tired and angry at having to run through the drop at a time he should have been sleeping that he made several mistakes—cycling the power for the avionics the wrong way, for instance, and giving them a jolt of electricity that scrambled them up pretty well. And of course the descent and restart broke up the continuity of the fuel consumption numbers we had worked out.

Once it was over, however, and we had settled back into cruise, we could finally address the real point of the flight: learning to live, eat, drink, and sleep in this airplane over an extended period of time.

Dick still couldn't sleep. And by that third night he was a little punchy. He was confusing some numbers, and the trailer transmitted the code that signified he was to wake me so I could check him out. The conclusion was that he was just tired, that he could continue, but things weren't looking good.

On night four, when Dr. Jutila came on for his questionnaire on how we were feeling, Dick had just gotten up, was irritable, and became snappy.

The doc ran down the list—headache? stomachache? tiredness?—asking for numerical evaluations, and Dick didn't respond. There was a long pause, and then he asked again. Finally Dick said, "Doc, is there something the matter with you?" And that was all he would say. Dick was still half-asleep, and the communication had caused him to nearly mess up a fuel transfer.

It took a couple of days for our circadian rhythms and work cycles to settle in. Dick was having difficulty relaxing and just letting me fly the airplane. I told him sternly he had to sleep, and he would try, but he remained restless, he wanted to be back at the controls. He felt an over-powering physical need to be in the seat.

He was constantly thinking about whether I was doing everything just right. Rationally he knew he didn't have to worry, but instinctively it was hard to stop.

I had brought a fleece to sleep on. Dick had an air mattress cut off to fit the space, and it kept leaking. Every so often his hip would bang into the floor and wake him, and he would get back up.

Since he wasn't going to sleep, I knew one way to keep him going: get him to talk. I told the folks on the ground, "Dick's tired. Set him up with interviews. Someone talk to him." Peter had lined up interviews via radio patch from all over the world, the networks in New York, London, even Australia, and now he began to put the connections through. I knew Dick was a ham at heart—he loved doing the interviews; they helped keep him awake and alert at night. He would describe seeing the Golden Gate Bridge with the lights of the cars going across or the sunrise brightening the haze across San Francisco Bay.

"What's it like up there?" they'd always ask, and finally Dick came up with an answer. "It's as dark as the inside of a cow up here."

It was a phrase I'd first heard years ago from Ken Thomas, an F-101B pilot from Texas. I used the line in the next interview, and the one after that, and pretty soon it became a joke—after a while, if I didn't talk about the inside of a cow in an interview, somebody remarked on it.

But when the sun rose and I would turn from the brightening colors in the east, that darkness to the west did not seem so funny. It was the dark cold wide Pacific, and next time we were in the air this long, we wouldn't be in the shelter of the land; we'd be heading out into that darkness.

. . .

We had planned to work on Jeana handling the pitch oscillations. I kept putting that off and putting that off, and finally at five-thirty in the morning, after nearly three full days, I decided it was time.

I got out of the seat very carefully, and Jeana slipped in. We set up the clip-on stick so I could reach around and catch it if she had trouble. And then all of a sudden I got a feeling of not caring—she's *got* to handle it. I don't know why—maybe it was just fatigue. I knew I was too tired to train her then and not sure I ever could. Or maybe somehow, for the first time, I knew I could trust her—I had to trust her. And I scrambled into the back, wrapped myself up, and was asleep as soon as my head hit the pillow—the first time I had ever slept in the airplane. I woke up five hours later, and she was handling everything fine.

. . .

It was the first time I had taken the controls for such a long time at this weight, and I was a little apprehensive. I looked over to see that none of Dick's straps had gotten caught in the control cables. To the right, the stick was moving back and forth in response to the control of the autopilot. I slid the seat forward so I could reach the V-bar that extended the pedals for my feet and adjusted all the gain controls on the autopilot. I checked the Omega system and confirmed that we were just coming up to the south turnpoint. I made the turn, checked the new heading, and soon I felt quite comfortable—but always alert, sensitive to any change in the plane.

In a couple of hours the sun began to come up, and beneath me there was no water visible, only the solid bank of the marine layer.

Every day going up and down the coast we watched as that marine layer, the clouds that topped the ocean up to a thousand feet or so, would gradually buin out to sea. But by noon the ocean was bare about ten miles out, and as the day went on and the air cooled, that layer would roll back in toward shore, flowing up into the bays and valleys. We marked our progress through the flight by this process.

That was how Bruce and Fergy found us, on the morning of the fourth day when they came out in the Beech Sierra for "the morning check" on Voyager. They set down at Paso Robles, a small airport nestled amid gently rolling fields of hay dotted with drying bales, about fifteen minutes from the coast, to wait for Voyager on our southbound leg. San Simeon, the William Randolph Hearst mansion, was plainly visible as they approached the ocean, which was neatly soft-wrapped under a cottony marine layer. Arriving a bit too early, they turned north to catch Voyager, and in a few minutes we came sailing serenely across their field of vision, above and to the right, gleaming in the sun.

"Hey, look who's in the driver's seat," Bruce said as he caught a glimpse of me.

Seeing me flying, they knew that Dick was relaxing a little bit, trusting me to fly the airplane. This, in fact, was the biggest breakthrough of the flight, and it made everyone feel better, on the ground as well as in the air.

Bruce swung the Sierra around and nosed in close behind to look at the rear engine. A small brown streak on the right side of the engine was the only thing marring the white fuselage. Fergy, using binoculars, reported the oil to be insignificant, just the expected run from the breather, and everything else looked fine. With the front engine shut down and the prop stationary, and the whirling disc of the rear prop looking tiny in comparison to its size, the airplane could have been riding some invisible rail or current. It seemed to be carried by the wind, but there was no apparent wind and no clouds there above the marine gauze.

Two chase planes a day generally made this inspection. They also carried photographers and a correspondent or two for radio interviews plane to plane. Bruce took up Major Moore, the officer who had arranged everything at Vandenberg, in gratitude for his help, and George and Irene Rutan went up on Monday night with Dick's daughters, Holly and Jill. Mom Rutan said it was the greatest day of her life "so far." On the last morning of the flight, Wanda Wolf went along for her first view ever of the plane from the air.

These were almost the only spectators. Los Angeles and Oakland air route control centers had been careful not to give out *Voyager's* position. The last thing anyone wanted was a curious pilot trying to get too close. We were slow and not very maneuverable. *Voyager's* white skin blended almost invisibly into the clouds, and from the side its silhouette was so low you could almost be on top of it before you caught sight of it. We did not want to have to dodge anyone. Only two or three planes ventured near, by guess or accident, and center warned them off.

A couple of times, though, Los Angeles Center did inform airline pilots that *Voyager* would be passing within sight of the plane, and the pilots, in turn, told their passengers. Some of them looked out their windows and got a glimpse of what must have seemed a very strange object sailing silently past them like a spaceship, whizzing along at a speed that, of course, had much more to do with the jet than with *Voyager's* eighty knots.

. . .

On Sunday night, July 13, Burt sailed into the trailer, back from a trip to the Midwest. He immediately asked to see the performance data and radio logs. He leafed through the notebooks and saw that there wasn't much written there. He was appalled; he felt we needed the data critically and didn't know how much we had been keeping in the airplane.

Burt began criticizing the radio people. "I expected to find two or three spiral notebooks full," he said. "Weren't we going to write down everything?" he asked. "His fuel and airspeed numbers? We needed all that."

Without knowing the fuel efficiency, there was no way to figure out the lowest-possible takeoff weight. And the weight problem, Burt said, was still critical. "Everyone keeps talking about this margin, this pad we have of extra fuel. But there isn't any. It's going to be close. Look how long it took to take off with just six thousand pounds the other day. For the world flight it'll be nine thousand pounds. If we add anything more," he said, "we'll be looking at nothing but a smoking hole at the end of the runway."

He was talking about the difficulty of taking off fully loaded even from the fifteen-thousand-foot runway at Edwards. There, at least, there was the dry lake at the end and the possibility of an abort if we couldn't make it. "The ace in the hole," Burt said, "is the reverse on the prop. Without that, there's no way." It was a concern that would grow stronger and stronger with Burt as time went on.

. . .

On the last full day of the flight, Lee Herron brought a bunch of cactus flowers into the trailer. Standing in a sunbeam amid all the computer terminals and video screens, they looked incongruous—an intrusion from the natural world outside.

Len Snellman had been hoping to find us some rough weather, some wind and rain, to give us all a run-through and to give him a better idea of what airplane and pilots could take. He knew that Voyager had not flown in rain since the vortex generators, those funny little fins, had been added after the near disaster in the rain shower. He saw an arm of clouds coming over the Pacific that he expected would give him that chance on late Sunday or Monday.

We knew we should find some rain to test how the canard behaved, but we were not eager to try it. And now, too, we were starting to get some lead buildup on the spark plugs.

We also noticed that our fuel transducers sometimes seemed 15 percent in error. It was a mystery; later on they worked fine. We rechecked the calibration later, but we never figured it out. As a result we missed an opportunity to fix something important. If we had paid more attention to what the airplane was trying to tell us right then, we might have saved ourselves a lot of grief later on.

On our last lap, at night, sweating it out, thinking after five nights that if we land short, we might have to do it over again, we heard the engine start to run roughly. The spark plugs were clogging up.

At high power, if the plugs get too hot, they preignite the fuel and can destroy the engine. If they run cool enough to avoid that problem, then they won't burn off the lead that builds up at low power.

Now, as we flew lighter and brought down the power, the lead buildup began to short out the plugs. If it happened on two plugs in the same cylinder, it shook like mad. When the engines started running rough, we would have to increase power to burn it out.

On our last lap, at the point of the course most distant from home, north of San Francisco, we started our turn, and the engine virtually quit, banging and shaking as if it would shake off its mounts. I had nightmare visions of a nighttime restart of the front engine.

Right away I grabbed the prop controller, increased RPM, and pushed the throttle up to change the combustion swirl pattern and clean it out. The engine shook and banged and clunked for five or ten minutes until it began to run clean. I was getting more and more anxious as we got toward the end of the flight, and that scared me badly. We went over the checklist and restarted the front engine.

But now we no longer felt we could run on low horsepower, or the same thing would happen again. For the world flight we would have to get better plugs, but right now we were only thinking about getting through the last lap and home. So without telling anyone in mission control, we left that engine running. We just wanted to get finished and get this airplane in the record books.

I was up all night after the engine hiccuped and had plenty of adrenaline to get home.

Burt and Mike and Sally Melvill came out in the chase plane to catch up with us halfway down the last leg. It was dark, and we sat there chuckling, wondering how long it would take Burt to notice the front engine running. They joined up on our lights, and as the sun began to rise and they got closer, Burt saw it. "Gee," he said, "I notice something a little different about the airplane."

We came off the south turnpoint of the last lap and then flew over Vandenberg—although we later found out the rules did not require that— and as we did Jeana came up close to the seat so we were almost side by side, and I could look over and see the satisfaction in her eyes.

There was a lot of weather between us and home, mare's tails sweeping out of the clouds, indicative of turbulence. We did fly through a little rain, just a light sprinkle, and the airplane seemed to pitch up.

They kept talking in the trailer about us getting into some more rain, but frankly we were no longer in the mood for that. We wanted to finish the record; we could do that test later.

We decided the smart thing was to keep it simple. Besides, we were almost getting comfortable in our little cocoon.

But that was not accounting for the winds of Mojave. We had put the gear down above Tehachapi, and coming over the mountain we ran suddenly into a mean rotor, a deadly, hovering swirl of air that shook the hell out of us. Jeana floated up, while I flipped off the autopilot, grabbed the stick, and tried to knock down the oscillations, leaning forward to block my view of the flailing wings and concentrating on getting the deck angle level. For just a minute we were almost out of control. The two chase planes on either side broke away hard, and the only part of them we could see was their bellies. Ahead of us, Doug Shane was being bounced in the Tiger, and I asked him to get the hell out of the way. Just as he sped up and moved away, we came out of the turbulence as suddenly as we had entered it.

"Oh, it didn't look that bad," Burt said from the chase plane. But to me it was some of the worst turbulence we had encountered, and even coming home, feeling triumphant about our record, it left a sinking feeling in my stomach. The feeling was caused less by that rough air than by the looming certainty we would have to fly into weather this bad on our way around the world. For most of this flight the air had been glassy smooth, but now we were reminded of how frail the craft was, how we hated the least turbulence, and how hard it was to get everyone back on the ground to understand what it felt like.

What the hell is it going to be like? I thought, and I felt a strong premonition that the chances of losing the airplane were very good. Here we could barely fly around a rotor right near home; how could we fly around the world?

The gray sky was growing lighter as we neared Mojave. On the ground we could see a good-sized crowd watching as four flecks appeared from the southwest: *Voyager* and her three chases.

There was a little shower and some convective activity over Mojave, and I turned on our approach to the runway a little high. My judgment was off: I had expected a bit more headwind. I pushed the nose over, but we still had too much airspeed, and I had to pull both engines back to idle.

Bruce in the chase plane radioed me that the approach looked too high.

"Yeah, I know," I said. "It'll be okay. I'm sure not going to come around again."

"Take a deep breath, Dick," Bruce said. He could tell I was a little hyper, fighting fatigue, still shaken up by that rotor.

And on the way in, something strange happened. When we were still five or ten feet off the ground, the airplane started drifting off to the left. I saw that we were heading for the landing lights on the edge of the runway, but I just let the airplane go. I knew the lights were there, but I didn't care.

Mike Melvill said, "Look left," and the comment woke me up. I corrected to the right and brought us in, a little long but safe. And I realized that even then I was subconsciously wanting to bang the plane up—not badly, but just enough so I wouldn't have to fly it again.

It was 6:37 a.m. Pacific coast time, July 15, and in 111 hours and 44 minutes we'd traveled some 11,857 statute miles—about the distance from Paris to Tokyo. And that doesn't count the miles to and from the course.

The seals on the airplane were checked, and the barograph was still running. Lee Herron took off the canopy, and we stood and waved in the cockpit. Then *Voyager* was pulled into the hangar with us still inside and weighed. One reason was that Burt wanted his performance numbers to be exact. But the other was that, if we were in bad shape, the hangar doors could be closed and we could be lifted out in privacy. Doc Jutila wasn't sure what condition we would be in.

We got out, sat on top of the fuselage, and raised our hands and started waving, feeling surprised at—well, not at how good we felt, but that we didn't feel worse.

We took our shower, and Lee Herron and Diane Dempsey put Hawaiian flower leis around our necks and pinned to our shirts *Voyager* wings that Lee Herron had made up. And an unplanned party started, with champagne spraying everywhere as if we had just won the Super Bowl.

But all that physical activity took a lot out of us. Doc Jutila knew Jeana was dehydrated; she was not supposed to be chased around the hangar. Now we were trotted out for a press conference. We were standing, and we should have been sitting down, because after a few questions Jeana began to get weak in the knees and had to be taken back inside. She had drunk less than a gallon of water in five days, and now it had come back to haunt her.

A few minutes later a thin little shower came along, and if you looked hard at the sky far to the southwest, you could see about a quarter of a rainbow against the clouds. The pleasure of the record was like that rainbow: it floated up there for a little while, and then the gray reality of what still lay ahead reasserted itself.

For several days Jeana felt weak. We went to Monterey Bay for a couple of days of R & R that the volunteers arranged and paid for. We did relax, walked along the beach and breathed the sea air, and looked up at the sky above us, out toward our record course. I got tired after just a short walk on the beach and needed a nap. It was a lesson well learned. I would make sure we both drank our water next time.

We were a little surprised at the attention the flight got. Newspapers all over the country and the world featured pictures of the landing. Whether we were able to fly around the world or not, we had established a major flying record. But it was the way it was accomplished that seemed to appeal most to the public. For the first time since before World War II, an absolute, unlimited category aviation record had been established—not by an elaborately supported military effort, but by civilians.

Hard as it was for us to believe, there had been people in the press who thought this thing was easy and that we were milking it for publicity, exaggerating problems, creating false drama. Jeana always said, "If it was easy, it would have been done a long time ago." But the coast flight convinced them otherwise.

What impressed them most, and was probably the chief factor behind the overwhelming public attention we received, was the can-do attitude that got us back in the air and back on the record course within twenty-four hours after the prop motor failed on us. The day we landed at Vandenberg, most of the reporters were automatically thinking of the delay to fix the problem in terms of months; all their experience with government and big corporations had conditioned them that way. They were so shocked when we flew again the next day that many papers and television organizations had to scramble their teams back to the base in a big hurry.

If we had not been able to push on and fly that day, we might never have flown around the world. Fiscally, we were hurting, and personally, we all needed a boast in morale. After the flight our VIP family grew dramatically, and we went back to preparing for the world flight with renewed energy.

The Last Rung
on the Ladder

The prop motors had held up all right for the rest of our record flight, but the problem with it was not just some fluke. It turned out to be a fundamental threat to the whole program.

Right after the coast flight we were demonstrating the feathering and unfeathering mode of the prop control motors when one overheated and failed again right in front of our eyes. We had reproduced the failure we had experienced in the air. We had just thirty minutes before the failure recurred. The magnet had not broken, but the wires of the bell-shaped armature were rubbing on the case. The centrifugal force drove the prop blade to flat pitch—something Gerd had said could never happen.

We took the front motor apart, too, even though it was still running, and found that it was worn and close to failure.

Discarded now were the initial theories that the motor had failed because of some vibration dynamic—that engine and prop vibration had struck the magnet at some fatal frequency.

The next day the motors were opened up and taken to Santa Monica Prop for analysis. The clearance between the wire-wound armature and the casing was minuscule: the centrifugal force of the engine—3,000 RPM or so—had combined with an equal amount from the motor itself to tug the winding wires out enough so they touched the case. They wore down, and the motor shorted out.

Once that had been discovered, Dick was livid, mustering the look of absolute incredulity that incompetence evoked in him. "We were staking our lives on these rinky-dink motors," he would say. "This prop system is absolute garbage, I can't believe it is on an airplane. I can't believe it is on my airplane."

The same day we dispatched a desperate telex to Gerd Muhlbauer: "The rear prop motor failed again . . . just like in flight during the world record . . . ***Please*** We must find why. Who are the manufacturers? . . . The world flight is in jeopardy!!!"

Gerd now began to show a certain Teutonic impatience. He had bought the motors off the shelf, not made them himself. He became evasive. He didn't know their capabilities or electrical specifications. "I am not an electrical engineer," he said several times.

Replacing the motors represented a major problem. Who made such motors? Did anyone make any that were better? Could we replace the entire electric motor scheme for adjusting the prop with another? It might take a year to install a whole new hydraulic or other system.

At the same time we got the name of the manufacturer off the side of the motor—a Swiss company, as it turned out, called Portescap. Peter got hold of the man in charge there, Hugo Wyss, on the telephone. When Peter had explained the situation, resorting to his French, Wyss expressed horror that the motors were being used under such temperatures—and at such voltage. They were designed to operate at temperatures no higher than 100 degrees Centigrade or so. In fact, the temperatures were more than 150 degrees. And the voltage had been much higher than specified; no one was sure just how high, but eventually we found out that these were nine-volt motors running in our twenty-eight-volt system.

Wyss had read about Voyager and the Vandenberg landing, and he knew that a prop motor had failed then. But he didn't know the motor was his. When he realized that, he became concerned and helpful. He offered to build, within a week, four motors that would meet specifications. They would be sent over on the Concorde and ferried west via courier. There was one proviso: they had to be thoroughly tested at Voyager and sent back for inspection prior to the world flight.

But we needed more assurance that we had motors we could count on. Ultimately we decided we were running out of time to test our new motors, even in their improved versions, so we went to TRW to provide new motors, built to military specifications.

Champion spark plugs came through with a solution to the fouling problems that had shaken us near the end of the coast flight. Most plugs require maintenance every fifty hours. Champion provided special fine-wire, iridium-tipped plugs that would handle both high- and low-power settings, without the fifty-hour maintenance requirements. These were mission-critical pieces of equipment. We couldn't exactly crawl out and change plugs every fifty hours.

There was another critical fix to be made. Lee Herron built a vent for the waste compartment, a little periscope-shaped tube that projected from the wing. He worked long and hard on it and was proud of the final product, which he named PPOGR—for "Poo Poo Odor Getter Ridder." These initials he painted beside the device. It was *Voyager's* do-it-yourself high technology at work again.

.   .   .

We also began to work in earnest on flight simulations in the trailer. Each day we would spend an hour or so with Larry Caskey and his team discussing philosophy and running simulations of various scenarios.

We worked out the uplink and downlink forms for the six-hour messages, trying to reduce the numbers that would have to be given back and forth on the radio. The uplink would give a thirty-six-hour course, updated each six hours: track, altitude, weather. The downlink from the airplane listed location, fuel, engine status, and physical condition.

We had to fight hard against what we called the black-line-on-the-chart syndrome. "There is no route," we would say. There was a course, which was determined regularly, each six hours, but no route written in stone. That was a critical concept, and most of the guys had military backgrounds, and in the military they never had responsibility for making route decisions. Operations and weather had to work together on that, and it was something new for most of them.

The criteria were set out in an operations manual: the factors in determining course were winds first, then weather, and only then red—politically sensitive—areas. I didn't want anyone running us through bad weather because they were afraid of a country. We were not going to be diverted for any political or diplomatic reason short of guns or missiles.

There was a plan worked out to keep either Mike Melvill or Bruce constantly available during the world flight. The coast flight began to show us that we wanted to have a trusted wingman in the trailer in case of emergency or extreme fatigue.

With the heat of the Mojave August sun shimmering off the pavement outside, we worked for hours inside that crowded little trailer. The team then was bare-bones: Don Rietzke for communications, Jack Norris for performance, Len Snellman for weather, and Larry Caskey (or stand-ins Mike Hance, Gil and Isabel Fortune, or Cob Harms) as mission control director.

I would go back into my office in the hangar and phone in a simulated six-hour message. It would describe fuel, winds, weather—the basics—and perhaps some emergency situation.

Then I would return to the trailer to see if the team plotted the message accurately and how they handled the situation.

When do you launch a search if communications are lost? How long do you wait, and whom do you notify?

What if we have an engine problem, have lost all our navigation equipment, but still have communications and are heading for the nearest airport? These were some of the possibilities we simulated.

We worked out plans for recovering the Voyager from various airports; Bruce was to have charge of any such operation.

A disturbing tendency to launch premature search and rescue missions emerged from the exercises. So we issued a special operations order detailing the policies: a communication search at the end of twelve hours without hearing anything, and only if there was no word after twenty-four hours should a rescue be launched.

If Voyager was over water and there was no word, there should be no search until twelve hours after the estimated time of our next landfall. I felt we had to train everyone to be conservative about launching a search that might prove to be unnecessary and embarrassing.

It was hard to make time for these exercises, with everything else that was going on, but they were as critical to success or failure as any mechanical component and were to prove their value again and again later.

. . .

While we waited for new prop control motors, Voyager was equipped with two new but still defective ones. We didn't want to shut everything down waiting; we couldn't afford to. Dick felt that the prop control motors would last fifty or a hundred hours. He planned to fly the next day, only for a couple of hours, even with the defective motors. There was too much to be tested—modifications made to the trim tab in the wake of the flutter episode, the new plugs, a new cylinder and other replacement engine components, autopilot, radios, and on and on. These were things that could not wait.

The prop motors were fitted with a new voltage regulator that Don Rietzke, the radio whiz, designed. Lee Herron took his Long EZ with the dragons painted on its side and dashed up over the windmills to Bakersfield to pick up the parts. He was back at Mojave in half an hour, and a few minutes later the regulator was in the airplane.

That might take care of the electrical problem, but we still worried about the temperature and the fact that the armature wires had spun out and shorted on the casing. It was another case of "cross your fingers." We simply didn't feel there was any alternative.

In the afternoon before a planned test flight the next day, Burt came by. He was very much against our flying.

"How can you fly with a part that has a known fault?" he asked.

Bruce, who had never liked the whole German MT prop system anyway, saw his point. "Dick, we have to consider what Burt is saying. We've got a motor that is a known bad guy."

The opposing argument was that we now knew it took the motors at least fifty and more like a hundred hours to fail, and we were just going to fly it for three hours. The three-hour flight would allow us to test the other systems. All this would make use of time that would otherwise be wasted waiting for the replacement motors.

But the real issue under discussion was larger. The program was at a critical juncture. We were under tremendous financial pressure; to postpone the world flight later into the fall might jeopardize the whole thing. With every day that brought us closer to November, things were less ideal. And if we slipped into next year, it might be impossible to get rolling again. Borrowed equipment would have to be returned and the backing of sponsors rearranged. And there were a lot of people who had lives to get back to.

But Burt, it seemed, was getting cold feet. He was now worried about the landing gear and whether it could take an abort onto the dry lake at Edwards. Edwards had been chosen because of that lake, the wide dry basin offering a margin of safety after the paved runway ran out. Now he was talking about drilling out a set of bolts on the landing gear and replacing them with stronger ones, something that could take weeks. We resisted. We refused to make a single modification for that sort of contingency.

Burt started talking about a man he had met a few days before, a man in his nineties who had been at Roosevelt Field in 1927. He told Burt that he had seen a number of Lindbergh's competitors attempt too great a leap in weight from their tests to their takeoff weight, only to find themselves too heavy to lift off. They ended up broken in a ditch at the end of the runway.

This was a very strange way for a man like Burt to be talking, a man who tended to discuss things in terms of known performance numbers and design factors. But his reputation was very much on the line, and when you are in doubt, you look for excuses not to try something. We had told everyone about the marvelous capabilities of the plane, and now it seemed maybe they weren't so marvelous. And, underneath it all, he was beginning to get worried about us and the chances we were taking. He did care.

Dick got everyone together and gave a sort of pep talk. "We are going to make an attempt to fly this thing around the world. If we can only take off at 8,500 pounds, we're going to take off at 8,500 pounds. If we get lucky and get good tail winds, we may make it. If we don't, we may have to land in Caracas or someplace. And we'll have a hell of a straight-line distance record, and we'll finally know for sure what the real range of the airplane is.

"It's the ninth inning now, and we're going to go whatever anyone else says. If we slip another year, we may not be able to get everything wound up again."

It was a question of reputation, responsibility, and readiness. When would the plane be ready? And ready was a matter of definition. Don Taylor, who had flown many record flights, listed it as an axiom: "The airplane will never be totally ready" before any record flight.

Burt was counting on the new props that John Roncz had designed, based on the performance tests done during the coast flight, and Gerd Muhlbauer was building to improve performance by 3 or 4 percent. But they might not arrive in time, and they would have the same sort of motors that had failed, the same blade retention bearings about which we had worried so much.

Against Burt's wishes, we flew the test flight with the bad motors. It went well and boosted our spirits considerably. We gained four days.

Burt was right about one thing: we checked the landing gear and found to our dismay that crucial bolts were in fact near failure. The gear had not been designed for so many flights. Glenn Maben drilled the bolts out and replaced them with stronger ones. And it took him not weeks, but days.

. . .

For all our resolve, we didn't make a world flight attempt in September; we couldn't. Things kept going wrong. Some were little things, but they all circled back to one big thing: a fundamental aerodynamic flaw in the airplane.

As we worked on takeoffs at higher and higher weights and the higher speeds necessary to provide lift at that weight, the old bugaboo of the flapping wings came back to haunt us: the pitch porpoise.

The danger increased as we built up weight and speed as testing progressed. With the airplane loaded up so full, the pitch oscillations went divergent and doubled amplitude in a cycle and half if unchecked—giving the pilot just seconds to control them before the airplane began to break up. We turned our attention to all sorts of ideas for correcting the problem.

The coast flight had gotten everybody's spirits up, but the emergence of this problem tested all our determination and enthusiasm. That flight had made us the first fliers outside of the military to hold an absolute aviation record since before World War II. It showed we could go at least halfway around the world. But there were more mountains to climb before we could make the world flight, and the next weeks turned out to be especially frustrating.

For me, the worry took the form of a bad dream. Jeana reacted differently. For her, the setbacks seemed to temper an even more intense dedication.

In my dream, I was climbing a ladder, rung by rung, slowly. Some of the rungs were shaky, but I got past them. Some of the rungs were absent and I had to put them in. Some of the rungs were broken, and I had to fix them. Finally I had climbed all of them but one. But the last rung was broken. I could not fix it, and I couldn't climb any higher.

It was a growing fear I had felt for a few months now: the fear that after all the months and years, all the nights in the hangar and all the early-morning takeoffs and exhausting eight-hour test flights and the turbulence and the glitches and the worry about money and equipment, that it would all fall just short.

Jeana would tell me, "We'll keep doing it until we get it right, however long it takes. We'll try so hard it has to work." And then she would burn off any frustration in hard work, rebuilding the offices, putting up walls, painting, mopping floors, moving furniture, paper work, inventory, accounting. And to forget it all, she would go down to the stables and saddle Gem and ride for a long while.

.   .   .

In mid-August Dick had said to everybody, "Let's push it. We're real close to the end of this thing. Let's go all out now. Let's make one gargantuan effort and do it."

Well, everybody did, and we only got 80 percent of the way there. That was disheartening.

At all the talks we had given, the same three questions had always arisen, and Dick began answering them before they could be asked. He answered the first by holding up one of the fecal containment bags and the second by saying, "No, she's not related to Chuck."

The third question was, "When will you take off?" In January, tired of saying, "When we're ready," I made a date up out of thin air: Sunday, September 14, at 0800—

But now that date was here, and we were not ready.

On September 13 we had a terrible flight.

During it, we smelled smoke—burning epoxy—and then later fuel fumes.

We had what looked like an oil leak. The alternator went south on us, and the aerodynamic performance was nothing to write home about, either.

Taking off at fairly heavy weight, we had a problem with the outer portions of the wings gaining lift before the inner portions—with control surfaces. This meant that the plane wanted to bounce up and down off the runway before we could really fly it. It was an unacceptable situation, and the problem would be even worse at full world-flight takeoff weight. If so, we might have a fireball.

Landing, the airplane was porpoising so much that I could barely control it. It was bouncing up and down in the big air waves. Coming in at fifty feet, I couldn't control the airplane to within fifteen feet. The only thing to do was guess and try to match the bottom of the bounce's arc with the runway.

The alternator failure was particularly disturbing. A man named Bill Bainbridge had specially built and carefully inspected this alternator. It was supposed to last two thousand hours, and it didn't even have two hundred hours on it. Had it failed on a world flight, we would have had to start the front engine. That would have cost us so much range that we could not have completed the flight.

We found the problem—one wire of a brush block had slipped out of a crimp joint—and sent that alternator and three others back to Bainbridge. He repaired them, and we never had the problem again.

Then there was the burning smell. The odd thing about that, we realized later, was that neither of us even considered coming down. The smoke, of course, meant fire—fire that any second could have turned into a huge and fatal explosion. But landing hadn't even crossed our minds. We simply continued with the test flight. Perhaps we were becoming inured to the danger.

I wrote up the smoke and fumes on the gig list, as if they were simply a few mechanical glitches. Dick said, quite matter-of-factly, "Well, if it had happened, it would have happened real quick and just gone all to hell."

Riding home from Edwards after the landing, with the twilight making the desert look even more desolate than usual, we both felt down. The next day was the day we had set long ago for takeoff on the world flight. It was an arbitrary date, to be sure, something pulled out of a hat, but there was a full moon on that date. A full moon was rising in the desert sky, the moon by whose light we had planned to fly around the world.

We sat down after we got back to Mojave and tried to figure out just where we stood.

Dick talked about that moon and how far we still were from being ready.

But Bruce and Lee and Peter Riva wouldn't take that kind of talk. "If we thought for a minute," Peter said, "that you were getting in that airplane when it was unsafe, we'd all be out of here. And that would be the end of that."

"We're not going to die," Dick said. "What we're going to do is fix this thing."

Dick talked to Burt, and Burt thought, as he always did, that we could fix it.

His idea seemed promising. We would lower the nose gear to lower the angle of attack—keep the airplane aimed down—until the entire wing had reached sufficient lift for controlled takeoff, then rotate up. And we would adjust the center of gravity forward to try to get the wings to dampen out their oscillations. And we would push on.

Peter Riva bought Dick a watch showing the phases of the moon—for luck, he told him. "You know, Dick," he said, "there will be a full moon next month, and the month after that."

. . .

Early the next morning I went running, and as I ran along the edge of the desert, startling jackrabbits off into the bushes, I began to feel better. What had seemed insurmountable the night before now seemed—after a good night's sleep and in the light of the morning—at least possible. And when we looked at the airplane, there were more tangible reasons to feel better.

The "oil leak" turned out to be nothing more serious than a pipe rubbing on the cowling and streaking it with metal dust. And a quick survey of the wiring in the cockpit revealed the source of the burning epoxy—I had left in place the wire leading to the old prop motor control and, ungrounded, it had fed right into the epoxy wall. Dumb, but easily fixed.

In the afternoon, Jeana broke some of the tension by riding Gem right past the trailer, down the flightline, and into the hangar, right up to me. The sight of the horse, this big living thing amid all the machinery, startled me. She had a little grin on her face, the grin that I had seen so much more of in the past and saw so rarely now. It reminded me how much I still loved her, and for the first time in a while I felt for what she was going through.

However frustrated I got with her attitude, I could also see a person who was working her heart out for this project. I stopped work, and we clowned around. I got on one horse, and she got on another, and we rode down the flightline for a little while, with everyone stopping to watch.

.   .   .

We flew again, with Burt's fixes, lowering the front gear, in flight moving the CG (center of gravity) forward by pumping fuel from the aft boom tanks. It worked pretty well—we confirmed that we had been operating with our center of gravity much too far to the rear—but it didn't get rid of the divergent oscillations of the wings. Dick still couldn't bear to look at them, waving and flapping out there. Flying the plane, especially as it got heavier, felt like herding a bunch of sheep around on threads. The sheep on the edge of the flock—the wingtips—barely paid any attention to you at all.

The new wooden prop blades finally came in, but they were not what was hoped. Somehow, the careful plans John Roncz had drawn up did not translate to wood and fiberglass. For one thing, the trailing edges were too thick. We compared them with Roncz's original templates, and they weren't even close. When we bolted them on and tested them, they gave good performance in level flight but lousy climb—which, when you're talking about taking off at 9,200 pounds, is the really big thing. That's what you get for having your prop designer in Indiana and your prop manufacturer in Bavaria.

Burt took a look at the props and came up with the idea of honing them back into shape. He took the original templates and with a router delineated the proper contours. Then Fergy, Bruce, Bruce's friend Al Nelson, and a couple of guys from Scaled spent two and a half days grinding the rest of the blades down to the proper levels. They laid new fiberglass up on the props, then cooked them in a makeshift oven: Bruce's Volkswagen van, parked in the sun with the windows rolled up. Bruce put up a big sign in the hangar: "Mojave Prop Works."

When they were finished and balanced, the props came out looking pretty good. But the big question was what they would do to the performance of the airplane.

.   .   .

Amid all the work and stress, there was one time when everyone could really relax a little bit: during the evening meals in the hangar. With everyone spread out along the big makeshift tables, these were a sort of combination family reunion, church picnic, and feeding the threshers on the farm.

We had good cooks in abundance—Mom Rutan, Suzy Bowman, Jeana's mother Evaree, and others. Lee Herron might make his chili and hush puppies. Doc Jutila would cook up the abalones he had gathered snorkeling on the rocky coast near Fortuna on his rare days off. And Sylvia Jutila was one of the best—the doc was always patting his well-padded stomach in testimony to that. She could cook all sorts of things, but most memorable were her breads and pies and cakes.

Someone put up a sign in the kitchen—"The Real Command Post"— and everyone who came in from the command post in the trailer had to agree they'd gotten it right.

One night before a test flight was scheduled, Bruce decided that the leading edges of the main wing needed to be sanded to assure better airflow. He had added a coat of paint before the previous flight, including a dark strip of paint inboard on the right wing so that we could more easily detect any airframe icing.

Everyone got straight up from the dinner table, and we did the job with a sort of human wave technique. Pretty soon we had about twenty people lined up on that wing, everyone from Doc Jutila to a woman named Turid Bjerke, who had just dropped in from Norway, from meteorologists to secretaries, everyone in the hangar with sanding blocks working away. The image survives as one that sums up the way the whole project had been done.

.   .   .

By the second half of September, the tension began to wear on everyone. To the favorite motto above his desk—"Life's a bitch, and then you die"— Dick added another preprinted sign: "The Unwilling led by the Unqualified doing the Impossible for the Ungrateful. We have done so much for so long with so little, we are now qualified to do anything with nothing." It was an expression of frustration, I knew, and not of the real situation.

In an even darker mood, I pinned up a quotation from Charles Lindbergh: "A coward can sit in his house and criticize a pilot for flying into a mountain in fog, but I would rather, by far, die on a mountainside than in bed. What kind of man would live where there is no daring? And is life so dear that we should blame one for dying in adventure? Is there a better way to die?"

One day Dick walked up to Lee Herron's desk and wordlessly placed down a note. It read, "If delay, then no moon over Indian Ocean. Not much to you, maybe, but my life to me."

As we were flying at heavier weights now, we began to take off on our test flights from Edwards. Our ground rules were to take off from Edwards at any weight above 6,500 pounds—the weight at which we could no longer stay in the air using just one engine. We did not want to risk the plane in case we lost an engine on takeoff. On Edwards's longer runway, in such a situation, we could abort, but not at Mojave. It was a gargantuan operation to move everything over to Edwards, but it was a safety rule we did not violate.

We would fly the plane to Edwards at lighter weight, Bruce's team would spend the night, fueling it up the rest of the way, and we would take off. The logistics became more complex, and at heavier weight we became more and more concerned with turbulence.

. . .

The tensions—the sudden changes in plan, the quick fixes—had begun to get to Bruce, too. On Saturday, September 20, we planned to take the plane to Edwards in preparation for a heavyweight dress rehearsal of the world-flight takeoff. Five in the morning came, then five-thirty, six, and still no Bruce. Lee Herron directed the rollout of the airplane. When Bruce finally appeared, it was with beer can in hand, loading gear into *Sky Slug*, his Vari Eze, and apparently just about ready to go to Mexico.

We flew most of that day, and in the early afternoon Bruce asked where we planned on landing—at Mojave or at Edwards, where we could set up for the dress rehearsal takeoff. We told him Edwards, and Bruce, being his most diplomatic, arranged everything with the air force people there.

Then, a few minutes later, we changed our minds: because of severe turbulence, we would land at Mojave.

Knowing how fragile Bruce's state of mind was, Peter and Lee Herron thought this might be the last straw for him.

Lee Herron went to Execute X-Ray, the private frequency, and dramatically radioed us in *Voyager*, "Do you know this voice?"

"Yes," Dick answered.

"Do you trust me?"

"Yes."

"Land at Eddie."

"Why?"

"I'm telling you because I know you should."

Ten minutes later we landed at Edwards. Bruce had agreed with Edwards on three o'clock, and now he was out getting a hamburger. We were two hours early.

What most bothered me was that I felt my ground crew was operating on emotion, not logic, and it was disturbing. I was upset that Bruce and even Ferg were going home if we didn't land at Edwards. It didn't bother me that they were tired, fed up, and ready to quit—I could understand that. What upset me was that they seemed ready to walk out on us before we could even get the aircraft back on the ground.

The problem was, we had landed right in the middle of the working day at Edwards, when they were trying to juggle all sorts of test programs. Bruce and Peter got chewed out by the Edwards people, and it made us look bad.

Bruce and Dick had a private powwow for twenty minutes. Bruce was fed up with taking the heat, he told Dick, tired of not being told things until the last minute.

"Bruce," I said, "when I was a young lieutenant an older officer told me, 'If you are ever in command, then command. You can be right or you can be wrong, but command.' The same thing applies to you: if you are the crew chief, you have to act like it, take charge."

"You mean act like an asshole?" Bruce said.

"That's right, hurt people's feelings if you have to."

"I'll practice. But I didn't ask for this job. Since I've got it, though, you're going to have to listen to me. No more of this jerking around."

The next day we took off at 7,500 pounds. We were supposed to come back in to Mojave.

These flight tests were exhausting—eight hours of flying and hard work. That day, as so often, the weather was too rough around Mojave, and we had to fly up into the quieter Central Valley toward Bakersfield to work. After flying all day, we would have to psych ourselves up for the landing, coming down through the gusty thermals coming off Tehachapi.

It was like a stuntman preparing to dive from a high building into a cushion. We put our parachutes on, Jeana would encourage me, I would buckle in, Jeana would brace herself, and I'd say, "Okay, you son of a bitch, here we come."

I'd put the back engine into reverse and head down, and sure enough we would get beaten to hell. I had to stay busy on the radio to handle the fear.

On this day, landing on runway 25, toward the town of Mojave, my ego overruled my fear—and my good judgment. We are going to have to be more courageous about these landings, I thought.

It was very turbulent, but I made it a personal challenge. There was a wind rotor right on top of Mojave but I told Jeana, "I'm going to land this son of a bitch or else." And on final approach I overshot dramatically because of the turbulence. By the time we came back around for a second try, we were way too high and rolling uncontrollably from left to right at the same time we were bouncing up and down.

I looked at Jeana and said, "How the hell are we going to fly this thing around the world when we can't even land at our own airport? It's a joke."

There was no way I could make a safe landing out of it. I started to get frightened, and then I felt completely out of control. As I went around again I almost went into a raging fit. This time I turned it in too close and had to go around again. The third time I could not even line the plane up with the center line of the runway. It became obvious I couldn't even crash the plane within the airport perimeter.

Finally I just said, "Fuck em, I'm going to Edwards."

Then off the line: "I can't believe I said that on the radio."

The ten-minute flight to Edwards was agonizingly slow and sickeningly rough.

Now I really needed Jeana for help. She braced herself against the bulkhead, and it was the two of us, plowing through the turbulence toward Edwards. Jeana reached up and rubbed my arm. "Okay, Rutan, it's okay," she said. "You're doing fine. Just don't panic. If you panic we're dead. Calm down. You can do it. Let's get our shit together and do this right." Then she continued down the checklist to the next item.

As the dry lake came into sight I thought, Forget the runway, I'm going to land this son of a bitch on the dry lake and never fly it again.

And then Jeana, as she had done so many times, came up to my shoulder and said, "It's not that bad, we're going to make it." She got the bottle of water out with a straw and gave me water, and she talked me into landing on the runway. Half laughing she said, "Don't hurt me, Rutan, I've got a lot of paperwork to finish up tonight."

The Edwards tower was reporting calm winds, but it didn't feel that way to us. On the landing, I overshot—it was one of the worst approaches I ever made—but we finally got the airplane down.

. . .

Once on the ground I tried to calm Dick down. It took everything I had to persuade him to come back to Mojave.

"It's a joke," he kept saying. "How the hell did we get ourselves into this? There is no way this thing can make it around the world. Who are we kidding? The longer we go, the deeper we get, the harder it will be to get out. Now we have no choice. The only out is death."

He had never been so frustrated, so ready to give the whole project up. He was talking about going off somewhere and changing his identity. I told him that would be nice but we had made a commitment to ourselves and to a lot of people. We had to finish what we started. We went on talking for an hour this way. I told him to get a good night's sleep and to see how things looked in the morning.

The flight suits were sent over to Edwards, knowing how much a uniform and an audience did to restore Dick's composure.

I reminded Dick that we had to get back to the hangar for our appointment with a television crew, and that we had to put on the dress-up-for-the-press flight suits.

He said he was not going to put on his flight suit ever again—as he was putting it on. "You aren't getting me in that monkey suit," he said, as he pulled on one leg. "I'm not ever wearing this again." Now his arms were in. And even as he zipped it up he swore he would never wear it again.

Back at Mojave, he talked to the press and was as professional as ever.

. . .

On Monday, September 29, we flew again, to test Burt's new idea: shift the center of gravity after takeoff to cut down on the oscillations.

The results were not encouraging. The problem persisted even with shifts in the center of gravity.

We came back to the hangar feeling very low. "It's a major setback," Dick said. I put the chutes down. I had a terrible migraine and sat down silently holding my head in my hands.

The oscillations had occurred again, and once more right between eighty-two and eighty-three knots. Dick had just barely fought off the porpoise in time, even at this weight. What would it be like at full world-flight weight? The shifting of CG had only confirmed that the problem was what is called aeroelastic, something to do with the shape of the airplane as it flexes, not with speed or weight distribution. This was our worst fear.

None of us was about to give up. We talked to Burt, and he came up with another idea, a new fix: a set of weights to be mounted forward of the wingtips in hopes of damping their vibration. Fergy was skeptical, but he and Bruce and Neal went about making the weights. They opened up some of the bags of lead shot we had used for weight testing, melted the shot, and poured it into paper cups to mold wheel weights. These were to be bolted to forward protruding plywood arms secured with clamps to the ends of the wings. The weights weren't finished before Dick left that night; the work would go on all night. But as I left in the early hours of the morning, I caught a glimpse of what the crew was attaching to the end of Voyager's sleek wings, and went cold. "I will not fly with those," I resolved.

When I woke up the next morning I felt uncomfortable and vaguely uneasy. It was nothing I could put my finger on. Sometimes I've had dreams or feelings about things that actually happen later. This was not a dream, but it was a strong feeling that seemed to be warning me of something. Whatever it was, something felt very wrong. Something was going to happen on this flight. But I got ready to fly anyway.

I woke Dick up and told him I didn't like what was being put on the wingtips. I wanted him to look at them closely when he went into the hangar. Dick mumbled something about Burt and Bruce and how they had worked out a solution. Dick arrived at the hangar and went to look at the weights. What he saw were ragged plywood fins, projecting forward from the wingtips, with crude leaden wheels bolted to them. They were strange and horrible contraptions that didn't look like part of any airplane—much less a world-flight airplane.

It was Rube Goldberg stuff: the plywood could come loose and tear off a winglet and make the airplane uncontrollable. There was no way Jeana or I would fly with those things.

I walked to the office, closed the door, sat down at my desk, and began to sob. The frustration all poured out. I felt let down by Burt, let down by a crew who had carried out some vague orders from Burt and ignored common sense to put dangerous objects on our airplane. Between the idea and plan and its translation into materials, something had gone terribly wrong.

Out in the hangar, others were equally appalled.

"These things," Lee Herron said. "These will kill them."

Ferg Fay sat grim-faced, drinking his morning coffee, and agreed. Even Magnamite, wandering through the hangar, seemed to wear an air of dismay.

So the tip weights went. Instead, we decided to see if we could dampen the oscillations with bob weights—something like clock pendulums—attached to the pitch control cable inside the nosewheel well. It had worked on an earlier plane we had tested called the Microlite, and it was worth a try here. It would cost twenty pounds, but we were running out of ideas.

We pulled ourselves together, mustered whatever optimism we could, and took off at heavyweight. We flew to the southwest, flew past Edwards, and were surprised to find that we really did have some luck with the bob weights. The oscillations were less extreme and the cycle longer. We flew for a couple of hours and were over a rough area not far from a little town called Willow Springs. We began to feel a little encouraged, for the first time in a long time. This fix might really work. If we increased the weight on the bobs, we might just be able to make this plane safe to fly.

We were also still testing the effects of shifting CG, transferring fuel out of the aft boom tanks into the feed tank—the largest shift in CG we could make. We were about halfway through the process and relaxed—as relaxed as we ever got in this plane—watching the fuel counters and waiting for the pumps to finish.

All of a sudden—Bang!—the airplane started vibrating violently. We couldn't read anything on the panel, but the cockpit was full of smoke. Everything was shaking. Entire instruments were coming loose from the panel. The radar screen popped out and landed practically in my lap.

I pushed it back into the panel, flipped off the autopilot, and grabbed the stick, thinking at first we had another flutter problem. But within a second we both knew it had to be a prop.

In grabbing the stick I set off the porpoising—a large oscillation—and I had to control that now subconsciously while my conscious mind went to work figuring out what had gone wrong.

The question was, which prop?

From the chase plane, Bruce saw it immediately. It sailed by, so close that it almost hit the wing. Bruce and Doug Shane and Jack Norris could see the blade going flying past. In the chase everybody stayed cool. Doug Shane very professionally turned the video camera on, had it aimed at *Voyager* within a couple of seconds, and recorded the whole incident on tape.

"You lost a prop, Dick," Bruce said.

"What is it?"

"You lost the front prop, Dick, take it easy."

"What prop?!"

"You're okay, shut off the front engine."

When the vibration started, Dick began talking in a high-pitched voice. I was on my elbows, head down, monitoring fuel gauges and preparing to record the fuel transfer in the log. Looking up, I could see his hands going in all directions and not really doing anything.

I smelled fuel and immediately started getting the checklist ready for emergency procedures, stowing things away, tugging up my chute—as on most test flights, Dick was already wearing his—while Dick was yelling to Bruce.

"You lost a prop, Dick." The third time Bruce told him I knew Dick hadn't caught it, and then I reached up and touched his arm. I was about to tell him "The front," but just then, he understood which engine it was.

It had taken eight or ten seconds. Jeana was telling me to stay calm. Everything was still a massive blur. I pulled the front throttle to idle, the mixture control off. The plane went into another wild pitch oscillation, and I fought that with my right hand on the stick and got it under control as I worked the engine controls with the left. I couldn't believe the front engine was still there. Now we had to make it stop turning.

The windmilling of the single remaining blade began to slow, and as the rotation decayed I could feel the amplitude increase and the vibration get stronger. I knew that the most dangerous vibration mode, the one most likely to take the engine off, was not the fastest but a slower one with a resonance that corresponded to the prop's natural frequency. So the engine might come off as the windmilling slowed.

I tensed myself, waiting for that to happen. I felt the oscillation increase in intensity, then pass through the dangerous frequency, and then I began to feel the amplitude going down and knew we were through the danger zone. It had taken fifteen seconds.

We were in control again. I had the presence of mind to tell chase to mark the spot so we could come back and get the prop blade.

Jeana rubbed my shoulders and talked to me calmly and slowly. "Take it easy, it's only a test flight. Just handle it professionally, relax. We're going to go through the checklist."

And that way we began securing the engine and preparing for landing.

We still smelled fuel in the cockpit and weren't sure that we didn't have major structural damage or that the airplane would not blow up at any second.

Bruce assured us the engine was still there.

I began feeling out the controls very gingerly, checking our ailerons, our elevators, our rudder—yes, everything was still there. I kept smelling the fuel, and as I looked to see if we had an active leak, I noticed that a part of our original, now discarded fuel transfer system was gone from the fuel bulkhead. That piece had been glued with Hot Stuff glue so tightly we had never been able to remove it, but the vibration had done the job. Boy, I thought, what an airplane, to take that kind of pounding.

We were amazed the engine was still there. In most airplanes, it would have been gone. The fact that the airplane had stood up to the loss of a whole prop blade was incredible. There was smoke and a little bit of a fuel smell, but no major leak. We could easily have ruptured a fuel tank, and the next time we transmitted on the radio the airplane would just have blown sky-high.

The engine was still there, the plane was still controllable, but what about a fuel leak? Bruce pulled the chase plane close to check; there was no leak he could see. I noticed we were losing airspeed, so I pushed the back engine up to full power. We were still very heavyweight.

I was breathing very deeply. My mind was working a million miles a second now—I was surprised how clear my head was—but there was a sinking feeling in my stomach.

Fortunately we were pointed right at Rosamond dry lake, a potential emergency landing site.

We tried to figure out where to land—Edwards Air Force Base or Mojave?

Bruce and I both had the same thoughts at exactly the same time.

I inclined at first to Mojave. We both knew that repairing what was almost certainly major damage would be harder at Edwards, without our tools. Bruce had the same idea. "We'll get a lot more done at home," he radioed.

It was a difficult choice to make, still reeling as we were with the shock of losing the blade. We assessed the situation: *Voyager* could sustain level flight, but if we had trouble at Mojave, on one engine we wouldn't have enough power to go around for a second try.

And then all of us at almost the same time thought of something else: debris might have damaged the back prop. The engine felt smooth, but Bruce pointed out that the back prop might be ready to let go, too, at any moment. We remembered our ground rule: Never risk the airplane unnecessarily.

"Let's worry about that on the ground," Jeana replied. We were still smelling fuel fumes in the cockpit.

You don't fly over a top-flight landing field with a long runway and emergency equipment.

We had a plaque just inside the door to our house that read, "The superb pilot is best defined as the pilot who uses his superb decisions to avoid situations in which he has to use his superb skills." That was the moral here: Don't risk a dangerous situation when you don't have to. There was really no choice at all.

The decision was Edwards.

We contacted approach control, declared an emergency, and got clearance to penetrate the restricted area. We were about twenty-five miles from Edwards, in a slow descent and just about lined up with runway 4, on which we planned to take off for the world flight.

We came down in a typical flame-out landing pattern. We had never landed this heavy before. I wanted to be careful not to come in too short and not too high or hot, either. It was time to rely on all the skills of a whole flying career. We didn't dare use the reverse on the back now that it was our only engine; landing speed would have to be right on the mark.

Jeana came up beside me. She had anticipated what we needed and had the checklist there.

We went through the checklist for landing: gear down, power reduced, prop set for high RPM go-around, mixture rich, fuel systems yellow up, fuel transfer boost pump on.

As we went over all the check items for the front engine, which no longer applied, we looked at each other, knowing we had now probably lost a year.

I began a shallow left-hand bank as we got clearance for landing.

I had to judge how fast we were descending, so I pulled the power way back to idle in order to be as close as possible for landing.

The Edwards tower had put all other operations on hold for our emergency. We were going against the normal traffic, and I saw an F-4 make a low approach and divert. A T-38 trainer on approach to runway 21 broke out of traffic to hold.

In the back of my mind I thought of all those jet jockeys up there, sucking up fuel and waiting impatiently for some civilian airplane to land.

We could still smell fuel and worried about those control surfaces. What if one was just barely hanging on? We were below bail-out altitude, and if anything came loose now, we were dead. There would be nothing we could do.

At two thousand feet over the field Jeana already had the main gear down, and as we came over the runway numbers, we put the nose gear down.

The approach looked a little high and a little fast, so I pulled the nose up and made a couple of S-turns to bleed off more altitude. With the engine at hard idle, we came down and flared out. Jeana called off the airspeeds and told me to take deep easy breaths. We were still five knots high; it seemed to take a long time to get down to our landing airspeed.

Not until we were down to fifty feet did we know we had it made. We would be a little long, but that was okay. Even that heavy the airplane still wanted to float. As we touched down I applied full forward stick to hold the nose on the runway, then reversed the back engine and slowed down with a slight touch of the brake. We rolled about 4,100 feet and turned off at midfield as the crash wagons came up to meet us.

I had a sick feeling. I wanted to look like a real pro to the Air Force, and I wondered what they thought. I felt a bit ashamed.

Jeana finished the checklist—battery off, mags off—and then she took the log and completed the flight entry: "Landed at Edwards."

She undid the back two latches and I did the front three, and we took the canopy and handed it to Bruce, who had landed just behind us.

The emotions were mixed: relief that we were down alive, respect for an airplane that had held together under extreme strain, but also sadness and a little bit of embarrassment.

We got out and walked around and saw the engine just lying in the bottom of the cowl. It had broken its mounts, but the steel tie cable (which Bruce had put on) had held. The front cowling was beaten up a little bit, and where the prop had gone into the spinner there was an ominous hole. With a flashlight, you could see the half stub the blade had left. Three of the attaching lag bolts had broken off. Jeana happened to have a camera along.

•

I took a few pictures. The sun was hot, and I sat down quietly under the airplane, while Dick, who was still shot full of adrenaline, went on explaining what had happened to all the air force personnel who had gathered around. I felt strangely comfortable; now I understood why I felt uneasy this morning.

We hadn't yet sorted out what this meant to the program, concentrating on the emergency, keeping our heads focused on the task at hand, but once I scrambled out of the cockpit, it struck me: this could be the end of things; we might not be able to put the pieces back together.

I thought, Well, we'll be grounded for at least three months. And I flopped down on the tarmac, in the shade of the wing under the right boom tank, feet toward the rudder, overcome with the exhaustion of the day, of the past few weeks, months, years, and settled my head onto the tire of the landing gear. I'm not going to die for at least three months, I thought, and a strange calm descended over me. Part of me felt good that the program was stalled, and another part felt bad for feeling so good.

An air force officer was telling me that we were blocking an active taxiway, and could we please move the airplane?

The air force took one look at the front engine and had visions of the rear prop blade coming loose and slicing through one of their expensive airplanes. They instructed us to keep the plane of rotation of the prop clear of the flightline. We got back in, had the rear engine hand-propped, and taxied almost three miles to the edge of the ramp, then pushed the plane another three-quarters of a mile, to a parking slot beside a giant B-52 Bomber.

. . .

As soon as he heard over the radio what had happened, Peter Riva came over to Edwards with an NBC camera crew that happened to be at the hangar, came through the press office, grabbed a public affairs officer, and dashed to the flightline. Knowing we were likely to be on the ground for a while, knowing we would have to scramble to reassure our sponsors to keep going, he wanted maximum coverage of the landing and what it said about a crew and an airplane that could survive such a near disaster. Heading for Edwards at seventy-five miles an hour, he had passed a traffic accident and caught a glimpse of two bodies lying under white sheets on the shoulder. It made him shudder.

· · ·

Dick was afraid we would have to make repairs before we could leave Edwards, and that it might take a month or more. But Bruce had already figured out what to do. He had called Ferg and had him bring the prop and extension from the first engines we had flown with, the rag-overhauled Lycomings.

Bruce and his crew turned the remaining blade on the front engine to feather and taped up all the holes in the cowling with duct tape. Then they replaced the rear prop with a fixed-pitch wooden prop Bruce Tifft had carved for the Lycoming and defueled and refueled the plane to a known center of gravity at a much lighter weight.

At dawn the next morning we ran down a checklist that was considerably shorter than usual, then took off, single engine, so light that the airplane just leaped into the air.

The fixed-pitch wooden prop felt reassuringly solid, the weather gods were merciful to us, and the Mojave landing was a piece of cake.

"It took bigger balls than I have to get back in that airplane," Lee Herron told me after we got back, and I smiled.

· · ·

Afterward we watched the videotapes that Doug had made from the chase and listened to the radio tape. I sat with my head in my hands, and Jeana sat on the floor with a hand on my knee. I heard how high my voice had become. "Why did it take me so long to get the message?" I kept wondering. And the more I thought about it, the more I suspected that it was my fear of the airplane and my desire to get out of this thing that had kept me from hearing. There was part of me that would rather have lost the airplane and even our lives to get it all over with.

If we found the prop blade, we could probably figure out just what had failed—and then feel either better or worse. We used the landscape features in the background of the videotape to give us an idea of just where we had lost the blades. Then we got the radar people at the Navy China Lake Weapons Testing Center to go through their tracks and come up with our flight track. Some guy on the night shift went through the whole computer and found it. You couldn't see the blade itself, of course, because it was wood and fiberglass, but you could track Voyager and mark the point where all of a sudden we lost about three hundred feet of altitude. That was when it had departed.

Larry Caskey and some of the troops from the trailer took the coordinates, and a Loran set out in a Jeep to look for the prop half. The Loran sat on a roll of sponge rubber on the console, powered into the cigarette lighter and with the antenna run all around the roof rack.

They located the area where we thought the prop had landed. There were some alfalfa fields around, and we hoped it had hit there, but no luck: the area indicated turned out to be all sagebrush. Hours on foot turned up nothing.

Finally they went up to the nearest house. It was surrounded by all sorts of junk—cars, campers, refrigerators, even a cabin cruiser, high and dry in the desert. Inside a fence guinea hens ran free, and two or three dogs came barking out from behind a pickup truck with a bumper sticker that read, "God Bless America and Please Hurry."

Larry waded through the dogs up to the house and talked to the lady there. No, she hadn't seen the plane or the prop. Yes, she would keep a lookout and tell the neighbors, but she didn't see how anyone could find something like that out there except by accident.

. . .

So we were grounded for a while. We sat down and tried to figure out what to do. The more we thought about Gerd's props, the less sure we were about them. Things kept emerging, negative things: Victor Haluska at Santa Monica Prop had been the one who talked up Gerd in the first place, and now he was telling about how some of his consultants, former FAA people, had been dismayed by the final product. "You would never get those props certified in the United States," one of them told Gerd over the phone, and the argument racing across the continent and the ocean had become so heated that I intervened. We did not want to anger Gerd. We hadn't entirely given up on the MT props—yet.

Maybe, Bruce suggested, it wasn't the prop's fault at all, but a bad bolt or something we did in recontouring them or even a bird strike. And there might not be anyone who could provide us with new props in time. It was Bruce's way to air alternatives, and we hashed it over for quite a while. But in the end we decided to give up on the MT props. "That rat bit me," was the way I put it. "I don't want to pick it up again."

Publicly, we took the blame for the loss of the prop blade, saying that we had not run adequate vibration torque and balance tests on the system. But this was only to protect Gerd's reputation and ensure his continued goodwill. In private, we were appalled at the quality of his engineering.

If those flights were hard on me, they had to be even harder for Jeana. I marveled at her calm—when the oscillations started, when the prop went. How, I asked myself, do you have enough guts to lie on that seat without any controls, getting flailed all around, and still be a functional crew member, keeping track of the fuel shifts and the engines? Jeana rubbed my neck and calmed me down. She was the one who got me home.

For her own part, Jeana threw herself into the work around the office. When she could slip off she went to ride Gem or go once in a while to the horse auction in Lancaster with Terri Smith.

One day Jeana and Terri and other volunteers put the horses in a trailer and drove to where we thought the prop had come off, west of Rosamond. They drove past ranches and trailers and wrecked cars and a place called the Last Chance Restaurant.

It was a beautiful, windless day—it would have been perfect for flying—and we rode for hours back and forth across the desert, searching and inhaling the spicy scent of the sagebrush. The prop could have disappeared into the middle of any one of thousands of bushes—you could have been five feet from it and not seen it. In between the bushes lay the white bones of calves and lambs and jackrabbits, bleached by the sun, and the rusty hulks of old tin cans protruded from the ground.

In the end, we found nothing. But the day out in the open was good.

Dick went out later in the Cessna-150 and looked from the air. So did Bruce, and both came back without finding anything.

"We'll find that prop," Bruce said, "when we stop organizing searches."

Rescue Mission

The loss of the prop turned out to be not just a blessing in disguise, but one of the luckiest things that happened during the whole program. "Fortune was smiling on us," Bruce said. If we had lost that prop out over the Pacific on the world flight, it would have been the end of the mission, and quite likely our airplane and our lives. The episode confirmed that these were not the props with which we wanted to fly around the world. They were being asked to do too much. "Those props," Bruce said, "have been trying to tell us something ever since we got them."

But it was hard to have to shut down the program on almost the very day we were to have begun the world flight. The chances for getting off in 1986 looked bleak. Len Snellman gave us discouraging weather prospects for the coming months. And another year made us fear losing sponsors and volunteers. Who could blame the sponsors if they began to get cold feet? And there was all that equipment in the trailer that people would soon want back—all those computers and radios. And there were volunteers who had jobs and families to get back to.

By great good fortune, the National Business Aircraft Association convention was going on nearby in Anaheim at exactly this time. Most of the chief executives of our major sponsors—the men who could make the decisions—were there. To get appointments with these CEOs and visit them in their offices all over the country would have taken a month. And the convention was an ideal negotiating environment with each CEO standing virtually in the eye of the aviation public.

We needed some help, and we needed it fast. So we flew down to

Anaheim with Peter and Bruce the day after the prop loss to rally the troops.

As we walked in the door, the Teledyne Continental booth was right in front of us, and hanging above it was a twenty-foot scale model of *Voyager*. The new line of liquid-cooled *Voyager* engines was the star of their display. We were counting on them, and their booth made it clear how committed they already were. They agreed to refurbish the engines as soon as we could get them to their facility in Mobile, Alabama and mate them to new props—if we could come up with the props.

The booth next door belonged to TRW Hartzell, the manufacturer at that time of metal props.

We had had a big meeting to figure out what to do about new props. We knew we wanted metal ones now, but we weren't even sure if it was technically possible to rig up metal props for these engines, which had never been designed for them. The engines would have to be drilled for a hydraulic system to allow the pitch changes we needed. Could that be done? Did a metal reverse pitch pusher prop even exist?

The best people to go to, we knew, were the ones at TRW Hartzell. Now we came to them a little sheepishly. After all, we had originally picked a German company over them, why should they help us out now? And Dick feared that the loss of the prop had put the credibility of our project in danger.

We had rounded up John Roncz, who had wanted metal props all along, had worked with Hartzell, was respected by them, and was eager to design new blades.

Peter planned to ask them to do the job in two weeks and was willing to settle for a month. Hartzell assured us the thing was technically possible but promised they could deliver in ten days. The only catch was it was a period of austerity at TRW, and they had to get an okay from higher-ups in the parent company. It turned out that the TRW executives, along with those of other firms, had seen the in-flight footage of the prop loss that was released the day after the episode, and it had left them, if anything, even more impressed with the airplane and the project. They gave Hartzell the go-ahead.

The weight penalty, including a hydraulic mechanism to change blade pitch, instead of the previous electric motors, would be around seventy pounds—or more than three hundred pounds of fuel. That would be a burden, but eventually we decided that the durability was worth it. And Roncz promised us that the improved performance of metal blades would more than make up for their weight.

To cut the two or three weeks it would normally take to get the engines to Mobile, we went to Beech. Peter approached Beech's CEO Jim Walsh, then asked for and received a commitment for airplanes, fuel, and pilots to ferry the engines to Mobile and back.

King Radio's booth was festooned with pictures advertising that its avionics were in Voyager—King's CEO, Fred Wenniger, agreed to check out all the instruments that had been so badly shaken in the vibration following the prop loss. We did not even turn the avionics on during the flight back from Edwards, but, amazingly, when we had plugged all the instruments back in on the ground, everything worked, but with the stakes so high King wanted to recheck everything.

The four of us literally ran from booth to booth to catch everyone. Peter boosted the program, wrapping us in the Stars and Stripes and practically telling them that the president would haul them up on treason charges if they didn't stick with us. They all held firm. Almost before they knew it, they had agreed to make a big push to help us out. Within three hours everyone had been lined up to help, a careful schedule had been drawn up, and "the great Voyager rescue mission" was under way. During the flight to Anaheim, we had discussed a realistic delay of six to eight months. But Peter was having none of that, and now the schedule was down to, if we were lucky, a month or two.

. . .

The pressure was still on, but the intense day-to-day pressure of the test flights just before we lost the prop was removed. Things were out of our control for a while now, in the hands of others. The time gave us an opportunity to recognize that we were not alone in this project.

We had to realize that the project was bigger than we were. We had to learn to let go and to trust the people who had stepped forward—Len and Larry and Peter and Mike and Bruce and Burt—to make sure that the airplane and the flight were safe, at least as safe as they could be made. We had started out working alone—two people out in the desert—and we were used to doing everything ourselves, but now we had so much of ourselves invested that we were in danger of losing perspective.

We came to understand that in a sense the lives of those working with us were on the line, too. Their lives would never be the same again, and if anything happened to us—through some mechanical problem, some problem in communications, some weather forecast that led us into danger— they would never recover. We also realized that the airplane we would take off in for the world flight would be far better than the one we might have taken off in before we lost the prop.

We had finally recognized that the wooden props had been a mistake. In surveying the available models and manufacturers, we had neglected to ask about the efficiency of the props. This was one case where we had overemphasized weight reduction. The metal props added about seventy pounds—a huge amount of weight. But as it turned out, because they could be machined more finely, their efficiency was higher than that of the wooden props.

We had other things to worry about, and we just put up with the MT props. We put up with them even after one came loose and tore through a prop blade in the engine test cell at Teledyne Continental in Mobile back in 1984, put up with them even though we had noticed that the main blade retention bearings were wearing at an alarming rate, put up with them even after the control motor failure forced us into the emergency landing at Vandenberg Air Force Base during the Pacific coast flight.

John Roncz, who had never been comfortable with the wooden props, went home, sat down at his computer on Thursday afternoon, and, aside from a scattered eleven hours of sleep, didn't come up for air until Monday, when he had worked out a new set of prop designs. He hooked his computer up with Hartzell's and zapped the new prop designs over to them, and they got to work turning metal pieces designed for an old Spencer Air Car—the only pusher-type pieces they had in inventory—into props for Voyager's back engine.

TRW Hartzell did a yeoman job of turning those out just as quickly as they promised. Hartzell is located in the little town of Piqua, Ohio, and the whole town seemed to pull together to do the job.

We'd been told that Hartzell wouldn't be able to meet our deadline, but they did: it took them ten days, ten days of everyone in that factory pulling together, working voluntary overtime, feeling that the reputation and pride of the company were on the line.

John Roncz went to work directly with the prop maker this time, to make sure his designs were accurately reproduced.

Two of the props were accidentally nicked in the anodizing tank, and although the nicks could easily have been filed out, without loss of performance and probably without anyone noticing, the workers were not satisfied. They would know, so they all went back to the factory and in two days built a new set—just in time for a formal presentation ceremony.

Jeana stayed in Mojave and I flew out to take receipt of the props. After John had given them the okay, the company broke out five big cakes and threw a party, with all the families coming in to celebrate. It was an inspiring performance, one of the most heartwarming experiences I'd ever had. There was no amount of money that could have made them work that well, that fast. It could only have been done by people who were working for nothing.

Bruce, Fergy, and Glenn got the engines crated up in about a day and a half and Ralph Meyer flew the engines back to Teledyne Continental in Mobile in a Bonanza lent by Beech. Even though it was a weekend, they went right to work checking them out, rebuilding the front to make sure there was no damage from the vibration of the prop loss, and carefully checking the rear, drilling it for the hydraulic prop control governors. While Bruce, Neal, and Ferg repaired the cowlings and rebuilt the mounts, Glenn flew down to TCM in Mobile. From now on the engines and especially the rear, which would run all through the flight, would be his particular responsibility.

I brought the props directly from Piqua to Mobile in a Beech Baron. There, they were mated to the engines in a test cell and run in. It was a frustratingly slow experience. These were thorough and deliberate engineers, and parts of the process could not be hurried.

We needed to break in the rebuilt front engine. The walls of its cylinders had been specially hardened to increase its durability, but that increased the necessary break-in time. The only way to do that was to just run it, run it twenty-four hours a day, but the engineers kept making all sorts of little adjustments that they thought would hasten the process. Meanwhile, time dragged on.

Finally the engines were ready. On the return trip from Mobile, carrying the engines and props back to Mojave, Peter Riva came along, and we flew through some god-awful weather. The Baron had a King color weather radar just like the one in Voyager's cockpit. We used it to pick our way through storms and rain so heavy we couldn't even see the end of the wings. We landed, and a man came up to Peter, thinking he was the pilot, and asked him, "What the hell were you doing flying? All traffic, military and civilian, has been grounded for hours."

It was the first time I had used that radar in such conditions and it provided a thorough course whose lessons I knew I would have to apply on the world flight.

. . .

The delay brought another, incidental benefit: it gave us time to install a backup autopilot. King wanted us to test out a new piece of equipment for them, the satellite-linked global positioning system, and we agreed to carry it. If none of the fixes for the pitch instability panned out, the redundant autopilot would at least give us an extra margin of safety. Before, if the autopilot failed, we lost the mission. And if it failed at a critical time, we might easily have lost the airplane and our lives to the pitch porpoise. And adding this equipment, too, was worth its weight.

On November 15 we were ready to fly again. We found that the metal props had a performance factor that was 3 to 5 percent improved—well worth the cost in added weight. It was an astonishing improvement in a business where people offer to sacrifice their grandmothers for a 2 percent improvement. We were overjoyed.

With the wooden props we had been limited in another way: there was a red zone band from 1,800 to 2,200 RPMs, where a strange and dangerous vibration set in, the result of interaction between engine vibration and prop vibration. This was right in the range where we needed to run for best economy, and we had never been happy having to put up with it. Now we no longer did.

And the metal props were extremely strong—they were rated for a three-hundred-horsepower engine, three times as powerful as our engines. We felt so confident that we removed the steel safety cables that provided a secondary attachment of the engine to the fuselage. Those cables were just about all that had held the engine on after we lost the wooden prop over the desert, but now we felt so good that we did away with them and saved a little weight.

. . .

On the very day we first flew again, a ten-year-old girl named Jennifer Burns, who lived near Willow Springs, was out with her father and brother, who had heard we were offering a reward for the lost prop. They had a map Terri and Kelly Chandler had given them, and they drove out to the desert. Jennifer took a toothpick in her hand and "flew it" over the map until she came over the indicated spot and dropped it. Then she and her father and her brother drove out to the location where the toothpick had landed on the map. Jennifer's father and brother decided to walk off in one direction to search, but Jennifer said, "No, I know it's over here." A few minutes later she found the prop blade not fifty feet from the mark on the map, sticking out of a bush beside a Joshua tree, without even a nick in it.

They came up to Hangar 77, where Jeana gave Jennifer her reward and some T-shirts, and we took a picture of everyone with the blade, which had fractured neatly across its base. Two lag bolts had come completely loose inside the prop hub. There was no other damage to the blade, no external cause for the failure, and any speculation about our having cracked the blade in reshaping or having hit a bird was ended. Our decision to get completely new props was confirmed.

.   .   .

We resumed flight tests with the new props and rebuilt engines. We had a few little problems, a leak in a fuel tank, an overheating oil problem, but they were quickly licked. We flew at 75 percent of world flight weight, but Jeana insisted on one more test flight.

We scheduled our heavyweight—8,600-pound—flight, our last test flight, for the first week in December. We would take off at 85 percent of our planned world-flight takeoff weight.

Fitz Fulton was there to fly chase. Fitz had just retired from NASA and was a valuable man to get on board—a member of the Mach 3 Club, a veteran of the B-58 and B-70 programs, and one of the pilots who flew space shuttles from Edwards back to the Cape on the piggyback of a Boeing 747.

There was a sickening moment when we rolled the airplane out for takeoff—only to find there was low oil pressure. We rolled it back into the hangar and found a little Teflon obstruction in the relief valve—an ornery little gremlin, but easily dispatched.

We took off, and for more than six hours Voyager flew so much better that when we landed we fairly bounced out of the airplane with happiness.

We were ready to go.

.   .   .

There was one other thing to do before we left. We made a videotape to be shown in case we died. I was insistent on making a record. No one knew more than we did the mortal risk this flight would involve, and we had some things to put on record—just in case. We asked Peter Riva to set up the video camera on the runway. He got the camera rolling and then walked off a hundred yards. We walked into the frame and up to the camera. I told the camera—told everybody—that we knew it was a high-risk deal, but that we thought it had been worth it. Everybody had done his or her best, and that's all we could ask for. Even though it might not turn out all right, no one should feel down about it. We should be proud of what we accomplished and preserve its spirit.

When we were finished we asked that if anything happened to us everybody should gather together and play that tape once. We didn't want anyone to feel guilty if something happened to us, and God knows we didn't want anyone to sue anybody.

It upset us to hear about the lawsuits after the *Challenger* shuttle disaster. We felt they disgraced the dead astronauts by suing the very people the astronauts had served and died for, and we made this point very strongly on the tape: there were to be no lawsuits.

.   .   .

We kept in mind Don Taylor's axioms, derived from his years of experience with record and around-the-world flight—two of them in particular: "The airplane will never be totally ready" and "The weather will never be as good as you want."

Dick had thought we might have to stand around, ready to go, for weeks. The drill for the last twenty-two hours before takeoff had been carefully worked out months ago. Bruce's mobile launch team would depart immediately for Edwards, taking the motor home that would serve as headquarters there, the fuel bowser, scales, wing support beds, toolboxes, and other equipment. Edwards security had to be notified, rescue and medical teams put on alert, hotel reservations activated, facilities for the press and public—including loudspeakers dotting two miles of runway edge—set up. Back in Mojave, the airplane would be rolled out of the hangar at exactly 12:27 and the engines started at 12:42; takeoff for Edwards was set for 12:49.

Once the airplane was loaded, we stood in readiness to start this schedule rolling. Every morning at ten exactly we would decide whether to move the airplane to Edwards that afternoon. We would open the doors, look out and see what the weather was, talk to Len, send Lee Herron and others up to see what the air was like on the path out of Edwards, and decide whether to launch the next day or not. If the decision was no, we'd delay exactly twenty-four hours. But if the decision was go, a carefully worked out, tight timetable started immediately. Ground launch team went to Edwards to prepare, and the clock started to tick—plane to Edwards, fuel up, press conference, final medical exam, last dinner with the families, bedtime. And twenty-two hours after the decision, at oh dark thirty, weather providing, we would take off from Edwards.

We were happy to have the colder, thicker winter air to take off in. We worried more about the thin summer air for takeoff than about any weather on the course. Due to a factor known as density altitude, a summer takeoff, at the same weight, from the same runway, might easily take 50 percent more ground roll. And we didn't have that to spare.

If we had postponed the flight into the early part of the year, the terrible Antelope Valley winds of winter and early spring, which blow so hard you could barely stand up outside, would likely have delayed us. And then we would be looking at summer again, and that thin air, for a more critical takeoff.

We declared the airplane mission ready on the night of December 12, and on the first day we looked out, we made the decision to go. It jolted some people. All of sudden it was "Are we going to go?" "Yes, wow, oh, shit, let's do it." And if we hadn't gone that day, the next time the weather was decent, it turned out, was the day we brought the airplane from Edwards back to Mojave, on January 6. When we needed it, the weather was there.

. . .

Dick was all wound up and seeing ways through the weather, and soon Bruce was, too. But I would talk to the weather people and hear something different, hear about how there were three typhoons out there, one dissipating, one full, and one forming.

I had already started to gear my thinking to keeping the program going into next year, preparing to take the knocks if I had to. If the weather didn't improve, hard as it would be, I was well prepared to dig in my heels and say we would not go. We would not go before we were ready and the weather was ready. I asked Bruce and Peter to back me up on this, and they agreed.

I had always thought that all of a sudden the airplane would be ready, the people would be ready, and the window would open. I didn't know how and I didn't know when, but I knew it would open.

And that's the way it happened.

It was the magic door effect at work again.

The weather had not really been good all summer and fall, there were typhoons and fronts and the works. But now with the airplane nearing readiness and everything falling into place on the ground, a way began to open. Dick and Bruce got enthusiastic about it, and I even began to think it was legitimate. It was a new track, farther north, but there was a path all the way around. It just said, "Here I am," and three days later we were airborne. Ready, set, go.

Len felt he could take us along the top edge of the ITCZ all right, and across the Malay Peninsula and the Indian Ocean at the latitude of Sri Lanka. On the way home, the winter storms meant we would almost certainly not cut across Texas and the West as planned, but cross Central America and come up the West Coast. There was a typhoon forming in the south Pacific, but Len felt he could steer us around it. "I like to see a typhoon there," he said, "because that means tail winds."

But there was no way, Len told us, that we could get across Africa. No way. Day after day they looked at central Africa and just shook their heads.

My strong feeling of the rightness of things, of a guiding pattern attending the whole course of the program, asserted itself again. I couldn't explain the feeling I'd had from the beginning of the program that it was going to succeed, but it was a strong sense that everything in the program happened just when it was supposed to. It was never easy. I would always say, "If it had been easy someone would have done it a long time ago." This enabled me to deal with the many delays. Seen in this light, they weren't really delays at all. When we tried to push too fast Voyager would tell us, "No, I'm not ready," as if she were a living thing. Losing the prop was the clearest example: she gave us a lot of hints; then, when we wouldn't listen, she told us right out: "I don't like this prop."

Understanding this, now I could see the time and prospects of the flight as part of a positive and unfolding course of events that had the whole up-and-down history of Voyager on its side, a momentum pushing for success.

. . .

We flew the airplane over to Edwards on the afternoon of Saturday, December 13. It felt terrific to finally be getting under way and to see that this whole program we had set up for six years was finally coming together and tuned like a Swiss watch.

We checked all the systems on the way over, and everything was running fine. Jeana sat up close beside me, we both felt great, and when we landed on runway 22 at Edwards it felt like a triumphant arrival—almost as if we had finished the flight itself. When we got out, Jeana was giggling, and I felt really up.

Now Voyager stood parked at runway 4, on the tab of pavement at the top of the runway known in aviation parlance as the hammerhead. Bruce and the crew had eight to ten hours to fuel it up and prepare it for takeoff.

Then we had a problem: Jeana had a miserable little sinus cold. She couldn't even clear her head, and something like that could get worse on the world flight.

Lee Yeager got a chance to see Jeana for a little while the day before we were to take off. He did not feel easy at all about the flight. It seemed to him we were taking off under less than ideal circumstances, going this late in the year. "I thought I taught my daughter to be a better poker player than this," he said.

With Dr. Jutila's advice, I decided to try to beat the cold by sleeping. I tried to, but everyone kept coming around trying to take care of me. Judy came to check on me, then Suzy Bowman, then Sally Melvill, then Dr. Jutila, then Peter, then Lee, then Diane and before long it seemed everyone had been by to visit. I felt so bad I just wanted to crawl into a hole somewhere and curl up and get rid of that cold. Everyone thought I was sleeping through the late-afternoon press conference, which naturally raised assumptions that I was too sick to fly. Judy, Sally, and I made some chicken soup at the house. Then, in the middle of the evening, Dr. Jutila and Suzy Bowman drove me over to the secluded room scheduled for me at Edwards—otherwise, I don't think I would have gotten any sleep. Doc gave me a cold pill. I smiled and put it in my mouth—then spit it out when he wasn't looking. I didn't want any more chemicals in my body. I took one-quarter of the sleeping pill they offered me—remembering what had happened when I'd had a whole pill before the Vari Eze record—just to relax my muscles and help me ignore the noises, and finally I found some quiet. Doc Jutila left me a specimen container to fill and went down the hall to give another one to Dick. Before I went to sleep, I went down the hall to Dick's room, knocked on the door, and just gave him a little kiss. "Tomorrow's the one we've been training for," I said. "See you in the morning." I fell asleep immediately, and the next thing I heard was the alarm clock.

. . .

While Jeana was resting, I went to dinner on the base at Edwards with the family. "Can you believe it," Nell said, "Burt and Dick are talking about airplanes and center of gravity and downward-bending movement."

There was one serious moment. Pop Rutan didn't know exactly how to say it, but he told me, "Well, if you have to stop short, you can always try again." What he meant was, don't do anything foolish.

The dinner was in the dining room of the enlisted men's club, and another party nearby was being entertained by a magician. As he pulled handkerchiefs out of his sleeves and juggled balls and ran through all his other tricks, he seemed a vaguely sinister and disquieting figure.

In truth, I had never thought we had a better than one-in-three chance to make it all the way "on the first try." We were fearful of some nutty little mechanical problem—"the five-cent screw," was the way it was referred to in the shorthand of the hangar—or some physiological problem. But we had no way out, no recourse, no other lives. If we didn't go, we had nothing—not even self-respect. A long time ago, we had both decided, whatever the odds, that we were getting in that airplane.

Increasingly I wondered whether there would even be a second chance if we didn't succeed on the first. It wasn't so much the survival and recovery of the airplane from an unsuccessful first try that I worried about, although there were plenty of doubts associated with that; it was my own patience and resources. I knew Jeana could push on, but I wasn't sure I would have the courage and strength, after so long, to try again.

I went to bed in my room at the base officer quarters—only to be awakened an hour or two later by Doc Jutila, who came to drop off a urine specimen container. "Doc," I asked groggily, "you woke me up to give me a cup to piss in?"

I had trouble falling back to sleep. The halls of the barracks—for that was really what it was—were full of sound. The heating was too hot, and when I closed the vent it made a whistling sound. I slept maybe three or four restless hours.

Bending the Bow

A big moon hung over the hammerhead, with occasional clouds sailing in front of it, and from time to time during the night the guys were startled to see showers of meteors shooting across the sky. "The Geminids," someone observed, but was unable to define any augury, either promising or threatening, in their appearance.

Suzy Bowman had cooked up some chili, and it sat with the ever-filled coffeepot inside the ground crew "headquarters"—a motor home parked by the edge of the hammerhead.

With his briefcase open in front of him like some junior executive, Bruce sat inside the motor home and carefully filled out his charts, showing exactly how much fuel was in each tank. We had decided to put in four hundred pounds more than previously planned in the roots and mids; the new props had shown we could take off with that much more fuel.

Burt's recommended takeoff weight was 9,400 pounds—a figure so conservative it surprised us. I thought we could reasonably get off with 10,000 pounds. But we had noticed that Burt had become more and more cautious as takeoff neared. After talking to the old man who had seen the crashes of Lindbergh's competitors, who had made too great a leap in takeoff weight, he seemed to be looking for excuses to postpone things; he mentioned eight months as the time it might take to fix the pitch stability problem. Earlier he had sometimes pushed us into things that were a little too ambitious. But by the fall he was thinking more of the ramifications of possible failure: what it would feel like to lose us.

I had upped the takeoff weight to 9,700 pounds. This figure was based on an intuitive feel for the plane derived from sixty-seven flights and 354 hours in the airplane. There was another factor at work, too. I wanted to give Burt an out in case we didn't make it, that it had been my decision to increase takeoff weight beyond his recommendation. I told Bruce, "If anything goes wrong, it is the pilot's fault."

The fueling went pretty smoothly—the biggest problem, aside from the deepening cold that crept through all sorts of garments, was a shortage of Styrofoam cups. "You can go from coffee to chili in the same cup," Neal Brown observed, "but not very well from chili to coffee."

The air force had stationed guards around the airplane—kids who seemed no older than the Civil Air Patrol cadets who provided a security force and other help back at Hangar 77, kids who seemed barely old enough to shave—and they brought out big lights called Lightalls that turned the hammerhead into something resembling a Hollywood set—with *Voyager* as the star.

After the inboard tanks were full, Bruce and Ferg and the others settled the wings onto the folding beds—like sawhorses with little "mattresses" of foam rubber—that supported the ends of the wings.

The crew worked through the night. The hammerhead, Bruce had promised, "will be the calmest place in Kern County," and everything was prepared quietly and efficiently. It could have been just another test flight—except for the large numbers on the scales.

The cold seeped through boots and jackets; breath turned into smoke. By nine or so frost began to form on the wings, and Bruce ordered the airplane covered. Bruce had anticipated this, and a volunteer named Flo Van Berkleo had phoned around to all her friends and gotten together a lot of bedsheets to drape over the airplane.

As they were spread across the wings, Fergy and Neal joked about how the government would have handled the covering task.

"They would have called it frost inhibition substance development and spent a million dollars and taken a year and a half."

Instead, we had the sheets, which looked like a clothesline had fallen down. There were paisley ones lapped over pink ones, green ones, blue ones, and striped ones.

After the fueling was done, the crew slept in the motor home. There were bodies scattered over beds, couches, and the floor, while outside, the *Voyager* snuggled under the mismatched sheets and the hissing lights.

When they woke up and lifted the sheets to look at the airplane, they found that frost had begun to build up on the cool wings. It was thin, an almost invisible layer, but Neal took his plastic identification badge, scraped it along the surface, and came up with a small pile of the stuff. The weight wasn't the problem, it was what the rough frost might do to the airflow. The baby-faced airmen wheeled up hot-air blowers to clean off the frost, big engines with tubes coming out of them like caterpillar heads. Ferg aimed the mouth of the hose at the wing, and Neal Brown swept along behind it with a chamois cloth in each hand.

The dawn was like pink granite: some scattered gray clouds, some pink veins of sky opening up behind them. But most important of all, the air was calm and smooth.

. . . .

I shaved, took a very quick shower, and started dressing. I was proud of myself for remembering to pack all the things I would need on landing: clean underwear and clothes and shaving equipment. I hoped they would end up at the hospital where we were to be taken after the flight.

I was wondering what that takeoff was going to be like. This was the morning all the cards were on the table and going to be played.

But this was not the way I imagined it would feel starting on this great adventure. I needed to share it, and instead I found myself alone.

It took the alarm to wake me up. I usually take awhile to get going in the morning, and I got in the shower and stood there letting it wake me up.

Suzy and Dr. Jutila picked me up and took me to the hammerhead. Somehow it didn't seem like the big day; it seemed like another test flight, just as the coast flight had. On the hammerhead, Dick seemed in a hurry, grumbling and snapping, jumping around. Suzy Bowman tried to feed us. I just stared at the food. I thought, I should eat, but I didn't feel like it. I didn't even drink the tea. For eight months now I had stayed away from all caffeine, saving its effects in case I needed a jolt during the flight. The only thing I got down was a little fruit juice.

Dick went to the plane, started the engines to warm them up, and then shut them down. Then he ate part of an omelet Suzy had cooked him while I loaded up some last-minute items, dancing through the bitter cold in my *Voyager* sweats and slippers. I hugged everyone on the ground crew, one by one. Each of them was special to me.

Dick, as always at the beginning of important flights, had given strict orders that he was not to be touched. He was concerned about a cold, too, but it was also a long-standing practice with him. He never liked to say good-bye.

I got in first, stowed some things away, then got out again to put on my parachute harness. Dick came out, snapping at everyone to hurry up. I looked up at him and told him I was ready. "Are you ready to start through the checklist?" I asked him, but he was silent. Finally, we both settled in and started down the checklist. We knew we had designed, built, and installed everything around us. Maybe we should have made it more comfortable, but we just hoped it had all been done right.

Mike Melvill directed the hose of one of the air blowers into the cockpit to give us a little warmth.

We were both in our pale blue running sweats, silk-screened with the name *Voyager* in my script, cotton underwear, wool socks over cotton socks, and fleece-lined moccasins direct from Carol's Western Wear Store, which has been on the main drag in Mojave since the days when it looked like Dodge City. We covered the moccasins' rawhide laces with gray duct tape so that they couldn't catch in anything. It was a curious-looking garb, but it was practical and comfortable.

The feeling was not trepidation, but relief that the moment had finally come, that a day we had many times over the past six years doubted would ever come had come at last.

Our mental preparation for takeoff had actually started the day before when we both began to slow down, to cultivate a calm, even lethargic attitude, to condition ourselves to disassociate mind from body, to relax and calm down and focus.

I hopped out of the plane and strolled off behind a couple of cars to take a last-minute leak at the edge of the desert. It should be noted that Kelly Chandler had sewn a critical modification into my sweatpants: a Velcro-sealed fly. Kelly was concerned about possible abrasive effects, and I had promised to report back to her.

For a while Burt hovered over Dick, discussing the numbers for a possible abort. Dick brushed him off—he had it all straight already. Burt got in the chase plane—the twin-engine Duchess—with Mike and Sally Melvill.

"Have you got all your Christmas shopping done?" Burt asked over the radio.

At the very last minute before the canopy went on, Dick relinquished his leather flying jacket and black cowboy hat. He put on his glasses, which gave him a strangely professorial look as he scanned the instruments and made sure his extra glasses were along. Rich Hanson of the NAA came up to officially seal the canopy and as he did he handed Dick two Confederate ten-dollar bills. This was an informal custom in the space program, dating back to the first Mercury flights: we would check the serial numbers after landing.

The ground crew gingerly eased the wings down off their supporting beds. They drooped down, and fuel ran from the tip vents—as it was supposed to, until various crew members stuck fingers in the vents.

We looked out the windows and saw the crew holding their fingers in the wings. To save weight the fuel vent system only worked in flight, when the wings were bowed up. Now, as they bent toward the ground, fuel was running out.

It was time for the Hemingway starter. Ferg, wearing his pads, got down on his knees and spun the prop. He ducked away and watched as it first spun, then slowed. He started to put his hands back in for another try when, just as it seemed about to stop, it kicked one more time and then, at the very last chance, caught—not to stop again for 216 hours.

The only people allowed on the edge of the runway were families, VIP Club members, and press. Loudspeakers at intervals along two miles of the runway edge carried updates from our press team and radio transmissions. The public had been arriving since the dark hours of the morning, and they filled a viewing area normally used for NASA activities.

Cliff Robertson, whom we had met at Oshkosh and who had been out occasionally to help out, stood at one wingtip.

The crew walked, then ran along, touching the wings, each one of them a little reluctant to let go and release the airplane, or the particular part of it he was responsible for. They looked like a funeral procession.

We were not surprised at how calm we felt, even taking off heavier than we ever had, with the whole thing on the line. We were ready, and we knew that what we had to concentrate on was speed—reaching that key target speed for takeoff.

We had to be patient, making sure that we were above that speed before Dick pulled back on the stick and eased the plane up.

It hadn't sunk in; in fact it never did. I didn't feel any different even though this was really it. That was probably good: I thought of it as just another test flight. I had stowed everything in the cabin as I did in the stable: so I could reach it by feel. I had every confidence in Bruce and his crew. I knew Bruce would go over everything again, and there would be no shortcuts.

We looked silently at each other. I was set on my elbows and knees, legs tucked under me, braced but not strapped in, where I could watch the airspeed and temperatures. It was time for me to quit looking out. I turned my watch around with the face inside my wrist, so I could read it as I noted down airspeeds and temperatures.

Controllability was the big question. The heavier and faster we had flown this plane, the worse it had controlled. Was that four hundred pounds a good idea? The airplane might start into its oscillations, and I wasn't sure I could handle them. And on the test flights, on just about every third takeoff, the plane had leaped into the air and overrotated. The wings would flex up, the nose would pitch up, and then the wings would rebound. It took full stick forward to get the nose down. We could not afford that at full world-flight weight.

We didn't know whether, at this weight, the oscillations might not begin right on takeoff. That might be the last rung on the ladder we had feared so long. We were taking a chance that we could leap over that rung and scramble up on the roof.

We ran over the procedures. Jeana was to key the mike quickly as she gave her airspeeds to leave plenty of time for any message from outside the plane. We were not thinking abort. The procedure was that, if the ground crew saw a problem, they were to come on the air and repeat "Abort, abort, abort."

Otherwise, the decision was totally ours.

They would call out only if they saw a massive fuel leak or fire. And our words on the radio would be mostly for the benefit of those on the ground, to let them know we were all right.

I looked out at the plane, and suddenly I was unable to believe this thing would fly at all. It looked terribly ungainly. I pushed the thought out of my mind to review what I would be doing.

With my left hand I would have to keep rotating the switches to display all the temperatures and pressures for Jeana to read. My right hand had to be limber so I could make the rotation smoothly. I flexed my hands and fingers and shoulders and got loose like a batter coming up to the plate. I would need to be smooth and sure for rotation about two miles down the road.

We got our air traffic clearance, but almost as fast as the frost could be cleaned off it reappeared, like moisture on a glass of ice water on a summer afternoon. One hot-air blower had stopped working, and the crew was trying to do it all with a single machine. Mist kept appearing on the inside of the canopy, too, and Jeana handed me a handkerchief to wipe it off.

With every minute we were eating critical fuel, and the temperatures in the engines, which had never been designed for ground cooling, were rising, approaching the red line. If they got too high, we would have to shut down and wait two or three hours for the engines to cool. The air was warming, too, and density altitude was going up, the air thinning.

Bruce saw fuel coming out of the left tip fuel cap. Bob Williams was yelling that there was still some frost on the wing. But we had to go.

Bruce was ready to stop the takeoff, and he almost did. After years of deliberate and careful effort, now suddenly it all seemed too hurried. There were lots of loose ends. All sorts of problems—the strange power surges, the sparks inside the fuel tanks, the fluttering sparrow strainer—these flashed through Bruce's mind.

But he realized that at last, go or not, it was time to give it all a try.

"Clear me, Bruce," I said, acknowledging the authority of the ground crew chief.

And Bruce did, despite all the doubts. "You're cleared."

"Let's go. We're on the red line here. We're overheating."

And so we did, just after eight o'clock—well after oh dark thirty.

I heard Jeana say, "Are you ready?"

My heart was beating a little fast, but I felt comfortable and loose.

"Okay, let's go over it one more time," I said. "You're watching airspeed and engine temps, and I handle the power and where we are on the runway."

"Well, here we go," I said, but so softly Jeana could barely hear me.

I released the brake and gradually pushed the throttles forward.

Ferg stood behind us, watching. Peter Riva, holding fuel in the forward left boom tank, was nearly swept off on a wing, practically run over, and had to drop underneath and let it pass over his head. Bruce held the left boom back by the tail to keep the airplane straight: we had found that when taking off at weights this high, the nosewheel, fabricated to be as light as possible for the job, bent slightly and pulled the airplane around to the right. We had to apply left full rudder for the first part of the takeoff run to keep to the middle of the runway. At first, that was barely enough to hold us on course, but as our speed increased I backed off on it and had better control.

I watched Dick carefully in my peripheral vision, making sure he was alert, and listened to his voice. He was calm; he seemed in tune with the airplane. I was listening to the airplane, too, trying to sense any change or anything different or wrong. You are not allowed to relax in this airplane, never, or to think about anything else or anywhere else. I was watching everything, trying to feel any little thing.

I was ready to hear over the air if there was any problem Mike and Burt observed from outside. I knew how it would come across the air— abort, abort, abort, over and over again—but it never came.

The only thing that felt different on this takeoff was a strange pulsing, a push and pull, a surging and shuddering and lunging that we had never felt before. I thought it was just because the airplane was so heavy, that it might be fuel sloshing.

As we picked up speed, those watching could see the wings bending down like a bow and the tips right on the pavement. But we couldn't. We didn't know or guess. It was unlike any of our other takeoffs, when the tips had lifted very quickly, almost as soon as they were out of the ground crew's hands.

Normally I would see the winglets peek up above the booms at twenty knots. Only subconsciously did I notice now that was missing and wondered why. It was not in priority consciousness.

The noise of the engines was strong, and they sounded good. We had set the governors three hundred RPMs above normal red line, and I could hear them kick in and feel the new props working well.

Then inside my head everything got very quiet. I was looking out at the runway distance markers going by and correlating them with the in- crease in the airspeeds that Jeana was calling off. Keeping the airplane straight was not easy, and my left hand kept working the switches. I was oblivious to the people out there.

There were three key checkpoints—distance markers beside the run- way. At the first we were a knot too slow, at the second two knots below.

The third checkpoint was at 7,500 feet, where Lee Herron stood and watched us approach. That was the last point that would leave enough runway to throw the rear engine into reverse and slow the airplane down enough so that it could run out onto the rough lake surface without the gear collapsing. We had agreed that if we were more than three knots short, he would advise an abort.

Lee listened to the airspeed numbers Jeana read off—fifty-five, sixty- seven, seventy-six. And when we passed Lee we were four low. He said nothing.

It was decision time: when Jeana called out that number, when we passed that last 7,500-foot marker, technically we should have aborted.

But I looked at the end of the runway, still more than a mile and a half away. The plane was accelerating smoothly, it felt strong, and I believed we had a comfortable margin even though we were slow. I felt confident we'd make it. I drew on my thirty-four years of experience and my feel for the airplane, and I felt we had it made easy. The only thing I was concerned about was lifting the nose smoothly when the time came. Even though the calculations stated that we could begin our rotation at eighty-three knots and lift off at eighty-seven, I wanted to wait until we had the full eighty-seven.

At the same 7,500-foot mark, our families were clustered along the side of the runway. Pop Rutan stood pulling his pockets up from inside as we came by. Lee Yeager aimed his video camera, with his Adam's apple bobbing nervously. Nell Rutan was the most volatile, yelling at the airplane as it went past, and then she started jumping up and down.

"We're low," said Bruce from the end of the runway—meaning low on airspeed.

Standing with his hands white with the fuel, Bruce's knees were about to give way under him: he was sure we were dead.

As we were taking off, Mike Melvill kept the Beech Duchess right on our wing, hanging in there at ten to fifteen feet of altitude, watching us.

"He's not going to make it," Mike said. For a moment, as we passed eighty-three knots, Burt thought we had some sort of control problem.

"Pull the nose up," he called.

The message didn't get through.

"Pull the stick back, Dick," he repeated.

Mike Melvill said, "He's not going to have enough."

"Pull back the stick, dammit!" Burt cried.

I heard them all right. If Mike had said, "Ease the stick back just a little," I might have paid attention. But not "Pull the stick back!" To do that would have been fatal. It would surely have set the plane porpoising.

My mind was just about saturated, and dumping that on me required more room than I had in my mental computer. I was thinking, Eighty-seven knots, eighty-seven knots.

Finally, finally, the airspeed crept through the eighties, eighty-two, eighty-three, and we approached the eleven-thousand-foot mark on the runway, eighty-four, eighty-five, and I told myself, Be smooth like you've never been smooth before, and as Jeana called eighty-seven knots, I eased back ever so gently on the stick, gradually starting the nose up to rotate, and the wings started to fly, coming up slowly, moving very deliberately upward.

The downward-bending bow of the wings reversed. Slowly, slowly, the curve turned inside out, and from bent downward the wings bent upward— much farther upward than we'd ever seen them before—and at ninety-two knots the airplane lifted off, and we were airborne. It had taken another 2,500 feet since I first began to ease the stick back.

"Lift, you bastard, lift," Bruce and the ground crew were yelling now. "Come on, come on, goddammit!"

Nell Rutan was jumping up and down and waving beside the runway. And everyone else was yelling.

I heard Mike Melvill on the radio say, "Whew, I really didn't think it was going to do it."

I sat up straighter, and I could feel that we were level, the wings were stable. There was no pitch oscillation. My right hand was stiff, and I tried to relax it and brace my arm hard against the right console. I flew now with the rotation of my fingers only, so I didn't transmit to the plane any kind of body motion that might set off a pitch oscillation.

We weren't out of the woods yet; we needed the extra lift you get in ground effect. I held us there—within the altitude equal to our wingspan— and we accelerated to the target climb speed. "A hundred knots," Jeana called out.

When he heard that number Burt cried, "Whoopee!" That was the number he was waiting for. We knew we could get up.

I eased back on the stick to maintain that speed and use the excess thrust for climb. The first thing we wanted to know was our climb rate. We locked on to 100 knots, and now we were 100 feet up, climbing at 200, 250, 300 feet per minute, climbing twice as fast as we expected.

"Look at that, Jeana!" I exclaimed.

Thank you, John Roncz, I thought, and thank you, Hartzell and new props. But then the other side of it struck me: Hell, if I'd known we'd have that much climb, I would have loaded up another few hundred pounds of fuel. It's an awful long way around the world.

Now we were out over the dry lake, and landing would be difficult. I put the airplane in a right fifteen-degree turn. I reached up to the front engine and backed off to just sixty or seventy RPMs to sync it up with the back. Temperatures, oil pressure—everything looked normal.

We needed to get that front gear up quickly, and get rid of its drag, so now Dick put the autopilot on, set to attitude hold, and made sure it was flying smoothly. There were two gear cables, an uplock and a downlock. I grasped one cable, and Dick grasped the other. While I kept mine in tension, he reached down and grabbed the tee-handle, unlocked it, and with a big sweeping motion of his left elbow pulled his cable back toward me. It was tricky. If he was not careful, he would hit me right in the face with his elbow—he'd done it on test flights. Now he locked the cable in place. The nose gear was up and locked.

With the gear drag gone, our airspeed crept up to 104 knots, and Dick pulled the nose up slightly to bring it back down to 100. Then we started a left turn to begin our orbit around the dry lake so we would be in a position to make a landing there if we had to. It would be risky, but if we lost an engine, it would be our only chance.

We charted ground track and evaluated abort possibilities. Dick could see the NASA facility below. We were lined right up with the shuttle runway and saw the compass rose on the dry lake where we were due to land in ten days. I could see for miles and thought of all the history that had been made in these skies. I thought of the X-1 and the X-15, thought of test pilots we knew who had flown here, of Scott Crossfield, Pete Knight, and of Doug Bennefield, who had lost his life at the B-1 at Edwards; directly under us was the runway where I remembered standing and watching as John Young and Bob Crippen brought the shuttle back from space for the first time.

We had planned to do a couple of orbits, spiral slowly up to altitude, but with our better climb we got the altitude we needed in one circuit.

After we came back over our takeoff point, the Edwards tower could resume normal operations. The first airplane to take off after us was a B-52, the holder of the world unrefueled distance record. It rose beside us in a great swirl of heat and noise and black exhaust and set up a wake like a powerboat. If it had hit us, it could have knocked us out of the sky.

"They told us," said Ken Brock, who fabricated the landing gear, "that the airplane would only have to make one heavyweight takeoff. What they didn't tell us was that it would be a fourteen-thousand-foot takeoff."

Somebody told us that we already had one record: for the longest takeoff ever from Edwards Air Force Base. To get off the ground, we had used up all but a thousand feet of the longest runway in the world.

.   .   .

Now as we turned and came back over, Pop Rutan saw it from the ground. "They lost the right winglet," he said, but no one believed him. Everyone thought he was seeing things. What he saw was the winglet wiggling on the skin that still kept it attached, folding inward.

In the chase plane Mike Melvill said, "Those wingtips are just ground away to nothing. Oh, God, that's a real nightmare. Terrible drag," he groaned.

The first we knew of it was hearing Mike say from the chase plane, "Don't be concerned, but the right winglet has failed."

Don't be concerned? Here we're planning to be in the air for ten days and fly around the world, and already we have parts of our airplane falling off. "We've got a damaged winglet, and there's a good chance of its coming off. Don't be concerned. You have some foam protruding."

The wingtips had been dragging. Now I knew what had caused the strange surging I felt: the wingtips dragging, holding back our acceleration.

I had not seen the winglets rise. Burt and Mike saw them dragging from the chase plane, taking off behind us. They saw a white spray coming up, and for a teeth-gritting moment he thought it might be fuel spray. In fact, it was fiberglass chips or foam dust.

Why had it happened? There were three reasons. First, we had cabled the nose strut down for a lower angle of attack. This would help keep the outboard part of the wings from lifting before the inboard—preventing the premature takeoff and "wahoo," which would likely collapse the front gear and be fatal at this weight.

Second, we had pumped the main gear struts up higher to increase tip clearance. And third, we were carrying more fuel in the front boom tanks, and the weight twisted the wings forward and down.

As a result the nose was too far down, and the angle of attack was negative. As the airplane lumbered forward and started flying, pressure built up on top of, not under, the wings, forcing them down, like a car spoiler. We were flying down instead of up.

It was something that had never happened in sixty-seven test flight takeoffs, something we never considered even possible. Three minor changes almost added up to one fatal mistake.

Now the tires were under a lot of extra pressure. Goodyear had provided us with carefully checked and X-rayed tires, which we filled to almost twice the rated air pressure—instead of 1,800 they were bearing 3,200 pounds each.

Normally during takeoff, as we rolled there was less and less weight on the tires as the wings took more and more of it. But now, as we started flying down, we were jamming the tires into the ground, overstressing them well beyond what we had planned. It says an awful lot for those tires that they didn't blow out.

· · ·

Burt was very cool about it all. He had been concerned about us just hanging it up right there, so he had said to Mike, "Start by telling him not to abort."

And strange as it may seem, we weren't worried. The whole thing was out of our hands.

Burt and Mike did a good job of reassuring us. Burt was calm and kept things in perspective.

We didn't even consider landing—but there were serious things to worry about. The first concern was for maneuverability—could we control the airplane? A quick check revealed all in order there. The second worry was about a possible fuel leak. So Burt and Mike slipped the chase plane in behind us to put any fuel mist there might be on their windshield. There were a few drops, but so few that we felt content they were normal overflow from the caps and not an indication that the tank had been ruptured.

The fuel vents run up through the winglet—were they working all right? The check from chase seemed to indicate no trouble. So we were going to fly around the world with no wingtips.

We had to get rid of the damaged winglets. Burt talked about knocking them off with the wingtips of the chase airplane, but we vetoed that idea. The interference of the airflow between the two airplanes' wingtips could get out of hand and possibly roll the lighter chase airplane right into the Voyager.

Instead, we would try to shake them loose. That right winglet, the looser one, was folded back now at an ungodly angle so that it almost seemed to touch the wing at the top. We'd sideslip the airplane after we got high enough to bail out, and that wouldn't be for a few minutes yet.

Halfway to Palmdale I pulled the chutes forward, and Dick told Burt, "Wait'll we chute up." We put on our chutes. We got the autopilot on and went over our bailout procedures. I was to get the back latch, Dick the two front, then we'd pull the canopy down, turn it, and throw it out. He would go out after it, and I would follow.

Now we applied right rudder to sideslip the airplane to break the winglet off. We wanted to fail the winglet outward to snap the top skin. If it failed inboard, it could peel the skin inboard and rupture the fuel tank.

At first, the winglet stuck. Then Burt said, "Let's put ten more knots on it. Let's get rid of that damn thing."

We repeated the maneuver, with more force. The winglet shook fore and aft, fluttered for about ten cycles, failed outward, clung for a moment, and then sailed free.

It ripped the top skin, all the way to the fuel tank, tore the wingtip light wires back into the foam, and left the fuel vent line inside the foam. We could see a foot-long piece of skin dragging beneath and behind the trailing edge. It was a hairy-looking thing.

"Good, super," Burt said. "It came off nice and smooth."

We couldn't believe this. Here was the designer of an airplane cheering as parts of it came off. "It'll fly better now," he said, "and handle better in turbulence."

But the airplane continued to fly just the same—lousy.

The wires from the wingtip running lights flapped around now—we were lucky they didn't spark. We kept the light circuit breaker off and crossed our fingers hoping they hadn't shorted anything out.

.   .   .

On the ground in Lancaster, a veterinarian's assistant named Margaret Garner was outside taking care of animals when she looked up and saw Voyager and the chase planes appearing overhead. She waved. She saw something fall toward her. Were we dropping something to her, she wondered—a picture, maybe? She followed the fall of the object to a spot in a field about 350 yards away. Then she watched Voyager until it was out of sight and went to retrieve the thing: the winglet, broken off neatly, with a piece of the blue Styrofoam of the wingtip beside it. She telephoned and brought it in to Hangar 77.

.   .   .

The highest point of land we would have to cross was Soledad Pass, at about 4,200 feet, where Highway 14 goes through the mountains toward Los Angeles.

If we had to abort now, we had Rosamond dry lake to the west and ahead of us, as we continued southwest, the long runway at Air Force Plant 42, where the B-1, SR-71 Blackbird, the Shuttle, and so many other airplanes had been built. We could see that the apron there was full of B-1's, like a new-car lot. But once we got above the ridges ahead of us, there would be no way to land until we got to the coast.

"What's the turbulence like up ahead?" we asked the chase planes. Three planes—Met One, Met Two, and Met Three—had been out checking designated areas for turbulence since before dawn. Met One told us the first ridge was clear and smooth. Mets Two and Three said there was

some light turbulence in the middle ridges. We asked the planes to find
us an altitude and area that would minimize that.

The airplane was flying nicely now, and we just let it fly, climbing
slowly to 4,600 feet. I slowly rolled the RPMs back to 2,900 and synced
the engines up. I could almost feel them breathing a sigh of relief; I kicked
off the autopilot in anticipation of turbulence over the pass.

We came over one ridge smoothly, and then another, and then hit the
turbulence. It shook us around quite a bit, and we got a little concerned,
but we just drove on through. Dick felt that he couldn't wait to get the
airplane over water. I thought how strange it was to feel less safe over land
than water. It ran opposite to all a pilot's normal instincts. And then I
looked out to the left and saw the left winglet was going.

I hadn't seen or felt it depart. Jeana saw it go, breaking more neatly than
the right one.

The damage to the left tip was not as bad as to the right, but we could
see a jagged piece of foam flapping in the breeze like a flag.

We started leaning the engines now, never too soon to save fuel, getting
on the mixture controls, leveling out at 5,800 feet and pulling down to
2,700 RPMs.

Burt was interested in performance; had losing the winglets cut into
it? Would we have the range now? Would we be able to make it?

We were south of Santa Paula now, and the Simi Valley unrolled beneath
us. We checked on the Omega—it would be our last chance until we got
to Hawaii.

We were beginning to make some minor deviations as we got into the
coastal weather. We gave Burt some numbers now on performance—it
looked good to him, nothing to worry about, but he told us he would work
out the figures when he got back to Mojave. He expected some loss of
range from the drag on the tips, but not enough to worry about.

Burt and Mike and Sally in the Duchess chase plane followed us out
over the ocean. We tracked the rate of fuel consumption and the distance
traveled and found Voyager was getting about 2.11 nautical miles per
pound—well on the performance curve.

As if we hadn't realized it already, losing the winglets served notice
that this was no ordinary airplane.

The tips looked like hell, like they'd been through a war. Out of the
ends stuck blue foam, like the material used to make picnic coolers or

surfboard cores. Now the foam looked like something washed up on the beach, all shredded and sharkbit. The tip running lights were gone, and frayed wires streamed out.

I caught a glimpse of the top of the wings and saw that they were wrinkling, rippling, like a washboard.

We were lucky that we had those extra few feet of foam on the tips, before the fuel tanks started. The tips had actually been added after we finished building the rest of the airplane. The final weight distribution had left it tail-heavy, and the added length corrected that.

There was, however, at least one thing wrong with having lost those winglets. The roughened wingtips, with bits of loose skin flapping and foam protruding, would naturally cause drag. Burt expected that any rain encountered would erode an extra foot or so from the tips.

There was induced drag, due to the rotation of the air set up at the wingtip and the removal of the air smoothing that the winglets would have performed—and parasitic drag, the pressure of the air on the flat hanging pieces of material. Burt worked up the numbers and found that the total drag might cut range by—at the worst—6 percent. That took away some comfort, but we could live with it.

There were lots of clouds above us and below us now as we got out over the ocean. Burt and Mike and Sally, who had flown beside us so many times before, could not fly beside us anymore.

"Jeana, how do you feel?" Burt asked.

"Pretty good," I said, "considering the morning."

We used the Omega to give Burt range and bearing back to Mojave; they wanted to stay with us as long as possible. But now they were getting to the edge of the Duchess's range.

We exchanged love-yous and good-lucks and took a last look at our friends as they banked away. And then we were alone.

We left them with a feeling of uncertainty. It was an emotional moment, because they all thought that there was a very good chance we might never see each other again.

Dick looked at me and said, "Well, this is the big one."

A silence crept over us. The reality was starting to sink in that we were going out across a big ocean. They kept in communication for a little while but then they had to change frequencies and talk to the ground controllers, and it went quiet. I began to write in the log—"feet wet, we're on our own," then data, numbers; but deep behind all that, I was thinking, We're committed, we're going to make it.

We'd finally started out, and in one way Dick felt glad we were on our own. The talk had been dividing our attention. Now I could settle in to fine-tuning the systems and lean the engines (decrease the fuel to air ratio). I rechecked everything: RPMs, engine temperatures, fuel. Dick, peering through the canopy, began to dodge weather; we would be doing it all the way around. We began to relax and settle into the grind.

For a while after Burt and Mike and Sally were gone, neither of us said much of anything. Despite all the noise of the engines, the cockpit was filled with a kind of strong silence.

Shooting the Curl

We picked up good tail winds just a few miles off the coast and began to settle in pretty quickly, just marking off the time, not saying much, trying to stick to routine. On the control panel we taped a strip of paper with the days to mark off—days of the flight on one side, Julian calendar days beside them—and we would cross them off with a pen, like prisoners chalking the days off on the wall of their cell.

All we saw for a while was clouds and clouds and clouds and very rarely any ocean, but that was what we'd asked for. "Here we are," I reported, "just bobbing along over the Pacific, not a care in the world, hah, hah."

I kept monitoring the radar for weather ahead. We were a few hours out when I saw a big cumulus go by and thought, Wow, where did that come from? It was then I realized for the first time that a lot of the storms did not have enough moisture in them to show up on the radar. That meant constant visual checks in addition to looking at the radar to see that we didn't run into any of those. More work, another thing to worry about. And what the hell were we going to do at night?

The experience seemed all very abstract to me. I knew all that was happening, but it seemed secondhand, indirect, something I had heard about rather than something real.

I had never operated on Julian time before—in which there are no months, simply the days of the year consecutively numbered—and now it left me without any sense of what day it really was. For hours of the day, we used Zulu—Greenwich mean time, which had little to do with the sun or moon we saw outside. Time was just a point on the chart for me, space just a fix on the map. All the days began to flow into one. It was like one long test flight over Mojave.

The lights kept the cabin bright even at night, and with my back to the windows, propped most of the time on one elbow, there was little that I could see outside. After a while, my neck was too stiff even to turn to look out. Besides, that was another world.

At one point, coming up on Hawaii, Dick saw something that looked like a rotor, and it startled him. From Mojave we knew these rotors well: churning eddies of air something like the sucking whirlpool of a sink drain that can take your wings off. They are "terrain-induced"—set up by some natural feature of the landscape that disturbs the flow of air. They don't usually show up on radar because they don't have enough moisture in them.

We reported it to Len Snellman, who said that it must be farther off than we imagined. After all, there was no terrain to induce any kind of weather between us and Hawaii. But whatever it was, Dick was sure he saw it, and it served as a reminder of how alert we had to be for any kind of disturbance that could wreck this fragile airplane.

The sun went down for the first time a few hours before we were to reach Hawaii. The track mission control had given us would have carried us twenty miles south of Hilo. But for our own comfort we needed a navigation fix to cross-check the Omega. The GPS (global positioning system) constellation of satellites came up, but our unit wouldn't lock on, so I deviated three or four degrees to the right to get close enough to Hilo to get a positive fix. Soon I got the coast on the radar and about forty miles farther picked up the lights of the island. The King Omega was right on the money.

During that first night, Bud Weisbrod and Pete Dawson flew out from Hawaii in a single engine Piper Saratoga to rendezvous and check us out. They were friends of Mike Hance in mission control, and Bud was VIP number one—the first name on the VIP list we carried on board with us now.

There was confusion about where we were to rendezvous. They thought it was to be on the north side of Hilo, but we were actually going to skirt the south side. When they discovered the error, we thought for sure we'd miss them. They were behind us now because of the error and ended up in an hour-long tail chase. Finally, though, they caught up with us. It felt good to have a friendly voice close to us again. Although they couldn't get too close in the dark, they reported that all looked normal. Then they had to head back. They banked hard right toward Honolulu. It was lonely as we watched their strobe disappear toward the northern horizon.

During the night, we flew through an eddy of turbulence caused by the air going across the islands—mild turbulence, but enough to ruin our sleep.

As the sun came up the next morning, we looked out and saw that we had lost the loose end pieces of foam from the left wingtip. We would just keep our fingers and toes crossed that it didn't go any farther.

Once I forgot to lower the aluminum pee tube that extended from the bottom of the airplane. It was connected to a long flexible tube that ran up to a funnel behind the seat. We had to be very careful that it didn't kink, and to save every bit of drag possible, we pulled it up when it wasn't needed. About half a cup of raw urine ended up on the floor, which had to be cleaned up and disinfected with Alcide, the germ killer we used on everything from our hands to headsets to the control stick.

Just a few hours into the flight, our headsets began to develop a cracking, popping noise. We turned off the Bose noise suppression electronics, but the set itself, with its form-fitting silica gel, continued to do a great job of protecting our ears. We didn't know it at the time, but the moisture from our perspiration was causing the electronic system to short out. The noise was much less oppressive than it had been on other test flights and the coast flight, before we got the Bose headsets—they were lifesavers. But we missed the high-tech sound suppression and knew the noise could be very fatiguing.

I learned well from the coastal flight the importance of water. I made sure that we drank all our water from the premeasured packets I had made up, but we ended up eating only perhaps three-fourths of our food. (Dick estimated about one-third.) It became a ritual: each morning we made sure to consume a big portion of that day's water ration. Most of the time Dick drank his water mixed with Shaklee Shake, Slim-Plan, or the split pea soup they made just for him. We had packed the water in plastic, each meal's ration with that meal, like a big solid bubble, which we punched with one of the little juice straws and drank. This forced us to drink it, because if we didn't we would have to deal with the thing leaking in the cockpit. So we were very good about water consumption, remembering how dehydrated we had become on the Pacific coast flight and knowing how good water was for potential shock situations.

I ate mostly crackers and peanut butter. Dick really liked the Yurika retort-packed meals, which were almost like home-cooked meals when warmed against the heater duct. We would heat one a day and split it, but Dick got the lion's share; sometimes I got a bit but most of the time he scarfed the whole thing—sometimes two packets. He needed the calories. I also gave Dick a lot of the fruit juices, because the sugars seemed to help him out, especially when he was waking up and trying to shake off grogginess. It was then, too, that we brushed our teeth—this little luxury did wonders to make us feel more human, and it was one of the few easy-to-make hygienic improvements.

The altitude and maybe the days on the shelf waiting for takeoff somehow caused the smell and taste of the plastic to transfer into some of the food, which tended to cut back on our dining pleasure. I had had everything ready since September except the liquids, although one of the juices had even managed to ferment due to a bad seal.

One thing benefited from the altitude, however. Dick kept telling the guys on the ground about how good this peanut butter and honey were that we were putting on crackers. In fact, it was just plain peanut butter— I had rejected honey as far too messy for the flight—and I loved it, too.

Dick liked to stretch out his meals—seeking a certain high-altitude leisure and elegance in dining—but I needed to police up and get the mess out of the way, so sometimes I had to nudge him to finish and clean up. This wasn't like a long drive where you could keep your burger on the dashboard and your coffee in the coin tray. Carelessness could be dangerous. A liquid spill could ruin a piece of electronics; a loose object could catch and slip a control cable off its pulleys. We didn't have much water for washing up; we mostly used prepared towels and Alcide disinfectant—in case we got a cut on a rudder cable or the rough carbon wall of the cockpit.

Dr. Jutila had given us a sort of oversized rubber band for exercising our leg muscles. I tried it once, somewhere over the Indian Ocean. It was pretty nice until it slipped off my toes, nearly smacking me in the eye. I decided our physical condition was more likely to suffer than improve using the band, so I put it away and never pulled it out again.

For the first three days, at least, Dick was to be in the seat. He found himself occasionally catnapping for thirty to sixty minutes. I watched the controls over his shoulder, in my makeshift "bucket seat" at the side of the instrument panel. My head was sideways, braced against the roof, and my cheek wedged against the console. My legs kept going to sleep under me, and every time I had to reach across the instrument panel I ran the danger of jostling Dick and waking him up.

The old problems with sleeping returned. Dick would tilt the seat back and try to catnap. He would put his head down and fall asleep, and then his tongue would relax and slip back into his throat, cutting off his windpipe, and he would wake up gasping for breath. Once, a couple of days into the flight, he felt that he couldn't sleep, and then he decided to give up: it was two hours later, but he had slept.

I slept only restlessly, too, in a half sleep at best, a catnap that never obscured constant alertness. I had to watch Dick and the autopilot and other systems. The autopilot had to work. We were going to sit out these first few days until the airplane got below eighty-two knots—the critical speed for the pitch porpoise—as we burned off fuel. If we let a fuel transfer run away or ran into turbulence and the oscillations got started, they would go into the divergent mode very quickly, and the airplane would come apart. Only fifteen seconds stood between us and death.

. . .

The shifts were long in the trailer, and many people stayed on beyond their appointed hours, tired but unable to tear themselves away. The activity was constant; printouts of weather maps coming in, updated information from the Lockheed Data Plan, fresh satellite pictures washing across the D-WIPS screens. There was no real time in the trailer, only the abstract numbers of Zulu time and Julian days. The Geochron clock on the wall gave a sense of the time of day where *Voyager* was: it showed the local time and the shadow of night creeping across the world.

A video camera had been set up in one corner of the trailer to show the press and public out in the hangar what was going on inside. It made some of the mission control people a little self-conscious, but after a couple of days had gone by, they began making crude banners showing distance and location, in mock NASA fashion, for the cameras to pick up.

Maps and papers covered the trailer walls. Clear plastic was laid over the big map so people could write on it with grease pencils, and our course was marked by yarn drawn over a succession of colored pushpins—checkpoints—and at the end of the yarn the airplane was represented by a gold *Voyager* tie tack somebody had brought in from the shop. There was a lot of blue on the map.

On the wall above the desk used by Jack Norris and his performance people were curves and graphs—fuel burns, gross weights, and so on—along with such inspirational slogans as "The slower it turns, the less it burns," and "Endurance is the key."

Before we had taken off, Len Snellman had shown us where a tropical storm was developing in the Pacific, and we had carefully rehearsed our plan to deal with it. Now the storm, centered on the Marshall Islands, had grown up and was called Marge. And Len was both happy—because the storm meant good tailwinds—and a bit anxious as we approached it.

We would turn northwest as we approached Marge—a clear pinwheel shape on the screens back in the trailer, hundreds of miles across—then come in on its top side, catching just enough of the edge of the pinwheel, spinning and swirling counterclockwise, to let Marge slingshot us forward. It was a dangerous game: if we got too close, or if we miscalculated just where we were, we could be torn apart.

Len was aiming to slot us right between two of the arms of the pinwheel—the storm's "feeder bands." It was like a surfer catching the crest of a wave—on the D-WIPS screen it literally did look like a wave. "Now it's time to shoot the curl," Len said.

It looked pretty simple on the weather screens and maps. But it took a lot of math to figure out the movement of those arms, just where they would be when we arrived, and the weather people sat down with calculators to do the calculus. Jack Norris, the performance engineer, who knew a lot about crunching numbers, stood and looked over the shoulders of the weathermen while they were doing it and was very impressed. But the key question was whether the numbers would come out right over the Pacific.

We had faith in Len, and we had discussed our plans many times, but still it made us a little uneasy to fly that close to Marge in this airplane, when we feared even the slightest turbulence. We trusted him, but . . .

Coming up on Marge, I slowed down and tried to mentally psych myself. I began to feel calm, almost subdued.

We knew Marge was there, but we had no neat pinwheel shape to watch. We couldn't see very far, and with clouds beneath us we could see the ocean only infrequently. It was not like looking off a mountain and seeing the thunderclouds rolling toward you. We had to depend on what they saw in Mojave.

Late on day two of the flight, Len saw that things were happening faster than he had counted on. Marge, he told us, was moving north, which meant that on our present course toward the Philippines, we would run directly into it.

What was worse, another system, a low-pressure system, was coming in from the north—an ugly piece of Southeast Asian weather. It was moving closer, forming a narrow channel between itself and Marge, a virtual tunnel that threatened to close up before we could reach it.

Len felt convinced that Marge's motion north would stop—that the pinwheel would be held off by the system to the north—and stabilize at about fifty degrees north latitude. This is what history and years of experience told him. But if he was wrong, then we would be in the thick of it. If we didn't run directly into Marge, we would be sandwiched between Marge and the front coming down, smothered in that tunnel as it contracted.

"We're in a real squeeze play," Len said. "This could be the toughest part of the flight.

"According to the textbooks, Marge should just about be done moving. But the big question is, is Mother Nature reading the same textbooks that we are?"

Suddenly everyone in the trailer was running. New courses were plotted, diverting us north.

Len told the guys in communications to reach us as soon as they could.

"This is no time to worry about the fuel curve," Len told us. "We've got to let that go to hell right now. The thing is to hurry and get that plane there as fast as you can, before that little tunnel closes up."

Because of the cirrus cloud layer on top of the storm, he couldn't be sure from the satellite pictures, he told us, about the exact location of the center of the storm or the feeder bands. So he wanted us to drive toward the center, divert north, and feel our way around. We had to do the fine-tuning on location. "Turn into it as much as you can," he said. "It's up to you to inch up to it, see how bad it is to the left, then move right."

Soon there were big banks of storm clouds on our radar—red-hearted monsters off to our left. We followed our plan and got as close to the clouds as we dared.

I had flown through a typhoon on my training flight to Australia with the ferry service, but now I was not even aware we were so close to Marge. Not looking out while Dick was at the controls, I concentrated on navigation and other log duties. Marge was actually smoother flying than some supposedly clear areas of the ocean.

There was surprisingly little turbulence. Off to the left Dick could see an intense wall of clouds extending from the ocean to fifty thousand feet and cirrus above it and above us. But there was another bank of severe weather on our right. The communication was good, luckily, and we explained what we saw to Len. It was a feeder band to Marge—just where he wanted us to be, right in its embrace. We would have good tailwinds there, but now it felt like running through a tunnel.

Len told us to inch over toward the left wall—Marge—and we made a twenty-degree turn. But the storm looked as if it extended in front of us, so we didn't go too far left. We didn't want to end up having to make an unnecessary turn if we ran into weather ahead. As Len had said, he'd gotten us to the green, but now we had to do the putting.

We came into some rain—for the first time since the nearly fatal day more than two years ago when we got ambushed by the mare's tail. This time *Voyager* didn't even leak in the cabin. And she didn't lose any lift or even show any perceptible pitch trim change.

After all the hassle fitting out the canard to handle rain, we had not ever been eager to go looking for it. We had planned to fly through rain, but the truth was we didn't want to fly through it until we had to. If John Roncz's vortex generators—those little shark teeth—didn't work, we didn't want to find out. It was all right to get killed on the world flight, was the line Dick used several times, but not on a test flight.

But now we did find out, and the news was good. John Roncz and the professors at the Ohio State wind tunnel had done a great job. "Thanks, John," we said, and told the guys in the trailer to let him know the airplane had handled the rain beautifully.

Instead of the neat pinwheel pattern, of course, there was a huge wall of weather off to one side and great towering clouds popping up individually ahead of us. They looked like redwood trees, with trunks and big tops. And the redwood trees were so tall we couldn't fly over them. Instead, we had to fly between them, dodging trunks all the way. It felt about as scary as if we were picking our way through real redwoods in the Long EZ. It reminded us of the scene in one of the *Star Wars* films where bearlike creatures on flying motorcycles go dashing through the forest.

Picking around those clouds, we made it through. The maneuver worked. We picked up a tailwind that sometimes went as high as thirty knots and really whipped us around; Marge shot us right up between Saipan and Guam before the gap closed up behind us. The benefits weren't all in the performance charts. There is nothing that gave us a bigger psychological boost than to be able to look down and see thirty free knots there. And by the same token, there would be nothing more depressing than fighting a head wind.

As the sun went down Marge was still off to our left at about the ten-o'-clock position. We were getting close enough to pick up Guam approach control very clearly on the VHF radio as it got dark. We were beneath the overcast—no moon, no stars—and it was very dark.

We wanted to be sure just where we were out in all this ocean. The experimental global positioning system was having trouble locking on to its satellites, and we were not going to fly close enough to any kind of island to get a land fix, so we altered to the left fifteen degrees to pick up some islands on the radar. But because there were so many and they were so little, we couldn't positively identify any of them.

At Saipan we saw lights and checked the Omega; it was so close we didn't even bother updating.

Len had told us after we left Saipan that we should have smooth sailing. After two and a half days in the air and passing Marge, we thought we had earned a respite, but it wasn't to be.

"Mother Nature threw us a curve," Len said. "We thought we'd be able to relax a little bit after Marge, but there's a lot of rough stuff ahead. We've shot the curl, but there's a bumpy wake ahead of us."

We were having a lot of trouble getting clear communications to the folks back in the trailer. Talking on the radio while trying to fly in the turbulence was exhausting. I wrote in the log in craggy letters that looked like some kind of seismograph trace, indicating how the turbulence was knocking me around: "Guessing game—repeat repeat and repeat again."

We flew on over Tinian, the island where the first atomic bombs were loaded up on B-29's, and toward the Philippines. We looked at the map of our course there, and Dick saw that it would take us almost directly over Cebu, which he remembered well from the early sixties when he was a navigator on C-124 Globemasters and would stage through there on the way to Vietnam, riding a leaky sampan with an antique engine across the lush bay to town.

But there was little time for such thoughts and less for talk. The weather seemed to offer no letup, and it didn't help things that Dick was feeling more and more exhausted now going into a third day in the seat, waiting for the sun to come up so he could get some sleep. Or that, as I marked our fuel numbers on the chart, we began to be concerned that the graph was showing we weren't doing as well on fuel as we should be. It made us think about whether those wingtips were turning out to create more drag than we thought. Twice we tried to shut down the front engine, but neither time could we maintain level flight on the rear engine alone. Why couldn't the airplane fly single engine? At our gross weight and altitude, it should have been able to. Maybe the airplane was heavier than the numbers showed. We started looking at the fuel graph—the how-goes-it chart that marked off our gross weight against the miles traveled—and it began to look less than rosy.

Something was wrong, somewhere, something in the numbers or in the fuel tanks or in the engines or in the airframe, and we didn't know what it was or if there was anything we could do about it. But for now that concern stayed in the background; in the foreground were too many other things, things we had to deal with immediately.

Flying the Profile

The autopilot had a flashing light and a beeping horn to warn us if we were out of trim up or down. That was the key to keeping the airplane at the angle of attack where we could fly most efficiently. But it was irritating as hell, going off all the time, and we had to listen to it twenty-four hours a day. I talked to it and threatened to rip it out by its roots. But I knew we needed it.

The light and the horn were linked to the elevator by two tiny microswitches. If the trim was too high, one signal was triggered; too low, and another went off.

Maybe the thing heard me and got irritated itself: before long, the "up" half of it failed. Although we still had the out of trim "down" warning, it meant we had to be that much more careful, work that much harder.

Many people outside the world of aviation got the wrong impression about the autopilot. "Oh, you had an autopilot," they would say, "so you really didn't have much to do." Hand-flying *Voyager* required almost all our concentration, and flying it on autopilot still required most of our concentration.

We constantly had to watch the angle of attack; any little change in air conditions would throw it out of whack so that we would be flying at a very poor efficiency. *Voyager* had tremendously efficient airfoils, but to fly the airplane with them at the wrong angle was like driving in the wrong gear.

The autopilot had to be adjusted to each different air condition we faced or when we shifted fuel and changed the center of gravity. The autopilot looks for altitude by measuring pressure, so when we flew into less dense air it would attempt to move us down. Its gains, or "rules," had to be reset.

If we turned the gains too high—made the autopilot more sensitive—it would work like mad. The stick would begin zipping back and forth, and there was danger of fatiguing the control systems. If we turned the gains down too low, the system became lethargic, with a long hunting pattern of two or three minutes.

We had the warning lights and horns because, unlike most autopilots, our autopilot had no autotrim control of its own. When the airplane got out of trim—and those lights and buzzing horns went off—we had to manually adjust the trim and bring our center of gravity back to the proper location. The key thing was to stay inside what the engineers call the "lift over drag bucket," the place on their graphs where we would obtain maximum fuel efficiency. Our job was to fly the profile, to stay in the Bucket, and that meant flying within just one or two knots of the optimum L/D speed.

If we got into turbulence or a different air mass, we would slip to what we called the backside of the power curve. Then we would have to hand-fly or descend while we adjusted the autopilot gains.

The airplane would fly along happily enough for an hour or so, right in the Bucket, and then all of a sudden we would look up and see airspeed bleeding off.

That was why I could not catnap without Jeana watching carefully. Every two or three minutes she would have to shift the autopilot from altitude hold to attitude hold to climb and get the airplane back in the Bucket, back on the profile.

The bottom line was that in turbulence we had to push the power up to hold the same L/D speed. The weather kept us higher, where airspeed had to be higher. That is why the trip took nine instead of ten days; we had more weather than expected, and we flew faster than expected—but not more efficiently.

The theoretical, still air range of the airplane was 28,000 miles; the flight was expected to cover 25,000 miles. And every time we had to climb or fly higher, we nibbled away at that 3,000-mile pad.

I was worried about keeping track of this as we got more and more fatigued, so after each hour's worth of fuel burned off I put a piece of tape by the airspeed indicator with an arrow marked on it.

Nor was it simply a matter of efficiency. If the center of gravity got out of position—if, say, we let a fuel transfer run away—the airplane could stall and become uncontrollable within twenty or thirty seconds.

But even with all our care to stay in the L/D Bucket, by the time we got to the Philippines, during the third day, we were almost down on the "how-goes-it" line and fast sinking below it. Something was clearly wrong somewhere.

We were finding that there was an awful lot of work to be done and a lot of irritations, aside from simply flying the airplane—and that was plenty by itself. Systems had to be watched and maintained constantly. The work load in the cockpit was much higher than we ever thought it would be. There was fuel transferring and logging to be done, controlling of the air intakes, monitoring of autopilot and radios, oil and coolant and temperature checks, food and water to be worried about. And to do any of the many other things we had to do—to program the Omega or talk on the radio—we almost had to use our elbows to fly the airplane.

It was not simply a matter of taking your turn flying the airplane and sitting back when off duty. We totted up all the things we had to do and calculated that *Voyager* constantly required 1.8 waking crew members.

While Dick flew, I had a lot of work to do monitoring systems from beside the seat, as well as carefully recording speeds, positions, winds, RPMs and all sorts of other information in the airplane log.

In addition, the fuel log had to be maintained, with its seventeen columns, every time we made a transfer.

The oil system had to be checked and, if necessary, replenished, a twenty-minute job, every four to six hours.

Oil had to be pumped into the engine with a hand crank. The pump was in the upper-right-hand corner of the rear bulkhead above the oxygen tank, and I had to lie on my back and reach over my right shoulder to turn the crank. It took four hundred cranks per quart to get the oil into the system, and in that awkward position it was tiring work.

There were the engine cooling intake scoops to adjust constantly. Cooling drag was about 20 percent of the airplane's total drag, and we had to keep it at the bare minimum if we were to make it around the world. We wanted just enough air moving through the radiators to take out the heat that was produced.

The way we varied the airflow was by opening and closing a hinged flap in the scoop. If there was too much air, there was too much drag.

To adjust it I had to crawl on my stomach to the back, open a door, and reach down into the lower compartment. There a protruding lever attached to the hinged flap, and I could adjust it up and down. The problem was that it took awhile to see if the adjustment was correct. I'd move it one click, and it would take twenty minutes for the effect to show up in the engine thermostat. And then I might have to go back there and move it another couple of clicks.

If there was too much cooling air, the engine would divert some of the coolant, wasting energy. To push all the coolant through the radiator, we ran the thermostat about five degrees above the normal threshold.

Navigation was another big job. Our trusty Omega computer handled our course only to the extent of warning us when we departed from the programmed route. But each time we got a new "six-hour message" from the ground, we had to write ten new waypoints on a sheet of paper and program each of them into the Omega's computer.

With all this to do, there was no time for idle conversation and no time to relax.

Because all our equipment had been pared down to the bone, any little failure meant even more work.

Just past the international date line, in the middle of the Pacific, the needle fell right off the deck angle gauge and just sat on the bottom of the housing, like a hand that had fallen off a clock. We would look over there instinctively and see that thing sitting there and really get irritated. That instrument was especially important because the arrangement of the cockpit, with the canopy off center to the right, gave a false visual orientation. We knew that we were looking from one side, but in flying the airplane it was natural to read the fuselage in front of the canopy as a horizon.

Being deprived of the deck angle gauge made it impossible to calculate the weight of the airplane, which we figured in part from whether we were flying nose- or tail-heavy. And looking at that broken thing staring dumbly out at us was frustrating. We finally got so fed up with it that we covered it with masking tape. It was a critical loss; if we had not lost it, we would have known for certain just how much fuel we had.

Part of all this was a consequence of our old fanaticism for saving weight. The fuel system, for instance, was monitored by just four transducers (or electronic gauges) and one sight gauge—a clear tube not much different from the one Lindbergh used in the *Spirit of St. Louis*. We could have used an automatic gauge on each of the seventeen fuel tanks and— as we had hoped to have at one point—an automatic fuel transfer and log computer. Instead, we had to set the transducers and record each transfer of fuel in a log by hand. We had to switch the gauge to the needed transducer, run the counter back to zero, and pump fuel.

Although we expected to spend a quarter or a third of our time on fuel, it turned out to be 160 hours, we figured out, or more than six days—four complete work weeks, or better than half the flight. It was a constant, dull refrain: select, switch, zero, pump, log.

. . .

We were getting irritated with all the questions and demands from the ground. They kept asking and asking. We called the same numbers over and over. We were losing badly needed sleep. At one point the performance people came on the frequency to get fuel numbers with the wrong chart. We gave them all the figures and then they would ask again as if we hadn't given those numbers, and the whole process had to be repeated.

Because the cabin was so small, I had to unfold the twenty-four-inch, eight-armed UHF satellite radio antenna while Dick talked, aim it at the satellite by hand, and then fold it up again when we finished and store it on top of the oxygen tank in back. We both had to be awake to use it. It was a spidery, awkward thing. The one we really needed didn't arrive in Mojave until the day after we took off.

It was also impossible to monitor HF radio, VHF radio, and UHF satellite radio all at the same time. And some of the frequencies in both the HF and the UHF interfered with the autopilot. You would be talking and the pitch channel would oscillate the nose of the airplane up and down. The trim warning horns would go off and lights would flash, and we'd have to turn off the radio or change channels and go calm down the autopilot.

To make out anything on the HF radio, we had to keep it tuned high enough so that there was constant background static, and after a while this became pretty painful to listen to. We picked up all sorts of strange interference on the radio. One thing we had to listen to halfway around the world was the intermittent tapping noise, tapataptap, tapataptap, that came from a Soviet "over the horizon" radar. The radio guys know it well; they call it "the woodpecker," which is exactly what it sounds like. And after a while it sounded like it was pecking on our heads.

We kept our VHF radio on all the time on an emergency frequency—121.5 Mc—in case anyone called us, and all of a sudden we got a call from a Singapore Airlines jet and heard the voices of Bruce and Glenn, eating lobster thermidor and drinking margaritas in the 747 a few hundred miles away. They had managed to persuade the pilot of their flight to let them come up into the cockpit and talk to us on the radio. It was great to hear their voices, although we were busy dodging some weather at the time and getting beaten around pretty well—as usual. We couldn't believe it: up to this point we had doubts that they would even be able to arrange transportation to the rendezvous point, and now they were on their way.

About three days into the flight we started noticing some noxious and unmistakable odors. Lee Herron's PPOGR vent was not doing its job.

We had forgotten something when we installed it. The whole leading edge of the wing was hollow, where the control cables and fuel lines ran, and it vented into the cockpit.

We'd discovered this before the coast flight when I told Dick I smelled fuel. I sniffed around near the leading edges and found the cause: there was a slight leak way out in the boom tank and about three or four inches of standing fuel. It wasn't much to worry about, at least considering all the other things we had on our mind, and we never even fixed it.

To correct the negative pressure that was drawing fuel smells in from the booms, we had installed a big vent up front by the pilot's feet. It drew hot air from the heater pipe in back. But as it turned out, it was so large that it also drew air from the PPOGR right by our noses. To alleviate that, Dick increased the pressure in the cockpit by opening up the vent on the canopy and covering up most of the foot exit vent with a map. That way there would be positive pressure in the cabin at all times.

But Dick never got around to explaining this system to me, and I would get in the seat and kick the map away while he was back sleeping. Fortunately, the smells didn't come forward that much.

. . .

Three days, five hours, six thousand miles out.

A couple of hours before we reached the Philippines, we tried to shut the front engine down again, without success; the airplane just wouldn't maintain level flight at 10,000 feet. All our charts said it should, but it wouldn't.

Either it was heavier than we thought, and we had more fuel, or—those winglets cost us more drag than we thought. Maybe the right wing was damaged more than we thought. Maybe that was why we were flying so strangely, maybe we had too much drag, and then it was all over, we'd never make it. There were two or three places out there that looked a little funny.

Weather was all around. I was getting even less sleep than expected because of bad weather. Now I was facing the prospect of being in the seat all day again after being up all night.

We tried again to shut down the front engine. It wouldn't hold altitude. The fatigue was mounting.

Was it all falling apart? Three times now we'd tried to shut down the front. We should have been running on the back engine by now. There was no way we were going to make it around the world on two engines.

We'd thought we'd have time to catch our breath and recover between bouts of bad weather. But it just kept coming at us. Looking at that weather, wiping the fog off the window, I knew that if I missed one of those thunder-bumpers, we were dead. We kept having to juke and weave and in some cases even make 180-degree turns.

Len Snellman was always talking about ridges and troughs, and we thought we'd have long troughs between the ridges. The good news was that we were getting more in the way of tail winds than in our wildest dreams. The bad news was that we were continually getting banged around in the turbulence. Jeana's knees and elbows were so sore she winced and grimaced every time she had to move on them.

Dick just had to get some sleep; he lay back in the seat and closed his eyes while I moved forward in my uncomfortable position to fly, reaching across him. I began to notice that every once in a while the airplane would turn off heading, then straighten itself out. It was the attitude gyroscope—the ADI unit—and as it started to roll or bank, the autopilot would follow, and we would turn off course.

It was something like a person's eyeball trying to stay awake: it rolled around, came back, tried to stay level, held on for an hour, then rolled back off. I reset it, and it held, but only for half an hour now, and then it would roll off to sleep again. Before long, it had become almost useless.

Autopilot failure! One of our worst nightmares. If the autopilot went out suddenly, we'd have only a few seconds to recover control of the airplane before it might shake its wings off. Thank God we decided—in the time between losing the prop and the world flight—to bring along a spare. It was another lucky benefit of the downtime after we lost the prop. The additional time allowed us to persuade King Radio to prepare an entire redundant set of autopilot components. Without that, the mission could have ended right there. There was just no way to fly *Voyager* for any length of time without the autopilot.

Badly as he needed the sleep, I woke Dick up and showed him the problem. It was time to change it, he said with a sinking feeling in his stomach. It was way too early for this piece of equipment to fail.

We had two identical ADIs, and we had practiced changing it on the ground. It was a matter of rewiring. Now, while Dick pushed the seat all the way back and put his feet up behind the rudder pedals to get his legs out of the way as much as possible, I rolled over on my back and scrambled up under the instrument panel, folding myself up and wriggling under the panel. I had to slide across Dick's left thigh, between his legs, and slip my head and shoulders under the panel.

It was an awkward and painful position, lying upside down on Dick's lap, with the compass stabbing me in the back. I removed two computer plugs from the primary ADI and plugged them into the standby, which was already in the panel for just this possibility.

It was not reassuring. If this one had failed one-third of the way around the world, the other one could fail two-thirds of the way. And it was not completely fresh. We had kept it powered up so vibration would not damage the gyro bearings. It might not last another two hours.

It was hard to see the standby ADI indicator—it was located way down in the corner of the instrument panel, at an angle that made it difficult to read. Meanwhile the primary ADI was still right in front of us, sitting there all cattywompus. Finally we put tape across its face. Before long, instead of the ADI, Dick began to use the two-inch JET Electronics emergency electric attitude indicator to fly by, a little peanut thing, but much more visible.

And I worried: What if something else goes? We really should have brought a second airspeed indicator. I looked at the needle on the indicator bouncing and shaking, and for the first time I realized the airplane could not be flown without it. If it failed, like the deck angle gauge, we'd have had it. We should have brought another one; it only weighed six ounces.

I had been up all night, and I tried to look at the situation rationally, only through a haze of fatigue. We might have a physiological problem here, I thought. I'd been up almost all night, and I was looking at an airplane that was really squirrelly to fly, just like it was when we took off— so I might be stuck in the seat all day. I was really starting to get pissed off and make basic mistakes. Things were falling apart.

I needed to go back and get some sleep, and I hoped maybe things would look better when I woke up. But right then, I had the feeling that things were falling apart.

We were still too heavy. We tried to shut down the front engine but couldn't maintain level flight. We decided to let me get some sleep and then worry about it afterward.

In the log Jeana wrote, "Dick badly needs rest. Not comfortable to let me fly until *Voyager* more stable."

"You need some sleep," she told me. "I can take it."

And finally I did go back.

On the ground in the trailer they were upset that Dick was still in the seat and held a big powwow to figure out what to do about it. He had gotten only five hours of sleep or so in the first sixty hours of the flight, the way they calculated it. Actually he had gotten more.

The severity of the pitch porpoise problem was still not common knowledge. So it was hard for the public and press and even some members of the *Voyager* team to understand why Dick kept flying. Some attributed it simply to "fighter pilot jockey." Others thought it reflected the inability of the veteran pilot to believe that anyone else was as capable.

I knew that it didn't matter what they said on the ground; he would get out of the seat when he got out.

The pattern was something like that of the coast flight, when Dick couldn't sleep for three days. Then, he'd been concerned about how he would do, flying the airplane for a long period. Now, the worry was about the autopilot—although it was so far doing yeoman service, aside from that ADI gyro—and the potential deadly danger of pitch instability.

By then, Dick wouldn't even answer Doc Jutila. Now, when the doc asked him how we were feeling, or if he was going to sleep soon, he answered curtly "doing fine" and asked not to bother him right now. Burt too was getting in the way of mission control, disrupting the procedures and dwelling on issues.

Sally Melvill took Burt aside and told him to stay out of the trailer and threatened to quit her job at Scaled if he didn't. It wasn't easy, ordering her boss around, but finally he listened.

What we found out only later was that Burt was so concerned about the fuel numbers—indicating as they did a potential massive leak or engine problem—that he had to be talked out of advising us to land in the Philippines.

We had discussed before we took off what should be done in this sort of situation. Mike Melvill was called, and he arrived as quickly as he could. Peter threw everyone out of the radio room, ruffling some feathers, and Mike and Burt got on the radio. The theory was that however fatigued, Dick would always listen to a wingman.

And Mike talked and came out with the news that it was all right;

Jeana was in the seat. At 142 Zulu, Dick had gone back to get some sleep. It would be only a few hours' worth, but the crisis they perceived in the trailer was over for the time being, and everybody relaxed a little bit.

"There's no question," Mike Melvill said, "that at this point the more capable pilot is flying." Still bad weather loomed.

There was talk of a diversion to better weather north—but that meant passing over Vietnam or Cambodia. Calls were made to our contacts in the State Department. The news that came back was not encouraging. The only way to fly over Cambodia or Vietnam was to land there—only then in cases of "life and death emergency."

"You had to pick the only two countries in the world we can't help you with," said the official at the State Department.

. . .

Dick rolled to the left so I could slip into the seat behind him and headed back for sleep. With the oxygen tank in the back now he could no longer even turn around in the hole, as he had been able to do on previous flights. He just took off the headset, hung it up, put in his earplugs, and wrapped a pillow around his head to fight the noise, leaving only a slight gap for his mouth. And almost instantly he was asleep. I reached back to pull the blanket over him and tucked him in.

Whenever Dick went in back it changed the center of gravity, and I had to make a fuel transfer right away. I selected an aft tank, looking at the key we had taped beside the seat, set the valves, zeroed the counters, selected the fuel transducers, turned on the pump and then the countdown timer.

As I was in the middle of the transfer, Mike and Burt came on the radio wanting to visit and chat. I felt like I was short with them. I don't know whether they thought I was being unfriendly, but I was just busy.

Flying for the first time, and surrounded by hostile weather, I was apprehensive. I just knew there were so many things that could go wrong and there were so many things that Dick didn't have the patience to teach me on the ground. Now I just had to know, and pull out of memory what I had overheard him tell Bruce, Doug, and Burt. Now I hoped all the systems would keep running all right. And that if they didn't, there would at least be enough warning to get Dick up.

We had a nice tail wind now, almost 30 knots, and we cruised along at 8,000 feet and close to 125 knots ground speed.

I began picking my way through the big storms that churned up from the Philippine Islands, great booming cumulus clouds that reached high above the airplane. It was tough weather, but I could handle it.

More difficult was dealing with the tangled talk of the local air traffic controllers, and after a few hours I got Dick up to deal with them.

. . .

Day four, December 18. We finally got the airplane to fly on one engine after the Philippines, but the weather was still lousy.

Len had expected it to be clear after the Philippines.

"All in all, we've been really lucky for this time of year," Len said. "If we had come through Marge two days later, it would have been a nightmare. The weather gods have been kind to us."

We were tracking along the Intertropical Convergence Zone with a squall line to our left. Our course had been chosen to take advantage of the trade winds, but with the trade winds came a price: running close to this band of storms that girdles the earth—the infamous ITCZ, the "Itch," as Len and his fellow weathermen call it. So far we had been lucky with the Itch. Planning our original, more southerly route, we had worried about finding a gap in it. Where we would go would depend on where a hole developed—if it developed. Now, we would be mostly skirting the Itch, directing our course to stay just away from it. The trade-off was typhoons and thunderstorms.

Now we were getting beaten to hell again, and the wings were flailing all around, the tips rising and sinking and the different waves from each wing meeting in the fuselage and fighting it out.

We kept switching off, changing positions. Dick went in back, and it felt as if he'd barely replaced his headphones with earplugs and wrapped the blanket around his head when the tug came on his leg: wake up, bad weather. Then it was like walking through motor oil, trying to get himself going again, everything about to go to hell any minute in a thunderstorm. Dick would say, "My God, how'd we ever get in a place like this?" and then get on the radio and ask weather to vector us away.

Other times the performance men came on, relaying through one of those stations with strange radio names like Orange Juice or Brandywine, and asked for all kinds of numbers. If the com was bad, we often had to repeat things five or six times. What should have taken just a couple of minutes would end up taking half an hour.

"Say again," they would tell us, "wait a minute, you're going too fast."

"Well, put it on tape and listen," Dick would snap back.

After a while we would realize we were cutting into our rest periods and finally Dick would just turn the radio off, angry and hurt and let down and frustrated.

Sometimes, though, when we had time and we finally got through on good clear channels and it was the middle of the night, there were moments when we could talk and joke with familiar voices back in Mojave. It was a good boost to our spirits. Then when we made contact with the over-flight team at Singapore, everything seemed more natural.

. . .

Bruce and Glenn had flown to Singapore along with Mark Greenberg, our photographer. They planned to fly up to an airport called Kota Bharu in a Piper Navaho to meet us. The rendezvous was to be in the dark, but we were hoping to at least get some kind of look over the wingtips and see if there was any sort of fuel leak or oil streak.

When they arrived in Singapore, they all three set their watches to different times. Bruce ran Zulu, Glenn went on local, and Mark on Pacific standard. Naturally they were always confused about what time it really was and worried about somehow mistaking the time for the rendezvous.

Mark took a taxi and told the driver to take him someplace where he could buy auto parts. The driver took him to an out-of-the-way place that was lined, for blocks it seemed to Mark, with auto shops. He went in and bought auto headlights. Then he went out to the airport and rigged them up to the borrowed rendezvous airplane so that they could look at the plane in the dark.

They flew up to meet us right on schedule, but the airport at Kota Bharu was socked in. So they went instead to Hat Yai, Thailand. It was a larger airport, with some Thai military aircraft.

There they found that an official had confused the information on the forms giving them permission to fly. *Voyager*'s tail number had been switched with the tail number of the local airplane they had borrowed.

The airport manager was less than sympathetic. He was officious—"the Guy with the Big Frown," Bruce immediately named him.

The assistant airport manager was more helpful. He had actually heard about *Voyager*—he even knew from the news that the wingtips had dragged on takeoff. He was very cooperative. Big Frown couldn't believe an airplane could fly nonstop around the world. "What do you mean? All the planes stop here," he said. He surely didn't think *Voyager* was anything but a military airplane, and he didn't believe our permits for Mark to photograph. With the Thai military planes around, he didn't like that at all.

Our local pilot knew an official in the capital, so Bruce suggested, "Well, why don't you just call Bangkok and check the permits out?"

"Can't use phone," Big Frown said. "We'll write a letter."

The problem was, *Voyager* was going to fly over his airport in just a few hours. There was nothing more to be done. Mark, Bruce, and Glenn were taken back to town in bicycle rickshaws that cost one bhat to ride, so Bruce started calling them "bhatmobiles." They were offered prostitutes. Their passports were taken away from them, and they were put up in a Vietnam-era hotel called The President. Once it had been luxurious, but now there were lizards running across its ceilings and the occasional rat strolling boldly across the dining room.

Finally they were allowed to return to the airport before we were due to fly over. Big Frown was gone, and the assistant manager agreed to let them sit in the tower and talk to us on his radio.

It was good to hear Bruce's voice come up so clear that night, so good we weren't even all that disappointed we couldn't meet up with them in the air.

We made contact at 15.45 Zulu Julian day 351, or December 17. I was in a complaining mood right then and bitched about the weather and the radios and the work load and how we had to repeat everything over and over again. "We're dealing with guys who can't talk on radios that don't work," I said with some exaggeration. Jeana was more patient, even though she was still suffering from her head cold.

As we approached, we called out distances, told them what we were seeing—a river, now, a town, yeah, on our right—and following their directions, we came right over the airport, not deviating but a tiny bit from the course the Omega was charting. "Listen, there's that little engine," Glenn said, smiling at the familiar noise, and then they saw us—our strobe light—for about ten minutes.

We verified the overflight for the record by turning the strobe on and off on command as we came overhead. While Bruce and Glenn were talking, Mark went out to the airplane, slipped his video camera out when the guards weren't looking, and tried to take pictures, but it was much too dark. He saw the flashing of our strobe as we came over and our silhouette against the almost full moon.

Glenn could tell how fatigued I was from the way I wanted to start the front engine just to climb over a cloud. He suggested, "Dick, why don't you just richen up the mixture on the back and get some more power out of it?"

"Oh, yeah," I said as if the idea had never occurred to me. "I guess that would work, too.

"What's the runway there like?" I asked, and they got the mistaken notion that we had some kind of idea about putting the airplane on the ground. In the background I could hear one of the guys saying, "Don't tell him it's ten thousand feet, tell him it's lousy."

"About fifteen hundred feet," Bruce replied, "and covered with boulders and water buffalo." I knew they were lying, but I didn't know why: they were afraid we might land.

"Hey, Dick," Mark Greenberg said, reviving my most ancient joke. "There's a Thai guy here says he went to high school with you."

Considering our fatigue at that point, it was amazing we actually got a chuckle out of that one.

We talked about the discrepancies in the fuel numbers, and Bruce knew there was only one thing we could do. He left us with stern words.

"Lean it out, Dick," he said. "Keep your RPMs down and push through that weather. Otherwise, I'll go ahead and book a hotel room in Grenada and wait for you there."

We took the message to heart and left encouraged—and determined. We were able to talk to them so long that when the communications started to fade, Bruce even made a formal sign-off, with each of them wishing us good luck, to send us on our way, rather than just talking until we lost contact in a swirl of static.

"Okay, babe," I said in signing off, "I've got the message. No more weaving around, we will go west, we will lean the engine and use lowest-possible RPMs."

At 17.30 Zulu Jeana noted in the log: "Good-bye to Bruce and Glenn and Mark. Radio contact out."

And then for some reason I had a vision of Bruce sitting in a folding chair on the runway apron at Mojave, just watching the sun go down, as we so often did when we were building the Voyager. I would grab a beer and Jeana her cola, along with some corn chips that would end up being our supper. And when we left for the day, Bruce would still be there, just sitting and watching. That was how I thought of him now.

The only thing we regretted was that we didn't get a close-up report on the wingtips, to see what the damage was there, or the engines, to see if we had any signs of an oil or fuel leak. That would have to wait until Africa.

Bruce was exasperated with Big Frown, but in the end he didn't feel too bad about not having been able to take off. He could easily have missed us in all the weather, and on the ground he was able to sit and talk with us at leisure, spreading out his maps and charts.

Sitting in the tower after we had all signed off, Bruce happened to glance at the airport log and noticed *Voyager*'s familiar tail numbers— "November two six nine Victor Alpha"—and seeing them inscribed there in strange handwriting in those alien pages gave him an odd sort of a thrill. We were all a long way from home.

I had always feared the Indian Ocean. I had heard too many bad stories about it in the military and known too many guys who went down in it not to fear it. It represented thousands of miles of open water with lousy radio contact, tracking along the ITCZ, which meant little storms popping up when you least expected them.

And sure enough, just as we coasted west of the Malay Peninsula with water beneath us again, we ran into rough stuff and had to start dodging storms. Bruce had reported that the locals said weather west of the Malay Peninsula was always better than in the South China Sea behind us. We were looking forward to that—God, how we needed a respite. But just the opposite was true. We went two and a half hours off the coast and found ourselves right back in turbulence, vectoring around weather, talking to the command post, trying to stay alive, as we had been from the beginning.

It was the ITCZ we were skirting on our left; as Len had warned us, the Itch was much farther north than normal, and it was pushing our course north with it.

We got hold of mission control so they could look at the satellite pictures and guide us to smooth air. The radios were working worse than ever, and when we finally managed to raise them, they told us to turn north. When we did we broke out of the weather, just like that, boom, into a nice, clear starlit night, and we thought we had it made for a while.

And then we hit a squall line.

Just after midnight, I was trying to climb a ridge between two big CB's and got the airspeed so low—way below anything we ever had flown before—that we should have stalled. I saw it just in time and pushed the stick full forward, barely catching it in time, and we descended into the wet, turbulent clouds below. We got beaten up for twenty minutes before we could get out of it, humping and bucking, running so lean the engine almost quit. Which was pretty unnerving over the Indian Ocean at night. And we could only get down to 4.4 gallons per hour. We were not sure what was wrong, but something surely was. We did realize that trying to deploy a low-altitude airplane in all this weather around the world was not the way to do it. We simply did not realize how much weather there really was at low altitude.

. . .

Our critical guide to whether we would have enough fuel to make it around the world was a chart bearing what we called the "how-goes-it" curve.

On its horizontal axis were marked degrees of longitude and on the vertical axis gross weight, which decreased as we burned fuel.

We'd been refining that curve for years. It marked nautical miles per pound of fuel, and how well our actual performance compared with the curve was the key to our success. The curve started very low at the bottom-left-hand corner, very low because starting out very heavy we would get low gas mileage. At the end of the flight, if we did well, the mileage would increase tremendously, so the curve soared up as we moved right across the page with time. If we were above the curve, we were doing okay; if below it, we would come up short.

Around Hawaii we were way above the curve, looking great. But by the Philippines we were just on it, which was barely acceptable, and we were going down. The curve Jeana plotted of actual burns was going off the page. We began to be concerned on day two of the flight, Julian day 349, at 07:22 Zulu, when Jack Norris radioed us, saying we were burning nearly 20 percent more fuel than we should be. But we would have Marge to worry about soon, so fuel wasn't our most important concern right then.

We attributed the poor performance the numbers and curves seemed to be showing to the loss of the winglets. It was a hell of a frustrating thing, to think that we had started out that deep in the hole, that we might have lost our chance to make it around the world even before we got off the runway. We worked hard to keep those thoughts at the back of our minds and tried not to look out at those bloody stumps of wingtips.

We also wondered—and tried to keep from wondering—if something to do with the fuel system might have been broken in the vibration resulting from the prop loss and never been detected.

The odd thing was that the airplane was flying as if it were much heavier than the numbers showed. The key figure was gross weight—the basic weight of the airplane plus the weight of the fuel. Our rates of climb indicated a heavier gross weight than our fuel logs. If we'd had the deck angle gauge working, it would have offered us another means of checking how heavy we were. Another indication was that twice when we tried to turn off the front engine and fly on the rear engine alone, the airplane failed to maintain level flight.

There were all kinds of theories about what could be wrong. Maybe a fuel flow transducer was out of calibration. We checked the transducer against the feed tank sight gauge—the only real fuel gauge on the airplane, a crude but certain physical device, and found a 10 to 15 percent error.

The least worrisome possibilities were that there had been an error or series of errors in the fuel log due either to the difficulty of writing in turbulence or to crew fatigue. Because we kept the log cumulatively, any error would be magnified over time.

"It would be easy," Ferg said, leaning against the bouncing wall of an imaginary airplane in turbulence, handling an imaginary pencil, "to write, say, a nine, and it comes out a zero. Or a five, and it comes out a two. Or any number of mistakes."

But if at that moment Ferg could have seen Jeana's log, he would have laughed at his own theory. Jeana was always justly proud of her fine and precise handwriting—the handwriting of the draftsman and artist she was.

Someone once told her, "Jack Norris has the tiniest writing I've ever seen."

"Well, you haven't seen mine. You have to have a magnifying glass to read it."

And you could have read it. The numbers in her log were all correct. Looking at them, you could see the effects of turbulence, to be sure, but it never changed a number or a letter. The loop of a six might show a jerky line, like a seismograph's, but it never made it anything but a six. Right there in those figures and on those pages was a visible record of the aerial rodeo we'd been through, but you could read every number.

Another reassuring theory held that the fuel Bruce added at the last minute—four hundred pounds of it—might somehow not have been recorded. The original plan had been to shift that fuel from the fuselage tanks to the mid wing tanks. It was decided, after takeoff, not to do that. That fuel could be in there.

The worst possibility of all was some sort of fuel leak. We had already noticed what looked like fuel streaming from the cap of the left tip tank. The loss of that entire tank, however, would represent only a hundred pounds, and it was fuel we planned to save for the very end of the flight. Our numbers now were showing a discrepancy in the range of six hundred pounds.

Or maybe something was wrong with the rear engine. Maybe it really was burning that much fuel. Mike and Fergy argued against this one, too. There were no signs of excessive oil burns or performance defects.

"If there's something wrong with that engine," Mike said, "then Dick would know it. He can hear it. He knows engines, especially that engine, inside and out."

One of the problems had to do with the difficulty of communications and the battle for radio time between the weather people and the performance people.

It was a battle, too, over our time, radio time, which, when communications were poor and things had to be repeated over and over, was at a premium.

Between performance and weather there was a natural conflict. The best fuel burns meant going in a straight line at steady altitude. But that implied running through all sorts of unacceptable storms.

Weather's job was to protect the pilots and the airplane and give us reasonably decent air. Weather was our lifeline.

At one point when Dick Blosser in the radio room came on to ask me, "Do you have time to talk to weather?" I answered, "I always have time to talk to weather."

But we didn't always have time to talk to performance. It seemed we always had to repeat the numbers for them over and over. What should have taken two or three minutes, with bad communications, ended up taking half an hour or forty-five minutes. We couldn't even work in our six-hour reports sometimes, because of the burden of the performance numbers.

The situation frustrated Burt tremendously. He was concerned that we might be in imminent danger—if the numbers were really this bad, we could be leaking fuel into the engine compartment, or we might have an engine that could stop working at any moment.

"We are spinning our wheels," Burt complained, "we're just not getting enough data. We've gone another twenty-one hours without performance data.

"I'd like to run those weather guys out of there and talk to Dick about his airplane."

Fergy couldn't understand what use all the numbers were at this point. He had very little sympathy for numbers people to begin with, and now it was no longer test time.

Ferg was convinced, from the way the plane was handling, that it had a lot more fuel on board than the number crunchers figured.

"I think there's just too goddamn much analysis going on," he growled. "Just fly the plane and do the best you can."

When Bruce got back from Thailand, he agreed. "You performance weenies may as well go home right now. There's nothing left for you to do. They'll fly the airplane as far as they can, and then they'll land it. That's all."

Spirits rose and fell according to the curve of each new graph the number crunchers turned out. By Wednesday night, day four, everyone in Mojave was feeling better. The discouraging fuel figures—"He'll just flame out on the runway," Burt said of his worst-case, no-tail-wind figures—seemed to be the result of either a faulty transducer or faulty bookkeeping somewhere down the line.

Mike Melvill was hopeful. "That fuel didn't just disappear. The burn rates will improve.

"Once they get back into the Caribbean or South America or someplace Dick knows, he'll lean that sucker out and push for home. We've never flown the plane as light as it'll be on the home stretch, and we'll see numbers we won't believe. The same thing happened on the Long EZ record—he turned in numbers that even the people who built the engine said were bullshit."

.   .   .

We didn't spend much time on theories; the only thing we could do was fly, as Bruce had admonished us: lean and stay in the Bucket. There was one thing to feel good about, however. We had now burned enough fuel that our optimum speed was below eighty-two knots—the feared point above which divergent oscillation could set in. There might be a lot of sharks in that blue-green water beneath us, but we had left the pitch porpoise behind for good.

Dick soon went back for some sleep, and I took over. He had left the CG aft, as usual, and I had to make another fuel transfer to keep us flying in the Bucket. There were also big thunderstorms to dodge as usual.

We were running the rear engine hot, trying to get above some of the weather. I opened the ramp halfway for cooling, but finally we had to start the front again.

More thunder-bumpers kept popping up. We ran right through the edge of one of those mothers when we both had our heads down.

We realized we had to watch the weather more carefully. The moon was a godsend, and another godsend was the starlight scope Jack Norris had gotten from Ed Green at Edwards Air Force Base.

The starlight scope was a high-tech little set of opera glasses that pilots clip on to their helmets. It magnifies the starlight and enables you to see things in darkness well below the normal sensitivity of the human eye. It is like a cat's eye, providing an eerie, grainy green view of the night, and the way the images glint and pop out made looking into it like looking into a dream or a ghost story.

The scope was my baby; Jeana never used it because of her height. It was a sensitive instrument, and you couldn't let any ambient light get into it or you would burn out the tubes. So when I used it she had to turn off all the cockpit lights and dim the instruments. To monitor the instruments she would work the flashlight like a strobe, taking quick frequent glances, then turn it off so as not to damage the night vision goggles.

My head and the scope would barely fit together in the canopy. I would take my glasses off, remove the covers from the lenses of the scope, and put it up in the canopy, then slip my head in behind it. I could only see straight ahead, and everything was black.

Then I turned it on, and a strange green world appeared, where I could see the clouds with very intense textures. I would try to memorize what I'd seen—big humper thirty degrees left, two more farther to the right. Then I would turn off the scope, put on the caps, drop back out of the canopy, and turn the lights and instruments back up. Then I would reset the autopilot for a course to dodge those things. And we did this over and over again throughout the night.

When the sun finally came up we could see that the water of the Indian Ocean looked different. It looked dirty; it looked more like a sewer.

As we approached Sri Lanka, we were flying much farther north than planned because the ITCZ had shifted upward. We began to plan our exact course over Sri Lanka and found that we did not have maps of this area. When the maps were cut down to size it was for the more southern route (Australia to the tip of South Africa, then back toward Texas). We couldn't carry a map for every part of the world, but we fortunately had anticipated deviations by bringing along many extra maps and charts in microfiche form. We carried microfiches of potential landing fields, as well as the diagrams and schematics for the Voyager. The microfiche reader was easy to use, but it was difficult to correlate the maps with the ground features. In an emergency, however, it would be quite functional.

Around midday we came up on Sri Lanka, which we were supposed to cross to the north, and the air controllers began giving us a hard time.

There seemed to be three or four control sectors in the area, with all the controllers talking on the same frequency at the same time in the same pidgin English. They wanted us to go south, but the weather people back in Mojave said to go north. We tried to change our flight plan, but we couldn't make them understand. We'd repeat and repeat and nothing got through.

Finally we said the hell with it and diverted straight across Sri Lanka just to avoid them, swinging past an eight-thousand-foot mountain called Mount Kandy. The big rock candy mountain—well, not hardly. We were over clouds and didn't see much.

The undercast finally ended over the western coast of Sri Lanka, and we passed a beautiful long airport. Good for a divert if we needed it, I thought. I began to fantasize about how nice it would feel to land, roll out, turn off that long runway, and go to sleep.

We started out across the Indian Ocean again. I was making some of my usual checks in back—looking at oil levels, adjusting the ramps, when I saw a few spoonfuls of coolant in the overflow reservoir bottle in back and brought it forward to show Dick.

Our engine coolant pump was a newly developed piece of equipment. We had had some problems with its seals and replaced them just before the flight. There was a seal to keep the oil from the engine, another to keep the coolant, a mixture of glycol and water, like automobile antifreeze, from leaking into the oil. Between the two was a hollow area with a drain tube. Some leakage, or "weep," was expected, and the tube normally ran overboard. But we had fed it into a little plastic bottle under the floorboard so we would know right away if anything was leaking. This is not one of those things you want to find leaking. I began checking on that bottle every time I was back there.

If the coolant seal was leaking, it was very bad news. A coolant seal failure never gets better.

"That means we've lost the mission," I said to Jeana. "No way to fix it, no way—it's all pressurized. If we've blown the seal, that's it." I felt a little guilty about my fantasy of landing, but I also thought, Well, now we have an excuse to land.

The prudent thing, of course, would be to turn around and land, right then, but we also knew we weren't going to. There was no point in talking it over. With Jeana I knew what her answer would be: we would go on. Of course I would be fooling myself to say I was going to land anyway.

If we turned around right then, we could make it back to that lovely long runway behind us; but if we went on, and lost the coolant and the engine farther out over the ocean, well . . .

And lo and behold, a few minutes later Jeana looked at the leak again, and there was no more! Maybe it was all right after all. Some of Jeana's magic door at work again. We formulated a plan to find out. We increased the pressure in the system by closing up the air intake and pushing up the power. Jeana tested the seal with saliva, the way you would check the valve stem on a tire. No bubbles, no leak. Then we cooled it way down to lower the pressure and see if it was leaking inward. No, there was no sucking leak, either. Somehow it had sealed itself!

Perhaps it was just normal weep from a pretty new system—but maybe it was some kind of progressive failure, a slow leak that would start up again and get worse as we got out over the ocean and left that nice airport behind.

From now on, Jeana would have to check that seal all the time, and we would both have to worry about it. Another thing to add to the constant fuel transfers and oil checks and cooling ramp adjustments. We never knew why it didn't recur—write it off to fate.

One more monkey wrench was thrown into the works. The bulb burned out in the fuel countdown timer. This was a simple little gadget that we used as a shutoff reminder for fuel transfers. We could set the timer, and it would light up flashing when the transfer was about done. In the meantime we could allow ourselves to do something else. But now we would have to watch that transfer with a reminder. If we missed the turn-off it could throw the airplane out of balance and even stall it.

There were three identical bulbs—one in the countdown timer, one in the landing gear down light, and one in the alternator warning light. I knew we wouldn't need the gear light until we got home, so I plugged it into the countdown timer—and it blew out. Then I had a hard decision to make. Not having that countdown timer was going to add greatly to the work we would have to do and the extra concentration we would have to pay. But if we lost the alternator and didn't have that light to warn us, we might not notice it until we had run the battery down with no way to start the front engine. That was a worse possibility, so I left the alternator light bulb right where it was.

At first I blamed Jeana for not packing the spare bulbs, and then I suddenly had a vision of exactly where they were: in the top drawer of my desk back at Hangar 77.

But worst of all, the fuel numbers gave us no hope of making it home. We were leaning it almost until the engine quit and still only getting 3.6 nautical miles per pound of fuel when we should have been getting 3.9. We didn't know why.

. . .

By the morning of Thursday, December 18, the mood was glum again in Mojave. Jack Norris's cruncher kids were working around the clock in the back office coming up with new curves, new scenarios, and every time they opened the door to bring out the latest graph, the mingled odor of sweat and Mexican food rolled out like a wave.

"If these numbers are right," Burt said, looking at the latest graph, "then we're going to have to recover him somewhere."

Suddenly everyone began to talk about worst cases, about potential landings at Ascension or Grenada. Was Trinidad better than Grenada? Was there any chance of making Puerto Rico, which was at least a U.S. territory?

A quiet gray sense of resignation settled over the hangar. And on the radio Burt told us the numbers we'd sent back were impossible unless something was very wrong. He was concerned that we not attempt to fly across Africa unless we also had fuel for the Atlantic. He had a strong suspicion that if we made it across Africa, we wouldn't be able to keep from trying to get across the ocean, too.

We reviewed plans made long ago to stretch the fuel to its utmost and still provide a margin of safety for crossing the Atlantic. It was a "fill and fly" plan.

We would fill the forty-two-gallon feed tank—this represented about six hours, or 1,218 miles of flying time, about the distance between Los Angeles and Kansas City—and fly until it was half-empty. If we could fill it and be looking at enough for Ascension, we went on. If there was no fuel left to fill with, then return to Africa. At Ascension, we would do the same thing.

So all that was left, it seemed, was to set the longest straight-line distance record we could.

"That was the original idea," Mike Melvill contended.

But of course it wasn't true, and Mike and everyone else in Mojave knew it as well as we did in the *Voyager*.

Lee Yeager had joked with Dick before the flight that if we were short, we could land in Texas, he'd put us up. That would be good enough, he implied. "No, no," Dick said. "Anything short of Edwards will be a failure."

. . .

We felt that way, too: everyone on the ground wanted an answer and kept badgering us for more numbers. We didn't have an answer. There was no way we could make the airplane go any farther than we were already, leaned out, sitting right there in the L/D Bucket, doing our job. But pretty soon we were going to have to face the possibility that the best we could do wouldn't be good enough.

Late that afternoon, halfway between India and the coast of Africa, we got the word that we'd passed the B-52's record. It was a nice milestone, but a lot of people could have broken that record. Tom Jewett could have broken it, if he had lived.

Clyde Evely, the B-52 pilot, sent a very gracious telegram from his home back in Apex, North Carolina, congratulating us. Compared with ours, he said, his flight was easy, and he saluted us. One of the volunteers back in Mojave had named his new baby Charles Richard, after Charles Lindbergh and Dick Rutan.

But all this just made us feel worse because we were being forced to face the fact that the fuel numbers were much too bad for us to have any chance of making it around the world.

We talked about it. I knew something was wrong, but in the back of my mind I still felt confident. The numbers were discouraging, but the airplane felt fine.

I had a slowly sinking feeling in my stomach for a while, and now as we faced it head on, my throat tightened and I wanted to cry. We were looking at failure.

"We can't even make the Atlantic Ocean," I said to Jeana. "And I'm leaning the devil out of it.

"If we really have this little fuel, we're not only going to have to land, it's going to be downright embarrassing." How were we going to face people? How were we going to face ourselves? To set out to fly around the world and barely make it halfway, we'd really look like jerks.

"No," Jeana said, "we can try again. We have to."

We had always thought about the possibility of needing another chance, about maybe not making it until the third try or so, but now I didn't think it was possible.

We tried to look at the bright side.

A great big straight-line distance record and the closed course before that. It was something we could be proud of.

But that was not what we set out to do. We set out to fly around the world. Anything short of that was not our intent.

"Recovering this airplane from some godforsaken part of Africa won't be any picnic.

"And, Jeana," I said, "I don't know if I could get in it again, sit on that runway at Edwards and face the whole thing again. I'm not sure I have another one in me."

"Well, I guess we owe it to ourselves and everyone else to do our best now, to go as far as we can."

. . .

The weather in the last half of the Indian Ocean was as bad as the first half. Now we monitored only the mission control frequency—8,822 megacycles. We had a relay through the U.S. base at Diego Garcia, in the Indian Ocean. At least we did not have to deal with the Sri Lankan air controllers; Mike Hance in mission control was making arrangements with them via telephone. We didn't even dare think of the phone bill.

Finally, in the dark hours of the next morning, Dick had to get some sleep, weather or not, and I took over for the run into Africa. We were coming into our fifth day, about halfway between Sri Lanka and the African coast.

In Mojave it was early afternoon of Thursday, December 18. Before he went back Dick asked on the radio that mission control plan "a conference" for the next day to "review the whole plan"—a three-way conference involving *Voyager*, Doug Shane, coming up to fly the rendezvous in Africa, and Peter, Mike, Len, Jack, and Larry Caskey in mission control. They all could tell in Mojave how down we were.

I told them, "If you can't find some fuel for this airplane, I'm going to put it down on the east coast."

The Dark Continent

Four days, seven hours: 11,250 miles to go.

There were strange-looking clouds ahead, and I didn't know quite what to make of them. Dick was in the back, and I had the engine leaned out and the airplane at just the optimal angle of attack—as best I could tell without the deck angle gauge—and I'd managed to save a lot of fuel. We were about eighty nautical miles off the coast of Somalia, approaching the African landfall we had looked at with a good deal of foreboding. We were leaving the Indian Ocean and entering Africa. Len and his weather people had always told us that Africa was impassable, that he had no idea how we'd make it across.

It was before dawn. I was carefully wading my way through the towering clouds. The moon was bright and most essential but suddenly I saw something I wasn't familiar with. A blackness in the dark gray.

I gave Dick a tug on his foot, and he stirred. "Good morning," I said, even though it wasn't morning.

He shook off his grogginess. We went through the acrobatics of changing positions. Dick caught sight of the squall line, with a lot of stratus, the kind of thing you often get a hundred miles or so off the coast.

We were almost in it.

Dick just barely got into the seat before we reached the weather. It was running almost perpendicular to our course. Dick turned but we couldn't avoid it completely, and we soon got into the weather. It was a heavy downpour and hurt our performance dramatically. We couldn't climb to get out of this stuff. As the airplane got wet Dick pushed up the power, trying again to climb, but still couldn't. Then he turned 90 degrees. We tried to climb again, but there was no way.

We finally got to clear air, and settled out for the run into Africa. Jeana was busy in the back running through her chores. Still groggy, I thought about all of our planning for taking on Africa, how we would have to keep away from the mountains, dodge thunderstorms—

Suddenly a light flashed on the canard. I looked back behind me and saw it: a landing light! It was an airplane! Coming up on the coast of Africa, and it was a fighter, tracking us!

"Jeana, come up here! We've got a fighter intercepting us! Do you see it? Come up and look."

I was busy getting the day's food and water set up. I left that to see what Dick was looking at. I looked out and saw nothing unusual. I thought he was joking. So I went back to the trivial jobs yet to be done. He kept on about the fighter and missiles. "Sure, Dick," I said.

I turned, and the light turned. I called back to mission control and told them we were being attacked, but the message didn't get through.

I watched that light for a long time and waited for the sound of a missile, waited for the impact.

There was nothing to do. I thought of all my fighter pilot training, evasion techniques. I remembered just the way a good fighter pilot would play it: pitch back up and into him, get him to overshoot, get him into a vertical rolling scissors and jink hard.

But in the *Voyager* that would be a joke. We were helpless. We just had to wait. There was no use even putting on the chutes, we would never get out, we would just be blown sky-high. The light was too bright to be anything else; it had to be a fighter.

Funny, they weren't even trying to get us to land, the pilot was not even waggling his wings, nothing. They didn't even plan to give us a chance, just take us right out, like that Korean airliner, same thing—I wondered what it would feel like. Would I see a flash, a jolt, anything at all? We hadn't seen any other airplane since the Saratoga had come up to look us over south of Hawaii. It had to be somebody looking for us.

Then I turned the *Voyager* as sharply as I could to the left and looked back over my shoulder to see him head on—and what I saw was not an airplane but a star. I realized that what I had been looking at was Venus, "the morning star."

It was no wonder we were nervous. Africa had long loomed as the biggest obstacle of the flight. We had originally planned to cross Africa in the south, to avoid the political complexities of the middle of the continent, but that had been back in September. Now that we had chosen the route farther to the north, what we faced was a corridor, limited by the dangers of guerrillas and hostile regimes and SAMs—from Vietnam I knew enough about those things, rising at you like flying telephone poles, to know I never wanted to get anywhere near them if I could help it. But there might be no choice. The corridor led over or through some of the highest mountains in the world and across the Great Rift Valley, the birthplace of thunderstorms that rose like time-lapse photography clouds, boiling to fifty thousand feet or more.

If the paleontologists were right, this was where man as a species had gotten his start, where zinjanthropus and the protoapes had roamed. The valley cut right down through the layers of stone to reveal signs of the world of millions of years ago in the fossils it had left. The footprints of our ancestors had been found here, turned to stone. If the geologists were right, this, too, was where Africa would one day break in two, as the plates of the earth drifted apart. The mountains we would have to cross were evidence of the power of the earth to reshape its own surface, and it was as if we were challenging that power head on.

. . .

We approached the continent near Mogadishu but didn't want to make our landfall immediately. We had been warned not to venture into Somalia, where a civil war was going on, so for about a hundred miles or so we tracked south/southwest, doglegging along the coast of Somalia. We wanted to go feet dry in Kenya.

There was not a single light down there. Not one. No wonder they call it the dark continent. There were no towns or resorts. Maybe the Omega was wrong. Maybe we weren't there yet. Hour after hour, mile after mile, we ran along looking to our right for some light over land. There had to be something, a town, a farm—hell, a campfire. We moved over close enough to get the coast on radar and cross-check the Omega. Yes, it was right on the money, the coast was right where it was supposed to be.

We kept cruising parallel to the coast, and when, a couple of hours later, we began to get the first sunlight, we could see why there were no lights—no one lived there. It was a no-man's-land. There was no place to live, nothing to eat—nothing.

There was nothing to support life. Or so it seemed from the air. It was all bush and sand and desert, just complete and utter desolation. It was an incredible place, more barren by far than the desert we knew in California.

Then, as we came cruising well into the continent, I happened to glance down and saw fuel bubbling through the clear plastic flow valves—flowing backward from the feed tank into the selected fuel tank, flowing when it wasn't supposed to be!

Right away I called to Jeana to come up and look at it.

This fuel tank select valve, remember, switched the feed tank so that it drew from any one of the sixteen tanks. It was made of clear plastic, and it resembled an oversized shower mix valve.

There were four transducers, two on the engines and two on the transfer pumps, but only one readout indicator for both sets, and we flipped a switch back and forth between the two. This saved the weight of one indicator. Now I immediately switched back to the fuel transfer transducers, and it hit me like a load of bricks: fuel was flowing backward from the feed tank to the selected tank!

That was why the fuel flow transducers had never returned to zero flow.

I turned off the emergency fuel flow valves, which kept the feed tank from overfilling and pumping fuel overboard, and we watched in amazement as the transducers immediately dropped to zero. That confirmed it: fuel was flowing backward. It was impossible, but it was happening.

That had always happened on the test flights, and I had told Dick and Bruce, and everyone said it didn't mean anything and ignored me. I had put it on the gig list every test flight with major fuel transfers. But no one had ever taken me seriously.

But sure enough, fuel was flowing backward, and that explained the aberration in the transducers. But why it was happening, we didn't know.

God, we were happy. We knew we had fuel. But we also knew there was absolutely no way to figure out how much.

It looked as if there were maybe two gallons an hour flowing back through, but there was no way to reconstruct the total figures. Accurate fuel accountability was lost. From here on it was just a guess.

Right away we got on the radio to share the news with Mojave.

I had been keeping a running tally of the overage of fuel just as in the test flights. So I suspected we had approximately 500 pounds floating around.

By the end of the flight we ate into my 500 and some odd pounds and were within 20 pounds of my estimate.

We looked at each other, and the implications hit us: we didn't have to land in Africa. I felt a weight disappear from my stomach and all of a sudden felt clean again, healthy, excited. Jeana was calmer, and I could see from her eyes that she had never really doubted we would be all right on fuel.

We should have known, from the angle of attack at speed, the way the airplane flew. We should have known.

We had been flying heavier than we thought—we were heavier, we had plenty of fuel; nothing was wrong with the engines or the wingtips! We were fine!

True, we had noticed on test flights that when we shut the pumps off, the fuel transducers didn't roll right back to zero. And at the end of flights— including the Pacific coast flight—we would sometimes come out with a 10 to 15 percent discrepancy. We didn't know why this was happening, and the discrepancy didn't seem that large at the time. We couldn't imagine any way we had fuel flowing back. Jeana had noticed the fuel in the tubing and kept mentioning it, but nobody paid any attention. There had been too many other things to worry about.

Now I noted in the log, "Everything points to being 1,000 pounds heavier. We have just decided to go as far as we possibly can."

. . .

About the same time, right after dinner on Thursday, day five, Julian 352, December 18 back in Mojave, Chuck Richey finished up his Chinese vegetable stew and went back into the offices. He had an idea: to run the fuel numbers from the transducers in gallons, not pounds. He charted the numbers and ran off the graph with a French curve taken from Jeana's drafting tools.

And the curve looked a lot better! Burt didn't really believe it, and it turned out that Chuck was very close to the exact amount, but we didn't find that out for a long time, and it didn't matter anyway. The point was that we had another confirmation that we had enough fuel.

Chuck was the brilliant engineer who had designed our landing gear— and it was a virtuoso engineering performance to turn out composite and metal gears weighing just twenty-six pounds that could support five tons of fuel-laden airplane. Chuck is quiet and calculating. He has an absentminded-professor air with an Abe Lincoln beard. This time he was right on. He said in his bemused way, "On one engine, the airplane won't climb. It has too much fuel. Very simple. At full throttle and 2,800 RPMs single engine, it will hardly sustain level flight. So it's too heavy. We should have known right there the numbers were wrong."

"But we always blamed that on wingtip drag," Mike Melvill said.

Mike took Chuck's numbers and tried to figure out a physical explanation for them. Finally he focused on the fuel return line. When we first installed the fuel system, the airplane had standard carbureted engines. But when we installed the final engines, the Teledyne Continental ones, the IOL 200 on the back was fuel-injected. And fuel-injection systems include a mechanism to remove vaporization. And this vaporized fuel was then sent back to the feed tank by a return line. On that return, it was running the transducer backward.

The transducer was a kind of little paddle wheel. Each turn of its paddles was counted by an electronic device something like the electric eye that opens the door to the grocery store. Each time the paddle passed, the transducer totaled it up, and the resulting number was turned into a measure of fuel flow.

But fuel going backward turned the paddlewheel, too, and the counting device didn't know direction, it only knew numbers. So the returning fuel was measured again. The error was double: the fuel was counted as having been burned once, when it went through going forward, and again when it went back. And in fact it had not been burned at all—it was back in the tanks, ready for another trip through the pump.

Mike checked his theory with Bruce, made a sketch, and had everyone pretty much convinced that he was right. He got ready to radio us the news we had enough fuel.

. . .

Not long afterward, equipped with Chuck's chart and already nurturing a theory about how the transducers were giving false readings, Mike Melvill radioed us, and the message came through all those different sets of electronics still laden with the sense of relief he had poured into it: "You have fuel for the Atlantic."

The com was not very clear, but our reply came back to the trailer across the miles: "Roger, we've got fuel for the Atlantic. Outstanding!"

We shared with Mike how we'd looked down and seen the fuel flowing, too, and thought how propitious it was that we'd found good news at both ends at just the same time. And we felt reinvigorated.

Now we had a chance to finish and get home. And all of a sudden the deep dark clouds of discouragement that had settled over us entering the African coast just vanished, poof—we had a shot at it again, a second chance, and our determination was born again, right there. We had just decided to go as far as we possibly could and land, and with that in mind we were playing out the string, running out the clock in the fourth quarter. But now it was a new game.

In checking feed tank levels against the transducers, we found errors in the area of 10 percent. So we knew we had more fuel than the log listed, but there was no way of telling for sure. Where had it gone? That knowledge might end up making the difference in whether we made it all the way or not.

Jeana converted one of the main wing tanks we knew was empty for the "miscellaneous" tank in her log. And she listed the "new fuel" as being in that tank, although we didn't know for sure where it really was.

When we rendezvoused with Doug we could do stall and rate-of-climb tests to get some better idea of the gross weight of the airplane—and a better idea of how much fuel we really had, what kind of a chance we really had of bringing this thing all the way home.

We anticipated that eagerly and with a bit of trepidation, too. When he came up and looked at us, we would know once and for all whether or not we had a fuel leak of some sort and just how bad the drag on the wingtips was. He would be able to see any oil streak we might have, indicating something wrong with the engine. One thing we knew, when we saw him and he saw us—our hearts were going to sink, or they were going to leap.

We crossed the coast near Mogadishu, just south of the Somalian border. The land below now looked more hospitable, with vegetation, roads, a small village here and there.

We were concerned about linking up with Doug successfully, especially after the problems in Thailand. We couldn't pick up the VOR (Visual Omni Range) station shown on the map but had to count on the good old Omega to bring us close. Already we could see that we were moving closer to the highlands. Little puffs of clouds were visible.

As we got closer to Nairobi, the brushy land of the coastal plain, without rivers or roads or towns, was beginning to give way to mounting uplands, grading from bumps at first to hills ranging up a thousand or fifteen hundred feet. They reminded me of the foothills of the Sierras we had flown over so many times.

The chase plane was supplied by Sunbird Aviation and piloted by Tim Sarginson, who so graciously turned the controls over to Doug for the actual rejoin. Also on board were Mark Hyatt, another Sunbird pilot, Martin Mayer, a Royal Air Force adviser to the Kenyan air force, and Gille Turle, a former government officer, both of whom could run bureaucratic interference.

We had wanted to arrive at the mountains just before dawn and cross in the morning—to get enough light, but also to avoid the afternoon, when the storms really got boiling. But now it looked as if we would cross in the midafternoon, the worst time of all. By then the sun would have warmed the jungle, and the rocks and the terrain would have heated up and begun to cook the big convective storms up into the atmosphere. But there was nothing we could do.

We did not know it, but mission control had sent us a message to circle before we came over the coast and wait until later at night to come across. We never got the message; ironically, if we had heeded it, we would not have had enough fuel to complete the flight.

On the VHF radio, we could hear guides running safaris on the ground, ordering in food and "petrol." The accents were British, and except for the fact that one guy was talking about the broken motor on his compressor, the voices might have come from a century ago. There was no sign of civilization, no roads, nothing. Except for those sounds on the radio, it felt even more lonesome, somehow, than being in the middle of the ocean.

We had the feeling that little had changed since the days of the great white explorers, of Livingstone and Stanley and Speke, seeking to discover the headwaters of the Nile back in the nineteenth century.

Doug and his pilot were due to take off from Nairobi and fly to a little airstrip with three grass huts called Samburu, inside the Buffalo Springs Game Reserve, about 150 miles northeast of Nairobi.

Beyond the edge of the airstrip, Doug could see herds of elephant and giraffe, and on the runway was a pile of elephant dung. Doug trained his video camera on the pile. "Want to take some home?" the pilot teased him. There was something else out in the grass. One of the local pilots referred to it as "a cat."

This time there were no problems with officials on the ground. The only difficulty was that we were late, and Doug and his pilot had to wait with the elephants and giraffes on the ground an extra five hours. They refueled the airplane from jerricans and took off to meet us.

Finally we got Doug on the radio and could hear his voice loud and clear. He explained why we were having trouble picking up the VOR station we were looking for: it was "ops normal" for Africa—out of service. And we gave him the good news on fuel.

The HF radio was crisp and clear, and we called out the miles. Twenty, fifteen, ten. Then he called: he saw us. He approached us head on and came around in a tail chase, turned, and slid in under our left wing, at seventy-five knots. It was about ten-thirty in the morning, and we were nearing the end of our fifth day in the air, when we caught sight of them—0800 Zulu, Julian day 353, near a town called Wajir, not far from the Buffalo Springs VOR station.

We saw Doug pull abeam under the left window about two hundred feet away. Five people were with him in the airplane, and with that weight it was hard for him to slow down enough to stay with us. He pulled the nose up. We could see the airplane shudder and buffet a bit and drop down. Then Doug, who is a great pilot, recovered and scooted ahead. We saw him look back over his right shoulder—a familiar face in this unfamiliar, threatening land and sky. And then his airplane shuddered again, and the nose pitched up, and the airplane began to turn in a slow rotation, a quarter turn classic spin entry—and he dropped out of view from our window.

One thing any good pilot knows is not to call somebody when he has his hands full of trouble. We just sat and wondered if he was okay. Should we search for him? Abort the mission? How long should we wait? It was a handful of seconds, but it seemed like an eternity.

Finally we could wait no longer. "You guys okay?" we asked as if there were something we could do about it if they weren't.

"We're fine now," Doug said, "but could you give me just a little bit more airspeed?"

We sped up to 83 so he could stay with us. And right away he alleviated our worries: everything looked fine.

There was no big ugly brown oil streak that might indicate some valve or ring problem, no big ugly blue streak that would show a major fuel leak, although the wing was smeared back behind the left outboard fuel cap, which was still overflowing when we took off. Doug said he saw no leak, but we still had our doubts. We would find out later who was right.

He saw a little brown streak, normal, from the oil breather. And a yellow streak on the right-hand side of the fuselage—a man-made phenomenon and also to be expected.

We knew our fuel was okay; we knew our airplane was okay, and we had a new impetus to drive on home.

The wires were still there on the wingtip. We had figured they would have fatigued and broken by now, but no problem.

We did some climb tests to try to get a handle on the gross weight of the airplane; the heavier it was, of course, the more power it would take to climb and the slower the rate would be. It was a crude way, but right then it was the best way of trying to sort out the fuel numbers.

We estimated a 5,257-pound gross weight. Jeana adjusted the log to call it 5,200, to be on the conservative side. And that placed us in the middle of the fuel curve on the how-goes-it chart!

We depleted a main wing tank and then found more fuel there— corroborating the theories and the good news.

We also ran another test—angle of attack versus airspeed. Our deck angle gauge had gone out, remember, but we figured how to make do with a kind of carpenter's bubble we had on hand. It was actually a device used to level off recreation vehicles, and it would work for us.

Burt was ecstatic to get solid numbers. He promised to check them against the curve and bring back the reports. But he never did, and we wondered why. It turned out that he didn't call because the news was bad: by that measure, the gross weight suggested we would not have enough fuel. For once, Burt just hoped the numbers we had given him were wrong—and they were.

They followed us toward Lake Victoria and up and across it.

Now it was time to climb. There was a stratus layer, and we had to stay on top of that. We saw thunderstorms in the distance. At fifteen thousand feet, we went on oxygen. We took off our headsets, looped the canulas around our ears, and replaced the headsets. Then we hooked up the Demand Oxygen Controller unit and activated the pressure chamber. We could see the gauges swing up to fifty psi. These were sensitive units— the pressure had to be just right to function—but all was working, and soon we got our first puffs of oxygen, watching the lights on the unit pulse with each breath. Until we were over the mountains, blinking lights would be registering our life's breath. We set the units according to the chart in our checklist book, the one we drew up testing them with Dr. White. We set them at first for a liter per minute.

But we were tired, Jeana still had the cold, and we were not absorbing the oxygen as efficiently as anticipated. We didn't know it, but from this point on, our bodies began to go into oxygen debt.

Now we had to restart the front engine and run through the familiar litany. Unfeather, prime, crank. I opened the ramps, and Dick started to prime and crank the engine. It didn't want to start. It fired, stopped, fired, and then caught.

As we climbed toward the mountains—seventeen-thousand-foot Mount

Kenya and its sisters—Doug reported that his airplane was beginning to ice up. I saw the engine temperatures going up—those engines were working hard now—and Dick looked out at the panel of dark paint we had added to the right wing—no ice there. We were at twenty thousand feet, over Lake Victoria now, and the chase could only make it to about eighteen thousand. They radioed their good-byes, dropped off, and headed back to Nairobi. We were on our own again. The first familiar face we'd seen—God, we hated to see Doug go. Time to face those mountains and clouds coming up.

.   .   .

In the trailer back in Mojave, the Africa crossing was being anticipated with considerable anxiety, and everyone wanted to be on the scene.

Mike Hance of mission control was trying to set up *Voyager*'s passage with air control in Nairobi. The man in the tower, a native named Patrick Oamuyo, had a hard time understanding everything. Mike spelled out our names—"Dick: Delta India Charlie Kilo"—but he could not get the fellow to understand that *Voyager* was an airplane that was going to fly around the world and—in a few hours—over his head, en route.

"What kind," said Patrick Oamuyo, "what kind rocket this is?"

Fergy, standing beside Mike and listening to this, shook his head. "I'll never bitch about the FAA again," he said.

The meteorologists were getting worried about weather over Africa, if they could have been more worried than they'd always been. And that was when they said it was impossible. Filling his big trucker's mug of coffee, Larry Burch shook his head on the way back to the trailer. "What I think I would do is shut off the transponder, get up high, and sneak through to the north. The way we planned sure looks awful."

It had been agreed that we would send no position reports on our way across Africa. But meanwhile Larry and the other weather people were looking at ugly storms coming out of the Great Rift Valley in their pictures, and they were disquieted. It was bright daylight in Africa, but well after dark in Mojave. The wind was beginning to whip around the antenna masts and shake the trailer.

"I think we'd better wake Len up," said Larry Burch to Conway Roberts, who was on duty in mission control. We were about an hour and a half from the lake—in the middle of our rendezvous with Doug, although no one in the trailer knew that—and Burch had already sent a message to be transmitted in the blind: "Thunderstorms over Lake Victoria. Divert to south."

When Len arrived and was briefed, he said, "I think that is an unfortunate message.

"We'll be adding miles out to the road, and we may not be improving things for them. What looks to us like it's boiling up here may have died down by the time they get to it, and what looks clear may be teeming with storms."

"I wrote the message," Larry Burch said, "so I'll take the heat for it."

"There's no heat," Len answered in a voice still thick with sleep. "If you can justify it, I'm with you.

"But to the north," he continued, looking at the red crosshatched area on the map of Africa—Somalia, Uganda, and Chad—"they've made it clear in all our briefings: it's no, hell no, triple no, and no squared. That's where you get shot down."

"Right," Conway said, "that's my point. We really don't want them going north. They should run around those things to the south."

"But that doesn't mean they have to divert south, either," said Len. "They just have to use their radar and pick their way through there.

"There is no way we can make this kind of judgment on the basis of a three-hour-old satellite picture. You know what kind of satellite pictures you need to plot a course here, with the storms boiling up like they do in this part of Africa? You need pictures every three minutes."

"Well," Conway said, "those storms are going to be picking up moisture over the lake and getting meaner."

"Baloney," Len said. "Baloney. Those storms are already loaded with moisture. The lake has nothing to do with it."

"Well, okay," Conway finally agreed. "Let's draft another message and send it."

. . .

We got Len's message, saying just to work our way through and not, repeat not, divert north. But we had already worked out our course on our own. The weather looked terrible in front of us, so, whatever the danger, we had decided to fly north—north over the red crosshatched danger zone.

There were three places we had been told never, never, never to fly. One was Somalia; the other two were Uganda and Chad. But now we were about to enter Uganda. We were going to fly right over Entebbe Airport, where the Israelis had staged their famous hostage rescue.

We knew that an airliner had been shot down up there—there were civil wars in both Uganda and Chad—only a few weeks before. But the weather was far more dangerous than any missile. Those huge storms meant sure death and anything and anyone on the ground was puny. We also knew that we would be coming over high enough so that it was almost impossible to spot us with the naked eye, and that whatever radar they had was probably pretty crude. We had never turned our radar transponder on over Africa.

So now we headed for the mountains, running both engines flat out and to hell with the fuel burn figures; the engines screamed as they tried to climb over this stratus layer.

The mountains were like some exaggerated version of the Rockies we had flown over often—and Voyager had flown over en route to Oshkosh—and steaming and boiling out of the valleys were huge mushroom clouds.

We picked our way among the clouds. We followed a canyon—it was a dead end! Nothing but clouds at the end. No way out now, except to turn around and try another way.

We were lucky that the orientation of breaks in the clouds was somewhat west, so that we were usually going the way we wanted to, even as we dodged and turned and diverted, trying to push it west but avoiding the worst, just running through the holes before they closed up, with the clouds boiling like one of those motion pictures where they speed up the action to let you see how weather works. Only this was not some photographic trick, it was real time, real life—our lives.

It was like flying around a bunch of A-bombs. Every move was a gamble, and the odds were ridiculous. There was no way we could win, we just had to choose a course and pray.

There were clouds to fifty thousand feet, where the jet streams knocked their tops off and sculpted them into strange and ominous shapes—just like anvils—flat on top, pointed where the jet streams swept around them. Those anvils looked as if they would drop on top of us at any moment.

We were crossing much too late in the day. We should have gotten here hours before. Now the heating on the jungle floor was pumping up the storms. We were really in trouble. This was the worst time we could ever be here. But there was nothing we could do except keep going.

The weather kept churning and boiling up. We would see one blue hole and try to put the airplane through it before the hole closed up, then look for another opening.

Because if we fell out here, we were history. Either the boiling thunderstorms would chew us up, or if we got in the stratus, we would begin to ice up and drop down into the storms and not have enough power to climb back. We'd just sink like a ship taking on water.

Lake Victoria was clear, but the storms surrounded it, lurking, as if just waiting for anything to come within their reach. It looked pretty clear on the far side. We decided to save some fuel and shut down the front engine and make a nice long descent across the lake on the rear engine only.

But this was a huge lake, an inland sea, really, and it wasn't long before I realized how wide it was and saw the weather closing in ahead. I began to feel guilty about having shut the front engine down. I was feeling a little light-headed, and I wondered if that was why I made a bad decision.

The clouds were moving a lot faster than we'd figured. There were clouds ahead, and we might have to restart the front.

We got three-quarters of the way across the lake. Damn, we waited too long to start the front. Now I didn't know whether we could climb fast enough to get through. It was a big mistake to shut down the front, a big mistake.

We had to restart, and the front engine was cold. I pushed the nose down. We switched the electronics to the backup battery pack, and we could only hope the Omega didn't lose its fix.

I primed and cranked.

"Come on, come on, start!"

Finally it started, stopped, ran, stopped, then ran. At twenty thousand feet, the temperature was about twenty degrees Fahrenheit outside. But we couldn't let the engine warm up. We had to push the power up right away, and we could hear it complain. The oil was thick and cold—thank God for synthetic oil, no way it would start without it.

Never have we seen thunderstorms so active and boiling as these. It was a movie of weather, run at high speed.

There was a saddleback in the clouds ahead. Could we get high enough to make it? That was our only chance, the only gap. It was closing in fast, a solid wall up to fifty thousand feet, where those giant anvils hung, ready to drop on us.

We blew it, we should have gotten across on two engines before it all went to hell.

The wingtips were scraping the clouds. We couldn't see the ends of them, we didn't want to look at them anyway, but we wanted to know they were there.

Wait, there was another opening, and we headed for it. It had closed in completely behind us. Now we pushed the engines for best power, forgetting range. We just kept going, kept hoping and praying, and remembered there was no way we could allow Voyager into one of those clouds. No way.

Right then I realized that Jeana wasn't saying anything. I watched her reflection in the radar screen while I flew, and I could see that her position was very strange. She was lying there just like a cat, on knees and elbows, hands forward, but with her face flat on the floor. I called her on the intercom, but there was no response.

"Jeana, you've got to stay awake."

She'd never slept like this.

She'd been trying to stay awake, help dodge the storms, but she just couldn't.

I reached over and touched her. She was cool to my touch. There was no blinking light on her oxygen! No light on the panel for her oxygen. She wasn't breathing!

Then, flying the airplane with my right hand, I reached over with my left to rub her back and neck. No reaction. I shook hard, rubbed her shoulders and neck, and shook again.

All of a sudden she came back to life, leaping up, almost hitting the roof. "What?"

"God, I thought you were dead," I said groggily, and I realized I wasn't feeling very good, either. "I didn't mean to wake you, I just wanted to see if you were alive."

She had a headache, and she dropped right back to sleep. The bulb was out. The goddamned oxygen indicator bulb on her unit had burned out. Now the only way to see if she was getting oxygen was to turn around and watch the pressure gauge in back to see her pulse. We really had to be careful with oxygen. She couldn't stay awake, and if you're not careful you don't ever wake up, or you wake up with a headache you have the rest of your life. I worried about this and whether I was in any shape to make sure she was getting oxygen while flying the plane and dodging thunderstorms. If she was dead, what would I do? Land, fly on with a corpse? I wondered, and I felt all alone.

We were still at twenty thousand feet—there was no way to descend—and I kept shaking Jeana every so often to wake her. It took awhile, but when she came back to life, she just exploded. "What, what, what is it?!" she said, and her eyes were darting back and forth in a way I'd never seen before.

But then I would have to turn my attention back to flying the airplane and dodging thunderstorms, and as soon as I did Jeana would fall right back down, on her hands and knees again, catlike, passed out with her face on the floor. It must have happened a half dozen times or more.

I wanted to hug her and hold her on my lap, but I couldn't. If I didn't do what I had to do—fly and dodge those storms—we were both going to die.

We had underestimated the oxygen. With fatigue and her cold she couldn't absorb enough, so I turned her valve up a little bit. Or did I? I thought. Did I already do that?

I fought to stay awake but I couldn't make my body respond. My eyelids closed; my muscles felt useless but my brain was still fighting hard to stay alert.

I tried to see the clouds Dick was telling me about. I watched helplessly as they rolled in behind us. And then I sank down again.

.   .   .

In the trailer there had been nothing to do but wait, nervously, with cups of coffee and jokes. Then a new position was relayed in.

"They're west of the lake already!" Conway Roberts said.

Conway couldn't believe it. He went over to the map and fiddled with the pushpins and then took out his flight computer and went over it.

"The message says they had a ten-knot tail wind."

"That wouldn't be out of the question," Len says. "Not at all. But jeez, they must have a rabbit's foot in their pocket to make it through."

Then Conway understood what we had done. He suspected it right away: there was a nice curve to the planned course around the south of Lake Victoria on the map, and Conway figured it out. We had just sliced that curve off and gone straight across the north side.

.   .   .

All the way from noon to dark it was a squeaker, and we were sweating it all the way. We finally started toward the plains, and it was time to wipe our brows and say our thank-yous.

The high mountains were behind us, and we began descending. At thirteen or fourteen thousand feet we shut off the front engine again and closed off its vents. No more dodging and juking: we were heading straight west, direct to the sea.

Jeana was stirring now, coming back to life. She had an awful headache, and her stomach was churning. It was still hard for her to stay awake.

We had been so high and cold and I'd been concentrating so much on flying that I didn't even notice I had let my feet get cold and wet. I couldn't feel them, and for some reason as I peeled off the wool sock and then the cotton, I was afraid that the skin and the cotton had fused together. I saw the feet were waxy and white.

I draped the socks and then each of the slippers over the heater pipe outlet in turn. I made a little tent of a blanket and fed in the hose from the heater and put my feet in it. Because of the hypoxia, it took nearly three hours of wriggling my toes and massaging my feet to get the feeling back in them.

We were coming downhill now, as the light was waning, getting away from the mountains just before the day ran out. But we still had twelve hours of Africa left and a dark, dark night ahead. An incredibly thick haze covered the plain—the Congo basin, the vast and sparsely populated jungle, the original heart of darkness. It was solid, and there wasn't any light on the ground. We couldn't see anything, even straight down, through the solid haze.

For some reason, maybe because I was still punchy from the altitude, the haze seemed filthy. I thought I could smell its stench. It was as thick as the smoke from an oil fire, and I was amazed the engine could keep running in such an atmosphere.

Only occasionally were there little breaks in the haze. I could look down and see little lakes and every now and then a shower giving the jungle a good dousing. But there were no signs of life. I kept my eye out for airports, just in case. There weren't any.

I talked to Lee Herron on the radio. "There's not a light anywhere," I said. "It's so dark, so dark."

"Well, Dick," Lee said, "there's a light at the end of the tunnel. There's a light here. You're coming home." But the stench seemed to stay in the airplane and my nostrils, until we were well out into the Atlantic.

The doc radioed that Jeana should still be on oxygen to purge her system, but I vetoed it—we might need the oxygen later. That was a mistake. She was still sick, still trying to shake off the effects of that hypoxia-induced sleep, and she could have used the oxygen.

The hypoxia and fatigue were getting to me too. I began to notice something strange. The instrument panel was bulging, it was growing out toward me, and the dials and screens were swelling. "We've never been this high before, maybe it does something to the honeycomb. Everything still seems to be working. I wonder if it will blow up? Nothing to do about it I guess." I reached over and shook Jeana's shoulder and said to her, "Look at that, look at that!" and pointed at the instrument panel.

"See how it's bulging all out? Do you see that? It may explode."

It was a foggy image, half hallucinatory, half reasoning. The instrument panel was bulging out toward me, swelling and widening. Beside it, a vertical member was bending outward. The radar screen was swelling into a big glass blister and the paper where we had been marking off the days was arcing forward, about to pop off. The tape covering the dead deck level gauge was straining.

The feed tank was bulging. My God, I thought, if the feed tank bursts it will all be over. It had never done this before, we never anticipated it, we just didn't know what this altitude would do, I guess. Crazy of us to go this high, crazy. We should have tested it.

Soon, I was sure, the faces of the instruments would crack and shatter, and then the whole panel would burst. I reached out to try to hold the panel in, to push it back into place.

I realized there was nothing I could do about it. I had trained myself not to worry about things you couldn't do anything about, and so a strange calm began to overtake my anxiety.

I reached over for Jeana, who was wide awake now.

"Jeana, look at this," I said. "You see how the panel is just bulging and swelling?"

"Well," she said, "it's—not—that—bad." She couldn't see anything wrong.

"See how it's bulging?"

"It'll be okay," Jeana said. "Don't worry about it. I'll take care of it."

Dick had been in the seat too long. He had to get some rest now. I had to talk him back into the rest area. He kept babbling about the panel and trying to push it back into place. I knew he was in trouble. At that point no one was flying the airplane. I moved forward and prepared for the changeover. I checked the instruments and verified our position, all the time talking to Dick, trying to get him to relax. I got back in the seat, flying at night for the first long stretch of the flight. I tugged my little throw-up bag along with me through the change gyrations and squirmed into the seat while Dick stumbled back.

My head was pounding, and the pain watered my eyes. I worried that this may turn into one of my incapacitating migraine headaches, days and days of pain, perhaps. My stomach was turning itself inside out. I took my little bag and began to vomit into it. Somehow I kept flying. I was in bad shape, but Dick was in worse.

Dick knew that there were two more mountains, one fourteen thousand feet, right near the coast, and before he had gone to sleep he gave me a point at which to wake him. "Be sure to get me up before Yankee Delta, the Yaounde nav point," he told me. But he neglected to mention the mountains.

I knew he needed all the sleep he could get, though, and I didn't wake him up at Yankee Delta.

Dick was just stirring, and I tugged on his leg. I gave him a drink of water and let him brush his teeth as he always liked to do when he woke up.

As Jeana curled up, I stumbled into the seat, careful that I didn't kick the accumulator valve off, and slid it back. When I put on the headset I could smell something funny and knew for the first time that Jeana had been sick.

I checked the log and pulled out the map. Glancing over at the Omega, I read the coordinates there and plotted them. And then I realized where we were: three-quarters of the way past Yaounde to the coast. The mountains! I glanced over at the radar, and they were right there, two big shadows.

The image got me going with a jolt, and I made an immediate left turn of twenty degrees to pull the airplane around Mount Cameroon. I was angry and frightened. "Why didn't you wake me?" I told Jeana. "You did not follow instructions. We almost ran into that thing."

"You needed the rest," she replied.

"But there's a mountain out there and we almost ran into it."

"Well, why didn't you tell me that earlier?"

"It's okay, you missed it."

The second mountain, Santa Isabel, was about fifteen miles away on an island, and I made sure we gave it a wide berth as we headed out over the coast, leaving the beautiful small city called Douala behind us, and into the Atlantic.

A few minutes later, at 0030 Z, I radioed for our position and gave a set of coordinates. Stu Hagedorn and Walt Massengale, in the trailer manning the radio, were puzzled and a little concerned. Somebody went scrambling to the maps to sort out the locations.

"We have you on the map, Dick," Walt radioed back, wondering if we were lost, if the fatigue was getting to me somehow, but trying to sound as if everything were under control.

"And what does that mean?" I said.

Walt was perplexed. "Say again?"

"What does that mean? It means we've made Africa, baby. We've made Africa, and we're on our way home.

"And you've got two people sitting here crying as hard as they've ever cried."

I looked over and was surprised to see Dick crying, big tears rolling down his cheeks, as if we were just coming up on Edwards for landing. "You're crying," I said, "you're really crying." I stretched my arms over his shoulders and gave him a big hug—and handed him a paper towel. The macho fighter jock who resists all emotion had vanished for a moment and the warm sensitive person who hides underneath came out in the open.

I wasn't sure why I was crying. Maybe it was just missing those mountains, but the realization we'd made it across Africa crept over me and sent a tingling down my spine.

Maybe it was the tension built up by all those storms, or the loneliness of the haze-shrouded plains, or the whole eerie experience of this continent we had crossed, or just the fact that we were still alive, but I cried.

Jeana reminded me not to get overconfident, that the race was not over until the last step, but I couldn't help feeling relief.

We had always thought Africa would be the hardest, and it was—up till then. For a moment I thought we were home free, and that flying across the dark continent was the greatest thing we had ever done in our lives . . . never mind that we still had a third of the world to go.

Red Light

Jeana was flying, and I was in the back with my parachute harness off and my pants down, about to apply one of our handy stick-on plastic bags to my rear end. It was not an elegant position. I lay on my side, head to the firewall, knees pulled up between the back of the seat and the bulkhead, left leg raised and relief tube in position. Jeana had a vanity curtain she taped up on such occasions, but I didn't have room for that. There could be no vanity for me.

It was then of all times that Jeana saw a red light go on: the oil pressure light!

A hell of a time for that, 165 miles off the African coast, making our way northwest between the coast and the offshore weather, and, while Dick scrambled frantically, I put the autopilot on attitude hold, pulled the power back, and pushed the nose down to get as much air as possible moving through the radiators to cool that oil and bring the pressure down.

Dick opened the cooling vent, slapping the sticky bag onto the ceiling, tugging up his pants, trying to slip the parachute harness back on—we might have to go over the side. That maneuver alone usually took ten minutes—it was like putting on a sports jacket while lying on the floor. The situation was ridiculous, and it would have been funny if it wasn't so dangerous. Dick scooted himself right away to the oil tank and cranked in a quart and a half, banging and scraping his elbows and knuckles in the process, then opened up the cooling ramps full to get more air flowing through the engines.

Dick yelled at me for not watching the system closely enough, and I ignored him because I knew he was venting his fear and frustration. It was the only time on the flight that happened.

It was my job to watch the oil level, and I knew I had checked it—I hadn't made a mistake. I suspected that what had happened was that Dick had decided to see if I was handling the oil correctly. He thought he added a quart of oil, but he turned the crank the wrong way, taking oil out instead of putting it in.

After ten minutes Dick scrambled forward with bloody hands, and we went through the switching gymnastics.

The oil pressure was slowly dropping, the temperature in the engine already rising, the engine maybe already on its way to burning out—and the airplane, if that happened, on its way to the South Atlantic Ocean, a couple of hundred miles off Africa.

"Mission control, this is *Voyager*, we've got a problem: Gulf six Alpha, REM two six two. Get Peter, Mike, Glenn, Bruce, and Dave Mayrose of Continental. Sorry to get you guys up in the middle of the night, but it's bright daylight here."

Dick started giving position coordinates, almost constantly, because we knew we were in deep trouble and wanted to make sure they could find us if we went down.

We were at twelve thousand feet and figured we had about three or four thousand feet to descend before we had to start the front engine—if it started. It had been cold and sluggish starting the last couple of times. And even if we got it started, it would probably mean the end of the mission.

In the trailer, they called Glenn Maben at the Camelot Motel, where most of the support crew were bivouacked, and got Dave Mayrose of Continental on the phone at his home in Mobile.

At his house in Tehachapi, Mike Melvill had been asleep for just a couple of hours. He'd been in the trailer constantly and gone home for a little sleep. Driving up the road to Tehachapi, after midnight, he'd fallen asleep. He was lucky to wake up and find himself on an embankment instead of at the bottom of some canyon.

But the call jerked him wide awake now. "Gulf six Alpha?" he mumbled.

"Engine problem," somebody said, and his stomach tightened. Engine problem in the middle of the South Atlantic! He tossed on some clothes and jumped into the car. He started it and put it in reverse—and the car spun all over the driveway. In his sleepiness he hadn't even noticed that the night had dusted the mountains lightly with snow and the pavement was slick. That woke him up for sure; he got straightened out and headed for Mojave.

Bruce Evans had no phone, and when Neal Brown knocked on his door and said, "It's a Gulf six Alpha REM two six two," the *Voyager* crew chief was just as much in the dark as everyone else. All these radio codes were a late addition to things. He was still exhausted from his flight back from Thailand. He knew it was trouble, but not what kind.

"What the hell is a Gulf six Alpha REM two six two?" he asked as he rubbed his eyes.

A lot of people in the trailer were asking the same thing. We had worked out a code system so that we could talk about problems that cropped up without alarming everyone who might be listening in who would then spread the word. Gulf six was the code designation for an engine problem, and alpha was the rear engine. REM 262 was the designation for the oil.

The whole point of the code was to protect our sponsors, at least give them a chance of getting their experts in the loop, and if they were going to take a hit on something, to let them know about it and help handle the problem. We knew that half the world was listening on the radio all the time, and those sponsors had all taken a big chance on us, gone out on a limb. So we owed them that much.

I thought that with all the hassles of crossing Africa, with the rendezvous with Doug and the weather and Jeana flying sick and with a headache, we might not have remembered to check the oil level in a day and a half. Every day, Jeana was supposed to check the level with an air tube and add any more oil that was required. Just like in a car, only we were running twenty-four hours a day. So somewhere along the way, I felt sure she'd missed a check. It scared me that we were forgetting things like that. That kind of mistake can put you in the water real fast.

We waited for the oil I'd added to get into the system, but the temperature stayed up. We talked on the radio to Dave Mayrose of Continental, and he was sharp: he figured what had happened and warned that it would take awhile to stabilize. When oil gets down low, air gets in, and it foams up. A vortex is formed, a sort of miniature tornado in the oil, and the oil gets aerated like a milk shake. Aerated oil lacks the necessary viscosity to function correctly. The new oil we added was mixing with the aerated oil, and now the whole mixture had to work out its bubbles.

Even knowing that, it seemed to take forever for the oil to get in there and start coating and cooling. "Maybe you guys want to go get a cup of coffee or something while this is getting ready to kick in," I told mission control. But no one left. They stayed clustered around the radio, groggy and nervous, in the dark, thinking about what was going on over the bright ocean half a world away. "I'll never leave the trailer again," Mike Melvill vowed.

Then the pressure was up, the temperature was going down. It had taken a full half hour.

We figured that in the initial confusion we may have dumped some oil overboard—we'd have given a million dollars right then for a chase pilot to tell us if we were losing oil. All we could do was check the reserve tank: we found that we had eight of the original seventeen quarts of oil. We were okay there, as long as we didn't make any more dumb mistakes.

The engine was okay, too; we hadn't burned anything out. But it was the closest—maybe the second closest—that we came to ending up in the water.

I had been getting ready to go to sleep when the light went on. I was afraid that now I wouldn't be able to, with all the adrenaline this little episode had rousted up, and I checked with the doc, asking him to okay a sleeping pill if I needed it. But Jeana vetoed that and as soon as I got in the back I dropped right off. In fact, we were proud that with all the drugs we had on board in case of emergencies, we never took anything stronger than a daily aspirin to keep our blood from getting too thick and (for me) a couple of caffeine candies—each containing the equivalent of a cup of coffee.

And I had forgotten all about that matter involving the plastic bag, still stuck to the ceiling in back.

Stormy Weather

So far the moon had been our savior. Without the good moonlight and the starlight scope, when it wasn't out, there was no way we could have made it. We always knew the moon would be important, but we didn't even have a glimmering of just how important.

For most of the flight we had enjoyed nearly full moon. But the moon comes up about an hour and a few minutes later each day. Now we had two or three hours of solid darkness before we got the moon, and it was then, wouldn't you know it, that we hit the most dangerous storm of the trip—at the worst possible time.

Burt had been on the radio, telling us he estimated that we would arrive on Tuesday with 230 pounds of fuel to spare. And as we were beginning to guess now, as the airplane slowed down and the hours stretched out, anytime anybody mentioned coming home it meant that whatever or whoever was running this little joyride was going to pop up some new surprise for us.

We had always worried about being near thunderstorms in this airplane. We had worried about being in the dark in this airplane. And we worried the most about being in a thunderstorm at night in this airplane.

It was only a few minutes after sunset, but already the sky was pitch black. Ahead, we picked out four or five cells of weather on the radar, bunched so there didn't seem to be anywhere to go. We were just north of the coast of Brazil, heading west/southwest, and we figured on a reasonably good ride through this part of the world, as long as we stayed away from the Itch—the Intertropical Convergence Zone. Now it was to our north. This was the dreaded wall of weather we had been dodging halfway around the world. But the Itch can also bulge and swell, and pieces break off into convective cells, as the weather people call them, and that was what had happened.

Suddenly we were in the midst of these cells, with all kinds of weather around us. "Hey, get me some help," I radioed. "I can't see anything. Get me outta here."

Back in the trailer, Rich Wagoner in weather was on duty and in a calm Texas accent guided us for a critical half hour, soothing us, telling us to vector left, away from the ITCZ. He was being so calming that we didn't even suspect he had no idea what was happening out here. He was waiting for a satellite picture to tell him. Meanwhile, he was going on instinct and experience, just getting us away from the ITCZ.

"Can we turn right?" I asked, looking at the shapes on the radar screen.

"Negative, negative," was Rich's reply. "You should stay on course, just thread your way through. If you have to divert, divert left. Repeat, left."

Jeana called off the distances to the great bumpers we were painting on the radar, now, right and left and dead ahead. They were getting thick, the screen was half-full of them, and now we were boxed in. One wingtip went through the clouds, and we got tossed, like a boat in a big wave. If that was just the edge, what the hell was the middle like?

And then we found out. All of a sudden the storm had us in its grip. There was nothing to do, the weather was flying the airplane. One wingtip went up, the other went down.

We rolled slowly toward inverted. We were just along for the ride. I tried to control the airplane, and for a moment the storm was simply more powerful.

I felt a strange calm come over me when I realized there was nothing I could do, that I no longer had control. Don't worry about what you can't control. I turned to Jeana, shrugging my shoulders, and said, "Well, babe, this is it. I think we bought the farm this time. Look at that attitude indicator. We ain't gonna make it."

But that was only for an instant, because as suddenly as it gobbled us up, the storm spat us out, and we could handle the airplane again. Now I instinctively went through the drill for recovery from overbank: push over to zero G, prepare to dive to regain control. But it was never planned for anything like this. This was ninety degrees, and we'd never banked more than twenty before; we never expected the airplane would hold up in ninety degrees. We figured the fuel whiplashing through the wing would break a bulkhead somewhere.

We didn't even want to think, though, of how those wings were flailing. We had to be very careful. You don't just roll out of this steep a bank in the *Voyager*, you have to turn it into a dive. If we put in aileron alone, the airplane would roll against it and bank the opposite way. The thing to do was unload the wings—go to zero G.

I pushed the stick forward, so the controls could work their best, not have to fight to overcome adverse yaw and dihedral effect, the eccentricities of this airplane, and now we were in the beginning of a dive. Things were almost floating in the cockpit when I began to apply full right rudder. I waited a moment for it to take effect, then slowly and gingerly fed in right aileron, carefully working it, modulating so we wouldn't go too far—if we rolled the other way, there was virtually no hope of recovery.

We had to stay right on the money. Don't load it up, I remembered, don't go negative G, either, keep it right on the mark, and now as the airplane headed down, we had to get the wings level. Then we could pull out.

We began leveling out—eighty degrees of bank, now seventy, sixty, fifty, forty—and the nose was falling very low, we were in the steepest dive we'd ever made, but there was no choice, it was the only way out of this—ten, fifteen, twenty degrees of dive.

Don't get impatient, I thought, and at fifteen degrees I eased back on the stick just a bit and began to pull out. At ten degrees we were up to half a G. I eased it back more, toward normal gravity and normal life again. We couldn't see the wings in the dark, but we knew they were flexing higher than ever before, and gradually as the nose came back up we pushed up the power to regain altitude.

"I almost lost it," I told Rich back in mission control. "I thought it was all over but the shouting.

"Just did a ninety-degree bank, can you believe that, ninety degrees in the *Voyager*?"

Jeana, braced against the bulkhead and console, looked at the radar screen. I saw that it was still full of thunderstorms, red-and-magenta monsters, laden with water, sure disaster if another one caught us. They were lined up, I thought, like two fleets of battleships squaring off for combat. And we were heading down the middle, right into the line of fire, and I called off the distances and directions ahead.

Rich was helping us. We just wanted somewhere to go. We turned and threaded through the first of the lines of weather we could see on the radar, and we were in smooth air at twelve thousand feet. And we felt better, felt some confidence that somebody back there knew something about something.

Rich was still calm, and through his Texas accent we could hear not a hint of panic. This saved me, that and Jeana reassuring me, "Take it easy, you're okay," but I knew I was right on the edge of panic, and if I had heard any uncertainty in Rich's voice, I was afraid I'd lose it completely. This had been the worst weather yet. I told Rich, "I'd rather turn around and fly back over Africa than go through that storm again."

I noticed a bright light—like a meteor—flashing by, an odd and miscellaneous intrusion.

"Wow," I radioed, "we just had something really bright enter the atmosphere up here."

"Is that a UFO report?" said Rich.

"Affirmative."

Jeana watched the radar carefully and kept calling out the distances to the storms for the guys in the trailer, regularly and precisely. To Rich Wagoner on the ground, her calm was astonishing. Her voice sounded to him like a piece of digital equipment.

Fortunately, the weather guys were just switching from the European weather satellite to the U.S.GOES satellite, and that meant they would have fresh pictures every half hour instead of two or three hours.

Now Rich had a picture, fresh off the satellite, and he could tell right away what had happened. A big bulge had developed in the Itch, and it swelled up and broke off and drifted right across our course. He could tell, too, that he had made the right call and directed us out of it.

And I realized, strangely calm, that I had never felt this unsafe before, not in combat or in bad weather, never before. Later we found out that the weather team had sent us a message, diverting us away from the storms that we ran into, but it had not reached us in time.

. . .

We had a few calm hours now. Dick handed over the radio. I had a chance to talk to my father and sister, just a few words, "fine" and "tired" and "we want to be home." I'd been worried about my father and the strain on him, and I was glad that he sounded okay. I don't know where Mother was, but my father told me everyone was fine.

Soon there was something else to worry about: we began to get vibration in the engine. On the radio, Bruce reminded us that the rear engine had been running for nearly 140 hours now, so it came as no surprise. We had also been running it very lean—on what we called "Dick's lean," a mixture so fuel-thin that it made the engine run a little rough. Also, we were beginning to get some lead buildup on the plugs. At this mixture and low power, there was more of the tetraethyl lead—used in aviation fuel as it once was in automobile gasoline to stop knocking—than the combustion required. The excess built up on the plugs and could cause fouling. These were special thin-wire, iridium-tipped Champion plugs, rated for a thousand hours—most plugs have to be maintained every fifty hours. At low power there was not enough heat to burn the lead off the electrodes, and it built up and fouled the engine.

We worried, too, what the vibration might do to the joints and connections in our cooling system. Some of the engine RPMs set off echoing, harmonic vibrations in the airframe and other systems. We had to avoid those. The cooling system was all brand new; we had already been jolted, coming off of Sri Lanka, by those few spoonfuls of leaking coolant, and we didn't want to run any risk of shaking something loose.

Burt came on and asked, "What was the RPM of the vibration?"

"About two thousand to twenty-one fifty."

"Let's try to get it down to about nineteen hundred for a while." We were slowing down now that we were lighter, staying on our maximum efficiency point, hanging right there in the L/D Bucket, and as we did, time seemed to stretch out, too. We were feeling the fatigue more, the cumulative effects of nerves and mind being drawn taut.

The doc could sense it. He advised us to go on oxygen to help with the fatigue.

Dick asked for the time of sunrise off the Brazilian coast. It was 0730 Zulu. Five more hours.

The engine kept running rough as we were coasting in to Brazil, and our progress seemed incredibly slow. Some of the maps of the area had been trimmed off in anticipation of our original route and I had to draw the latitude/longitude grids on them so we could check our position.

Dick had brought along a little credit-card-sized AM-FM radio, and for the first time in the flight he could pick up something on it: South American music. He left it on for a little while, wishing we'd had room for the Willie Nelson tapes he once planned to bring.

We felt the storm had given us enough adrenaline for the rest of our lives, but now the fatigue had caught up. While I tried to sleep, Dick talked to keep himself awake, making it impossible for me to get any rest.

·

The Omega kept flashing a request to be "relaned," which was the navigational equivalent of shifting from the right to the left lane of the freeway.

"I'm just going to flip a coin." And I made a choice. We were out of position to use the global positioning system, our satellite reference link—we would have to wait until the satellites came back over—so the Omega was all we had. There was no other system to check it by. All I could do was guess.

"I don't know—that means we've got to get a fix someplace. I may sneak over to get close enough for a fix off one of the VORs in Brazil."

Jeana woke up and heard my voice and was concerned. "Everything is working," I told her. "Go on and get some sleep."

The autopilot had been acting up again. Another little scare. The ADI—this was the replacement one—was precessing, rolling off, every now and then.

"Hell, I don't want to mess with it. I want to eke out every last bit of performance even if it's just an hour or so. We're close enough to home right now that if it quit, we'd probably hand-fly it—which would be one of the most incredible feats that two people would ever have to perform. I'm looking forward to having to hand-fly this airplane like I'd look at the electric chair or something. I've got my fingers crossed saying, 'Oh, God, please don't do that to me.' Hang in there, autopilot, hang in there, baby. . . . Oh, no! It wants to be relaned again. I don't know what to tell you, Omega. Well, here goes, wild choice. . . . Another little bite out of the shit sandwich. . . . Two more full nights left. I don't even want to think about it. At times I feel real good, other times real fatigued.

"Boy, we made a lot of mistakes planning this thing. Low altitude is crazy, there's just too much weather. Oh, Omega! Come on. Well, if it quits, it quits. Nothing to do about it. It's been a long flight."

I just kept talking, trying to stay awake. There was always plenty to do. Just before sunrise the engine started fouling again. The oil temperature ran up, and we had to pull back again, to 1,800 RPMs.

Now we were running really lean. We knew there would be head winds for the last part of the flight—could things move even slower? we wondered—and Burt was beginning to be worried again about our fuel. When the sun came up we could see the big clouds of the ITCZ off to our right.

By midday we were flying in bright sunlight and through good weather.

I shouldn't have been flying then. It was clear sailing, and I hadn't slept in so long I couldn't remember, and Jeana had been trying to get me to go back.

That's when I hit the wall.

One minute I was fine, and the next minute I couldn't remember how to do anything. I was in a haze, and I could simply not make my mind work.

I held my hands out in front of me. "How do I make them do something," I wondered, "turn a switch, punch in a number, adjust a knob?"

I sat there, not knowing how to do anything, and I didn't care. None of it mattered anymore.

"What is that beeping? What is it you want, autopilot?" I said to the instrument panel. "Stop that damn beeping. Who cares about your beeping?"

Now the fog was thickening. It was slow and hard to move through. It was turning into a liquid, like molasses, sweet and thick, and I was getting comfortable now. I was floating and drifting, peaceful and warm and blissful.

I looked at some of the other things on the panel, and I realized I didn't understand any of that either. All the knowledge that was automatic was simply not there anymore. I could see the stick moving—that meant at least the autopilot was still working.

And then from far back in my mind, there was a faint glimmer of something, a thought that kept slipping away again and again until I saw Jeana's reflection in the radar screen and got it: It doesn't have to be this way, I don't have to do this. Jeana is here.

"Jeana, I need help!"

I heard the urgency in his voice and felt him tug on my leg. Not the gentle "come spell me" tug, but the "get the hell up here now" tug.

"I'm right here. What's the problem?"

"I don't know how to do anything and I don't care. I just don't care."

"You're okay," I told him. "Come on back now, it'll be okay. Trade places with me."

"Let me tell you, I've been sitting here, and I can't remember how to do anything. I can't make the calculator work or the autopilot or anything, and I just don't care. I've really hit the wall."

"You're okay, Dick, I'll help you. You need sleep, then you'll be okay. Come on back."

We talked this way for an hour. I moved forward, and while Dick talked I looked over his shoulder checking our position, the performance charts, the fuel logs, and prepared the cabin for a changeover. He just kept talking.

Finally Dick lurched forward and to the left, half out of the seat. He took off the headset. The engine noise was tremendous. He threw himself against the left wall and stretched back. His head was back in the hole. He put the plugs in his ears, hung his glasses on the radio stack, pushed his head up against the oxygen cylinder, and, as soon as he lay down, he was asleep.

I climbed over Dick's legs and rolled into the seat. I put on the headset, slipped the seat forward, and gathered the scattered charts. I double-checked position and fuel, adjusted the autopilot, then reached back to pull the blanket quietly over Dick.

I tucked my legs up under me, put my hands on the consoles, and pulled myself up inside the canopy so I could look around. I was surprised to find that it was bright daylight—back in the hole daytime and nighttime were the same. I could see some clouds ahead, towering cumulus. They were big battleships of clouds, and they were on the radar screen, too, an abstract painting of yellow and red and magenta. Perched on my toes, legs aching, I began to dodge them.

. . .

Three hours later, Dick was back up. He'd had very good sleep. But now he was starting to feel grubby, and his beard was getting itchy. Little hairs were cutting into his lips. "God," he said, "I'd love a shave." I realized he hadn't changed his clothes at all, while I had been scrupulous about cleaning up every day. Maybe it's not worth it, I thought, to clean up. It just makes my nose notice him more.

Until the Fat Lady Sings

Six days, eighteen hours, 4,800 miles to go.

The last legs of the flight seemed to take forever. From Brazil to Trinidad seemed like three-quarters of the way around the world, and then as we came across the Caribbean and Central America and turned back toward California, we would encounter head winds for the first time and slow down even more. We had had terrific tail winds most of the way, and we'd gotten spoiled.

The Caribbean water was a crisp, lovely aqua in places where it shallowed, and it reminded us of our stops in the Caribbean when—once upon a time—we landed in Grand Turk after my flight from Alaska and when we stopped for those idyllic few days in St. Martin on the way back from Angel Falls.

We had always hoped to get back to the United States as soon as we could, fly home over Texas and the West. But now, in the winter, with big storms moving west to east, it was out of the question. Len worked out two alternative crossings of Central America—one over Costa Rica, one over Panama. Jack Norris and his number crunchers were comparing the efficiency of the two routes. Then we would turn up the coast and head for home.

But every time we even thought of that word, "home," and every time we started to relax the least little bit, something happened.

We didn't realize the attention we were getting; we didn't dare to think about what was going on in Mojave and the rest of the world—about anything outside the airplane and the trailer.

We did know that the flight as seen from back in Hangar 77 was as consuming and exhausting as in the airplane. Everyone was tired, everyone's nerves were strung tight.

We had always worried that the ground crew would get less rest than we would. The crew had a bet going: Who would get less sleep, Peter or Dick? For most of the flight, Peter was winning. Lee Herron, Larry Caskey (a composer who wrote a song about Voyager), and Mayo Partee, on loan from ABC, helped out with the constantly ringing phones in the press office, fielding inquiries from all over the world.

Each morning of the flight there was a press conference, and Burt was called on more and more to brief the press. At first his talk was all technical, but soon he was mixing the technical talk with off-color jokes, and by the end his emotions were evident—he had become more and more conscious of the human factors involved, the lives on the line.

A camaraderie developed among the press in the hangar: most of the reporters seemed happy to have an upbeat story to cover for once, and they soon felt almost like part of the family. More and more computers and typewriters and cameras appeared in the hangar, and the telephone man was kept busy installing new phones. There were constant interviews with family and volunteers—with everyone in the hangar, it seemed, except perhaps Magnamite the cat.

CNN kept its trailer outside throughout the flight, and the networks kept sending crews around. Greg Lamotte, the CNN correspondent, had a hard time tearing himself away from the place. He came back a few weekends later, bringing his family to see the airplane.

The momentum was building, interest was growing. The aura that Jeana had always felt hung about the project seemed to radiate out with every report and news story, and people became drawn to the adventure. In Las Vegas, the bookies even had a line going on whether we would make it—just like the World Series or Super Bowl. "Should have had that in the command post," Bruce said, "to keep guys on their toes."

Peter set up radio interviews for us, but things almost always seemed to crop up for us to do just when they were scheduled.

Here we were, at the beginning of our eighth day in the air, approaching Costa Rica and being treated to one of the most gorgeous sunsets of the whole flight. There was a whole set of lush pinks fading into this intense blue studded with stars, and, for once, incredibly smooth air, like molasses, with only lower level clouds around.

Dick on the radio was waxing poetic on this subject when the engine coughed again. We couldn't run down at 1,800 RPMs, our projected best efficiency level, without the engine getting rocky and starting to shake the hell out of the airplane, so we kept it at about 2,200. Still, it gulped and tried twice to quit on us.

The decision was made about Costa Rica—it was a little longer, but Len anticipated some bad weather off the coast of Panama. Dick saw that the six-hour message from the trailer, giving us our course across Costa Rica, had us coming within about five miles of the border of Costa Rica with Nicaragua. We didn't like that idea at all. Not now when the Omega might only have been accurate to forty miles or so. "Let's give those guys a wide berth," Dick said. We would cut the track south of what they gave us to allow ourselves plenty of leeway, put some distance between us and whatever sort of missiles or guns that might reach down across that line.

Dick went back to get some sleep, and I took the seat as we came up on the coast. I felt bad for him: he was very fatigued, and it seemed the weather never gave him more than a couple of hours' sleep at a time.

I kept thinking about the fat lady and knew that the race was not over until the very last step, and I tried to listen even harder to the airplane, trying to pick up any little sign. I watched the temperatures and the CG. I knew that there were still a thousand ways we could lose this thing.

And sure enough, before long we ran into the typical weather you find a hundred miles or so offshore: long lines of thunderstorms. Dick wanted to fly, and I went back to make my daily checks. The oil was fine, and there was no further coolant pump seal leak. I made sure the air ramps were set right, updated the logs, and cleaned up.

As we ran through clouds about eighty miles from the coast, Dick flipped the radar to the mapping mode to see if we couldn't dig up some landmarks and cross-check the Omega against a map. We couldn't pick up any VOR station, and Dick now wished we had an automatic direction finder. We started painting the coastline. The radar was not as good for landscape as for weather, but years in the military with cruder radar had taught Dick how to interpret the images. As we got close to the shoreline the radar started painting the coast, and we could pick out some details and the curve and cut of the coast and the cumulus buildup over the land.

The controllers were helpful and very friendly—a welcome change. They knew we were coming. Mike Hance had been on the phone to them, and they greeted us very congenially and somewhat formally, extending the best wishes of the people of Costa Rica. Some of the domestic airliners coming into the airport at San José also said hello. We turned on our radar transponder for the first time; that made us feel like we were back near civilization. Now there was even a VOR, one that worked, and we flew right over it and cross-checked the Omega. Sure enough, despite all that relaning and worrying out in the Caribbean, it was in good shape.

Costa Rica is divided by two ranges of high mountains. To be safe, we stuck to the big valley of the San José River, right up the middle of the country. "We're coming right up the warsh," I told the trailer in the tones of an old cowboy actor, and as we came up the valley we could see Lake Nicaragua, over the border to the north, and the lights of the city of San José off to our left. It was a beautiful, rich, and peaceful-looking landscape, and along with the warmth of the people on the radio it lifted our spirits.

Back in the trailer Walt Massengale decided to get even with me for scaring him out of his wits coming over the African coast. I had really shaken him up, shaken them all up, asking, "What's my position, what's my position?" Now, as we came out over the Pacific again, Walt asked, "Have you reset your altimeter? Time to adjust it twenty-two feet"—the difference in height between the Atlantic and Pacific oceans.

It seemed they were routing us pretty far out to sea, but everyone was concerned that we end up with a nominal distance of over twenty-five thousand miles. In fact, of course, we had flown much farther, but only the distance between sighted points officially counted.

We wanted to stay a good fifty or sixty miles west of the coast as we came north up past Nicaragua. The closer we got to home, the more conservative we became. Dick must have checked the position of the lake a hundred times.

I kept reminding him that we had to avoid "get-homeitis"; we tried to be prepared for anything. He asked the command post for information on surface conditions and kept making sure alternate airports were lined up. Maybe we were even getting a little paranoid. "It still seems our heading is too far west. What if the Omega is off?" Dick wondered, even though we'd just checked and I showed him the map, and he inched back toward land a little to pick up the curve of the coast on the radar and check it. It was fine, of course.

In the trailer they could hear Dick showing fatigue. He stumbled over some words. For some reason, for instance, he couldn't remember the word "peninsula." He was getting irritated with the turbulence. "We've got good weather," he said. "What the hell is causing all this turbulence?"

We were down to around eighty knots, and the engine was starting to show the effects of constant lean running. Then we began to get the head winds, slowing down to about sixty-seven knots ground speed. It was too early for that. Len had led us to expect we wouldn't pick them up until we were at least halfway up the coast. We watched the wind slowly track right around from the tail to the nose. It was fairly weak at first, five knots, and then it grew to ten and fifteen. Dick's spirits sank. Those extra knots in our face were the same thing as extra miles; it was as if someone had reached down and stretched out the map.

The Pacific felt familiar, and I had the impression we were getting close to home—until I looked at the tape on the panel and saw that there were two more nights and a day still to be marked off.

"Gee, we're slowing down? We may be tight on fuel—"

"This would be really tough," Dick said, "if we had to sweat fuel. You know how I hate to sweat fuel." Hah, hah. Little did we know.

The guy in charge of this gauntlet we were running was not going to let us home free. He was going to make us sweat every damn mile.

"Well," I kept reminding Dick, "remember it's not over till the fat lady sings."

"Every time we think about our arrival time or what we're going to do on the ground," Dick told mission control, "something bad happens. Well, you can think and talk about it back there, but do not talk to us about it anymore.

"We're getting kind of superstitious."

I got on the radio to home and heard from Terri that Gem was fine, that Terri had gone riding with some of the guys from weather, that Gem missed me. I wanted to know everything was fine at home, and that my support team was holding together, but I didn't want to talk about coming home, not yet.

Right now, I just wanted to get to the United States.

We had a good talk with Burt, and we told him the second attitude indicator, the ADI we had switched over to replace the original one just before coming up on the Philippines, was acting up occasionally.

"But, Burt," Dick said, "if it goes out, we're going to hand-fly this baby home, whatever it takes."

Hearing that moved Burt deeply. As the flight had gone on, he had become more and more emotional. On the day of takeoff he had worn his cool engineer's demeanor. "You tend not to think about how you feel," he had told reporters who asked him about his emotions on seeing the plane take off, "you tend to concentrate on the set of data in front of you."

But now, after all we had gone through, hearing this really got to him. He seemed to realize that we had come through, for him as well as for us, and it touched him.

His throat was so tight he could barely get an answer out.

"You can do it," he finally managed to say, "you've got the Velvet Arm."

. . .

And then we were thrown another curve ball. We were into our last day, Julian day 357, zero forty-seven; I had gotten back in the seat. We still had more than twelve hundred miles to fly. It was the middle of the night, and we were still bucking the strong head winds—now thirty knots—almost due south of Cabo San Lucas, the tip of the Baja Peninsula. We could no longer be confident that we would have enough fuel. We were running a lot higher than we should have been because of the head wind, although our ground speed, of course, was slowing.

The nose was lower, and it was not our most efficient speed. We had to be more and more careful now as the airplane lightened to stay in the L/D Bucket.

The command post had told us that we could make it with twenty-eight gallons in the feed tank. Could we find twenty-eight gallons? If so, then we could finally put one of the big unknowns of the flight behind us. So we started to glean all the remaining fuel out of the tanks. We began on the left side and got two-tenths of a gallon out of the forward fuselage tank. There was a gallon in the forward boom tank—good news. Jeana logged it and zeroed the counter again. Now the left main—nothing there, we'd long since emptied it. A little bit in the aft boom.

Now it was time to open the solenoid on the left tip tank to get all of that fuel—but the tank was nearly empty! Ever since we took off, we thought the cap might be leaking, but over Africa Doug Shane said he saw no leak. In fact, we'd been oozing fuel out of that tank all the way around the world, and now 123 of its 170 pounds were gone. And without that fuel, we might not have enough to make it. We were quiet, focusing our attention on the fuel log.

Then we began to glean from the tanks on the right side. Jeana zeroed the counter and set the valves, and I turned the electrical transfer pump on, and right away I could hear it overspeed. No fuel was moving. I turned it off, reached over and tapped it with a screwdriver, and tried again. The same thing: it was running fast and not pumping. We had been concerned about these pumps, they were supposed to run for five hundred hours. But now the right pump had failed. I figured right away that the shaft had probably sheared.

The pumps were located up in a cavity in the left front of the cockpit where we could see and hear them.

We talked with Burt about changing the pumps out. We were concerned that fuel smells would make us sick if we tried it, and that the engine might quit in the middle of the operation.

Burt's advice was to change the pump, but to be sure to turn the front engine on before we did anything. I didn't want to change it.

I had built that fuel system, and I was proud of it. I had thought of just this sort of eventuality: the system had been designed so that the engine pump could draw directly from the feed tank.

"I have a backup system," I said, "and it's working. Why change procedures now?" I knew this system by heart, while the guys in the trailer had to pull out the diagrams and spread them in front of the radios and try to figure out the best way to handle things.

Burt, Bruce, and Mike kept pressuring me to change the pump. I could tell they were getting pretty exasperated with me, but I stuck to my decision and they finally gave up. "I'm going to shoot him forty-nine hours after he lands," Mike threatened, recalling our old joke about having to survive the landing by forty-eight hours.

We ran the engine on its own mechanical pump for several hours, direct from the right side tanks. We ran two tanks dry, and each time when I began to see bubbles come through the clear fuel line I switched quickly back to the feed tank. The engine hesitated and gasped, but it kept running. I switched to another tank, and the engine quit—the tank was empty. I switched tanks again as quickly as I could, and in a few seconds the engine started again. Whew.

Now we were drawing from the right canard tank, and I was talking to Pete Mueller about whether or not we could find some better winds at lower altitude. I wasn't looking closely at the lines and Jeana was busy in back. I thought the canard had a lot of fuel in it, and I didn't see the bubbles before air got all the way back to the engine. The engine coughed, and I switched to the feed tank, but it was too late. There was so much air in the line now that the poor little pump could not reprime. I pushed the nose down, hoping the engine would start right up, but now the fuel was lower than the pump, and without the power of the engine it could not draw.

The only sound was the wind and an eerie dull roaring in our ears where the engines had always been. Now we were at eight thousand feet with no engine.

I saw that Dick was not moving. He did not seem to be concentrating and I heard him say something like "Now we've lost it." I began to read the checklist but there was no response.

And I moved up and put my hands on Dick's shoulders and said, so quietly and insistently that it seemed to Dick like a voice in the back of his own head, "Be patient. This is going to take awhile. It's just another test flight, just another flight. It will seem longer than it actually is. The time is going to go by very slowly. We have plenty of altitude. So just take a deep breath and be patient."

We began to go down the checklist together.

"Fuel selectors yellow up."

"Check."

"Mags on."

"Check."

"Mixture to full rich."

"Yes."

"Throttle cranked."

"Yes."

"Alternator off."

"Yes."

"Recheck feed tank selected."

"Right."

"Recheck fuel level in feed tank."

"Okay."

It seemed so slow, like waiting for a train to get off your toe. The moon, Dick noticed, had just come up over the horizon over his right shoulder. "Take a deep breath."

The plane headed down. The rear prop was still windmilling, causing a lot of drag. The airplane had always been right-wing heavy, and now with the left side nearly empty of fuel we were being pulled off course to the right. The moon was ahead of us now; we had turned almost 120 degrees off course. We were going down in a spiral, going down—but forget that, the thing was to get the engine running—we better get that alternator off power, everything down, save that battery for the front engine restart if we need it—

The time went on. "Seventy-five hundred feet," Dick told mission control.

All of a sudden we got a little tweak; it looked as if it was going to start. "Here it comes," Dick yelled, "here it comes."

But then it was gone. We waited. "Take a deep breath."

"Seven thousand feet."

"Start, baby, start." For the first time in the flight, I was physically starting to sweat.

"Six thousand feet."

"Come on, Jeana, make it start."

"Five thousand feet."

Nothing. It must have been some sort of vapor lock. Bubbles in the tank? Who knew?

"Negative fuel flow," I radioed Mike Melvill back in Mojave.

"Negative firing."

"Dick," Mike said, trying to sound as calm as he could. "Why don't you start the front engine?"

Yeah, yeah, I knew that time was coming up. We were running out of altitude. We might be able to get the back going if we pulled it up, got the airplane a little nose up so the fuel could run back. But if we did that, I thought, we might also stall out the windmilling—and then we'd never get that back engine started again. The windmilling was our only starter, and if we lost it, we would lose the mission. We could well go into the water, too. No, we couldn't do that.

If we started the front, we might still lose it. If we could get it started. But now we had to try. It was either that or get wet. I had always prayed, If we fail, let it be on the first day, not the last. To lose the whole mission so close to home . . .

We continued down the list, and Jeana read and marked each step as I carried it out.

"Open cowl doors.

"Autopilot off.

"Avionics down.

"Alternator off.

"Fuel selector to green.

"Boost pump, front on.

"Avionics to auxiliary battery power.

"Prop control set high RPM.

"Prime and start."

The process was made harder by the fact that the unfeathering accumulator wasn't helping. There was no way that Jeana could scrunch up into the seat without it slipping forward and knocking off the switch for the unfeathering accumulator, the device that built up energy to rotate the prop out of feather. We had to start with the prop in flat feather. Then, as the engine built up oil pressure, the prop would unfeather.

"Pump on.

"Mags on."

We switched the avionics to backup battery pack—otherwise that starter surge would throw them for a real loop, and we would lose the Omega fix. I shut off the autopilot. Elbow flying time, elbow on stick, hands on starter and panel.

I was sweating, feeling damp, smelling myself now for the first time.

"Take it easy, Dick," Jeana said. I opened the front cowl ramps and Jeana began to call out the altitudes as I began to nose the airplane over: ninety, ninety-five, one hundred knots.

"Come on, baby." The front began popping. Pop . . . pop . . . pop. And it quit. "Come on, goddammit!" Then it came to life.

"Sorry, engine," I said. "No warm-up tonight. Hate to do it to you, but you gotta go to full duty right away."

And nothing from the back.

"Take a deep breath."

"Four thousand feet."

"Thirty-five hundred feet."

The front caught!

I slowly pushed the power forward, the oil pressure came up, and as it did the prop unfeathered, and we started to level out.

"The rear is running," Jeana said. She could feel its vibration through her feet, braced against the rear firewall. The fuel had flowed back down to it. And that sound, so familiar, returned, the sweetest sound we'd ever heard. Now we could make it back home.

And now I realized, "Hell, if I'd just leveled it off, the rear would have restarted right away.

"The back engine could have sucked fuel out of the feed tank and fired. The nose was so far down, that little pump couldn't suck the fuel uphill to the rear engine."

Afterward, Mike Melvill, sitting at the radio, put his head on the desk. He was exhausted and in tears.

"That," he said, "damn near tore the heart out of my body. Look and you'll see teethmarks on my heart."

We couldn't bring ourselves to shut the front engine down again. We left both engines running and leaned it way down. Now that we no longer had to worry about leaving ourselves room for restart in case an engine quit, we could stay down lower, and we were able to find a reduced head wind. Even with both engines running now, that might make the difference in getting home.

But why hadn't they let us fly down there before? Dick was irritated. "Why didn't we come down here before?" They said they knew the winds were better down lower: they just wanted us to have security if we had to start the front engine. We were a lot more likely to go into the drink from not having the fuel than from losing an engine.

We'd figured out we could make it if we kept to a target of 3.9 gallons per hour, but that was figuring on one engine. It was all worked out. We needed just twenty-eight gallons to make it home, twenty-eight gallons in the feed tank. Now, on two engines we leaned all we could to see if we could still hit that number.

From the Omega we had figured out exactly to the tenth of a gallon how much fuel it would take us to get home. But then Burt had told us to push it up and take care of the engine, that we had plenty of fuel. We could have leaned more then.

We were still eighteen gallons short.

If we were going to make it home, we would have to replumb the pumps now. "You know," Dick said offhandedly, "Burt was right." I got the little bag of tools out and assembled what we would need—pliers, wire cutters, some paper towels, Alcide, and some safety wire. The pumps were set in a kind of pit by Dick's knee. I had to clear out a lot of maps and charts, pens, pencils, and Dick's glasses while Dick moved the steel cable for the front landing gear out of the way. He did that very carefully, not wanting to bump it and possibly create a spark. It was a tense moment; there were a lot of bare wires around the fuel transfer area, and after eight and a half days we couldn't be sure there wasn't some broken or frayed wire that could set off the fuel fumes.

It was easier than we thought it would be. Dick realized that he only had to change one piece of tube instead of four, just move the input line from the right to the left. I had only one free hand—the other was always beneath my body—so Dick did the switch. I took a flashlight and taped it above the pit where the pumps were so Dick could see to untwist a wire, pull the plastic tube loose, and pinch it between his fingers. Then he removed the other tube, switched the two, and twisted safety wire around them for clamps.

He didn't even clip the ends of the safety wire—another chance for a spark—but simply wrapped them in close around the tubing. Meanwhile, hanging on his shoulders, I kept casting glances over at the altitude, the autopilot, the airspeed, and the pressures and temperatures to make sure all the other systems were holding on.

Then I policed the area—paper towels to absorb the little fuel we lost, Alcide to disinfect—and put the whole mess in a plastic bag and cleaned our hands. There were still some fuel fumes, and they made us gag a little bit.

At 1118 Zulu, just after three in the morning, with about five hours to go until landing, we finished changing out the pump. Unless it worked—unless we could get fuel from the right side—we couldn't make Edwards. Even if we could, it was iffy.

Dick turned the valve to the setting to pull fuel from the right side. But nothing happened.

It scared the hell out of us.

Our fuel system was complicated even when we were awake and had time to study it, but we were tired. So it took a handful of minutes to remember that the way we'd rigged it, we had to turn the valve to the setting for the left side to get fuel from the right side. I made the switch, and it worked: there was fuel flowing!

God, we were happy. Now with the good pump we could glean the tanks on the right side.

Before, we were finding that we had more in the tanks than we expected. Now we were finding less, and it was taking a meat axe to all our estimates. We had gone all the way around the world, and we might get home with five pounds of fuel.

We had to slow down and just sit there and agonize and figure and refigure what we had, and hope we had it in each tank. We were just sitting and sweating blood.

What we needed now were just twenty-eight gallons, twenty-eight gallons we could look straight at in the feed tank in front of us.

I opened the solenoid that controlled the right tip tank and began drawing that fuel. Unlike its twin on the left, it was full.

The level in the feed tank slowly rose. It took a good half hour, creeping slowly by, as the level went up and up. And then we had it!

And just as soon as we got the twenty-eight gallons in the feed tank, we knew we had it made. I switched off all the valves. I turned off the autopilot to check our balance. The airplane felt good, very controllable. And I turned the autopilot back on.

We're going to make it, boy, we're going to make it.

But we were still afraid to mention it. We were still looking at some weather through the starlight scope.

I could see the lights of Ensenada, Mexico, off to the right, just a hazy kind of a glow through the clouds. The moon was up, but we couldn't see it because of the clouds. With the starlight scope I could begin to see the lights of airplanes going in and out of Lindbergh Airport at San Diego and Miramar Naval Air Station—renowned base of the *Top Gun* pilots.

It looked as if we would get home the first thing in the morning. The day before, I was able to get three rest periods instead of one, and Jeana had flown the night before.

Doc Jutila urged us both to use oxygen for the rest of the flight, just to finish it up, and it was a good thing we did. It really helped with fatigue.

The good news was that although my sleep had been cut short, I felt great. After that engine quit, we both had enough adrenaline to last us for about six months.

So we came limping home, hoping the engines and the fuel would last. We wanted to get to somewhere in California, at least.

Compass Rose

It's like stretching a rubber band out from your face, I thought. Pull it out a little bit and let go, and it won't hurt much. But pull it way out and let go, and it'll hurt like hell. There was nothing we could do now except push it all the way, make San Diego if we could, then try for Los Angeles, then hope for Edwards.

We weren't taking anything for granted, and neither of us said anything, but when we finally got the feed tank up to the twenty-eight gallons we figured we needed to make it, there was a moment when we each let out an internal sigh and dared to hope that this time we really did have it made.

The HF radio was very clear now. Mission control told us that Burt and Mike and Sally Melvill had taken off in the Duchess to meet us.

Soon we could hear them on the radio, too, expressing some concern about the weather. There were layers of stratus clouds ahead of us, but excellent arrival conditions forecast.

Mission control advised us of a routing change: we were to fly off the coast and only then vector back in to Edwards. The command post was particularly concerned about unauthorized intercepts by Sunday pilots who might just decide to fly up for a look.

I was not so worried about that—we knew how hard it was to spot the *Voyager*—and I vetoed the route. We told them we were going directly to Edwards AFB.

On the radio, we worked out a rendezvous with Burt; we would track on the Seal Beach VOR station, south of Los Angeles, being sure to keep five hundred feet of altitude between our two airplanes. I couldn't see anything ahead. I got out the trusty starlight scope one more time and looked up ahead. I could see a half a dozen airplanes over the L.A. area. To distinguish the Duchess I asked Mike to turn his landing light on and off. I could see it, green and grainy, flashing out there, a strange and distant welcome. I dropped back down inside the cockpit and turned the cockpit lights back on with a warm feeling in my heart.

As we approached, we called out our distances from the VOR station, and as we both said sixty-four miles, we realized we'd passed each other. They made a hard left turn and came up behind us in a tail chase. A few minutes later, because their speed was double ours, Mike finally spotted what he thought was our strobe. To confirm, he asked me to flash it on and off. And when they saw the strobe disappear, then reappear, all hell broke loose in the Duchess. Joy, joy, joy!

It would be another twenty minutes before the sun came up and they could actually see the Voyager, so Mike slowed down and synced his speed with ours, flying offset to the left just as I had trained him.

We had no running lights, of course; we lost them with the winglets. "You know," I said, "the airplane flew just as well without running lights."

Burt sat there for a while, just looking at our strobe light and then, as it got a little brighter, between the glow of Los Angeles and the rising sun, he told us he could just barely see the black outline of the Voyager. "Those wings are a lot flatter now," he said. He had last seen them bent upwards, laden with fuel, and now they were almost level. And as the light came up some more Mike told us that everyone in the Duchess was crying with joy and I began to get misty myself.

Now we could see each other. Jeana stuck her head up by the window, and we all waved.

We could see the glow of Los Angeles now. At first it was just a soft yellow smoggy glow, and then, as we came closer, we saw the whole wide grid of the city burning beneath the haze. Seeing it, we felt warm all over, almost a physical warmth. In Mojave, Los Angeles seems like a long way away, it's "down below," but seeing it then, the network of lights arranged around the familiar freeway arteries gave us a fantastic feeling: we were almost home.

.   .   .

In the dark early hours of the day a light snow began to fall on the Edwards dry lake, swirling in the TV spotlights, and the lit lake took on the air of a giant ice-skating rink. The wind was gentle but cold and persistent.

People pulled their coats tightly around them, wrapped their hands around steaming cups of coffee, and stamped their feet to stay warm. The 747 that ferries the space shuttles back to the Cape was brightly lit in front of the NASA hangar behind them. Across the way, there was a constant stream of headlights from the vehicles coming into the viewing area: a world-class collection of motor homes and recreational vehicles and two dozen television dishes generating enough microwaves to cook dinner for everyone in the Antelope Valley.

All we heard, though, was that traffic was backed up going into Edwards, and still we didn't dare to think about anything like that.

. . .

We came across Chavez Ravine and I could see Dodger Stadium down below and to the other side the Hollywood studios.

At the northern end of the L.A. basin we started up over a layer of stratus clouds, and pretty soon we were sandwiched between two layers of them.

"We're turning left now," I told mission control, "and we'll fly directly to the Van Nuys VOR, then directly to Magic Mountain and right up the valley."

Larry Caskey, back in mission control, was upset. "Dick," he said, "don't tell everybody in the world just where you're going."

But in fact we were turning right, not left, and the chase planes knew that what we were saying was to throw potential gawker pilots off the track.

What we really did was fly over Mount Wilson and then on into the Antelope Valley across the mountains. There on the edge of the clouds we saw what looked like very bad rotor activity, a bed of clouds all turbulent and boiling.

We had a whole entourage now, the Duchess, Bruce and Glenn and Doug in the Sierra, and Fitz Fulton flying Mark Greenberg and his cameras in a Cessna. I felt a little bit uneasy. The Voyager was so light that turbulence could jostle us, and the chase planes seemed a little close. I had to resist the urge to tell them to back off.

"You know, Jeana," I said, "we left the car back at Mojave. How are we going to get back home?"

She didn't even pretend to laugh. We knew Dr. Jutila and Suzy Bowman were going to drive us home.

We thought we would get bounced by turbulence coming back over the mountains, so we told the chase airplanes to back off. And seeing those rotors developing, we knew we were back in the familiar rough air of the high desert. We were afraid we would really get nailed, but this day it was kind to us. We only felt a few bumps.

There was still time for one more argument with Burt. He kept insisting that the numbers said the airplane's center of gravity was too far forward, and he pressed us to adjust it. But we knew the Voyager better than anyone and could feel that the CG was actually too far aft. We ran some minimum speed handling quality evaluations to verify CG. The plane handled fine. We had it out with him for a while, and then I declared, "This airplane is within CG limits, and we're going to land."

We called Edwards tower to find out about other air traffic. "None," they told us. "The whole place is shut down for you."

It was time to find out just where we were. They were telling us Edwards was clear, but we were on top of clouds. There were clouds for as far as we could see, with an occasional mountain peak. Still, we were a ways out.

As we approached the base, Jeana saw out the window that suddenly there were no clouds within the Edwards complex. The sun was shining on Edwards, the Voyager, and all the awaiting people. The magic door had opened for us again.

.   .   .

At 7:32 a.m., Pacific coast time, December 23, 1986, Voyager appeared above Edwards Air Force Base. The cheers from the crowd began as a scatter and then swelled to collective applause as more and more people caught sight of the white airplane against the blue sky.

We came in right over the edge of the Edwards restricted area and saw the whole Edwards complex in front of us and where we would land: on the dry lake by the compass rose, marking true directions so pilots could adjust their compasses before taking off. So many airplanes had landed here: X-planes, space shuttles, strange prototypes.

We'd never seen Edwards like this: nobody, nothing was flying. One whole side of the dry lake was full of people.

We had no idea what was going to happen at home. Thinking always about the fat lady, we had refused to let anyone tell us about it.

I told Jeana to police up the back area. She didn't say anything, and it made me angry. "Why not?" I asked. More silence. She had already taken care of it. After that we didn't say anything we didn't have to say. And for the first time I realized how little we had said, beyond the necessary things, throughout the flight.

.   .   .

I began to talk about getting the gear down, but once Dick had seen all those people on the ground, it was show time.

I rubbed Dick's arm and warned him not to show off too much. Don't get careless now, don't do something stupid, we've come too far. Take it easy; your legs may not have as much strength or control as you think.

But Dick knew right away that he wanted everyone to see this airplane.

"Those people have come a long way and been out here all night. I don't want them to catch the first glimpse of this airplane all dirtied up with the gear down. They came to see *Voyager*."

"I want to make some solo flybys," he told the chase planes. "You guys break it off. I want one solo parade lap."

We had a hell of a time getting Fitz to move away. He was carrying Mark Greenberg with the video camera, beaming back down to the microwave dishes and into the network trailers and into millions of television sets, and he took his responsibility as the eyes of the nation very seriously.

Fitz said, "Negative, this is live TV coverage, and I can't leave."

"Fitz, turn hard left and break off."

And Mike Melvill in the other chase came on and said, "Fitz, break it off."

Dick repeated part of the number he did at Oshkosh, showing the airplane off like he did after its first cross-country flight more than two years ago.

Since this was not an airplane he could bring in with a series of snap rolls, Dick, the ham, settled for a nice low pass—say, fifty feet. And just a couple more orbits.

But the engines were loaded up and getting a little rough.

"I don't care," he said. "Even if the engines quit, I can still land gear up if I have to."

Of course that might be embarrassing, worse than falling down getting out of the plane. Maybe we shouldn't.

So reason and prudence overcame showmanship. We came over at about four hundred feet. We made one pass alone, and then the chase ships rejoined us and we made several more.

"Dick, time to land," I said. "We're running low on fuel." The gauge on the feed tank said 8.4 gallons.

And, legs crimped up under me, the circulation cut off, I started the tedious and uncomfortable cranking down of the gear. Meanwhile Dick replaced the bulb we had borrowed from the gear lamp. He took the one out of the alternator warning lamp and installed it.

I had to take my parachute harness off to extend the gear. There just wasn't enough room; besides, it was uncomfortable. I was folded up, facing backward, working in the small cavity between the console and the bulkhead to the back. I remembered why I had cut my long hair.

I took the crank handle to the sailboat winch that raises the gear and the key to the uplock plate and set to work. I hoped the air stayed smooth; if we hit a gust the gear could swing back and add another number to the gear counter—the gear counter was our proof that we didn't land. I cranked; it was eight minutes before the gear popped over center.

The green light came on the panel and Mike visually confirmed: "One main down and apparently locked." Then I reached down to crank the other gear. After it too was locked I went to the back, turned around, and lay there letting the blood flow back into my legs while Dick started extending the nose gear. Then I scooted forward to help him. He gave the cable a big hefty pull, barely missing my head with his elbow. I held the cable as he pulled the gear into the locked position. Now we had all three green lights—gear down and locked.

We'd never landed on the dry lake, and we weren't sure if Dick's depth perception was all right, not sure if his coordination had deteriorated, not sure that his legs and hands were really talking to each other. We'd never flown the plane with this little fuel, not even in tests, and it was really floating.

"Okay, boy," Mike Melvill said, "go get it. This is the big one, the one you've been training for."

And we did it: we came in almost hanging there for a long time, smooth and level and lined up. "Fifty-eight knots," Jeana called out. "Forty-four." And now Mike called out our altitude—"thirty feet, fifteen, ten, six, three, two, that's it"—touchdown, completing the first nonstop, nonrefueled flight around the world: nine days, three minutes, forty-four seconds.

We could hear Bruce say, "Welcome home, Voyager, welcome home."

We didn't know where to put the airplane. I was a little confused. I thought we were going to taxi toward the hangar. "Where do you want this thing?" I asked. I got no answer and thought at first the radio was not working until I heard Mike say, "Turn hard right." Just then the back engine quit, by itself. I pushed the front engine up because I didn't want to be embarrassed by both engines quitting and having to restart. It coughed but kept going, and I slowed down with the nosewheel hand brake.

Finally I heard Lee Herron say, "Follow me," and, as he had done so many times before, he led me in with hand signals. We made a 180-degree turn so we could dismount on the right side toward the cameras. We pulled to a stop in front of the cameras and press. Lee Herron gave the cut signal.

As usual after landing, I had trouble getting Dick to finish the checklist. It was important; if we ever left a mag on, say, somebody might get hurt. You aren't going anywhere until we finish this checklist, I told him.

This time I almost welcomed Jeana running through the checklist. It gave me time to psych myself for dealing with the people out there, time to enjoy for a few moments what life sounded like without the noise of an engine.

The ground crew brought up two ladders, so they could put a pole between them and haul us out if necessary. I worked my legs around, and they seemed to feel as good as the day we left.

Rich Hanson and his wife, the NAA officials, came up and checked and photographed the canopy seal, confirming it was unbroken, and as soon as he gave the okay we undid the latches, and Lee Herron took the canopy and handed Dick his black hat. Dick stuck the two Confederate ten-dollar bills out of the plane, and Hanson took them to match the serial numbers in joking proof that this was the same aircraft and crew that took off nine days ago.

Jeana reminded me about the barograph behind the backrest. That jolted me; for a moment I'd forgotten it. I pulled it down and saw that it was still running: our descent and landing were clearly marked on the altitude line. After Rich had photographed the seals on it, I turned it off, disconnected it, and handed it to him. Right then it was as precious as gold—without it, we wouldn't get credit for flying around the world. Just to be sure, there were two backups in the wheel wells.

I got up and removed my parachute harness and sat on the top of the fuselage. I called Jeana to come out and soon she was there too.

While Dick was coming out I still had to finish my job. I gathered up the maps, cleaned up everything loose in back and completed the log—"Arrive, Edwards Air Force Base"—and when I emerged I felt my legs were rubbery, but they worked. I could control them. They were more cramped from folding myself on top of them to get to the landing gear crank than from anything else.

While Jeana sat on the side of the *Voyager*, I extended my legs and touched the ladder—and then jerked them back as if the ladder were hot.

I felt woozy, and I couldn't believe it despite all the tangible evidence: the legs wouldn't work. I started to feel for the ladder rung and thought, Something's really wrong here. They had felt fine in the airplane, they weren't asleep, the blood was there, but now they just didn't want to work.

"Doc," I said to George Jutila, "I think I'll just sit here for a while." So I slipped myself along the fuselage forward of the hatch on my hands and sat up real straight, working my legs like crazy—toes, calves, thighs—trying to get them working, sitting on the top of the airplane as if that was how I planned it.

Somebody said, "Why don't you wave?" and I thought that sounded like a good idea. "Wave, Jeana," I said and we both started waving.

And we heard a noise, which may have been cheers and clapping but sounded a lot like the fat lady.

I thought, If I fall down, I'm going to look pretty stupid.

My legs were rubbery, but they were working now. And I wasn't going to give up the chance to walk around the plane and inspect it. The tough part was ducking under the canard—I wasn't sure I could make it—but I bent my head and went under, and my legs were still barely working.

I gave Burt a big hug and remembered when I hugged him—for the first time in our lives, probably—after our first record, back at Oshkosh in 1975.

As much as I feared this airplane, I respected it now, and I was proud of it. We had built it, and I felt a oneness with this thing that had carried us so far, and I thought of all those nights and days in the air when we would have given anything to look at the outside of this airplane.

I looked at Fergy and said, "Well, there are a lot of things wrong with it, and the neat thing is, we don't have to fix any of them."

Sitting on the fuselage, I wondered how well my legs were going to work; I remembered how weakened my body was after the coast flight. I put weight on my legs and stood up. I felt like a duck—calm on the outside but paddling like hell underneath. I waited for Dick to get down to see how well he did: not very well, it seemed. I ventured down and was surprised to find my legs felt pretty good. I wanted to move around but Suzy Bowman was right there to wrap her arms around me.

Suzy wanted to make sure I didn't fall, but there was no danger of that. My legs felt fine. The only problem I had with walking was that because Suzy was tall she was holding me too high, all but carrying me, and I had to walk on my toes. I just wanted to hug everybody, all my people—friends and family—and finally I had to break loose and give one very special person—Bruce—a big hug. That was important to me and began to make me feel I was home.

There was an ambulance ready for each of us, and I got in one of them and we waited for Dick—and waited and waited.

The reality of what we had done hadn't sunk in. I sat there thinking, We did it, we really did it—why don't I feel it's been done yet? I felt wonderful, I knew I had done it, but I didn't feel like it really happened.

While Dick was slowly working his way around the airplane visiting with everyone I felt a little jealous. I wanted to say hello to everyone too but I couldn't escape. Suzy and the doctors had me in their custody.

The doctors couldn't wait to get their hands on us. It was a good long ride to the base hospital, and on the way they handed us hot towels. Boy, nothing ever felt so good!

When we arrived at the base hospital, they made us get into wheel-chairs. Dick, in the black hat, with a gray stubble of beard like some outlaw, tried to resist but finally gave in. My doctors were going to let me walk in until they saw that Dick had been seated. Better follow the rules, they said. Oh well. We were wheeled upstairs.

The hospital felt like a big fishbowl, with everyone staring at Dick and staring at me. I felt great. Then they started putting the needles in. It took them five tries and three vampires to find a vein in my arm. Pretty soon I had needle marks all up and down my arm, and a bloody trail from the near misses.

On a television in the corner of the room, CNN was replaying the landing over and over, and Dick kept watching it in a kind of haze.

We were weighed, I'd lost nine pounds—about 10 percent of my body weight. Dick lost six pounds. But the doctors found us in very good shape. Our hearing was better off than it was after the Pacific coast flight.

At the hospital, I wrapped an arm around Jeana. It made a nice picture, but at the same time I felt a twinge of emptiness and loneliness. The moment of my greatest triumph was mixed with my greatest disappointment: in the end I did not really have the person with whom I would most have wanted to share the moment.

Jeana went off for her shower, and I went for mine. They had assigned a medical corpsman to watch me constantly, in case I fainted, I guess. He followed me practically into the shower, and it began to get on my nerves. I washed hard with heavy-duty disinfectant soap, and then I washed again and again. I figured washing nine times would catch me up.

The kit I'd packed before takeoff made it to the hospital all right, but the shaving was hard work. The beard was like wire, and I didn't like the idea that so much of it was gray. I figured that there was a gray hair for every time I'd gotten into the airplane and a dozen more for every time I'd brought it down into the Mojave winds for landing. No wonder.

The families had laid out a whole buffet of food for us: raspberries and other fruit and lobster and shrimp and steak. Dick did a pretty good job on the food, but my stomach had shrunk so much I couldn't eat much of it. What I really looked forward to was seeing my family, and soon they came in: Evaree, my mother, and her husband, Doug, and Lee, my father, with his wife, Frances, and my sister, Judy. My dad came up bashfully, not wanting to get in the doctors' way, and gave me a box of yellow roses—sent from my high school in Commerce, Texas.

Two hours later, after Dr. Jutila had given the okay, we got dressed in our blue flight suits and trotted out to the press, installed on bleachers in the weight and balance hangar, where the old x-airplanes used to be mated to their carrier airplanes. It was a vast space arched over by great silver girders, and any sound seemed to be instantly sucked up into its high corners. That, in combination with speakers and cameras, made the whole experience—facing this bleacherload full of reporters, lined up as if they were at some high school pep rally, entirely surreal.

But before we mounted the platform we first had hugs for everyone, family, friends, and volunteers. Throughout the whole press conference it was hard not to look back over our shoulders at them and at the roped-off *Voyager*, sitting where an air force tractor had towed it, looking tiny in the huge hangar. Behind it stood Fergy's black Ranchero, an incongruous vehicle beside the sleek silver airplanes and blue Air Force vehicles.

A plaque was pressed into our hands—from the National Aeronautical Association—recognizing the flight as a U.S. record. It was tangible evidence that the flight had really happened, an object that felt as strange as the realization itself. Dick took it.

The plaque made me uneasy—nothing was official yet—and I really didn't know what to do with it. I handed it to Burt. And we both hugged Burt one more time.

Answering the questions from the press, I had a hard time changing tenses—I'd been talking for so long about what we were going to do that now it was unfamiliar to talk about the flight as what we had done. It would take weeks to make that transition.

Afterward we mingled with our family and friends. "You saved our lives," we told Len Snellman, and it was true. Sally Melvill had found rocks embedded in the foam at the bottom of the wingtips. "Can I please have one of the rocks that went around the world?" she asked.

I was determined to unload the airplane myself, even though the doc and Jeana tried to persuade me to stay away. I was concerned about the two remaining barographs and felt almost irresistibly drawn back to *Voyager*. I couldn't seem to tear myself away. Finally, after Jeana came over and persuaded me to leave so everyone else could leave, and that Mike and Sally were going to take care of everything from the airplane, I allowed myself to be led back to the car.

We drove over to the Officers' Club. I was still restless and wanted to get back to the airplane, but no one would let me. Doc went over to the hospital to check us out and gather our things. Jeana ordered me a beer and herself and Suzy a cup of tea. The beer mixed with all the adrenaline, and the fatigue began to melt away. By the time Doc returned, I was still hyper but not so angry anymore. We went back to the Weights and Balances Hangar and, just as promised, Mike and Sally had gone in and cleaned out the various compartments in the *Voyager*.

I thought that now I could relax, it was over. But as I looked around, I felt drained and empty. That ride back to Mojave was one of the loneliest times in my life.

We wanted to talk to the volunteers, see our friends. That was our number-one priority. Many of them were going home the next morning, some that night. Back at Hangar 77, we told them how proud we were of them and what we had done together and the spirit we had created and what we had proven not just about airplanes, but about what people working together can do.

In the background was the sound of one of the barographs printing out the record of the flight.

We'd always talked about the biggest party of all, when we came back. The truth was that we were all too tired to do much partying. There was a sort of collective collapse and daze around the hangar, abetted by champagne and beer.

Conway Roberts and others in mission control had outfitted a tricycle to present us. It had droopy cardboard wings, and there was a sign on the pedal: "Place foot here if engine quits."

We hung around the party for a while. I left when I found I couldn't hold on to my third beer; it just slipped right out of my hand. So I went home and slept for eighteen hours straight. Jeana stayed up later, and of course visited Gem before she turned in. She got about eight hours and was back in the office the next morning, as usual. Reporters came to the house looking for an interview, but Judy fended them off.

It was appropriate that we had landed on the compass rose. That is the pattern marked on the ground for pilots to check their compasses against— to find true north—to get their true bearings. And after six years of thinking about nothing but *Voyager*, after finally achieving a success that so often seemed beyond reach or reasonable expectation, it was time for us, too, to check our bearings. During the flight, we had neither the time nor the desire to think about coverage of the flight in the newspapers or on television. It wasn't the purpose. That may sound surprising, but much of it came as a shock to us when we landed.

Gradually we found out what had happened, watched TV tapes, saw those winglets waggling and then flipping off, saw what we looked like over Africa, gazed at the newspapers with pictures of the just landed airplane on the front page and us sitting on the airplane and Fergy, looking dapper, right behind us, and the doc in the foreground looking happy.

We found that millions of people watched the landing live on television, including the president. Later, Mrs. Reagan told us the president said "Why don't they just land it?" as we made our passes over the dry lake. The president's hands were going up and down in front of the set. "What are they waiting for? Just land it, land the damn thing!"

We understood that something special had happened, something that widened the circle of the *Voyager* family way out beyond the hangar, beyond Mojave, beyond the VIP Club, beyond the United States, into just about every corner of the world. *Voyager* was even covered in *Pravda* and the dailies in the People's Republic of China. It was a stunning realization of a phrase Jeana had spoken early in the program, one that summed up the original dream and vision: "one flight, one world."

It took awhile to dawn on us just how much people had gotten excited, and caught up, and inspired at Christmastime. It was a Christmas gift, people said, to a country that, after a year of terrorism and scandal and the *Challenger* disaster, badly needed good news. Perhaps, Jeana thought, that was the why of the when: so it could be at Christmas.

Long lines of people appeared at Hangar 77 within a couple of hours of the landing. It was all that Dan Card and Gary Gunnell and everyone in the shop and offices could do to keep things moving. Weekday afternoons were soon busier than the best of Sundays had been before the flight.

On Christmas Eve, Bruce Evans worked alone on his airplane in the dark and now deserted Hangar 77 by a single light. He was exhausted and drained—he had given the project everything he had, and it had brought him close to his limits. He was going to Baja in the morning, and that night he came by to say good-bye—and to share another thought.

He was thinking, he said, of *Voyager* sitting over in the hangar at Edwards, in the dark, under the huge silver arches.

"That airplane probably feels kind of lonely over there," he said.

"It must be thinking, Jeez, what are they doing letting all these owls shit on me? At home if a single sparrow got in the hangar, they'd shoot it.

"There is no way that airplane should have made it," he said. "And it should never fly again."

"Well," Dick said, "we've got to get it back here."

"All right," said Bruce, "then take off, make one left turn, and just come back home. Don't touch a thing. Don't even turn on a lot of electronics. And then don't fly it anymore.

"It was built to go twenty flights, and you went sixty-eight.

"And remember all those things we just decided to cross our fingers about?

"Remember the arc of electricity we saw in the right forward fuselage tank? It could still be lurking in there.

"Remember the times when smoke would just all of a sudden start coming out of the console from places that were nowhere near electricity? We never did find out about that. Remember all the fuel leaks?

"Lindbergh's was a straightforward, regular airplane. There's nothing regular at all about the *Voyager*. It's not an ordinary airplane, or else it wouldn't have flown around the world."

Bruce was right. It was a damned close thing. Any number of factors could have made the difference between success and failure, between landing on the compass rose and landing on some Caribbean island or being plucked out of the Atlantic Ocean or of vanishing forever into the middle of the Indian Ocean.

We thought of all the close moments. Any one of a number of small factors could have made the critical difference. What if we'd had a few more bugs on the wings? John Roncz had surveyed the airplane carefully in the hangar at Edwards and was proud to find only 68 insect streaks: his design had performed magnificently. What if we had flown with the old props? Without the increased performance of the new props, we might have landed in South America. What if we hadn't had winds averaging five knots better than our most optimistic predictions?

. . . .

We spent Christmas quietly—and separately. At the house everyone pitched in to make Christmas dinner: my father and Frances, my mother and Doug, Judy and the volunteers who were still in Mojave. Dick and Burt went to Mom and Pop's for their traditional family dinner.

If Dick felt mostly relief it was over, I began to worry about my people, wishing that the Voyager family did not have to disperse just yet, that I could keep everyone together.

Four days later, on December 29, we put on our best duds and went to meet the President and Mrs. Reagan at the Century Hotel in Los Angeles. To us and to Burt they presented the Presidential Citizens Medal.

"With all of America," he said, "Nancy and I followed the Voyager's progress along each leg of its fabulous flight, with alternating feelings of nervousness, and hope, and fear, and elation—but mostly an overwhelming pride in these two courageous Americans and their historic mission.

"On December 23, 1986, the name Voyager joined the distinguished family of airborne technological breakthroughs that began with the Wright Flyer and includes the Spirit of St. Louis and the Glamorous Glennis, and three men, or new names, I should say, will be added to the column headed the Right Stuff. Along with Orville and Wilbur Wright, Charles Lindbergh and Chuck Yeager, history will now record Dick Rutan, Jeana Yeager, and Burt Rutan."

It was a ratification of what we had all done, and we felt good that with us that day were as many of the people from the hangar and mission control center and supporting companies as could possibly come.

But still it took a while to sink in. A week or so after we landed we began to make public appearances. Only then, with all those people around us, did the reality begin to come home to us. They had been rooting for us, they had shared the flight with us—they had felt the impact of what we had done before *we* did.

What was more important than the fact that we had finally done it was that we had done it our way. The airplane would be going to the National Air and Space Museum, where, so long ago, we had stood with Burt and told each other, "We want not only to fly around the world, but to look back on the way we did it with pride, and to all still be friends in the end."

We had done that. It had not been easy, but we were friends with Burt again.

The Burt to whom we returned was a very different man from the one we had left. He had become more and more concerned about us in the weeks before we took off and more and more conservative in his calculations for takeoff. And during the flight, he had become more and more emotional.

"He couldn't work at all," Mike Melvill said with astonishment.

And not long after we landed, Dick and Burt went off together for a weekend in Las Vegas, the two brothers having fun together for the first time in years, probably since they were kids in Dinuba, California.

. . .

On January 6 we flew the airplane back to Mojave, spending a couple of hours in the air while the cinematographer Clay Lacy shot some footage. It wasn't easy to get back in that airplane and give it another chance to pull something on us. I wore my old parachute, which I felt more comfortable with than the lighter world-flight chute, and we double-checked everything.

My instincts were warning me not to stay in the air any longer than necessary. And I missed not having Bruce do the preflight check; he was in Baja. That made me uneasy. Peter and Clay Lacy talked about flying to the coast to get some footage of the *Voyager* over water. I refused. My gut feeling said, stay within gliding distance of an airport or lake bed and just get the *Voyager* back to Mojave. My instincts told me *Voyager* should never be flown again.

There were mixed feelings—hearing Bruce's warning and feeling my own warning, wanting not to press our luck, but also feeling some strange responsibility to this airplane that had tested and endangered us so many times, yet ultimately had also done so much for us.

After we landed I noticed that the coolant seal had failed completely—the one that I had been watching so carefully since I first saw it leaking in the middle of the Indian Ocean. A mix of oil and coolant was now in the reservoir bottle. It had held on to the last moment—and no longer. "The warranty is about up," Mike Melvill joked. "Twenty-five thousand miles or ten days, whichever comes first." We had totaled up the fuel left in the tanks, and Mike had won the pool on how much remained: 18.3 gallons, enough for about 800 more miles. Jeana's fuel log was accurate to within 20 pounds. We got back with 1.5% of our takeoff fuel.

The whole gang was there to meet us at Mojave, and we all celebrated: the last was the sixty-ninth flight for N269VA.

. . .

"Now what will you do?" people kept asking. "What will you do next?" But the project was far from finished.

We had a debt to pay—some $300,000 to $500,000—and we had to go on the road to pay it off. We had obligated ourselves to appearances on behalf of our sponsors, and there were dozens of groups that wanted to hear our firsthand account of the flight and the whole program.

And here the story turns almost into a blur—London, Rome, Paris, Tokyo, Frankfurt, New York, and home again, to crisscross the country.

But there were also debts we could never repay—to the volunteers and the VIPs and the other contributors. And we had more friends than we ever dreamed we would have. People everywhere kept coming up to us, and we didn't know quite what to do for them. Dick felt odd, signing autographs, and it irritated him sometimes; he'd rather talk to somebody or tell a story, share that. I could sense that they wanted something but didn't know just what, maybe a handshake, a chance to say a few words, so I smiled and listened and shook the hands and wanted to offer something more, but I wasn't sure what.

The things we said were no less true for the fact that we were called on to say them again and again: that what Voyager represented was the power of people working together to realize a dream—even if achieving that dream meant constantly skirting the edge of nightmare. That a free society was the medium in which those dreams could grow—even if it meant constant struggle and living on a shoestring and in danger. And that records were set to be broken. But we also knew that while records could be broken, milestones could not.

We began to notice that everyplace we went people kept asking us the same question, "Would you do it again?"

"No, no," we would say, "once was enough. Not again."

It took awhile to catch on to the fact that what they were really asking was, "Was it worth it?"

And yes, it was, we immediately answered, worth all the work and sweat and patience, worth the physical discomfort and the danger and the fear.

And still yes, but an answer that was not as easy, yes, worth all the travail and heartache, and the strain and the distance it put between us and the other paths of life we didn't take, and the imprisonment and the fear and the reduction of life to a hangar and then a cockpit-sized space.

It was worth the friends we gained and the nerves we touched in the wider circle of friends, worth the technological lessons, although they were the least of it, much more worth the human lessons of dreaming and work and determination. And it would have been worth the effort even if we had failed or lost the *Voyager*, or lost our lives.

This was the last first in aviation, we had always said, a milestone, and that made it unique.

Would we do it again? No one can do it again. And that is the best thing about it.

Glossary

ADI (Attitude Directional Indicator) The attitude input to the autopilot

Airfoil Any aircraft lifting surface, such as a wing; the curved shape of the wing that produces lift

Angle of attack The angle between an airplane's longitudinal axis and the airflow; a critical factor in flying efficiently

Attitude indicator A device that indicates the pitch and roll angle of the aircraft

Autopilot A device that automatically adjusts the control surfaces of an airplane. *Voyager*'s autopilot could be set either to maintain a certain angle of attack ("attitude hold") or a certain altitude ("altitude hold") and to control the airplane's heading

Avionics The electronics used in flying and navigating an airplane: radar, autopilot, guidance computer, radios and engine instrumentation

Boom tanks Long fuel tanks partway out on *Voyager*'s wings, to either side of the fuselage, connecting the tips of the canard to the main wing; a tank set outboard from the fuselage on the wing

Canard A secondary wing set in front of the main wing, often called "a front tail"

Center of gravity (CG) The centerpoint of an airplane's weight distribution, which must be kept within a specific range for stable, efficient flying

Circadian rhythm An individual's normal waking and sleeping pattern, which can be disturbed by a change in routine resulting in "jet lag" symptoms

Compass rose A series of marks on the ground showing magnetic north and used to calibrate flying compasses

Composites Materials combining woven fiber—either glass, graphite, Aramid, or other materials—with epoxies or other resins and used instead of metals in advanced aircraft design

Deck angle gauge A device that shows the airplane's pitch angle with reference to the earth's horizon. In level, stable flight it can be used to determine the angle of attack—critical to the performance, range, and stability of the airplane

Delta P The engineering shorthand for the difference in pressure from one side of a cooling device (radiator) to the other; determines airflow through the radiator and hence the cooling capacity

Density altitude Air density at any altitude, reflecting the combined effects of temperature and altitude on the thickness of the air. Air thickness affects the performance of the aircraft—the higher the density altitude, the lower the performance

Divergent oscillations Wavelike motions of a wing that increase in amplitude—when divergent oscillations are extremely dangerous

Feather To immobilize a propeller in flight for minimum drag. Once the engine has stopped rotating the prop blades are twisted edgewise into the airflow to reduce drag

Flutter The rapid, uncontrolled flapping of an airfoil or control surface, usually leading to its destruction—an extremely dangerous situation

Gains In an autopilot, the control settings for its sensitivity in responding to turbulence. The stronger the turbulence the more aggressive the autopilot must be and vice versa

Ground effect An added measure of lift, beyond the normal lift provided by an airfoil, provided within an altitude equal to the airplane's wingspan, by the pressure of air between wing and ground

Gyro Gyroscope, used to establish a reference horizon for the autopilot

Hypoxia Insufficient oxygen in the body

Induced drag The force of air retarding the flight of an airplane created as a result of the production of lift (see also *Parasitic drag*)

Lateral stability The steadiness of an airplane around the longitudinal axis of its fuselage or rolling stability

"L/D Bucket" The speed at which the airplane is flying most efficiently—any faster or slower, and drag and the thrust necessary to oppose it would increase. So called because the graphs of lift (L) and drag (D) form a bucket shape at this most efficient point

Longitudinal stability   The steadiness of an airplane around the lateral axis of its wings or nose-up, nose-down, pitching stability

Mixture   The relative proportions of air and fuel fed to an engine; if "rich," the mixture is high in fuel; if "lean," it is lower in fuel

Omega/VLF   A long-range navigation system using high power and Very Low Frequency (VLF) radio signals, employed in *Voyager* as the primary navigation system

Parasitic drag   The force of air retarding the movement of an airplane caused by its basic shape (antennas, airscoops, canopy, etc.); any drag not associated with lift (see also *Induced drag*)

Pilot-induced oscillation   A wavelike movement set off by the pilot's unsuccessful efforts to control oscillations

Pitch oscillation   A wavelike, upward and downward pitching movement of an airplane, sometimes called porpoising

Spanloading   The even distribution of weight along a lifting surface. The more effectively spanloaded, the less airframe structure is needed

Torsion   A twisting force

Trim   The setting of an airplane'e elevators and ailerons to maintain stable flight

VOR *(Visual Omni Range)*   The basic short-range aviation navigation system, using very high frequency (VHF) radio waves and ground stations

Windmilling   The turning of an unpowered propeller in flight (produces much more drag than either a fixed or feathered propeller)

Winglet   A vertical airfoil at the tip of a wing to reduce wing tip vortices

DAVID BOLTON

Journey Without End

'There is something elusive and compelling about the waterways that urges you back and back again.'

David Bolton and Lynda Rolfe decided to throw up their jobs in central London and explore the rest of England in a seventy-foot narrow boat called *Frederick*, traditional in style yet luxuriously equipped.

From the Nene at Peterborough to the Mersey at Ellesmere Port and into the deep south-west at Gloucester and Sharpness, they spent eighteen months covering the inland waterways, mooring near beautiful Oxford colleges and grimy city docks. We share the acquaintance of the many different people they met, including those who still remember life on the old working boats; the unique view of landscape, townscape and wildlife; the problems of breakdown and the pleasures of life on the water.

'Makes you ache for the sound of the wind in the willows.'
Daily Mail

'Enthralling and absorbing . . . stands head and shoulders above other "Living and cruising on a boat" publications.'
Canal and Riverboat

'Rich with the gentle pleasures of cruising' *Books*

A Selected List of Non-Fiction Available from Mandarin Books

While every effort is made to keep prices low, it is sometimes necessary to increase prices at short notice. Mandarin Paperbacks reserves the right to show new retail prices on covers which may differ from those previously advertised in the text or elsewhere.

The prices shown below were correct at the time of going to press.

☐	7493 0000 0	**Moonwalk**	Michael Jackson	£3.99
☐	7493 0004 3	**South Africa**	Graham Leach	£3.99
☐	7493 0010 8	**What Fresh Hell is This?**	Marion Meade	£3.99
☐	7493 0011 6	**War Games**	Thomas Allen	£3.99
☐	7493 0013 2	**The Crash**	Mihir Bose	£4.99
☐	7493 0014 0	**The Demon Drink**	Jancis Robinson	£4.99
☐	7493 0015 9	**The Health Scandal**	Vernon Coleman	£4.99
☐	7493 0016 7	**Vietnam – The 10,000 Day War**	Michael Maclear	£3.99
☐	7493 0049 3	**The Spycatcher Trial**	Malcolm Turnbull	£3.99
☐	7493 0022 1	**The Super Saleswoman**	Janet Macdonald	£4.99
☐	7493 0023 X	**What's Wrong With Your Rights?**	Cook/Tate	£4.99
☐	7493 0024 8	**Mary and Richard**	Michael Burn	£3.50
☐	7493 0061 2	**Voyager**	Yeager/Rutan	£3.99
☐	7493 0060 4	**The Fashion Conspiracy**	Nicholas Coleridge	£3.99
☐	7493 0027 2	**Journey Without End**	David Bolton	£3.99
☐	7493 0028 0	**The Common Thread**	Common Thread	£4.99

All these books are available at your bookshop or newsagent, or can be ordered direct from the publisher. Just tick the titles you want and fill in the form below.

Mandarin Paperbacks, Cash Sales Department, PO Box 11, Falmouth, Cornwall TR10 9EN.

Please send cheque or postal order, no currency, for purchase price quoted and allow the following for postage and packing:

UK	55p for the first book, 22p for the second book and 14p for each additional book ordered to a maximum charge of £1.75.
BFPO and Eire	55p for the first book, 22p for the second book and 14p for each of the next seven books, thereafter 8p per book.
Overseas Customers	£1.00 for the first book plus 25p per copy for each additional book.

NAME (Block Letters) ....

ADDRESS ....

....